"I am pleased to recommend *The Deuteronomy Project: A Journey into the Mind of God.* This is an altogether new and exciting way to approach both the art of Bible study and the task of writing biblical commentary. In the persons of Hal, the retired pastor, and Chris Green, the inquisitive seeker of Christian understanding from the Scriptures, we do indeed have both a guide and an explorer who walk so easily through the book of Deuteronomy that one would think it was a New Testament book! Many will instinctively identify with Chris, for he asks all the right questions. I recommend this work to all who want to see what a whole new approach to studying the Scriptures would be like under the tutelage of not only Hal, but Richard B. Couser's creative pen. The writing style is beautiful and the narrative and explanations are captivating and convincing. While not professing to be academic or sectarian in its approach, which of course it is neither, *The Deuteronomy Project* is neither a popularization of Deuteronomy nor is it a foil for easy answers. Its profundity and its clarity will amaze you."

—Walter C. Kaiser, Jr.
President Emeritus
Colman M. Mockler
Distinguished Professor of Old Testament
Gordon-Conwell Theological Seminary

"Richard Couser is a distinguished attorney and a deep Christian thinker as evidenced by his book *The Deuteronomy Project.* I'm delighted that he is my friend. For those who have a passion to discover, worship, and serve the one true God of the Bible, Couser's book will be a powerful incentive to spiritual growth and searching thought."

—Gordon MacDonald
Author and pastor

"The Word of God best transforms us for good when it catches our imagination and shows us how to apply its teaching to our daily lives. Just as a picture is worth a thousand words, *The Deuteronomy Project* unfolds a deep and unforgettable story of two men learning from one another and the Book of Deuteronomy what the good purposes and true meanings of our lives can be. Here's a story that you not only can read fruitfully yourself, but also together with your friends. As someone who for years watched how Richard Couser's study of Deuteronomy changed him, his family, his clients and his legal practice for good, I am delighted that we can all now share from Dick's insights and be inspired by this worthwhile journey of a lawyer in search of higher authority and a retired pastor who has devoted his life to understanding the mind of our just, but also ever-loving Creator God."

—**Samuel B. Casey**
Executive Director and CEO,
Christian Legal Society

RICHARD B. COUSER

all the best
Dick Couser

THE
DEUTERONOMY
PROJECT

A JOURNEY *into the* MIND *of* GOD

WINEPRESS WP PUBLISHING

WinePress Publishing (PO Box 428, Enumclaw, WA 98022) functions only as book publisher. As such, the ultimate design, content, editorial accuracy, and views expressed or implied in this work are those of the author.

Unless otherwise noted, all Scriptures are taken from the *Holy Bible, New International Version®, NIV®*. Copyright © 1973, 1978, 1984 by the International Bible Society. Used by permission of Zondervan. All rights reserved.

Scriptures quoted in Chapter 25 are reprinted from *Tanakh: The Holy Scriptures: The New JPS Translation to the Traditional Hebrew Text*, copyright © 1985 by the Jewish Publication Society, with the permission of the publisher.

ISBN 13: 978-1-57921-938-3
ISBN 10: 1-57921-938-1
Library of Congress Catalog Card Number: 2007939799

Dedicated to my wife, Lindie, the best spiritual director a man could have, and to the men and women of the Christian Legal Society, who do not neglect "the more important matters of the law—justice, mercy, and faithfulness" (Matt. 23:23).

CONTENTS

PREFACE

The Deuteronomy Project is a study of the mind of God, seen as a story. Deuteronomy becomes the basis for a relationship between the principal characters. Christopher Green, the narrator, is a young attorney, a new Christian, and a seeker of understanding. In the style of Dante's Virgil, Hal, a retired pastor, becomes to Chris both a Moses figure and a guide through Deuteronomy. Hal and Chris, and others as the story progresses, explore the story of the entire Bible and the Christian faith. Great texts like the Ten Commandments and the Shema, and obscure passages like the law of the bird's nest, become portals for seeing into the mind of God. In a surprising ending, the epilogue brings the story together in a way that ties the text to the lives of the characters.

Hal, Chris, and the other characters in *The Deuteronomy Project* are entirely fictional, as are the events of their lives that they experience together or discuss with each other. Nevertheless, I have drawn on my life experience as a Christian believer—and my experience with many others, Christian and otherwise—in composing the fictional aspects of the book. The expository aspects of the discussion, however, are not fictional. All of the theology is rooted in Scripture and in the many commentaries noted in the bibliography at the end of the text.

The Deuteronomy Project is a valuable resource for those who long to understand the Scriptures but are reluctant to read dry, academic, or narrowly sectarian commentaries. Its story is intended to draw in readers and appeal to contemporary interests in spiritual themes. *The Deuteronomy Project* will inform evangelical, Catholic, and mainline churchgoers as well as spiritual seekers with no Christian affiliation. Hal's wisdom is deep. Through his practical examples, Socratic dialogues, responses to questions, lifetime of experience, and prayers—all presented in a variety of settings—readers will be led, like Chris Green, to see the created order in a new and holier light.

Most of the hundreds of thousands of churches in America, especially the evangelical churches, have small groups and Bible studies eager to explore and understand the Scriptures. And most Christians want to understand their faith, whether or not they are part of such church-based groups. There is no lack of commentaries and Bible study guides for these people and groups. There is, however, a great void in reader-friendly Old Testament works. Commentaries are read mostly by scholars, students, and pastors, and are difficult for people in the pew to access. There are few Bible study guides on Deuteronomy. Most that exist are simplistic, dealing with a few high points of the book rather than plumbing its depths. The spiritual resources of the Old Testament remain inaccessible to most modern Christians.

Despite the lack of literature to make it accessible to the people in the pew, Deuteronomy has been seen by its scholars as a colossus at the gateway of Old Testament theology. It grounds the teachings of Jesus and is the most-quoted Old Testament book in the New Testament. Understanding it is foundational to understanding the teaching of the entire Bible. As *The Deuteronomy Project* reveals, it is no less than a journey into the mind of God—given to a particular people for a particular time but containing a way of thought and understanding that is timeless for God's people.

The Deuteronomy Project is a new approach to biblical understanding and Christian spirituality, using the following means to draw readers into a deeper and fuller contemplation of Deuteronomy:

- Using characters who tell the story and explore the Scripture in a fashion lay Christians—through meetings, questions, thoughts, and discussions—can understand
- Centering the story on the Moses figure of Hal, the retired pastor, who serves as a guide through the text, and Chris Green, the new Christian who seeks understanding to bolster his faith
- Telling the Scripture as story rather than verse and commentary, while including the entire text of Deuteronomy for reading and reflection

- Teaching through thoughts presented as Chris reflecting on his studies, or Hal educating Chris, that explore particular aspects of the text, the Bible, and Christian history
- Placing the discussion and exploration of Deuteronomy in settings that become metaphors for the message of the passage
- Relating the text to the teachings of Jesus and the New Testament writers

Readers become familiar with the characters of Chris, the narrator, and Hal, the mentor, following their thoughts from chapter to chapter. Hal connects thought to thought, chapter to chapter, ancient to modern, Old Testament to New Testament, teaching to practice, mundane to spiritual. The story, the characters, and the text of Deuteronomy merge and flow, drawing readers along through texts in which most Christians did not expect to be interested—exploring the revelations of nooks and crannies they may never have known were there. Through them and Hal's wisdom and spiritual riches, the mind of God emerges out of the obscurity of the laws of an ancient people.

The Deuteronomy Project will help readers gain the following:

- An understanding of the mind of God, by exploring his will for his people as expressed in Deuteronomy
- A perspective of the whole Bible as one book with one author telling one story
- Insight into biblical geography and history
- Identification with characters whose questions and perspectives may be much like the reader's own
- Meaning and relevance for laws that seem archaic and inconsequential
- Entry into the spiritual depth and wisdom contained in Old Testament texts

The Deuteronomy Project is, as the subtitle indicates, *a journey into the mind of God.* In a way that keeps readers reading through new insights, this book makes it possible to tour God's mind via the book of Deuteronomy. From prologue to epilogue, through the thirty-four chapters of Deuteronomy, the story of the Creator and his people unfolds in settings to which every reader can relate.

This is a journey that every believer longs to take. My prayer is that this book will enable them to do so.

ACKNOWLEDGMENTS

I acknowledge with deepest gratitude the constant support and advice of my wife, Lindie, the best spiritual director a husband could ever have; the partners of Orr & Reno Professional Association, who allowed me the necessary extended leave from a busy law practice to write most of the original manuscript; my colleagues at the law firm of D'Amante Couser Steiner Pellerin, P.A., who supported and encouraged the completion of this book, especially Genevieve Van Beaver, for many years my able support person and paralegal; and the men and women of the Christian Legal Society, who have cared for me in this project and in many other ways with an everlasting love worthy of the Lord himself.

PROLOGUE

This book wasn't supposed to be about Hal. Looking back now, I can see that most of my life hasn't been about what it was supposed to be about, so I guess this book is no exception. You see, the problem is that I've always been the one who decided what was supposed to be—for me, and usually for everyone around me as well. It's a problem with which I still struggle. Until I came to know Hal, I didn't know I had a problem.

I had first seen him playing the piano in our rural New England church when the regular pianist was away. He was not a graceful musician. His old fingers moved stiffly and awkwardly about the keys. But he knew the tunes, the old tunes, and he loved them. I identified with his off-key voice as he sang them out amidst the little congregation. His love of praising God with voice and music overcame the insecurity that most, like me, would feel at betraying our lack of excellence. With time, we became acquainted, as one does with other people in small churches and small towns.

Hal was a long-retired pastor who had spent his life in small independent churches in northern New England, places where simple faith often mixed with dirt poverty. In these churches there was no avoiding the hardscrabble counseling of marriages gone wrong, of parents who buried their children, and of families who came to the church for food when the unemployment checks ran out. He knew Christ on the ground, in the tough lives and flinty faces of a rural people. And he knew the Bible from which he had preached so well that phrases, even whole verses and short passages, flowed from his mind like ordinary speech and thought. Scripture was ingrained in him, so that he saw people through the lens of God's Word, rather than God's Word through human eyes. God's Word was a language to him, like speaking Spanish or French. As I was to learn, it was his first language.

I wasn't planning to visit Hal that afternoon that first began my journey with him. But I knew he lived alone since his wife had died years ago. His daughter was in Massachusetts, somewhere in the Boston area, and didn't see him often. Perhaps it was a sense of duty—or perhaps a nudge from some spiritual resource of which I was hardly aware—that made me pull into his driveway that late summer Saturday afternoon instead of passing on to my intended destination.

The dirt drive led through a brief, untamed stretch of woods before ending at the narrow end of an ancient cape-style house surrounded by shrubbery nearly as high as the roof. The outside of the house looked a little shabby and unkempt around the edges, and needed paint. In the driveway was a Buick he had owned since long before Edith, his wife, had died. The door to the house was open, and an unlocked screen door was the only barrier to entry. My finger pressed the doorbell repeatedly, but no sound from within, bell or occupant, responded. Knocking was no more successful, so I walked around the side.

I could smell the flowers before I saw them. Roses of every shade and color were everywhere. I heard the pruning shears and saw the green snake of a hose that led me to Hal in the midst of the garden. A floppy tan hat shaded his face, and his shirt and pants were long, despite the summer heat. I wondered if he owned a pair of shorts or a bathing suit. He lowered his shears and smiled as I approached. "Chris Green," he said with an affection that exceeded how well he actually knew me. "Welcome to an old man's garden." A pastor's heart lay beneath the warmth of the greeting.

He insisted we tour the garden. Roses, I learned, were not just roses but a family of flowers, and every variety had its own name. As we strolled among them, the names rolled off his tongue like familiar friends: pink Pristines, pink and red Paradises, the deep red Timeless, the light purple Angel Faces. Then the yellows: the St. Patricks and the Pilgrims. As we walked under lattice arches, he introduced me to his climbers: the deep pink-and-white Handels, and the red, orange, and yellow Joseph's Coats. Each variety differed in color, height, and habits; in preferences for climate and moisture; and in resistance to insects, fungus, and disease. A good gardener needed to get to know them, he said, to learn their ways; what made them prosper, and what made them decline. In our northern climate some were harder to keep than others, but success was possible with enough attention.

Amid the talk of roses, Hal deftly shifted the topic to me. Christopher Green, he'd learned, was a thirty-nine-year-old lawyer, educated in the best of schools, and working for one of the best New Hampshire law firms. Wife: Anna, an artist and musician. Two children: Elizabeth and William, ages ten and eight. Grew up going to a church that would today be called "mainline," in a time before such distinctions were known or even necessary for most churchgoers. Followed the star of rationalism and let his Christian roots, shallow already, die for lack of nourishment. Always believed, or thought he did, in "The Great Whatever," but let his outwardly successful life drift into moral and spiritual chaos. In his late thirties began to question his life. Found that rationalism didn't have all the answers, or, properly applied, led to different answers than most rationalists thought. Began to read the Bible and go to a church where the Bible was taught and believed. Bright, in his way. Curious. Confused.

Eventually I realized that the talk, other than roses, had all been about me. Pastors are public figures who, with their families, live in fishbowls. Why didn't we ask them about themselves when we talked with them? Why did we see their only role as being to shepherd us? How could I get into Hal's life? I turned the talk back to roses. How did he get interested in them? Where did this profusion of beauty come from? And why did he spend so much time keeping it that way?

"It's really Edith's garden," he told me, looking around him at the sweep of color that surrounded us. "She chose them for the names. It helped her to think about things that were true, pure, and lovely. She always said that if you surrounded yourself with these kinds of things to think about, your thoughts would be uplifted. The trick was planting them so the colors blended together, and keeping the more southerly types alive.

"She loved them," he went on from under the brim of his hat, settling onto the bench near the middle of the garden from where we had begun our walk. "I only planted one after she died." He pointed to a three-foot high bush next to the bench, thick with a profusion of perfectly formed pink-white blossoms. "It's called 'Little Darling.' It does well in a tough climate . . . it reminds me of her. Keeping up the garden is a way of remembering her, staying in touch in a way.

"It was her garden," he repeated, "and she was the one who kept it up. I was too busy with the people. Forty years of pastoring . . ." He paused. "She said the roses were her flock to shepherd, not that they had souls like my flock, but tending the garden was keeping a little corner of the Lord's creation healthy and beautiful. In a way, we did the same thing, only I did it with the people's souls."

He never asked me why I came or what led me to stop that day. But for several hours we sat together on the old wood slat bench in the middle of the garden he'd shared with Edith and talked about his life as a country preacher. He talked about how a preacher is always walking a tightrope between the people's hearts and God's heart, and how he had longed to shorten the distance so he could hold on to what was at both ends and knot them together. That was his life's work, and, in the end, he said, he had failed. But preaching was the one profession where failure was guaranteed. That's why we need the Book, and Jesus, to cover over all our failures, he told me. Everything we needed to know to live was in the Book, and whenever he despaired and grieved, he took refuge in it. Now, alone, in the evening of his years, he loved it still. You are never truly alone if you have Jesus, and the world is full of great books by people who learned that, in monasteries and concentration camps and wheelchairs and hospitals and nursing homes and houses that no longer sing with the songs of children, and in places full of people who don't know you or care about you. And at the end of the afternoon, I knew two things: I would need to make another trip tomorrow, because a more important mission had taken my time today; and I needed to sit with Hal in a place and a time where I could absorb the wisdom that would too soon be gathered, as the Scriptures say, to his fathers.

I asked Hal if we could meet again.

CHAPTER ONE

A Greek friend once taught me a traditional Orthodox prayer known as "the Jesus Prayer." It is simple; a single sentence: "Lord Jesus Christ, have mercy on me." The extended, continuous repetition of this sentence is said to bring believers into a deeper, even mystical, communion with God. I don't know what effect such repetition has on mind or body to add to the spiritual force that must spring from absorbing the message of the prayer into one's soul. Its seven words contain all that is needed for spiritual life: confessing the Lordship of Christ, the sin of the believer (without which there would be no need for mercy), the plea for mercy, and the certainty that the Lord Jesus can and will provide it to those who ask.

I knew a little, but very little, of such things when I first met Hal. I had heard it at an early stage of my adult life as a believer of the practice of "praying the Scriptures"—taking a word, a phrase, or a verse and focusing meditation and prayer on it until it was absorbed into the soul like the Jesus prayer. Despite my intellectual knowledge of spiritual matters, my own life of prayer and meditation had been engaged lightly and infrequently. I had never experienced the mystical union with God from such prayer or meditation claimed by saints like Teresa of Avila, Madame Jeanne Guyon, or John of the Cross.

Even at the "book-learning" level, there were times when my poor and inconstant study of the Bible became stuck, wheels spinning in the proverbial rut, at a point that seemed insurmountable. Deuteronomy is a little-visited book, and it was just there that the mountain of Scripture was planted in my path, with no way around. A visiting preacher in our church asked once, only half in jest, if any of us could find Deuteronomy in our Bibles. Like too many people in the pew, even those who were biblically literate, I could find Deuteronomy, but I almost never found myself in it. The book is long—and long before Christ. For much of its length, it seems to bog down in detailed laws that no longer apply, at least to Christians. It consisted of Moses' speeches and teachings, but we had Jesus. It expressed the "old covenant," but we had the "new covenant." It was, in short, too old, too long, too Jewish, and too irrelevant. What was the point of studying it?

Yet many things about Deuteronomy intrigued me. It was Moses' end-of-life speeches and teachings, summarizing everything he had learned from the Lord and taught Israel for forty years. Surely the last words of such a monumental figure in religious and world history were worthy of attention.

It was also, I could see, a transitional book, marking the end of Israel's Exodus from Egypt, when the forty years of desert wandering were over and the conquest of the Promised Land was about to begin. Israel was camped on the Plains of Moab, east of the Jordan River, and Joshua was about to assume leadership. The historical books of Joshua through Second Kings would continue the story of the movement over the Jordan and the life of God's people in the land, a story of promise, failure, and ultimately destruction and exile in Babylon.

And, I read in my study Bible, it was a covenant—a contract or treaty document expressing the relationship between God and a special people he had chosen to serve him and to exemplify to the nations what a righteous nation under God is like.

I knew Deuteronomy to be a book embodying much of the law of ancient Israel. A literal translation of the Greek title was the "second law" or repetition of the law, and the title was appropriate. In Deuteronomy, the laws Moses had given Israel in the three preceding books—Exodus, Leviticus and Numbers—were sometimes repeated, sometimes summarized, sometimes abbreviated or expanded. Modern Christians have little interest in studying Old Testament law. But could the accounts of people and events in both testaments of the Bible—including the teachings of Jesus and his controversies with Jewish groups and leaders of his time—gain meaning from understanding the law contained in Deuteronomy?

It was also, commentators said, a book of deep theology. One writer called it "The theological colossus that guards the entrance to Old

Testament theology."[1] From beginning to end, it was a document of teaching and preaching, filled with instruction and understanding on right living and relationships between people and God, between people and their community, and between people and other people. It contained the Ten Commandments. It is the most often quoted Old Testament book by Jesus and the New Testament writers; it grounded their understanding of what the universe was all about. If it was that important to Jesus, perhaps it should be more important to me.

My mind turned over and over its opening phrase: "These are the words. . . ." Like the beginning of the book of Genesis, or of the Gospels of Mark, Luke, and John, it held a promise of depth in what followed that kept one at the beginning, as if peering into a well of pure water whose shiny surface reflected back the face of the viewer and needed to be penetrated to taste what lay beneath.

I decided to visit Hal again to explore these thoughts.

"These are the words . . ." (Deut. 1:1).

Anna and I had stopped on a couple of Saturdays but hadn't found Hal at home. I took her for a tour of his rose garden, knowing he would want me to share it with her. Some of the names of the varieties had stuck with me, but Anna saw color and composition rather than words, beauty rather than thought. The garden, she told me, was a reflection of the gardener. She told me to call Hal and find a time to get together with him. She encouraged me to spend as much time with him as I wanted. She sensed this was important to me and to my personal spiritual journey. Her own lifelong journey in the Spirit told her this was the right thing to do, the right time to do it, and the right person with whom to do it. Hal was happy to oblige my request.

I found Hal in his study on a late summer evening, when the early chill of fall was in the air. He was sitting in a deep red chair, facing the hearty flames of a fireplace. A soft, dim light flowed from the floor lamp over his shoulder. Two other lamps, on a table and a desk against opposite walls, helped illuminate the room. The study walls were floor to ceiling bookcases on every side, broken only by the entrance door, two west-facing windows with small panes, and the space where his desk was set into the bookcases between the windows. Like a condensed library in an English manor house or an expanded office of a university professor, bathed in the suffused orange of gentler light, it spoke as the dwelling of one who lived by words.

Hal invited me to sit in the shallower and harder green chair across from him. Would he help me study and understand Deuteronomy? I had purchased some commentaries by various academics and others about the book, and I was willing to read them—in fact I had already begun to do so. But I wasn't getting to the spiritual heart of the book, so I pressed my case with Hal.

He needed little persuasion. He didn't have a lot of people to pastor anymore, he told me. It would be a joy to his heart to share what he could with me. He asked me to commit to meet with him regularly and to prepare for the meetings, not just by reading Deuteronomy but by reading some background on it, studying it so we could talk at more than a superficial level. When I assured him I would, he reached for his Bible resting on a nearby table.

"Open your Bible to Deuteronomy and follow me while I read," he said.

"Moses proclaimed to the Israelites all the Lord had commanded him concerning them. . . . The Lord our God said to us at Horeb. . . . Then, as the Lord our God commanded us. . . . When the Lord heard what you said, he was angry and solemnly swore. . . . Because of you the Lord became angry with me also and said. . . . But the Lord said to me . . ." (1:3, 6, 19, 34, 37, 42).

"You see, Chris, that's only the first chapter of Deuteronomy, and already the words you are reading have been given six times as the very words of God. You are not reading the great American novel. And this is not a 'page turner' to hold you breathless until the next fictional adventure. Rather, you have come onto holy ground, where the author of all that is—the only final and ultimate reality—has shared with you a glimpse of that reality. You are peering into God's mind more surely than the scientist who studies the far reaches of the universe through images from great satellite-mounted telescopes, or one who teases from DNA molecules the secrets of the chemistry of being. And your author is about to take you on a journey that will carry you farther and reveal more to you than journeying to outer space on a rocket ship.

"Contemplate the very term *word*. The acts of creation themselves occur as spoken word—'God said'—let there be light, an expanse between the waters, dry ground, living creatures, man in our image. God reveals himself to humanity through both word and deed, but the deeds in turn are remembered and told and retold through the word. Word is communication, and communication is the essence of the triune God: Father, Son, and Holy Spirit. 'Word' expresses thought, logic, rationality, relationship, feeling, and finally becomes the expression of God himself: 'In the beginning was the Word, and the Word was with God, and the Word was God.' It is in this—the living Word—that all things hold together. Martin Luther wrote, 'But to hear God is bliss, even if He were to sound out the same syllable all the time.'[2]

"In your soul, you have sensed what 'the words' really are and are really about. You're afraid to see God. You're afraid to know him. That's why you're stuck in your journey. You aren't the first, but you have this—few who read these words have any understanding of the Awesome Presence in which they stand. You have felt the fire and seen the cloud. Don't turn back. Press on!"

It was enough for the evening. I was seized with awe and a dread. I thanked him for his words and fled into the night journey home. Hal had pried the scales a little bit loose from my eyes. I tried to see into the dark, beyond the short range of the headlights, all the while keeping my mind on worldly things enough to stay on the right side of the road and not be blinded by the oncoming masses of glass and steel.

"Moses spoke to all Israel in the desert east of the Jordan—that is, in the Arabah—opposite Suph, between Paran and Tophel, Laban, Hazeroth and Dizahab" (Deut. 1:1). The words echoed in my mind. Many Rabbis believe Moses' words in Deuteronomy were not all spoken on the plains of Moab, east of the Jordan. Rather they were accumulated speeches given in the villages along the route of travel—Suph, Paran, Tophel, Laban, Hazeroth, and Dihazeb, perhaps supplemented, summarized, or finalized in Moab. Others believe that the villages referred to are among the many nameless tells, those ancient mounds that were cities or villages in millennia past that dot the Middle East, no longer identifiable by name. Still others try to find modern villages in the area and transfigure the current name into a variation of the ancient biblical name and speculate that these mark the boundaries of the location of Israel in the time of Deuteronomy.

I saw none of these that night. As I drove through the little crossroads and village squares of the several rural New Hampshire towns that lay between Hal's home and mine, I counted off their names as the biblical towns of Deuteronomy: Barrington Suph, Northwood Paran, Epsom Tophel, Chichester Laban, Loudon Hazeroth, Concord Dihazeb. I had seen these villages before, from hills overlooking Cardiff in Wales, and Monaco in southern France, as well as San Francisco, Los Angeles, and Albuquerque in this country, and from the windows of a hundred airplanes flying over every part of America and much of Europe. They were every town, and all of their inhabitants stood on the edge of the Jordan, on the plains of Moab. Instead of deserts, forests, farms, lakes, and ponds filled in between the villages. It didn't matter. What lay around me was as dry as those dusty plains where Moses spoke.

> These are the words Moses spoke to all Israel in the desert east of the Jordan—that is, in the Arabah—opposite Suph, between Paran and Tophel, Laban, Hazeroth and Dizahab. (It takes eleven days to go from Horeb to Kadesh Barnea by the Mount Seir road.)
>
> In the fortieth year, on the first day of the eleventh month, Moses proclaimed to the Israelites all that the LORD had commanded him concerning them. This was after he had defeated Sihon king of the Amorites, who reigned in Heshbon, and at Edrei had defeated Og king of Bashan, who reigned in Ashtaroth.
>
> East of the Jordan in the territory of Moab, Moses began to expound this law.
>
> —Deut. 1:1–5

Monday morning came and the workweek swallowed me. Telephone callers demanding return courtesies, letters to read, letters to write, reports to digest and act on, projects to move, meetings, people with questions, people with needs, bills to send, the sweat of my brow by which to earn my bread. The bright fluorescence and busyness of the office environment could not be more distant from Hal's warm library. I was on the phone when the "notification" box flashed on my computer screen. It was an e-mail from Hal. My heart quickened, remembering our recent evening together. I clicked on "read" while still talking to my client.

> Chris: God speaks in rhythms as well as in words. Just as the molecules and atoms and subatomic particles that make up your being and everything else in the universe are bound together in a vibrating dance held together by forces that we give names to and try to measure but don't really understand, so does the Scripture cohere in ways we rarely see. The Bible is a whole book, not a series of disconnected texts. Like all good stories, it has a beginning, a middle, and an end; protagonists and antagonists; a series of scenes in which the main character, Adam, strives toward a goal that he is frustrated in reaching, until he finds the path. It is, of course, *the* good story, not *a* good story. But the music of Scripture is writ small as well as large. Bars and measures have patterns within themselves that go together to make up the whole symphony. Look for God's patterns in it. Read only the first five verses of Deuteronomy until you see the pattern. Then tell me what it is. When you can see the small rhythms, you will begin to be able to see the large. Blessings—Hal.

I rushed home that night and plunged into the text after dinner. It took an hour, but eventually I saw it. The text began with Moses speaking the words, progressed through a description of space ("east of the Jordan")—where the words were spoken—then time ("in the fortieth year")—when the words were spoken, to the core message, "Moses proclaimed to the Israelites all that the LORD had commanded him concerning them." Then in perfect rhythm, it reversed order, speaking to time ("after he had defeated"), then space ("east of the Jordan"), to where it started ("Moses began to expound this law"). I picked up the phone and called Hal with my discovery. His voice on the other end of the phone betrayed his pleasure at my discovery.

"The technical term for what you've found, Chris, is a chiasm. It's a concentric structure of music or text that can operate on any level, from the few verses you are studying, to the book of Deuteronomy, or the Bible as a whole. You can see the logic of it in an English translation. The poetry and music only come through fully in the Hebrew. The liturgical churches understand, intuitively at least, something of this, more than my own evangelical tradition. Truth and goodness are communicated through beauty. The music and poetry of it awaken our sensitivity to meaning. The Holy Spirit is not a hack writer. I think you're ready to go on."

I had a practical question for Hal first. "Why does God insert verse two in here, Hal? The reference to the eleven days it takes to go from Horeb to Kadesh Barnea seems out of place."

"The point," Hal said, "is to contrast the ease of God's way with the difficulty of man's. Horeb is Sinai—where the law was given. Kadesh Barnea was the place they were supposed to jump off for the Promised Land. You are about to read that part of the story, but the bottom line is that because of their lack of faith, it took the Israelites thirty-eight years to make a trip they could have made in eleven days if they had followed the Lord's command. His yoke is easy and his burden is light. Keep reading."

> The LORD our God said to us at Horeb, "You have stayed long enough at this mountain. Break camp and advance into the hill country of the Amorites; go to all the neighboring peoples in the Arabah, in the mountains, in the western foothills, in the Negev and along the coast, to the land of the Canaanites and to Lebanon, as far as the great river, the Euphrates. See, I have given you this land. Go in and take possession of the land that the LORD swore he would give to your fathers—to Abraham, Isaac, and Jacob—and to their descendants after them."
>
> —Deut. 1:6–8

Hal was in a Socratic mood when we met next. He sat across from me at a small table in the little coffee shop down the street from my office. The business day had not quite begun. To enhance the beginning of their workday, people drifted in and out, picking up take-out cups of flavored and specialty coffees. We sipped our own brew with bagels and strawberry cream cheese, though we didn't really want to eat but felt obligated to purchase something to justify occupying the seats.

"Tell me about your education," Hal began.

I recited my history: public school through the tenth grade, very ordinary, followed by a couple years at a private preparatory school, four years of undergraduate education, and three years of law school.

"Why did you spend nineteen years doing all that?" he asked next.

The early years were easy; I had, as did all children, to learn basics that enable one to function in the world. After that, I was more goal-oriented, with the learning gradually becoming more focused on what would be my life's work in the law, work I could not have done without everything that went before.

"How did you feel about education when you graduated from law school?"

I recalled it well. I had been in school long enough. It was time to leave school and practice the things I had learned. I was eager to start my first job—to be a real lawyer, with cases and clients, helping people, participating in the affairs of life through my chosen field of knowledge.

"And what does that have to do with the next three verses you are studying in Deuteronomy?" Hal brought his brief quiz back to the Scripture. I understood at once.

My schooling was the mountain where I had dwelt "long enough." When I finished my schooling, it was time to "break camp and advance." The Lord had put a world before me and prepared me to take possession of it. The time for sitting at the learning desk was over—it was the time of life to act. Deuteronomy 1:6–8 was every graduation speech I had ever heard. I'd heard it at my own graduation; no doubt my children and their children would hear it at theirs.

"But what does it teach spiritually?" Hal pressed.

His question led me on. We should move beyond being taught the basics of the faith to act in the world as the Lord taught us to act. There comes a time when sitting at the Lord's feet, at "the mountain," is no longer where we belong. There are lands before us to conquer in his name.

"It's the life goal of every pastor," Hal said, "to bring his flock away from the mountain and lead them into acting on the promise. I hear it in Moses throughout Deuteronomy, and in Paul when he says of himself, 'When I became a man, I put childish ways behind me,' and in the writer of Hebrews when he scolds his readers for still living on milk like infants, and not being ready for the solid food of maturity. Most people in the pew spend their life at the foot of the mountain, being hearers of the word but not doers. I used to plead with God to give me one congregation or one board of elders that could leave the mountain before my ministry was over, but he never did. There were some very deep and committed believers I knew over the years, some who moved on spiritually to deeper levels, and some who took possession of the promises God had laid out before them. But if success in ministry means leading people beyond the elementary level, I've been one of God's colossal failures as a servant."

His eyes were beginning to tear, and I was about to begin reassuring him that he must be wrong, that he surely had led many to a deeper understanding, that pastors always had to deal with the lowest common denominator in the congregation—the new people constantly coming in who needed the milk of elementary teachings of the faith. But before I could speak, he pushed his chair back, signaling the end of our talk. "You'll be late for work," he said abruptly. "We'll talk more about Deuteronomy later."

I e-mailed Hal that afternoon to ask if he was all right and to tell him I was eager to discuss the next section of the text. Verses nine through eighteen were about government, designation of leaders, judges and judging, things I thought I knew a little about. Hal quickly set me straight.

"You're not ready to talk about what you think you know," he replied by return. "The subject of government will come up in the text again, and we'll talk about it then. Just read the rest of chapter one, verses nineteen through forty-six, and the first verse of chapter two." So I did. Later, Hal e-mailed me and told me to meet him in the fast-food area of the airport for coffee the next evening.

Then, as the LORD our God commanded us, we set out from Horeb and went toward the hill country of the Amorites through all that vast and dreadful desert that you have seen, and so we reached Kadesh Barnea. Then I said to you, "You have reached the hill country of the Amorites, which the LORD our God is giving us. See, the LORD your God has given you the land. Go up and take possession of it as the LORD, the God of your fathers, told you. Do not be afraid; do not be discouraged."

Then all of you came to me and said, "Let us send men ahead to spy out the land for us and bring back a report about the route we are to take and the towns we will come to."

The idea seemed good to me; so I selected twelve of you, one man from each tribe. They left and went up into the hill country, and came to the Valley of Eshcol and explored it. Taking with them some of the fruit of the land, they brought it down to us and reported, "It is a good land that the LORD our God is giving us."

But you were unwilling to go up; you rebelled against the command of the LORD your God. You grumbled in your tents and said, "The LORD hates us; so he brought us out of Egypt to deliver us into the hands of the Amorites to destroy us. Where can we go? Our brothers have made us lose heart. They say, 'The people are stronger and taller than we are; the cities are large, with walls up to the sky. We even saw the Anakites there.'"

Then I said to you, "Do not be terrified; do not be afraid of them. The LORD your God, who is going before you, will fight for you, as he did for you in Egypt, before your very eyes, and in the desert. There you saw how the LORD your God carried you, as a father carries his son, all the way you went until you reached this place."

In spite of this, you did not trust in the LORD your God, who went ahead of you on your journey, in fire by night and in a cloud by day, to search out places for you to camp and to show you the way you should go.

When the LORD heard what you said, he was angry and solemnly swore: "Not a man of this evil generation shall see the good land I swore to give your forefathers, except Caleb son of Jephunneh. He will see it, and I will give him and his descendants the land he set his feet on, because he followed the LORD wholeheartedly."

Because of you the LORD became angry with me also and said, "You shall not enter it, either. But your assistant, Joshua son of Nun, will enter it. Encourage him, because he will lead Israel to inherit it. And the little ones that you said would be taken captive, your children who do not yet know good from bad—they will enter the land. I will give it to them and they will take possession of it. But as for you, turn around and set out toward the desert along the route to the Red Sea."

Then you replied, "We have sinned against the LORD. We will go up and fight, as the LORD our God commanded us." So every one of you put on his weapons, thinking it easy to go up into the hill country.

But the LORD said to me, "Tell them, 'Do not go up and fight, because I will not be with you. You will be defeated by your enemies.'"

So I told you, but you would not listen. You rebelled against the LORD's command and in your arrogance you marched up into the hill country. The Amorites who lived in those hills came out against you; they chased you like a swarm of bees and beat you down from Seir all the way to Hormah. You came back and wept before the LORD, but he paid no attention to your weeping and turned a deaf ear to you. And so you stayed in Kadesh many days—all the time you spent there.

> Then we turned back and set out toward the desert along
> the route to the Red Sea, as the LORD had directed me. For a
> long time we made our way around the hill country of Seir.
> —Deut. 1:19–2:1

Manchester Airport is a busy regional airport. Tens of thousands of flights and several million passengers pass through it every year. The next evening, as I took my place across from Hal with a cup of McDonald's coffee, the security lines for the evening flights were formed, and travelers by the hundreds were moving in and out of the terminal, a steady wave of humanity on the way to or from some business or family or recreational destination. Someone has observed that all stories ever told could be titled either "I Took a Trip" or "A Stranger Came to Town." The story contained in the Hebrew Scriptures—the Old Testament, the Bible that Jesus read—is of the "I Took a Trip" nature, a journey story of God's revelation to humanity, focused into the journeys of men and women of faith and then of a people chosen to be a people of faith. The story told in the Christian Scriptures—the New Testament, the part of the Bible written about Jesus by those who walked with him or learned from others who had—is of "The Stranger Who Came to Town."

Hal sipped on his coffee and I on mine as we watched the flow of people for a time.

"I thought we should discuss this section somewhere that we could get a sense of journeys," Hal began. "Watch the people going by. Think about what the journey is, for each one—where they've been, where they're going—now, tomorrow, next week."

I recognized the journey motif easily in the passage that made up the rest of chapter one. The travel from Horeb to Kadesh Barnea on the edge of the Promised Land, the mission of the spies, the rebellion against entry into the land, the change of heart after it was too late and the unsuccessful attempt at entry, and the thirty-eight years of wilderness wandering. It was an abbreviated recapitulation of the journey story told at great length in the earlier books, and a reminder to the people of where they had been. In academic terms—I had learned from the commentaries—it was part of the "historical prologue" that preceded the requirements of the law that was to be given in Deuteronomy and made part of a covenant between God and the people. But Hal was not interested in academic analysis. After my summary, he plunged in.

"Journeys," he said, "are not just travel in space. The journey of Israel in this passage is a journey in space and in time, like these people around us. But, more importantly, it is the journey of the spiritual experience of the people. It covers most of the wanderings before the entry into the land—a period of thirty-eight years—and the experience of a failure of faith. They have been brought out of the bondage of Egypt, led through hardship to the edge of plenty, and promised success by the Creator of the universe. Yet they refuse to go in, blaming their unbelief on God's evil motives toward them. Although God saved them by bringing them out of Egypt, they claim he intends to destroy them at the hands of Amorites. Although God loved them and carried them 'as a father carries his son,' they claim that he hates them. It's the psychological phenomenon of 'projection,' where a person attributes to another the same feeling that he or she has toward that person."

"You mean they really hate God?" I asked.

"What else can you conclude?" Hal answered my question with a question of his own. "At every turn, they do the opposite of what he asks. Every time he shows them why they should have faith in him, they are unfaithful. Then the consequences of their unbelief are brought to them. He sends them back toward the desert and tells them they will not see the good land; only their children will. This is, in effect, a death sentence—to wander in 'that vast and dreadful desert' for the rest of their lives. Faced with the consequence of their sin, they repent and try to make it up by doing what they're no longer commanded to do—a further rebellion—and the result is utter failure. At every point, they act contrary to God, and the result is that the blessings are withheld and given to a generation that will accept them."

I wondered aloud with Hal about how I should find the story relevant to my own life—or to the lives of people filing by. Was it just about a nation, or does it apply to individuals? Is it of interest only as history? Or as moral teaching? Or does it represent something more?

"The Hebrew scripture of Deuteronomy," Hal responded, "is written with 'you'—the people to whom it is addressed—in both the singular and plural. The shift from addressing the individual to the group 'you' occurs throughout the book, often within discrete passages. Since both are translated simply 'you' in English, you don't see the difference in English Bibles. In biblical studies, the technical term for this is the 'Numeruswechsel.' Both singular and plural 'you' appear in this passage. You don't need to remember the technical term, but what's important is that the message is addressed to both the nation and to individuals."

"To me *and* my country, then, right?" I asked.

"For you, Chris, that means it is addressed to you personally and to every other individual human being. But the heir to the Israel of Moses is not the modern state of Israel, nor the United States, nor any other contemporary nation. It is the church—in the words of the Apostles' Creed, 'the holy catholic church,' the church universal, the community of believers, or at least those who associate together and profess to be believers."

"So it's really for me and the church," I said. "But how is it relevant?"

"As for its relevance," Hal said, "this would be a good time to talk a little bit about how we should interpret Scripture. We'll need to deal with this all the way along in our study together. The story we are reading now is, first of all, history, and we can learn from its example. It is, of course, history with a moral. The story is not told just to tell it, and not just because it happened or is interesting. It is a story with a point, a teaching, something we need to absorb and by which we need to be guided. Acting in faith and in accordance with God's will brings success, while unbelief and hesitancy in the face of God's clear command brings defeat, disaster, and wandering without hope in a wilderness. As the saying goes, 'Those who do not learn from history are condemned to repeat it.'"

The security lines were growing short. Most of the evening flights had loaded and left; the sojourners within them were on their way to the next stage of their journey, or to their destination.

"What else?" I asked. "This sounds like a literal understanding. Simple enough. The Bible tells a story, the facts are true, and there are lessons to be gained. Are there other ways of understanding it?"

"There are," Hal said. "Beyond the literal historical sense—and the moral or example we can take from that—are the allegorical, typological, and anagogical senses of Scripture. These are not the same, but people use the terms somewhat interchangeably, and everyone doesn't always mean the same thing when they use them. They must be used with care."

"I think I know about allegory and types," I said. "But what's the difference?"

"In allegory," Hal replied, "whole stories or sections of Scripture are sometimes seen as symbolic or figurative of something else, ways of expressing truths about God and humanity. Stories that don't fit well with our current human understanding, such as the early chapters of Genesis, or the books of Job or Jonah, are often seen as allegorical. A great danger in allegory is that it can lead to flights of fancy where the true meaning of the Scripture is lost in human imagining and we hear man and not God. Another danger is that allegorical interpretations become focused on words, or, worse, numbers, and find hidden meanings in the text that are supposedly known only to some inner circle. This is the stuff that leads to cults."

"And the allegory here?"

"The story of Israel is the story of humanity," Hal replied. "God does great things for them, and they turn away from him, afraid to follow his commands, blaming him for their fears. In the end, they deserve only wilderness wanderings and death."

"And what about typology?"

"In typology," Hal said, "particular historical events are seen as prefiguring or symbolizing something that comes to full significance in Christ. The crossing of the Red Sea prefigures baptism; Jonah prefigures the resurrection of Christ. Typology is usually grounded in the Scriptures themselves, which often make these connections explicit. Jesus taught that the Law of Moses, as well as the prophets and the psalmists, all wrote of him, so we are not off base in seeing these connections. Moses is a type of Christ in many respects."

"You had something else, too," I said. "A word I've never heard before."

"Anagogical," Hal replied. "In anagogical interpretation, one finds—beyond the literal, moral, allegorical, or typological—a spiritual and even mystical sense in which the scripture has eternal significance in leading believers to the true homeland. The anagogical sense of Scripture is better felt than taught; it's what comes from the depth of contemplating God in prayer and meditation in light of the Scriptures. When you understand Scripture in an anagogical sense, you will have gotten beyond the milk of elementary teachings and will be eating real spiritual meat."

The last evening flights had landed and their passengers disembarked. As Hal and I parted, we passed through the crowds on their journeys through the world, briefcases in hand, suitcases trundling behind them, and children in tow. I had much to contemplate. History with a moral. Israel as an allegory of humanity, its journey that of Everyman. Moses prefiguring Christ. And that other word—anagogical—the deeper spiritual meaning. I could think of far too many events in my own life—and in that of churches of which I had been a part—that were troublingly similar to the story of the spies, the rebellion against taking God's promise, and the resulting exile in the spiritual wilderness. I watched the travelers in the airport making their way past, to cabs or cars or shuttle vans, carrying the baggage of life to wherever they were going. Every one was a human soul on a journey—in time, in space, and in their spiritual life. How many, I wondered, were wandering in the wilderness? How many standing in disobedience to God's clear commands? How many on their way to the Promised Land? How many—indeed, were there any—who knew God's words in their truest spiritual sense? Did I? Could I?

I was glad I would be meeting with Hal again soon.

CHAPTER TWO

In most of our churches, the Sunday after Labor Day is the most highly attended church service of the year, more so than even Christmas and Easter. People are rested and full of energy and resolution and commitment for the months ahead. Children are in school and in Sunday school. The excuses they used to drift away in previous years are forgotten. This year, things are going to be different. As the weeks and months go by, they never are. But in September, we can pretend we have been born again into another year.

Hal and I agreed to settle in to the new year—like the rest of the world in its new year—with a pattern. We would meet Friday nights to continue our study unless one of us had another commitment we couldn't break. We would try to cover a chapter a week. We would commit the year ahead to the study, but we would not ramble on indefinitely. The next Friday night, I headed for Hal's, fresh with my study of chapter two of Deuteronomy.

Perhaps part of my freshness came from the time of year. The end had come to the all-too-short New England summer. It is a time when life slows down, and this summer had been no exception. Business was conducted intermittently, vacations were taken, weekends were spent on lakes or at the beach, and activities, from cooking to sports, moved outside. We took our annual Sabbath rest from the intensity and busyness of the other seasons. Labor Day had just passed. In New England, it's the real New Year's Day. The year by which people live their lives began then and continued to the end of the following August. Children were back in school, and life had a serious purpose again. The crisp, dry feel of fall was in the air. My homework was done, and I was ready for the professor.

Then the LORD said to me, "You have made your way around this hill country long enough; now turn north. Give the people these orders: 'You are about to pass through the territory of your brothers the descendants of Esau, who live in Seir. They will be afraid of you, but be very careful. Do not provoke them to war, for I will not give you any of their land, not even enough to put your foot on. I have given Esau the hill country of Seir as his own. You are to pay them in silver for the food you eat and the water you drink.'"

The LORD your God has blessed you in all the work of your hands. He has watched over your journey through this vast desert. These forty years the LORD your God has been with you, and you have not lacked anything.

So we went on past our brothers the descendants of Esau, who live in Seir. We turned from the Arabah road, which comes up from Elath and Ezion Geber, and traveled along the desert road of Moab.

Then the LORD said to me, "Do not harass the Moabites or provoke them to war, for I will not give you any part of their land. I have given Ar to the descendants of Lot as a possession."

(The Emites used to live there—a people strong and numerous, and as tall as the Anakites. Like the Anakites, they too were considered Rephaites, but the Moabites called them Emites. Horites used to live in Seir, but the descendants of Esau drove them out. They destroyed the Horites from before them and settled in their place, just as Israel did in the land the LORD gave them as their possession.)

And the LORD said, "Now get up and cross the Zered Valley." So we crossed the valley.

Thirty-eight years passed from the time we left Kadesh Barnea until we crossed the Zered Valley. By then, that entire generation of fighting men had perished from the camp, as the LORD had sworn to them. The LORD's hand was against them until he had completely eliminated them from the camp.

Now when the last of these fighting men among the people had died, the LORD said to me, "Today you are to pass by the region of Moab at Ar. When you come to the Ammonites, do not harass them or provoke them to war, for I will not give you possession of any land belonging to the Ammonites. I have given it as a possession to the descendants of Lot."

(That too was considered a land of the Rephaites, who used to live there; but the Ammonites called them Zamzummites. They were a people strong and numerous, and as tall as the Anakites. The LORD destroyed them from before the Ammonites, who drove them out and settled in their place. The LORD had done the same for the descendants of Esau, who lived in Seir, when he destroyed the Horites from before them. They drove them out and have lived in their place to this day. And as for the Avvites who lived in villages as far as Gaza, the Caphtorites coming out from Caphtor destroyed them and settled in their place.)

"Set out now and cross the Arnon Gorge."
—Deut. 2:2–24

The setting for chapter two, I had learned, is the land on the eastern side of the Dead Sea, traversed south to north by ancient trade routes followed by the Israelites on their journey. The Dead Sea, or Salt Sea as the Bible often calls it, is the lowest water body on earth. Unlike other lakes or inland seas, it has inlets, principally the Jordan River, but no outlets. As a result, it is six times saltier than ocean water and nothing lives in it but a few bacteria that can tolerate the conditions. Sodom and Gomorrah were located on its south end, where pillars of salt can still be found. The fortress of Masada—where the Jewish garrison committed suicide rather than be taken by the Romans in the time of the revolt in 70 A.D.—is on the west side, as are the caves where the Dead Sea Scrolls were found. On the east are the ancient kingdoms of Moab, and, north of it, Ammon, as well as the fortress of Machaerus, where the historian Josephus relates that John the Baptist was imprisoned by Herod.

Viewed from above, the Dead Sea is a fifty-mile-long lake within the Great Rift Valley, a separation of earth's plates that has left a depression beginning at the Sea of Galilee, following the course of the Jordan River south to the Dead Sea, then down the valley known as the Arabah that runs from the south end of the Dead Sea to the Red Sea, continuing south through the Red Sea and into East Africa, and ending in Mozambique. Its 4,000-mile length, the longest such valley in the world, is replete with biblical and human history, from Jesus' recruitment of fishermen disciples along the Galilee shores to the Olduvai Gorge in East Africa, where anthropologists have unearthed early fossils of what are claimed to be human ancestors. It was to the east of the valley, along the Dead Sea—"along the desert road of Moab"—that Moses led the Israelites when God told them to "turn north."

Two watercourses enter the Dead Sea from the east: the Wadi Zered and the Wadi Arnon. The Zered runs into the south end of the sea from the wadi's origins to the southeast, and was, in Moses' time, the boundary between Edom to the south and Moab to the north. The Arnon enters the Sea at the midpoint of the easterly side and marks the northerly boundary of Moab. Both represent significant transitions on the journey of Israel to the Promised Land.

The crossing of the Zered is the point at which the "entire generation of fighting men" who had refused to fight (in the rebellion against entry into the land) had perished. The Lord's promise that none of them would see "the good land" and that he would give it to their children was now ready for fulfillment. The crossing of the Arnon Gorge represents another significant transition. The gorge itself is a spectacular geological feature, cutting a swath with depths up to 3,000 feet into the surrounding plateau. When Israel crossed the Arnon, it was no longer within territory of its "brothers," or of peoples God had told them not to provoke because he had given the land to these nations. It was now venturing into hostile territory where the current generation would have to take up arms.

All this I had learned in my study, preparing for my next meeting with Hal. The geography of the journey and the significance of the points of crossing—the Zered and the Arnon—captured my attention. I was pleased with my learning and feeling fresh for the study ahead.

I told Hal about my observations—about the significance of the crossing of the Zered and the Arnon gorge. He agreed that these were signal crossings in the journey. The sin of the earlier generation had been wiped out with the Zered crossing, and the Arnon crossing was when the people began to come into the promise. But when we talked about the geography and the Great Rift Valley, Hal had a different message and a different vision.

"Do you see, Chris, how mired in the clay your feet still are? When you read this passage, you saw geography—geography that has significance in the physical and spiritual journey of God's people, but still geography. You looked up maps and facts, but you didn't look up to God. See the valley instead as the source from where the good news of God's salvation first welled up. Moses led God's people along the road, on the high ground on the east side of the valley, to get past the Dead Sea. On the west side lay the Promised Land, and they needed to cross the valley to reach it. From there, God's promise to Abraham that all the nations of the earth would be blessed through him would be fulfilled. Jesus would be born there, baptized there by John the Baptist, and begin—and spend—much of his ministry there. From him would come the grace and truth that would fill the valley and spill out to Africa in the south, Asia in the east, and Europe and the Americas to the north and west, until it fills the whole world and all people have heard the good news. This is not a local thing of wadis and water bodies; it's the heartbeat of creation waiting, in the fullness of time, to pump life-giving blood, living water, to nourish the whole earth."

Hal's vision of the passage swept me beyond the geography of the Valley. It occurred to me that it approached the anagogical meaning of the Scripture we had discussed earlier, while I was still looking at the literal and historical. As I contemplated this, Hal stood and walked across the room. He took a globe off a bookshelf, brought it back, and set it on the coffee table in front of us. He spun it slowly and then reached out his hand to stop it when the eastern hemisphere was

"Don't miss something else here, Chris. God's chosen people are marching through occupied territory. They are instructed to treat the inhabitants fairly, paying for what they receive, and to deal with them peaceably. As Paul says in Romans, 'If it is possible, as far as it depends on you, live at peace with everyone.' This describes the relationship we should have with those around us as we journey through the world of nonbelievers."

The evening was wearing on. "We'll save the rest of the chapter for another time," Hal said. "Pray with me."

We had not prayed together before, and he didn't ask me to pray. But Hal prayed, and his prayer was more than sufficient for both of us. He did not thank God for our time together, or for the Scripture, or ask for wisdom or health for us or our own. Rather, he prayed for all the people of the world. He prayed over Africa and South America, Europe and Asia and Australia, islands of the Pacific, and the lost souls of North America and everywhere in between. He asked God to fill again the empty cathedrals of Europe, and to bring knowledge of himself and mercy without measure to those who worshipped gods that were not gods and were deceived by every false religion and philosophy humanity could invent. He cried out to God for mercy on the ignorant and disobedient peoples of every land. He praised him for the glories of his creation, but especially his creation of human beings, and called on God to bring them to himself as he had brought Israel to himself thousands of years earlier. He prayed that God's kingdom would come on earth for every person and for all peoples.

In the center of Russell Square in Savannah, Georgia, is a statue of John Wesley, preacher, evangelist, and founder of Methodism, who spent two years in that city (1736 and 1737), while traveling from England. Inscribed at the bottom is a quote from Wesley: "I regard all the world as my parish." Although Hal had never pastored a church outside northern New England, it was clear to me that he had moved into that small group of men of God like Wesley whose parish was the whole world. I was thankful to be one of his closest parishioners.

The hour was late; it was time to part. We had already failed in our first resolution—we had not gotten through chapter two. But some things more important than keeping on schedule had happened.

Hal's prayer stayed with me for weeks. It came back to me as I worked out in the exercise club, traveled to appointments, woke up in the middle of the night—those times when your body is idle or on autopilot and the mind engages with the ideas that are waiting in the shadows for an opportunity to be thought, studied, examined, and perhaps fondled. The world is full of peoples and nations that pursue false philosophies and false religions, that do not know their Creator, or see him only dimly or imperfectly through human imaginings, or that know of him and choose not to follow him. It has always been thus. And yet he made them all, was sovereign over them all, and exercises that sovereignty whether they know it or not. Should we conclude that there are indeed many ways to God as some claim? What level of ignorance does he forgive? And to what level of accountability for ignorance does he hold those who know him and have the truth? These questions troubled my mind as I recalled Hal's prayers. They were questions I would meet again before we completed our study.

Hal told me to read through chapter three, verse eleven, before I came to see him again. In our next session I was to get another jolt to my thinking about other peoples.

> See, I have given into your hand Sihon the Amorite, king of Heshbon, and his country. Begin to take possession of it and engage him in battle. This very day I will begin to put the terror and fear of you on all the nations under heaven. They will hear reports of you and will tremble and be in anguish because of you.

> From the desert of Kedemoth I sent messengers to Sihon king of Heshbon offering peace and saying, "Let us pass through your country. We will stay on the main road; we will not turn aside to the right or to the left. Sell us food to eat and water to drink for their price in silver. Only let us pass through on foot—as the descendants of Esau, who live in Seir, and the Moabites, who live in Ar, did for us— until we cross the Jordan into the land the LORD our God is giving us." But Sihon king of Heshbon refused to let us pass through. For the LORD your God had made his spirit

stubborn and his heart obstinate in order to give him into your hands, as he has now done.

The LORD said to me, "See, I have begun to deliver Sihon and his country over to you. Now begin to conquer and possess his land."

When Sihon and all his army came out to meet us in battle at Jahaz, the LORD our God delivered him over to us and we struck him down, together with his sons and his whole army. At that time we took all his towns and completely destroyed them—men, women, and children. We left no survivors. But the livestock and the plunder from the towns we had captured we carried off for ourselves. From Aroer on the rim of the Arnon Gorge, and from the town in the gorge, even as far as Gilead, not one town was too strong for us. The LORD our God gave us all of them. But in accordance with the command of the LORD our God, you did not encroach on any of the land of the Ammonites, neither the land along the course of the Jabbok nor that around the towns in the hills.

Next we turned and went up along the road toward Bashan, and Og king of Bashan with his whole army marched out to meet us in battle at Edrei. The LORD said to me, "Do not be afraid of him, for I have handed him over to you with his whole army and his land. Do to him what you did to Sihon king of the Amorites, who reigned in Heshbon."

So the LORD our God also gave into our hands Og king of Bashan and all his army. We struck them down, leaving no survivors. At that time we took all his cities. There was not one of the sixty cities that we did not take from them— the whole region of Argob, Og's kingdom in Bashan. All these cities were fortified with high walls and with gates and bars, and there were also a great many unwalled villages. We completely destroyed them, as we had done with Sihon king of Heshbon, destroying every city—men, women, and children. But all the livestock and the plunder from their cities we carried off for ourselves.

So at that time we took from these two kings of the Amorites the territory east of the Jordan, from the Arnon Gorge as far as Mount Hermon. (Hermon is called Sirion by the Sidonians; the Amorites call it Senir.) We took all the towns on the plateau, and all Gilead, and all Bashan as far as Salecah and Edrei, towns of Og's kingdom in Bashan. (Only Og king of Bashan was left of the remnant of the Rephaites. His bed was made of iron and was more than thirteen feet long and six feet wide. It is still in Rabbah of the Ammonites.)

—Deut. 2:24–3:11

"Where do we get our language?" Hal asked, sinking into his old red chair after handing me a cup of freshly brewed decaf.

"Ummm . . . Latin . . . and German?" I was reaching into language courses I hadn't thought about since high school.

"The English language," Hal replied, "is a composite of Norman French, in turn derived from Latin, and German, with words borrowed from many other languages, one of which is Hebrew. Do you know any Hebrew words we use?"

Most of the Hebrew words I could think of were first names for people. According to a survey I recalled, Jacob was the most popular name for boys in the United States. Other biblical names are in common and familiar use, names such as David, Jonathan, Isaac, Adam, Paul, Stephen, John, Micah, Noah, etc., for boys, and Mary, Elizabeth, Sarah, Rachel, Rebecca, Abigail, Deborah, and Priscilla for girls.

"All good biblical names," Hal said. "And there are many more. The early settlers here used a lot of biblical names for places as well." He called to my attention New Hampshire towns named Canaan, Hebron, Goshen, and Bethlehem. I mentioned the Hebrew praise term *Hallelujah*, which we use in music and worship, and *Amen* to end prayer or affirm statements. Other terms are familiar from Jewish practice and culture: *shalom, Rosh Hashanah, Yom Kippur, kosher.*

"Where are we going with this, Hal?" I asked. It seemed far from the scriptures about the battles with Sihon, King of Heshbon, and Og, King of Bashan.

"I'm going to teach you a Hebrew word that has not been borrowed," Hal said. "First, do you know what the word *harem* means?"

"Sure. That's where Arab sheiks or the sultans keep their women."

"Another borrowed word," Hal said. "This time from Arabic. We think of it as the place where the women are kept, but it has a more generic meaning—a separated, maybe even sacred, place, set aside for a special purpose. Arabic and Hebrew are similar languages. The Hebrew cognate for *harem* is *herem*. Look back at your text. *Herem* is the word translated 'completely destroyed' in chapter two, verse thirty-four, and chapter three, verse six. It's a biblical word that hasn't been adopted into our language. The concept of *herem* is so foreign to us that we lack a suitable word to translate it."

"Well, it is translated," I said. "Completely destroyed."

"Yes," Hal said. "But here Moses is talking about people; all the people, women, and children as well, not just the city. It refers to the irrevocable devotion or sacrifice of things, including people, to the Lord—a holy massacre. The term is used later in Deuteronomy in instructions to the people as to how to conduct war in the Promised Land. The practice of herem was not confined to Israel. The 'Moabite Stone' is a three-foot-high inscribed basalt stone, dated to around 830 B.C., which records the triumphs of the Moabite king, Mesha, including his practice of herem in devoting, or sacrificing, the 7,000 inhabitants of the Israelite town of Nebo to the Moabite deity."

"I see why we didn't borrow that word," I said.

The slaughter by herem of the people of Heshbon and Bashan, and later of Jericho and other locations west of the Jordan, was, in modern terms, genocide—a holocaust with a holy rationale. I could understand how surrounding peoples, worshipping false gods, could fall into such practices. But God's people, acting under God's instructions—how could this be? I imagined the terror of the inhabitants of these cities, especially the helpless women and children after the defeat of their armies, as the Hebrew soldiers rampaged through the towns, dragging them from hiding places, slaughtering them in their homes and in the streets and fields as they fled in panic. The horrors of the Holocaust visited by the Nazis on the Jewish people of Germany and central Europe were in my mind. The murderous philosophy of the perpetrators of the September 11, 2001, attack on the World Trade Center, and other terrorist outrages, seemed to share the same ground—a conviction that they were serving God by indiscriminately slaughtering people because they were Americans, or Jews, or Westerners, or happened to be where such people were. In a lifetime of church-going, I had never heard these biblical issues addressed by a pastor. And I was sure they were never taught in Sunday school. I was troubled.

"Help me out, Hal," I said. "How should we understand this? I can't believe it came from the mind of God."

Hal turned on his computer and took me on a virtual tour of the Holocaust Museum in Washington, D.C. We discussed how the Nazi Holocaust of Jews was rightly understood as perhaps the greatest evil that has arisen in the modern world, and how the Holocaust Museum and other memorials in Israel, Germany, and elsewhere keep alive the horror of it so that humanity will not again fall into such genocidal thinking. We discussed the many books and movies that had preserved the memory of it in our culture (*Schindler's List, The Pianist,* and others), and the stories of heroism of those who resisted the evil, hid and protected Jews, and smuggled them out of Nazi Europe. Hal pointed out that though the Nazi attempt to impose the "final solution" on the Jews was the most poignant such evil of our time and the most imprinted on the Western conscience, it was not unique. In modern times man's evil had, because of education, socio-economic status, or ownership of land, imposed slaughters on countless millions of Russians, Chinese, Cambodians, and others under Communism; on Tutsis and Armenians because of the ethnic group to which they belonged; and on Muslims in Kosovo and Bosnia and Christians in Sudan and elsewhere, because of their religion. Twentieth-century slaughters had corrected those Pollyannas who thought humanity was making moral progress.

"All these were great evils," Hal said. "Our revulsion at them is justified. Why God in his sovereignty allowed them to occur is something we should discuss, but that is for another day."

"So what is going on here in Deuteronomy, Hal?" I asked. "If God hates genocide now, how could he have ordered it then? Is this really what Scripture teaches?"

Hal rose and walked to the window. The last touches of day were fading, and his gaze seemed to follow them as darkness eclipsed the world. He turned back toward me, his head low.

"First, Chris, accept that this is real. God really did direct the total extermination of certain peoples at a certain time and place in history. You need to understand why and what it tells you about God's nature. A lot of Christians hide under a rock when they come to this subject. They find it inconsistent with the God of perfect and complete mercy and love; the God of grace, who extends undeserved favor on us; the God of whom Jesus taught. This Old Testament God, they say, must be a historical artifact—the imperfect and erroneous understanding of a primitive people echoing the barbarity of other people and cultures around them, or a later invention of a history that never really happened to make a theological point of how Israel should keep itself pure of corrupting influences, or an allegory of the extermination of sin in the life of the believer."

He returned to his seat. "All of these deny the authority of the Bible and put human wisdom ahead of God's revelation of himself in the Scriptures. They would allow us to pick and choose what we like in the Bible and ignore the rest. The Scriptures become simply a convenient well to dip into when we need a quote or a rationale for what we want to do rather than a constitution and framework for understanding the universe and how we should live in it."

"OK," I said. "So how do we understand it?"

"From the time of Adam and Eve, death has been the lot of every man and woman. God has his own reasons, which we can't always know, as to why some people die early and some late in life . . . some in circumstances of injustice, pain, fear, or even horror, and some peacefully in their sleep. Keep an eternal perspective on this—death in this life is entry into the next; we were all made for eternal life. Physical death is a passage, not an end. It's a tragedy only for those who have rejected God and have no hope of life with him in eternity."

"We all die," I said. "I understand that. But that doesn't make killing right."

"Of course not," Hal said. "But the slaughter of the Amorite peoples in the Promised Land at the command of God is not a unique circumstance in the Bible. Remember the flood? God saw how great the wickedness of mankind had become and how 'every inclination of the thoughts of his heart was only evil all the time.' At that time he destroyed all humanity except for one man and his family. That was a much greater destruction than the 'herem' of the conquest of Canaan.

"And remember Sodom and Gomorrah? Because of their wickedness these Canaanite cities were also destroyed totally, except for one man and his family. The waters of the flood and the burning sulphur that rained down on the sinful cities wiped out pregnant women and children, people of all ages and degrees of guilt.

"The only difference between these events and the herem destruction of the Amorite people in Deuteronomy is that in the latter event God used a human agency rather than natural forces for the destruction. But God used human agents later against Israel itself, sending the Assyrian and Babylonian armies to slaughter and take captive a disobedient people.

"As to the idea that the New Testament God is above all these things, one need only read Jesus' words on the Mount of Olives in Matthew twenty-four, or the book of Revelation, to understand that such things will happen again. The return of Jesus at the end of time will not be for teaching and preaching but to gather his own and bring death and destruction to his enemies. He will tread 'the winepress of the fury of the wrath of God Almighty.' It will be a time of total destruction of those who are not believers."

I was beginning to see a picture here. Hal was putting it in the context of the whole Scripture. And he was on a roll. "Do you remember how we talked about the several senses or ways of understanding Scripture the other day? So far we have talked only about the literal. If you want to get the moral sense, or at least some insight into it, read the eighteenth chapter of Leviticus." He turned to it. "There are eighteen verses of descriptions of improper sexual relations, including incest, adultery, homosexuality, and bestiality, as well as child sacrifice. These were the practices of the nations God was going to drive out before them. And then he uses one of the most arresting figures of speech in the Bible: 'The land vomited out its inhabitants.' And, lest the Israelites miss the point, he goes on to promise them that if they engage in the same practices, it will vomit them out too. The herem destruction of the peoples of that land is the vomiting out of a people who had fallen into such unholy and abhorrent practices and ways of living that God in his righteous anger decreed their destruction. The only solution, as in Noah's time, was to wipe out the entire culture and start again with a God-fearing and God-honoring culture, this people of Israel that he had chosen for the purpose. That is the literal and historical meaning of the 'herem' sacrifice of the Canaanite people when Israel entered the land."

The image of a land vomiting out the people who lived there to cleanse itself of sickness gave me pause. Many of the practices that were mentioned in the passage from Leviticus were current in our own place and time. But Hal was moving on.

"In the typological or figurative sense, the destruction of the Amorites is like the destruction of all ungodly people that will occur in the end times. It's a judgment and a notice of what lies ahead when history is over. How many of the people around us understand that they live under the sword of God's judgment? Whom do they serve . . . really serve? The false gods of Canaan, concealed in their modern garb? Or their Creator and Redeemer? How many have some pious, sentimental view of God and heaven, expecting him to make everything all right for them in the end after a lifetime of displaying their unbelief by ignoring him or disobeying him? How many understand that, even if we don't live in the end times when these things will be fulfilled, we live in our own end times when we will have to meet the King of Kings and Lord of Lords at the end of our own lives, which could come at any moment?

"And in the allegorical sense, the utter destruction of this sinful people is a figure for the Christian destroying the vestiges of sin in his or her life, what we sometimes refer to as the 'old man' in us after we become believers. Like Israel in Canaan, we never quite get there and some vestige always remains. But the command to utterly destroy what is ungodly in us stands."

"And the anagogical sense?" I asked.

"In the anagogical or spiritual sense," Hal said, "the wars of conquest of the Promised Land were wars that transcended the human and earthly. The land before Israel was in the grip of wickedness and spiritual darkness. The inhabitants were hopelessly and irrevocably in rebellion against their Creator. Their idolatry was a declaration of war against God, a proclamation of other supernatural powers that should be worshipped. God used Israel to invade and reclaim from the forces of evil and darkness a portion of what belongs to him." He paused and then added, "Don't ever think that those forces are not real and are not still at work in the world. They are real, and they are still here."

Hal rose to refill our coffee cups. When he came back with the pot, I had a question.

"When the Israelites were passing by Edom and Moab and Ammon, they were taught to be peaceful and treat these people fairly. You're teaching me that these are principles to live by—that they teach universal truths for believers. But after that, these people of God were told to slaughter the present inhabitants of the land they were being given. Why isn't that the universal principle? Are we just deciding that we like the peaceful, fair principles more than the genocidal principle as a personal preference? How can we distinguish these?"

"When I was in seminary," Hal said, "we were taught a phrase to help in understanding Scripture: 'Text without context is pretext.' To illustrate, one could accurately say that the Bible states, 'There is no God.' But the full quote, in context, is this: 'The fool has said in his heart that there is no God.' The full message is very different.

"With respect to your question, the context is the whole book—the entirety of Scripture. The principles of peacefulness, fairness, and helping others run through the whole book, from the law to the prophets to the teachings of Jesus, Paul, and the other New Testament writers. But nowhere in the later texts does God command his people to slaughter other peoples. The fate of the Amorite people who occupied the Promised Land was a one-time event, not a guideline for dealing with others in the future. We have no biblical warrant to carry out the 'herem' on any people at any time since the conquest of the land in the time of Moses and Joshua. It was a one-time event, but a lesson for all times."

"And the lesson is . . .?"

"God's patience is not inexhaustible" Hal replied. "Sin can become great enough in an individual or a nation that his wrath overflows on it; in the end, he will take back what is his."

I was sobered but not quite out of questions. "What about the part where God makes Sihon's spirit stubborn and his heart obstinate? It sounds like God is setting him up for the fall. It doesn't seem fair."

"God can, of course, act in his sovereign will to harden men's hearts," Hal said. "As Paul says in Romans, he 'has mercy on whom he wants to have mercy and hardens whom he wants to harden.' He can make some persons as 'objects of his wrath—prepared for destruction.' But to understand this passage we need to go back to the other 'hardening the heart' scriptures in Exodus. When Moses confronts Pharaoh and demands that he let the Israelites go, there are a number of references to God hardening Pharaoh's heart. But they are preceded by other references to Pharaoh hardening his own heart. God doesn't turn an innocent person into an evil one; rather, he acts on the person who refuses to acknowledge him."

Hal went on, "There is another passage in Romans that may help you to understand this. It's one of the most frightening statements in the Bible. In Romans one, verses twenty-six and twenty-eight, Paul writes that God gave some people—those who steadfastly denied him—over to 'shameful lusts and to a depraved mind.' He is talking about people who deny the natural knowledge of God, who exchange the truth of God for a lie, and who worship created things instead of the Creator. This tells us that there can come a time for individuals, and even societies, when it's too late—God gives up on them, their rejection of him becomes irretrievable, beyond redemption. I've seen it in my pastoral ministry. When people practice sin, it becomes easier and easier to do it. At some point, what began as a hesitant and guilt-ridden departure from innocence becomes a part of who they are, their way of life, perhaps even an addiction. They stop viewing their behavior as wrong and find ways to justify it, convincing themselves that their wrongs really are right. They search for ways to reinterpret the obvious meaning of the Scriptures so they won't be condemned by God's word. Or they find ways to argue that the Scriptures really aren't God's word and don't need to be followed anyway. They fight furiously to resist any change or interference with their wickedness. And, finally, they are beyond repentance. God will always hear those who call on him, but these people are no longer able to speak the words."

And then he told a story. "I once counseled a man on his deathbed. His wife was a believer who was in church every Sunday and was deeply grieved that he persisted in his rejection of the things of God. I spent hours with him; I persuaded him to see the sin in his life and his inability to save himself—all the things needed to come to God. But in the end, he couldn't cross over. He wept, but he couldn't pray. I asked him to accept Jesus, and he looked up at me through his tears and said, 'I can't.' He was utterly defeated in his life but unable to grasp onto the one thing that could save him. He died in his unbelief."

I could see Hal was tired. The energy of the discourse had left him depleted. I had stayed long enough. The evening was over, and I moved to leave. As I came to the door, he took my arm. "Keep short lists with God, Chris. Confess sin regularly. Don't ever convince yourself that you're all right in ways you're not right with God."

I stored his thought but had one last question: "What about the children in those Amorite cities, the ones not old enough to know right from wrong? Did they go to hell? Should we understand that all of those people are in hell, or will be, after the judgment? People who had never been taught right conduct or about the true God or given a chance to repent?"

"Deuteronomy is about living in this world, not the next," Hal replied slowly. "God is perfect justice and perfect mercy. Trust him to do the right thing with them."

CHAPTER THREE

The sun was setting earlier and earlier, and I was running late. It was dark when I drove into Hal's driveway. To my surprise, no lights were on. When I went to the door, I saw a note pinned to it: "Chris, if I'm not here, go down the road about a half mile to a house being built on the right and find me.—Hal"

I went back to the car and followed Hal's directions. Floodlights from a temporary electrical connection, allowing the project to continue into the evening hours, lit the half-built house. Several men were working on the upper level. As I pulled into the dirt drive that led to it, I saw for a moment—just a moment—a silhouette. A man, stooped and bent, was carrying a timber about ten feet long over his shoulder. The timber was too heavy for him, and the back part dragged on the ground behind. The floodlit house was behind him, and I could see only the black outline where he passed before it with his burden. As he passed in front of a small leaning tree, the trunk formed a crosspiece with it at a perfect right angle. In that instant, the dark vision of another man bearing another timber 2,000 years ago was before me. And then it passed. The crosspiece fell behind and, as the laborer turned toward the house, the shadow of the timber melted into that of his body. When he passed the outside floods, the blue of his jeans, the red of his shirt, and the unmistakable white tousle of hair were illuminated.

Hal greeted me warmly. After delivering his timber to the stronger arms of younger men working on the house, he made his excuses to them and we returned to his place. The men were building a house for one of them, he explained. The family had a lot of children and couldn't afford the kind of house they needed at current prices. The project would take a year, maybe two. He helped as much as he could, though he had little in the way of carpentry skills. Sometimes all he could do was move materials so those who knew how to use them could do so. Yes, it was heavy work for his tired old frame, but that was all right. As long as he could do it, he would rather be engaged helping someone than sitting in a rocking chair.

"Read me the next section," he said as we settled in to talk.

> Of the land that we took over at that time, I gave the Reubenites and the Gadites the territory north of Aroer by the Arnon Gorge, including half the hill country of Gilead, together with its towns. The rest of Gilead and also all of Bashan, the kingdom of Og, I gave to the half tribe of Manasseh. (The whole region of Argob in Bashan used to be known as a land of the Rephaites. Jair, a descendant of Manasseh, took the whole region of Argob as far as the border of the Geshurites and the Maacathites; it was named after him, so that to this day Bashan is called Havvoth Jair.) And I gave Gilead to Makir. But to the Reubenites and the Gadites I gave the territory extending from Gilead down to the Arnon Gorge (the middle of the gorge being the border) and out to the Jabbok River, which is the border of the Ammonites. Its western border was the Jordan in the Arabah, from Kinnereth to the Sea of the Arabah (the Salt Sea), below the slopes of Pisgah.
>
> I commanded you at that time: "The LORD your God has given you this land to take possession of it. But all your able-bodied men, armed for battle, must cross over ahead of your brother Israelites. However, your wives, your children and your livestock (I know you have much livestock) may stay in the towns I have given you, until the LORD gives rest to your brothers as he has to you, and they too have taken over the land that the LORD your God is giving them, across the Jordan. After that, each of you may go back to the possession I have given you."
>
> —Deut. 3:12–20

"What do you make of it?" Hal asked when I finished reading. He was still unwinding from the construction work.

The land east of the Jordan, I told him, that had belonged to the conquered kings Sihon and Og, is now divided among the tribes of Reuben, Gad, and "the half tribe" of Manassah. The story summarized in the third chapter of Deuteronomy is told in more detail in the thirty-second chapter of Numbers. The tribes of Reuben and Gad have livestock and see that the newly conquered land is suitable for grazing. They come to Moses and Eleazar the priest, who had succeeded his father, Aaron, and ask for it, and to be relieved of crossing the Jordan. Moses chastises them for proposing to stay in the land while their countrymen cross the Jordan for the war ahead. He sees their mindset as similar to the now-deceased older generation whose reluctance to go into the Promised Land, described in chapter one, brought on the Lord's anger and the long desert sojourn. In response to the chastening, the Reubenites and Gadites propose an alternative: They would rebuild the cities, build pens for their livestock, and leave their women and children there. The men would not only cross the Jordan with the other tribes, armed for war, but would go ahead of them. Only when the land west of the Jordan is subdued would they return to their possessions. Moses agrees with their proposal. Realizing he would not be around to enforce it himself, he communicates it to Joshua, who would succeed him, and to Eleazar and the tribal leaders, with a warning to hold these tribes to their commitment.

When I paused for a breath, Hal commended me. "Good. I see you've been doing your homework. You looked back at the story in Numbers, where it's told in more detail. Deuteronomy is often like that, summarizing what appears in more depth in the earlier texts."

But I wasn't through. Eager to show him my learning, I went on to tell what happened.

"Later, after the war of conquest west of the Jordan, Joshua praised the eastern tribes for their faithfulness and sent them home with a reminder to love the Lord and serve him with all their heart and soul. In their zeal to do so, they built an altar near the river, which the other tribes mistook for a pagan altar. In the twenty-second chapter of Joshua, representatives of the other tribes—prepared for war to preserve the holiness of the land—confronted them. The Transjordan tribes explained that the altar was not for pagan worship but to remind the descendants of their generation that, despite the Jordan River boundary between them, they are part of the Lord's people. Their relatives were satisfied that they hadn't fallen into apostasy, and war was averted."

"It would make a great movie, wouldn't it," Hal said. "The Bible is full of great stories, Chris. I don't know why those people in Hollywood don't make them."

"It hasn't been the same since Cecil B. DeMille," I said. "Still, sooner or later, someone will figure it out."

"And what about the geography? I'm sure you studied that, too."

I had. The tribes of Reuben and Gad received the southerly portion from the Arnon Gorge, where Israel had first crossed into hostile territory, east of the Dead Sea, north through the southerly half of the area known as Gilead, and east of the Jordan. Gilead is the source of the familiar phrase "balm of Gilead." In Genesis 37:25, the caravan of Ishmaelites who bought Joseph from his brothers and took him to Egypt came from Gilead with their camels "loaded with spices, balm, and myrrh." Apparently the balm, which had medicinal properties, was the product of trees that grew in Gilead. The prophet Jeremiah uses the balm of Gilead as a metaphor for the healing that is not available to a sinful people.

The half-tribe of Manassah, more accurately half the tribe of Manassah, one of Joseph's sons, received the northerly territory of Gilead and Og's territory in Bashan, still farther north, and to the east of the Sea of Galilee, a region well known for its fertility and grazing capacity. Bashan appears frequently in later Scriptures as a metaphor: Psalm 22:12, a Messianic psalm, says, "[S]trong bulls of Bashan encircle me" in describing the assaults on the one who would be crucified. In Isaiah 2:13, "all the oaks of Bashan" are among a series of metaphors for the proud who will be humbled. Jeremiah 50 describes the return of Israel from exile as a return "to his own pasture and he will graze on Carmel and Bashan." Ezekiel 39 describes a time in which the birds and wild animals will eat the flesh and drink the blood of the mighty men and princes of the earth, "all of them fattened animals from Bashan." And Amos 4 condemns the wealthy women of Israel who live in luxury while oppressing the poor and crushing the needy, referring to them as "cows of Bashan."

Later Bible passages indicate that the lands east of the Jordan River proved the hardest for the Israelites to hold on to. They are part of the modern kingdom of Jordan.

As I talked and Hal listened attentively, I felt a twinge of guilt. He had chastened me only two weeks earlier for focusing on the geography instead of the spiritual meaning of the text. And here I was, talking about geography again—Bashan, Gilead, the Arnon Gorge, all of the rivers and towns and mountains east of the Jordan. But what spiritual message was there in the division of the land? It was just history, I thought. The geography made it more interesting, and I wished that I'd had the time to trace what happened in those lands from the time of the defeat of Sihon and Og, the Amorite kings, to the present. But it was just geography!

Hal must have read my thoughts, but he didn't reprimand me again. Perhaps he realized I was already chastising myself. Instead, he gently turned the discussion to the spiritual significance in the text.

"Here," he said, "is a model for one of the most basic and consistent teachings of the Scriptures: Help your neighbor. The three tribes that are allotted land east of the Jordan have come into their inheritance. The enemy is conquered, wiped out. The land is there, and it is theirs. But they are not to rest in it until all the other tribes have their possession too. They are to actually cross *ahead of* the other tribes for the battles to come. Only when the other tribes have their possession are these tribes to return to their land."

It was true, Hal acknowledged from the account in Numbers, that Moses had to shame them into it. Their inheritance was conditioned on helping others gain theirs. But still they were obedient and did the right thing. They didn't grab for it, or plant themselves there, or defy their leader. Apparently they were willing and even enthusiastic to do their share for the others by crossing the Jordan to fight with them.

"The message," Hal said, "is the same as Jesus' teaching of the second greatest commandment: 'Love your neighbor as yourself.' It's repeated in Paul's letters when he tells the Philippians, 'Each of you should look not only to your own interests but also to the interests of others.' Paul also told the Corinthians that 'Nobody should seek his own good, but the good of others.' It's a common theme of popular morality, from the Boy Scout code to the first President Bush's 'thousand points of light'—the volunteer activities of millions of Americans to build a better world. It's the foundational principle of all government programs to aid the less fortunate. And it's the universal biblical obligation."

"Like retired pastors who help other people build their houses?"

"Oh, I'm just keeping myself busy," Hal replied, and then went on to talk about another message in the passage.

He directed me to the verse 20 reference about God giving "rest" to the people in the new land. "The New Testament is often referred to as a commentary on the Old Testament. Here's a good example. In Deuteronomy, entering and conquering the land brought physical rest, a respite from battling enemies, from the harsh life in the wilderness, from the nomadic existence they had for forty years. In the third and fourth chapters of Hebrews, the idea of rest in the Promised Land becomes a type or figure for the rest found in eternal life. As the theologians would say, rest is despatialized and spiritualized. The disobedience of the earlier generation of Israelites was the product of unbelief; as a result, they didn't enter the new land's rest. Now, rest means life with God for eternity instead of life in the new land. Those who believe and obey will enter 'God's rest.' And you don't have to wait until you die to enter God's rest. Paul says in Philippians we can have 'the peace of God, which transcends all understanding,' even in the most adverse circumstances. Paul wrote those lines from a jail cell."

"Did Moses have that peace?" I asked. "From the rest of the chapter, he didn't seem too content."

"Let's read it," Hal said.

> At that time I commanded Joshua: "You have seen with your own eyes all that the LORD your God has done to these two kings. The LORD will do the same to all the kingdoms over there where you are going. Do not be afraid of them; the LORD your God himself will fight for you."
>
> At that time I pleaded with the LORD: "O Sovereign LORD, you have begun to show to your servant your greatness and your strong hand. For what god is there in heaven or on earth who can do the deeds and mighty works you do? Let

me go over and see the good land beyond the Jordan—that fine hill country and Lebanon."

But because of you the LORD was angry with me and would not listen to me. "That is enough," the LORD said. "Do not speak to me anymore about this matter. Go up to the top of Pisgah and look west and north and south and east. Look at the land with your own eyes, since you are not going to cross this Jordan. But commission Joshua, and encourage and strengthen him, for he will lead this people across and will cause them to inherit the land that you will see." So we stayed in the valley near Beth Peor.

—Deut. 3:21–29

"So Moses was going to die here," I said. "God's greatest man, of that time at least, was going to die without seeing the fulfillment of what he had been working toward for forty years."

Hal's eyes were twinkling. "Let's go for a ride," he said.

We got in his old Buick, and he drove down the road, turned once, then again, and finally slowed and turned into a large old community graveyard. A near-full moon illuminated the silent city. Hal pulled up and stopped several rows in. He turned off the headlights and ignition.

"There's a flashlight in the glove compartment," he said.

I found it and clambered out after him. He led me to a large but weathered monument and asked me to shine the light on it. I could barely make out the name, but underneath it read "Governor of New Hampshire, 18**." The dates were more illegible than the name.

"Graveyards," Hal said quoting an aphorism, "are full of indispensable people. This man served as governor of the state, the biggest man in New Hampshire, so to speak, for a couple of years. Then he lost the next election. I don't know why—probably something to do with slavery and all that."

He looked around at the acres of gravestones, large and small, some just a marker in the soil.

"None of them got everything they wanted in life," Hal said. "None of us do. Maybe because we want too much, maybe because we don't deserve what we want and the Lord isn't going to give it to us. And if we get too much, we die disappointed because we have to leave it all behind."

He sat in the grass, resting against a larger monument.

"He won't mind," Hal said. "I'm sure he'd be glad to know someone was getting a little rest out of his gravestone right now."

I shined the light on the engraving. "It's a she, Hal."

"All the better," he said. "Edith always said I was soft on the ladies."

"So what's going on in this passage we read before we came out here?" I asked. "Moses had the vision and led the people to the edge of the land. He did it for forty years. But God refused to let him enter."

"Well," Hal said, "first it shows that Moses is obedient in the duty of a good leader to prepare his successor and turn over power at the right time. He must have seemed indispensable to the Israelites. But he commissioned, instructed, and encouraged his successor, Joshua, who would carry on after him. The selection and commissioning of Joshua for leadership is referenced in three other places: Numbers chapter twenty-seven and Deuteronomy chapters one and thirty-one. With the Lord's guidance, he made sure someone who was capable of doing so would carry on his mission."

"But he says here that not being allowed to enter the land is 'because of you.' He's blaming the people for it. Doesn't it say in other places that it's because of his own disobedience?"

"It does," Hal said.

"So which is it? Is the Bible inconsistent?"

"Both are true," Hal said. "This all goes back to an incident at a place called Meribah; it's recounted in the twentieth chapter of Numbers. Meribah is in a desert area, the Desert of Zin, near Kadesh Barnea, where they had been nearly forty years before. It's near the end of the Exodus, when they're about to turn north to conquer the land. There's no water for the people or the livestock, and the people were complaining that they'd die there. Moses and Aaron went to the Tent of Meeting and fell facedown before the Lord. The glory of the Lord appeared to them, and the Lord told them to take the staff and speak to the rock, which would pour out water for the people and their livestock. Moses took the staff, and he and Aaron gathered the people. Moses then spoke angrily to them, calling them rebels, and struck the rock twice with his staff. The water gushed out, and the moment was saved. But the Lord had told Moses to speak to the rock, not strike it, to bring forth the miracle of water. Instead he struck it, not once but twice, and appears to have done so in anger. The Lord was angry with Moses for not honoring his holiness in Israel's sight. It's this disobedience that causes the Lord to deny Moses—and Aaron as well—the opportunity to enter the land with the people."

"And how is that the people's fault?"

"When Moses says he is forbidden to enter on account of them," Hal replied, "he means that their rebellious spirit and complaining required that he bring the matter to the Lord—and for the miracle. And they also provoked his anger and impetuousness in striking the rock, as if some natural means were being engaged to release the water instead of speaking the water forth from it. There is a very human side of Moses here, not unlike Adam. When Adam was disobedient in eating the fruit of the Tree of the Knowledge of Good and Evil, Adam blamed Eve for luring him into it. So Moses wants to blame the people who caused his anger and disobedience, and they do have blame. But God doesn't allow the buck to be passed that easily, especially by those who should know better."

"It seems a minor failing," I said, "for such a major punishment. And God didn't show mercy, even when Moses asked for it. He led Israel all that way and prayed for the chance to enter the land, only to have God deny him."

"I agree," Hal said. "But if God would take so seriously what may seem to us a minor failing, how much more should we fear the consequences of our major failings?"

While I thought about that, with some difficulty Hal raised himself from his seat by the woman's gravestone. As he ambled back to the Buick he said, "Moses had seen God's mighty works firsthand. And the more you see of God's glory, the more you want of it. The eleventh chapter of Hebrews tells us that the heroes of the faith in times past didn't receive the things promised but only saw them from a distance. Even God's great men don't always receive what they want."

"Have you received what you wanted from God?" I asked, and immediately regretted the question as I remembered his eyes tearing in the coffee shop earlier.

Hal didn't answer my question directly.

Back in the car, Hal replied, "A great preacher named Matthew Henry once said we should never allow any desires in our hearts that we cannot in faith offer up to God by prayer. Moses offered this desire to God in prayer, and he was innocent in doing so. And even though God said no, we should learn something about this from the New Testament. When Jesus took Peter and James and John up on the mountain where he was transfigured into his glorious state—a story told in three of the gospels—Moses and Elijah appeared with him. You see, Chris, in the life to come, Moses did enter the land.

"As Paul wrote in Romans, 'I consider that our present sufferings are not worth comparing with the glory that will be revealed in us.'"

We drove back to Hal's house in silence. On the way, I experimented with prayer. It was not something I was used to doing. But Hal was at the wheel, and the darkness lent itself to concentration. Paul teaches that we should "pray without ceasing," and nothing in Scripture says that prayer can only occur when we are kneeling and have our eyes closed.

I prayed I'd be a good neighbor; as good as Hal and the men who were helping his neighbor build a house. I thanked the Lord for their commitment to others. I thanked him for the moment of vision in the silhouette before the floodlights when I saw Christ in the simple activity of a helper who sacrificed his own time and energy for another. I tried to identify all of the large and small lusts and greeds and covetousness and fears and ambitions that had marred my obedience to my Lord in recent days and asked his forgiveness for each of them. It took all the time I had—I was still working on them when we reached Hal's driveway and turned in.

As we parted, Hal said, "Praise him that the opportunity to enter his rest isn't dependent on the perfection of our obedience. If it were, I fear none of us would get there—in this life or the next."

CHAPTER FOUR

Hal's e-mail arrived on Monday morning: "Have you read chapter four yet?"

I replied that I had not but promised to do so that night.

"Read it every night this week," came the response. "And read it several times a night. Then think about it, reflect on it, meditate on it. This is one of the great theological chapters of the Bible. If you had no other Scripture but this, you would know a very great deal of what God wants you to know and what you need to know to be one of his children."

That night, when the kids were in bed, I told Anna about the e-mails. "Let's read it together," she suggested. And so we did, each night, she reading the whole chapter to me, and then me to her. The words became more real as we experienced them, and the thoughts they expressed in both the reading and the hearing, and in the repetition. Gradually, through the week, they became familiar, like the Lord's Prayer or the twenty-third Psalm—passages we had known from childhood.

> Hear now, O Israel, the decrees and laws I am about to teach you. Follow them so that you may live and may go in and take possession of the land that the LORD, the God of your fathers, is giving you. Do not add to what I command you and do not subtract from it, but keep the commands of the LORD your God that I give you.
>
> You saw with your own eyes what the LORD did at Baal Peor. The LORD your God destroyed from among you everyone who followed the Baal of Peor, but all of you who held fast to the LORD your God are still alive today.

See, I have taught you decrees and laws as the LORD my God commanded me, so that you may follow them in the land you are entering to take possession of it. Observe them carefully, for this will show your wisdom and understanding to the nations, who will hear about all these decrees and say, "Surely this great nation is a wise and understanding people." What other nation is so great as to have their gods near them the way the LORD our God is near us whenever we pray to him? And what other nation is so great as to have such righteous decrees and laws as this body of laws I am setting before you today?

Only be careful, and watch yourselves closely so that you do not forget the things your eyes have seen or let them slip from your heart as long as you live. Teach them to your children and to their children after them. Remember the day you stood before the LORD your God at Horeb, when he said to me, "Assemble the people before me to hear my words so that they may learn to revere me as long as they live in the land and may teach them to their children." You came near and stood at the foot of the mountain while it blazed with fire to the very heavens, with black clouds and deep darkness. Then the LORD spoke to you out of the fire. You heard the sound of words but saw no form; there was only a voice. He declared to you his covenant, the Ten Commandments, which he commanded you to follow and then wrote them on two stone tablets. And the LORD directed me at that time to teach you the decrees and laws you are to follow in the land that you are crossing the Jordan to possess.

You saw no form of any kind the day the LORD spoke to you at Horeb out of the fire. Therefore watch yourselves very carefully, so that you do not become corrupt and make for yourselves an idol, an image of any shape, whether formed like a man or a woman, or like any animal on earth or any bird that flies in the air, or like any creature that moves along the ground or any fish in the waters below. And when you look up to the sky and see the sun, the moon and the stars—all the heavenly array—do not be enticed into bowing down to them and worshiping things the LORD your God has apportioned to all the nations under heaven. But as for you, the LORD took you and brought you out of the iron-smelting furnace, out of Egypt, to be the people of his inheritance, as you now are.

The LORD was angry with me because of you, and he solemnly swore that I would not cross the Jordan and enter the good land the LORD your God is giving you as your inheritance. I will die in this land; I will not cross the Jordan; but you are about to cross over and take possession of that good land. Be careful not to forget the covenant of the LORD your God that he made with you; do not make for yourselves an idol in the form of anything the LORD your God has forbidden. For the LORD your God is a consuming fire, a jealous God.

After you have had children and grandchildren and have lived in the land a long time—if you then become corrupt and make any kind of idol, doing evil in the eyes of the LORD your God and provoking him to anger, I call heaven and earth as witnesses against you this day that you will quickly perish from the land that you are crossing the Jordan to possess. You will not live there long but will certainly be destroyed. The LORD will scatter you among the peoples, and only a few of you will survive among the nations to which the LORD will drive you. There you will worship man-made gods of wood and stone, which cannot see or hear or eat or smell. But if from there you seek the LORD your God, you will find him if you look for him with all your heart and with all your soul. When you are in distress and all these things have happened to you, then in later days you will return to the LORD your God and obey him. For the LORD your God is a merciful God; he will not abandon or destroy you or forget the covenant with your forefathers, which he confirmed to them by oath.

Ask now about the former days, long before your time, from the day God created man on the earth; ask from one end of the heavens to the other. Has anything so great as this ever happened, or has anything like it ever been heard of? Has any other people heard the voice of God speaking out of fire, as you have, and lived? Has any god ever tried to take for himself one nation out of another nation, by testings, by miraculous signs and wonders, by war, by a mighty hand and an outstretched arm, or by great and awesome deeds, like all the things the LORD your God did for you in Egypt before your very eyes?

You were shown these things so that you might know that the LORD is God; besides him there is no other. From heaven he made you hear his voice to discipline you. On earth he showed you his great fire, and you heard his words from out of the fire. Because he loved your forefathers and chose their descendants after them, he brought you out of Egypt by his Presence and his great strength, to drive out before you nations greater and stronger than you and to bring you into their land to give it to you for your inheritance, as it is today.

Acknowledge and take to heart this day that the LORD is God in heaven above and on the earth below. There is no other. Keep his decrees and commands, which I am giving you today, so that it may go well with you and your children after you and that you may live long in the land the LORD your God gives you for all time.

Then Moses set aside three cities east of the Jordan, to which anyone who had killed a person could flee if he had unintentionally killed his neighbor without malice aforethought. He could flee into one of these cities and save his life. The cities were these: Bezer in the desert plateau, for the Reubenites; Ramoth in Gilead, for the Gadites; and Golan in Bashan, for the Manassites.

—Deut. 4:1–43

On Thursday, Hal e-mailed to cancel our Friday night study. He had to go to Boston, he said, without further explanation. He said he'd be back on Sunday and asked if I wanted to come over after church. The kids were scheduled to attend a friend's birthday party that afternoon, and Anna and I were not needed for supervision. I accepted Hal's invitation for Sunday afternoon and asked if Anna could come with me, since she had been reading the Scripture with me all week. Hal e-mailed his approval.

Sunday was one of those bright, crisp fall days that trumpet the beauty of creation. New England was near her best. The maples were well into their annual transformation from summer green to the spectacular reds, oranges, and yellows that make Columbus Day weekend the most heavily trafficked of the year. The deep red of the Sumacs in little shrubby mounds preceded the maples, and the oaks and poplars were showing the more subtle yellows and deeper hues of maroon that would mark later fall when the winds from the north would herald the imminent snow. We clung to those days, knowing how soon nature would shut down and how far away April really was.

Hal met us on his porch and suggested we take a walk. Hunting season wasn't on yet, so we could still walk safely through the woods. He stuffed a small Bible in the pocket of his jacket and set out at a brisk pace. A few hundred yards beyond the rose garden, as we passed out of a wooded area, through the opening in a stone wall, and reached the open crest of a small rise, we could see row on row of hills rising to the northwest. It was like viewing the entire world as the greatest of all artists' canvas. The swathes of reds, oranges, and yellows were punctuated by splashes of green where the evergreens clung to a sense of permanence and reminded us of the summer past. Each row of hills grew lighter in a tint of blues and purples, obscuring the brighter fall colors, until they blended into the distant skyline. It was just there at the crest that Hal halted our march. After we had gazed in silence for a minute or so, he turned and asked us quietly, "Where is God?"

"In heaven," I answered, too quickly.

"And where is that?" Hal asked.

"It's a spiritual place; another dimension."

"When I was a boy," Hal said, "I used to think it was up there." He pointed to the sky. "If I had a big enough rocket ship, I could go there. Some people still think that way—science can solve all our problems;

it's all a matter of making enough progress and getting everyone in on it."

"I would have said that God was right here," Anna offered, looking out over the hills. "This is close enough to heaven for me."

Hal nodded. "Let's sit down. It's time to learn a little theology.

"Theologians," he said, after we had settled in the unmown grass, "have been thinking about what the two of you just said for many centuries. Your thoughts about God have names. The names are 'transcendence' and 'immanence.'"

Transcendence, he explained, is the understanding that God is above and distinct from the world, beyond the limits of human understanding, more wonderful than we are able to comprehend. "It's what you mean, Chris, when you say he is in heaven."

He fished the little Bible out of his pocket and found Deuteronomy chapter four. "Transcendence is what Moses was talking about in the verse thirty-six when he said 'From heaven he made you hear his voice to discipline you.' In verse thirty-nine, he says the Lord is God 'in heaven above and on the earth below.' Or, as Isaiah says, 'As the heavens are higher than the earth, so are my ways higher than your ways and my thoughts than your thoughts.' It's like what we were talking about in the last chapter, when Jesus took Peter, James, and John up the mountain, and Moses and Elijah appeared to them. God's transcendent glory was revealed in Jesus there when he was transfigured. His face shone like the sun, and his clothes became white as snow. Transcendence is God in his awesome and unimaginable glory, what theologians sometimes call 'wholly other'—that is, other than us."

"And my notion that God is all around us must be . . ." Anna hesitated.

"Immanence," Hal said, finding the word for her. "It's what Moses meant in verse seven: 'The Lord our God is near us whenever we pray to him.' And in verse thirty-nine, when he says God is God 'on the earth below.' It's our knowledge that God is with us, near us, and accessible to us individually. It's probably what Jesus meant when he taught in Luke 17 that 'the kingdom of God is within you.' It's not a physical place to go to but a spiritual experience of relationship with God that can be enjoyed in all circumstances. It's the same as when Isaiah and

Matthew called Jesus 'Immanuel.' Immanuel means 'God with us.' And it's what evangelical Christians mean when they say Jesus is their 'personal Savior.'"

Anna had a slight frown. "I don't know. I mean, when I said God was here, I don't think I meant it literally. I just meant that we could see him through the beauty of nature, of the creation."

Hal replied, "We do have to be careful when we think about God being present. There's a common heresy that grows out of the concept of God's immanence. If God is with us, or within us, or in the world, so the logic goes, then we ourselves must be divine. Man and woman created in God's image become man and woman as God. Maybe you've seen pictures of these 'New Age' people twirling around in ecstasy, saying, 'I am God.' The heresy isn't new—it's the oldest one in the Bible. The serpent's temptation of Eve to eat the fruit of the Tree of the Knowledge of Good and Evil was so that 'you will be like God.' It's the same temptation we see in Isaiah fourteen, the temptation that brought down the King of Babylon, whom some think represents Satan. 'I will make myself like the Most High.' Some environmental enthusiasts have another variation: the earth, rather than its inhabitants, becomes a god, or, more likely goddess, having divine qualities. The heresy is the age-old shame of people worshipping created things rather than the Creator. A God with whom you can have a personal relationship is still the transcendent eternal God, not a created person who has become a God."

Hal continued, "I have found that most people are more comfortable with God's transcendence than his immanence. In transcendence, God is far away—up there . . ." He gestured toward the sky. ". . . somewhere. We can keep him at arm's length. We don't have to involve him in our lives very much, in the hard, nasty little details of what we're about. He's a much more disconcerting companion when he's sitting beside you in the room."

Hal asked us how often we contemplated God's presence in us or the people around us. When we hesitated to reply, he waved the question off. "Most pastors are no different," he said. "We busy ourselves with organizing the church or the service or our sermons; we meet with boards and committees; we attend to the details of life that everyone else has to attend to. And we keep God up there—in heaven, where he belongs.

"In my first church, I was determined to have a great success. There were only thirty or forty families, and I meant to make it many times that size. I tried every program I could think of: programs for kids, for men, and for women. We put fliers out into the community and got on radio stations. But no one came. Five years later, I was still ministering to the same thirty or forty families, give or take a few that had come and gone. I didn't know how to bring Christ into the hearts of the people, how to teach them to pray, to love the word, and to love the Lord and bring him into all of their lives. I didn't know how to help them find God's immanence."

I sensed his sadness at the discouraging memory. "Shall we walk some more?" I asked.

We got up and proceeded across the open field at a more leisurely pace than we had begun. Hal had the Bible open and read the first two verses of chapter four aloud: "Hear now, O Israel, the decrees and laws I am about to teach you. Follow them so that you may live and may go in and take possession of the land that the LORD, the God of your fathers, is giving you. Do not add to what I command you and do not subtract from it, but keep the commands of the LORD your God that I give you."

He kept a finger in place as he lowered the book and continued to talk.

"Notice that knowledge of God is communicated by words. It's like where we began in chapter one—in thinking about the word. Moses gave the people decrees, laws, commands, and stipulations. The people heard his voice, the sound of words. The Ten Commandments were given to them written on two stone tablets. The words we're talking about aren't just communication. They have special value, sacred value. Verse two says, 'Do not add to what I command you and do not subtract from it.' This command is repeated in Deuteronomy chapter twelve, and in Proverbs,[3] and at the end of the Bible in Revelation.[4] We are in holy literature here."

"Did Jesus treat the Old Testament as holy literature?" I asked. "I mean, didn't he add to it?"

"Jesus grounded his teaching about himself in the Old Testament scriptures again and again. So did the apostles. He is the fulfillment of what went before, of the words written here or elsewhere in the sacred Scriptures. There's a lot less that's new in the New Testament than most Christians think."

"But surely he added to Deuteronomy, at least," I persisted.

"The principle of not adding to or subtracting from," Hal said, "refers to the Scriptures as a whole. Our task is to interpret and understand what God reveals about himself and right living in the Scriptures. The warning here is not to substitute our own ideas or philosophy. The human mind has achieved many great things in literature, art, science, and other areas of thought and understanding. But the central truths of the universe and human existence are not up for reinventing or reimagining.

"That's one of the reasons why the academic study of the Scriptures is dangerous for many people. It isn't that there's anything to fear from knowledge. All truth is God's truth, and knowing more truth will not diminish God. But in the academic world, there's a built-in pressure to find something new. People advance to their doctoral degrees—and in the estimation of their peers—by being innovative, by coming up with a theory or way of looking at something that no one has thought of before and then writing theses or books about it. Deuteronomy itself is a good example. Every decade brings a new scholar who has a new idea about it, when it was written, why it was written, by whom it was written. That becomes the prevailing wisdom for a few years until someone else comes along and knocks the last theory over. You can read in some study Bibles or commentaries things like 'most scholars believe' this or that. But a review of the history of academic study of the Scriptures will burst any bubble of confidence anyone might have in what 'most scholars believe.' In a little while, they'll believe something else. Too often they're adding to or subtracting from what God has revealed. I wouldn't want to stand before God having done so."

"Don't you think God would forgive you for being wrong about something in the Bible?" Anna asked.

"Of course . . . to a point," Hal replied. "Believers have always disagreed about this or that understanding. That's why we have different denominations and church traditions. But you can't be wrong to the point of defying God himself." He read the next two verses (four and five). "You saw with your own eyes what the LORD did at Baal Peor. The LORD your God destroyed from among you everyone who followed the Baal of Peor, but all of you who held fast to the LORD your God are still alive today."

"These verses are directly connected to the first two: the command not to add to or subtract from the Scriptures. They give an example of the consequences of that particular disobedience. The people who followed the Baal of Peor were people who chose another god. That story is told in the twenty-fifth chapter of Numbers, where the Moabites induced Israelites to engage in sexual immorality and sacrifice to their gods. There is a consequence to rejecting God. In this case, the result was death. Those who followed God's commands and held fast to him gained life."

We had reached the other end of the field. A wood road beckoned us on. A young couple was walking up it toward us, with two children darting around them like yo-yos. We exchanged greetings as we passed.

"If you had the opportunity," Hal asked as they passed out of earshot, "what would you say to them to persuade them to become believers? Assuming they're not, but rather just people who may vaguely think of themselves as Christians while paying little attention to God in their life."

"I would tell them about Jesus," I said, "about his miracles, his resurrection, how he died for our sins."

"And what about you, Anna?" Hal asked.

Anna did not answer immediately as we walked. At last she replied, "I think I would tell them about Anna—how God has worked in my life, what Jesus has meant to me, how I'm different because of him."

"Two good answers," Hal said. "What happened in history and what happened to me. This chapter is full of that sort of stuff. Let's hear Moses tell some of it." He read:

> Ask now about the former days, long before your time, from the day God created man on the earth; ask from one end of the heavens to the other. Has anything so great as this ever

> happened, or has anything like it ever been heard of? Has any other people heard the voice of God speaking out of fire, as you have, and lived? Has any god ever tried to take for himself one nation out of another nation, by testings, by miraculous signs and wonders, by war, by a mighty hand and an outstretched arm, or by great and awesome deeds, like all the things the LORD your God did for you in Egypt before your very eyes?
>
> You were shown these things so that you might know that the LORD is God; besides him there is no other.
>
> —Deut. 4:32–35

"These were recent events," he went on. "God showed himself to them by all of the awesome events associated with the Exodus. This is real apologetics."

"Apologetics?" I said.

"Another theology lesson," Hal said. "You should know this word. *Apologetics* doesn't mean apologizing in the sense of our modern English usage. It comes from a Greek word that means giving a defense, or explaining. First Peter three-fifteen says," he turned to it and read, "'Always be prepared to give an answer to everyone who asks you to give the reason for the hope that you have. But do this with gentleness and respect, keeping a clear conscience, so that those who speak maliciously against your good behavior in Christ may be ashamed of their slander.'

"That is the essence of apologetics—giving a reason for the hope that's in you, why you believe. It's what evangelical Christians sometimes refer to as giving your testimony. The Jewish and Christian faiths are unique among world religions; they aren't based on human thought or words alone. God has acted and does act in specific and dramatic ways in history. We have a historic faith that is based on things that actually happened, that were done with and for and in front of real people who observed and reported them. There is a powerful apologetic in this chapter—an answer to skeptics, a 'reason for the hope that that you have,' as Peter says. Over and over, Moses speaks to these people and through them to all people about the historic evidence of God in apologetic terms: what their eyes have seen, what was done before their eyes, and the things that were shown them. They heard the sound of words, and God spoke to them out of the fire. Moses is talking here about the great events they'd experienced throughout the Exodus, in Egypt, at Mount Sinai, in the wars they fought, and in the miraculous signs and wonders. They saw what God did at Baal Peor. They didn't have to make any 'leap of faith'—their faith came out of their personal experience."

"Just like the apostles," Anna said.

"Oh, yes. It's the same with Jesus in the New Testament. Take, for example, the beginning of First John." Hal turned to it and read: "'That which was from the beginning, that which we have heard, which we have seen with our eyes, which we have looked at and our hands have touched—this we proclaim concerning the Word of life.'

"Other New Testament writers speak similarly from their personal experience with Christ. Paul talks about encountering Jesus on the road to Damascus. Peter says, 'We were eyewitnesses of his majesty.' Luke begins his gospel by telling of his careful investigation from the beginning of the things that were fulfilled among us. John, Peter, Luke, and the other New Testament writers speaking of Jesus—and Moses speaking of the experience of Israel—all testify to the real-life experience of seeing, hearing, touching—with their eyes, ears, hands—the revelation of God. This isn't just a mental experience, a philosophy, a bunch of ideas. This is hands-on religion."

Hal was rolling. I hardly noticed that we had emerged onto a paved road and turned back along the side in the direction of his house. A dog in a neighbor's yard yipped at us as we passed.

"There is an explicit purpose to all this," Hal continued. "'You were shown these things so that you might know that the Lord is God; besides him there is no other.'"

"But, Hal," I protested, "the people he was talking to weren't all at Sinai or Horeb forty years earlier. In fact, they couldn't get to the Promised Land until the generation that saw those things had died off because of its rebellion."

"It's true," Hal said, "that Moses was talking here to the next generation of the people who were in Egypt and at Mount Sinai, although the present audience had been in Moab during the events of Baal Peor and did see that part of it 'with their own eyes.' But he spoke here as though they were all there during the earlier times; there is continuity in the community of God's people. They are to teach what they have heard and seen—both the personal experience of the believing community and the words of God—to their children so these things won't be forgotten. The command to teach the children, to transmit the knowledge of God's acts and requirements to future generations, is one of the most repeated teachings in Deuteronomy."

We walked in silence for a few minutes.

"Immanence, transcendence, apologetics," I said. "Maybe I'll go to seminary."

A white house, set back from a well-trimmed lawn on our right, was flying a large American flag. Hal ignored my weak joke about seminary. He looked over at the flag. "Are you patriots?" he asked.

"Of course," said Anna. "But why do I think you're about to teach us something more about chapter four?"

"What makes this country great?" Hal asked.

"Freedom, democracy, justice," I replied.

Hal had the book opened again.

> See, I have taught you decrees and laws as the LORD my God commanded me, so that you may follow them in the land you are entering to take possession of it. Observe them carefully, for this will show your wisdom and understanding to the nations, who will hear about all these decrees and say, "Surely this great nation is a wise and understanding people." What other nation is so great as to have their gods near them the way the LORD our God is near us whenever we pray to him? And what other nation is so great as to have such righteous decrees and laws as this body of laws I am setting before you today?
>
> —Deut. 4:5–8

"So what does God say makes a nation great?" he asked, repocketing the text.

"Obedience and prayer," Anna replied.

"National greatness is described in these two attributes. Neither has to do with military power, economic success, cultural domination, or contributions to secular knowledge. Verses seven and eight describe the greatness of the nation as grounded in nearness to God in prayer, and the righteousness of the body of laws that govern it. Right relations with God and other people are what is required. Our Gross National Product and standard of living may be consequences of some collective obedience to God within our nation . . . I'm not saying they are, but they may be. But they are not what make us good or great. Our prayer life as a nation and our righteousness are what counts with God. Freedom, democracy, and justice are consequences of following God's righteous law. But they are a result, not a cause. When we get to chapter seventeen, we'll look at these issues again in the instructions given to the king."

We had come full-circle in our walk and passed down Hal's driveway and into the house. He found some cold cider in the refrigerator and some cookies to share. We went out to his porch and settled down as the afternoon heat gave way to the cool of the coming evening. I asked him to talk about the idolatry that is discussed in the middle of the chapter.

"Ah, idols," he said. "The Bible talks so much about them. In biblical times—both Old Testament and New Testament—worship of idols was the common religious practice of surrounding peoples, and it was a constant temptation to God's people. Modern people either brush it off as irrelevant or use it as a reason to condemn our Roman Catholic and Orthodox friends, whom they see as idol worshippers."

"Aren't they?" I asked. Seeing people bowing in prayer before statues had troubled me.

"Not if they understand it correctly," Hal replied. "It's not our way, we Protestants. But sacred art has a long and honorable history, and sculpture is only one form of art. When I've had the opportunity to visit great cathedrals, the beauty of the images has inspired me, whether in stained glass, paintings, or statuary. Beauty can communicate truth and goodness, and that's what the artist is doing. John of Damascus, one of the early church fathers, wrote, 'The beauty of the images moves me to contemplation as a meadow delights the eyes and subtly infuses the soul with the glory of God.' Churches that use them as part of the atmosphere of worship distinguish between idols and icons. An icon is an image. Churches that use icons say they honor or venerate the icon but never worship it. It's merely an inspiration to contemplate the reality that it represents, and any honor or veneration passes on to that which is represented. When they say they venerate certain icons, they don't mean worship. They mean respect or deference or reverence. I don't see the use of icons in worship as an issue to stand between those who should be one in Christ."

"Is the whole discussion of idols, then, irrelevant to us?" I pressed.

"Not at all," Hal replied. "The New Testament shows us that idolatry is placing any part of our earthly nature before God."

He turned to Colossians 3:5 and read, "Put to death, therefore, whatever belongs to your earthly nature: sexual immorality, impurity, lust, evil desires and greed, which is idolatry." He paused. "How do you invest your thoughts, your time, your money, your energy? What comes first? Where is your Creator, the Creator of all that is, the One who is alone true and good, who is responsible for every good thing you have or can ever hope for, in your priorities? *That* is the question of idolatry for modern people."

I had a sinking feeling that I was not as free of the temptation to idolatry as I thought. Clearly we were no longer dealing with the worship of Canaanite or Greek or Roman statues.

"What else do you see in this chapter, Hal?" Anna asked.

"A lot," Hal said. "But let me leave you with just two more points. First, there is powerful literary and liturgical art in this chapter. The first forty verses are in three parts and form a chiasm, like we discussed earlier, a rhythmic pattern where the central section—verses fifteen to thirty-one, about idolatry—are framed by generic sections in verses one to fourteen and thirty-two to forty about the nature of God and obedience to him. Each of these in turn can be broken down into similar patterns. We don't have time to study these patterns, but you should know that they are there and they speak—as the saying goes—volumes about the nature of Scripture and how God has communicated to us. These patterns and rhythms may have been memory aids, ways of communicating epic truths in a time when the written word was rare and hard to access for most people. They were told and repeated in homes, around campfires, in worship times; they become engrained in the people's memory and knowledge.

"There are other patterns here worth noting. The order of the images that the people are prohibited from making or bowing down to in verses sixteen to nineteen is the precise reverse order of the creation in Genesis chapter one. This was not an accident. Moses intentionally recapitulated the categories of created things here. God creates, and man tears apart the creation. It's like Paul says in the first chapter of Romans, 'Although they claimed to be wise, they became fools and exchanged the glory of the immortal God for images made to look like mortal man and birds and animals and reptiles.' We are to worship the Creator, not the created things.

"Then notice what the punishment is for making and worshipping idols: 'The LORD will scatter you among the peoples, and only a few of you will survive among the nations to which the LORD will drive you. There you will worship man-made gods of wood and stone, which cannot see or hear or eat or smell' (Deut. 4:27–28).

"As the saying goes, 'Be careful what you wish for.' Those who wish for false gods are likely to receive them."

"And the second point?" I asked, aware of the late hour.

Hal read verses 29–31: "But if from there you seek the LORD your God, you will find him if you look for him with all your heart and with all your soul. When you are in distress and all these things have happened to you, then in later days you will return to the LORD your God and obey him. For the LORD your God is a merciful God; he will not abandon or destroy you or forget the covenant with your forefathers, which he confirmed to them by oath."

"Verses twenty-nine to thirty-one are the beginning of hope for those who have failed in their obedience to the Lord. He promises that, no matter how great their failure and how desperate the resulting circumstances, if they will seek him with all their heart and soul, they will find him and be returned to him because he is merciful and will not abandon or destroy them or forget his covenant.

"This is the grace and mercy that always gives us hope. It's a message that Moses will come back to later. The promise is renewed in

Jeremiah, chapters twenty-nine to thirty-one, and is fulfilled in Jesus. Jesus himself taught in similar terms. He said, 'Ask and it will be given to you; seek and you will find; knock and the door will be opened to you' and that we should forgive others 'seventy-seven times' so that God will forgive us also. And John wrote, 'If we confess our sins, he is faithful and just and will forgive us our sins and purify us from all unrighteousness.'"

The sun was near the horizon; it was no longer warm. As Anna and I made our good-byes and headed for home, I recalled Hal's e-mail that had started the week: "If you had no other Scripture but this, you would know a very great deal of what God wants you to know, and what you need to know to be one of his children."

CHAPTER FIVE

The roaring fire filled the old colonial fireplace in Hal's study. It had been built in a time when heat and not decoration was its primary function. It was only a little smaller than the kitchen fireplaces of that era—almost big enough to walk into. Hal had a pile of three-foot-long logs beside it. He heaved one more on for good measure, and the sparks flew up the chimney as he hastily replaced the screen to keep them from escaping into the room. The heat from the blazing logs radiated across the room. He pulled around his old red-wing chair and my green chair until they faced the fire at slight but opposite angles, accents to the open furnace before us. The winged sides captured the heat so well that I peeled off the sweater Anna had insisted I wear to ward off the chill. "He'll have you running around outside," she had said. "I've got to look out for you. It's too early in the season to get a cold."

We were back to our Friday evening routine, just the two of us.

"Talk to me about fire," Hal began the conversation, his eyes half closed, basking in the warmth.

"It's one of the four elements of the ancient Greek philosophers," I began. "Earth, air, fire, and water."

"What else?" he asked.

"It transforms, consumes, destroys," I said. "We depend on it for heat and cooking, but we have to control it or it will destroy us."

"What else?" he asked again.

I reached for more thoughts. "People are fascinated by it. Children want to play with it. Some of my best memories from my youth are campfires where we told stories, sang songs, roasted hot dogs or marsh-mallows, cooked meals on wilderness trips, shared good times with friends."

"What does the Bible say about it?"

"Our God is a consuming fire. I can't remember where that comes from."

"Hebrews," he said. "The whole verse is that we should worship God acceptably with reverence and awe, for our God is a consuming fire."

"What else?" I asked, becoming the questioner.

"Lots," he replied. "John the Baptist taught that the one who came after him would baptize with the Holy Spirit and with fire. Jesus said he had come to bring fire on the earth. On the day of Pentecost, the Holy Spirit descended on the disciples in what seemed to be tongues of fire that separated and came to rest on each of them. Paul teaches us not to put out the Spirit's fire. There's a lot more."

"All metaphors for God, I expect."

"More or less," Hal replied. "They all work. Warming, consuming, transforming, destroying. Making what we consume healthy and acceptable. Fascinating, but not totally approachable. It all starts in Deuteronomy, of course."

I was silent, unsure of his drift.

"Well, Deuteronomy and Exodus," he went on. "What happened at Sinai, or Horeb, as Moses calls it in Deuteronomy. And in the Exodus. God appears as fire, speaks out of the fire. Let's read."

We read chapter five, beginning with the introduction at the end of chapter four.

> This is the law Moses set before the Israelites. These are the stipulations, decrees and laws Moses gave them when they came out of Egypt and were in the valley near Beth Peor east of the Jordan, in the land of Sihon king of the Amorites, who reigned in Heshbon and was defeated by Moses and the Israelites as they came out of Egypt. They took possession of his land and the land of Og king of Bashan, the two Amorite kings east of the Jordan. This land extended from Aroer on the rim of the Arnon Gorge to Mount Siyon (that is, Hermon), and included all the Arabah east of the Jordan, as far as the Sea of the Arabah, below the slopes of Pisgah.

Moses summoned all Israel and said: Hear, O Israel, the decrees and laws I declare in your hearing today. Learn them and be sure to follow them. The LORD our God made a covenant with us at Horeb. It was not with our fathers that the LORD made this covenant, but with us, with all of us who are alive here today. The LORD spoke to you face to face out of the fire on the mountain. (At that time I stood between the LORD and you to declare to you the word of the LORD, because you were afraid of the fire and did not go up the mountain.) And he said:

"I am the LORD your God, who brought you out of Egypt, out of the land of slavery.

"You shall have no other gods before me.

"You shall not make for yourself an idol in the form of anything in heaven above or on the earth beneath or in the waters below. You shall not bow down to them or worship them; for I, the LORD your God, am a jealous God, punishing the children for the sin of the fathers to the third and fourth generation of those who hate me, but showing love to a thousand generations of those who love me and keep my commandments.

"You shall not misuse the name of the LORD your God, for the LORD will not hold anyone guiltless who misuses his name.

"Observe the Sabbath day by keeping it holy, as the LORD your God has commanded you. Six days you shall labor and do all your work, but the seventh day is a Sabbath to the LORD your God. On it you shall not do any work, neither you, nor your son or daughter, nor your manservant or maidservant, nor your ox, your donkey or any of your animals, nor the alien within your gates, so that your manservant and maidservant may rest, as you do. Remember that you were slaves in Egypt and that the LORD your God brought you out of there with a mighty hand and an outstretched arm. Therefore the LORD your God has commanded you to observe the Sabbath day.

"Honor your father and your mother, as the LORD your God has commanded you, so that you may live long and that it may go well with you in the land the LORD your God is giving you.

"You shall not murder.

"You shall not commit adultery.

"You shall not steal.

"You shall not give false testimony against your neighbor.

"You shall not covet your neighbor's wife. You shall not set your desire on your neighbor's house or land, his manservant or maidservant, his ox or donkey, or anything that belongs to your neighbor."

These are the commandments the LORD proclaimed in a loud voice to your whole assembly there on the mountain from out of the fire, the cloud and the deep darkness; and he added nothing more. Then he wrote them on two stone tablets and gave them to me.

When you heard the voice out of the darkness, while the mountain was ablaze with fire, all the leading men of your tribes and your elders came to me. And you said, "The LORD our God has shown us his glory and his majesty, and we have heard his voice from the fire. Today we have seen that a man can live even if God speaks with him. But now, why should we die? This great fire will consume us, and we will die if we hear the voice of the LORD our God any longer. For what mortal man has ever heard the voice of the living God speaking out of fire, as we have, and survived? Go near and listen to all that the LORD our God says. Then tell us whatever the LORD our God tells you. We will listen and obey."

The LORD heard you when you spoke to me and the LORD said to me, "I have heard what this people said to you. Everything they said was good. Oh, that their hearts would be inclined to fear me and keep all my commands always, so that it might go well with them and their children forever!

"Go, tell them to return to their tents. But you stay here with me so that I may give you all the commands, decrees, and laws you are to teach them to follow in the land I am giving them to possess." So be careful to do what the LORD your God has commanded you; do not turn aside to the right or to the left. Walk in all the way that the LORD your God has commanded you, so that you may live and prosper and prolong your days in the land that you will possess.

—Deut. 4:44–5:33

"There are a lot of references to fire," I observed.

"Fourteen times in this and the last chapter," Hal replied. "The New Testament images of God as fire—or acting with fire—are rooted in the literal experiences of Israel in the chapter we just studied and the one we're studying now."

He looked down at his Bible.

"In your Bible the heading on chapter five of Deuteronomy is 'The Ten Commandments,' and that's what this chapter is about. It's one of the most familiar sets of teachings in the Bible. Virtually everyone knows about the Ten Commandments, even if they can't recite them and don't know much about their background. But the Ten Commandments aren't just a set of good rules that may be posted on a church wall—even if they can't be in our schoolrooms or public buildings any more. God himself spoke them—out of fire—to all the people on the mountain."

He paused as we gazed into the blaze before us. The heat remained intense. I pushed my chair back a bit.

"Imagine the awe and fear!" he said. "The mountain blazes with fire up to the sky, black clouds and deep darkness surround it, and out of fire and clouds and darkness, the very voice of God speaks to the people and gives them these commandments."

Hal's eyes closed. He bent forward, tensed as if he knelt on the mountain in the face of the fire and the voice of God. "And what was their response?" He opened his eyes and looked up at me. "They retreated. They were afraid. They sent their pastor to listen to God and tell them what he said. Face to face with their Creator, they fled and sent Moses to find out what else God had to say to them. 'Let someone else have the experience of the Holy; it's too much for me. You tell us what God wants from us and we'll do it, but let us out of here.'"

"Do you think people still have experiences like that?" I asked.

Hal rose from his chair and shuffled over to his bookshelves. He pulled down a thin paperback volume and returned.

"Charles Finney was one of the great evangelists of American history. He was born in the late 1700s in Connecticut. He passed up an opportunity to attend Yale and instead studied law in the office of an upstate New York attorney and became a lawyer. In his autobiography," he patted the book on his lap, "Finney tells the story of his own conversion in the back room of that small-town law office. He had a vision of meeting the Lord Jesus Christ face to face. That meeting broke him down to tears and confessions. Listen."

He opened the book, which I could see was well-thumbed, and read:

> I received a mighty baptism of the Holy Spirit. Without any expectation of it, without ever having the thought in my mind that there was any such thing for me, without any memory of ever hearing the thing mentioned by any person in the world, the Holy Spirit descended upon me in a manner that seemed to go through me, body and soul. I could feel the impression, like a wave of electricity, going through and through me. Indeed it seemed to come in waves of liquid love, for I could not express it in any other way. It seemed like the very breath of God. I can remember distinctly that it seemed to fan me, like immense wings.
>
> No words can express the wonderful love that was spread abroad in my heart. I wept aloud with joy and love. I literally

bellowed out the unspeakable overflow of my heart. There waves came over me, and over me, and over me, one after the other, until I remember crying out, "I shall die if these waves continue to pass over me." I said, "Lord, I cannot bear any more," yet I had no fear of death.[5]

"When a client came to see him the next day, Finney told the man, 'I have a retainer from the Lord Jesus Christ to plead his cause and I cannot plead yours.'[6] Finney went on to become an evangelist, preaching the gospel to millions in an age before the advent of mass media, serving as a leader in the movement for the abolition of slavery and in the founding of Oberlin College in Ohio."

"Sounds like Finney felt the fire of God's presence," I said.

"And did you ever hear of Dwight Moody?" Hal asked.

I had heard the name but didn't know much about him.

"It was later in the nineteenth century," Hal said. "He was converted in a Congregational church near Boston at the age of seventeen and became perhaps the most successful and best-known evangelist of his day. The story is told of Moody that once on a city street he was so overcome by the Holy Spirit that he, like Finney, couldn't bear it anymore and prayed for the Lord to lift the experience from him."

"Great men of God," I observed. "But those things don't happen to most people."

"They happen to more people than you might think," Hal said. "I know pastors who could tell you a lot of stories. I could tell quite a few myself. But most people are like the crowd around Moses. The experience of the Holy is too much for them. They don't want to be that close to the fire. They want the pastor or the priest to do it for them. 'Just tell us what to do, but don't expect us to get that close to God.'"

I knew, in a small way, what Hal meant. Most believers have learned how few people want to talk about the things of God. Stony silence or polite deferral greets most attempts to bring up the subject. The "religious" person is called upon for appropriate occasions, such as saying grace at a meal, but is not welcomed for anything deeper. The popular maxim is that one should not discuss politics or religion. They are thought to be too controversial, too likely to give offense, and perhaps they are. People of faith have learned that their faith is not always as welcome as they are.

But, I wondered, how does God view it? Does he think it inappropriate to discuss him in polite conversation or acknowledge him in public? Is he in the same category as pornography or bodily excretory functions? Should we be dependent on our Moses to teach us and avoid our own contact with the holy and sacred? Is it only pastors and priests who are to be in touch with God on our behalf? Are we afraid to be engaged with the Holy?

Hal brought me back to reality. "God recognizes and accepts people's weakness in the face of his holiness." He was more relaxed now, retreating from his own vision of the Holy to his pastoral role. "The people's desire to send Moses to hear the rest of the message is good. If they can't bear the encounter themselves, at least they want to receive God's words, and they do promise to obey them. And God's words in this chapter are the Ten Commandments."

We turned to the Ten Commandments, sometimes called the Decalogue. They were, Hal pointed out, originally given in Exodus, chapter twenty. They are recapitulated with minor variation in this chapter of Deuteronomy. They have been thought of as the very moral and legal core of the Judeo-Christian tradition, hence of Western civilization itself. Many students of Deuteronomy think the laws of Deuteronomy that follow chapter five, up to the end of the giving of the laws in chapter twenty-six, are a commentary on the Decalogue, an outworking of specific meanings and applications of the general principles stated in it.

Hal said, "They are the only words recorded in the Bible that are actually written by God himself."

We talked about the Ten Commandments and their significance to civilization.

For much of American history, the Ten Commandments have been posted in public places such as schoolhouses and courthouses. They represented a code of righteousness honored by consensus. Only recently had anyone assumed that it would not be a good thing for children to learn them, judges to honor them, and citizens to look to them as a moral if not legal code.

In the mid-twentieth century, the moral consensus in the United States that supported public display and respect for the Commandments began to crumble. Libertarians and atheists brought court challenges over their display in public schools and other government buildings, citing the language of the United States Constitution that forbade government "establishment of religion." Courts had to acknowledge the logic of the challenges—it is too hard to argue that the Ten Commandments are not religious, and to do so denies the most compelling part of their message. To the dismay of large numbers of Americans, the commandments were removed from many government buildings. The nation was, it seemed, turning its back on God. The principle of government neutrality in matters of religion enshrined in the Constitution seemed at odds with the history and beliefs of most of the people.

Hal reshelved his Charles Finney. "You will have to be my teacher on the legal issues involved in public display of the Ten commandments," he said. "I don't understand the legal elements. They didn't teach us constitutional law in seminary."

"Most people who feel strongly about these issues," I said, "don't understand them either. But let's talk about the commandments themselves, and not American church-state law. I get enough of law all day in the office."

Hal agreed, but made me promise to come back to the subject.

"You know," I said, "I always thought of the Ten Commandments as just the stone tablets. I never knew God had actually spoken them out of the fire on the mountain. But why the tablets? Why were they written down?"

"They were written down for the same reason you write down contracts for your clients in your law office, Chris," Hal said. "The Ten Commandments are more than commands, they are also a covenant—call it a contract in more current language. God's part in the covenant was to free the people out of their bondage in Egypt. Their part in return was to obey the commands. As long as they did, God would continue to show love to them, and they would prosper in the land he was giving them."

"Five commandments on each tablet?" I asked.

"Is that how you write contracts?" Hal asked. "Half of it on one document, and the other half on another? No, the covenant was written on tablets to preserve it for posterity, and for evidence when the people of the covenant broke their promises, as they would. But the whole of the Ten Commandments would have been written on each tablet. There are two tablets because each party to the contract should have a copy, just like you do in your law practice.

"And it's not just a contract with the people who were at the mountain with Moses—their descendants as well have been freed from the bondage in Egypt by God's gracious acts. Moses is specific here—it is a covenant 'with all of us who are alive here today.' That can still be said."

"How so?" I asked. "I mean, I can see it for Jews—their history goes back to the Exodus. But my ancestors were probably throwing spears around the woods in northern Europe while Moses was writing the Torah."

"Christians have always understood that for them the bondage in Egypt is their slavery to sin, where they were held before they came to Christ. God frees them from that bondage, but he expects them to follow and obey him thereafter."

I'd known the Ten Commandments from childhood. But what else could Hal teach me about them? "What," I wondered aloud, "did God have in mind when he said he would punish the 'children for the sin of the fathers to the third and fourth generation of those who hate me' in the command against idolatry?"

"Remember from last time that idolatry includes all the disobedience of sexual immorality, greed, and other things that we saw in our last meeting. The only way to understand it is that the consequences of this kind of sin inevitably affect future generations. At the time of Deuteronomy, extended families lived together, so the third and fourth generation would be in the household of the idolater and affected by the sin. But it's common sense. Children are always affected by their parents' disobedience, sometimes tragically. Contrast this warning with the promise to show 'love to a thousand generations of those who love me and keep my commandments.' Probably neither of these numberings of generations should be taken literally, but as figures of speech to show how much greater the power of God's grace and love is—the triumph of mercy over justice."

As the evening wore on, the great fire settled gradually into coals and embers. Heat still radiated from the bricks and hearth that had absorbed it from the flame. And Hal radiated the wisdom of that greater flame from which he had absorbed all that he had to teach.

He showed me that the commandment against using the Lord's name in vain was not just about blasphemy or swearing. "Remember that the commandments are addressed to God's people. Misusing God's name can include false worship, using God's name in magic, or in a calculating or manipulative way of dealing with God. People who seek to gain personal advantage over others from God—or who seek to use him to satisfy their own greed or improper desires—violate this commandment." As Hal said this I made a mental note to pray for justice rather than victory when I went to court.

I asked, "What about the common uses of the name of God that you hear on the lips of all kinds of people who don't think they're swearing? I hear people say, 'Gawd' or 'Omigod' twenty times a day in private and public conversations. People use it like they used to say, 'Wow.' It seems to have become a culturally acceptable expression of surprise or pleasure."

"Yes," Hal said. "And people who use the Lord's name that way are often good people, people who go to church, who wouldn't think of coarser ways to misuse his name. But the culture has been cheapened and coarsened, and this is a commonplace witness to this cultural coarsening. Remember Charles Finney, Dwight Moody, the voice of God speaking out of the fire at Sinai, the flames descending on the believers at Pentecost? God is a consuming fire, too holy for us to even look upon. Using his name like bubble gum shows how far we are from any sense of holiness before him, or even understanding the meaning of the commandments, which most Americans still think are the moral heart of our civilization."

We turned to the commandment to "observe the Sabbath Day by keeping it holy." Hal pointed out that the commandment to observe the Sabbath was specific in extending to the whole household, including children and servants. The "boss" is not to take a rest while the subordinates have to continue working. It is, among other things, a statement of good employment practices. Both work and rest are the province of everyone, in the home and the workplace.

I was troubled by this commandment. "Most Christians honor the commandment not to misuse the Lord's name, even in culturally acceptable ways. But the Sabbath command seems to me the subject of massive disobedience. Christians work on Sunday and do everything else then. Children's sports teams practice on Sundays, even during normal morning church hours. Stores are open, and people buy and sell on Sundays. But God puts this in the middle of the same commands as not to steal, murder, or commit adultery. Are we, even in the church, defying God on this matter?"

Hal led me through the Scriptures that addressed the Christian understanding of the Sabbath. I learned that although Exodus taught that violation of the Sabbath was an offense that merited death, Jesus had healed people on the Sabbath and gathered grain with his disciples when they were hungry. When he was challenged on these practices, he taught that he was "Lord of the Sabbath," thus affirming his divinity and authority. He told the people that it was lawful to do good on the Sabbath, and that the Sabbath was made for man, not man for the Sabbath. Unlike other commands of the Decalogue, neither he nor the other New Testament writers affirmed the strict commands of Sabbath-keeping contained in Deuteronomy and Exodus. This has led many to think that the Sabbath commands apply only to Jews or are repealed in the New Testament era.

From the earliest time, the church moved its gathering and worship day from the last day of the week to the first day—from Saturday to Sunday—commemorating the day of the week on which the Resurrection occurred. In Acts twenty, verse seven, they came together on the first day of the week to break bread, presumably a communion meal. In First Corinthians sixteen, verse two, they brought offerings on the first day of the week. When John says in Revelation chapter one, "On the Lord's Day I was in the Spirit," he was undoubtedly referring to Sunday. Paul taught in his letters to the Romans, Galatians, and Colossians that observance of special days, including Sabbaths, should not be a matter of judgment between people but should be a matter of individual conscience.

Hal said, "The New Testament teaches us to gather together, and that there should be times of rest, worship, prayer, and communion. The Christian consensus has been that Sunday is the most appropriate day for that to happen. But the strict application of the Sabbath-keeping laws of Exodus and Deuteronomy are not carried forward. The Commandment to observe the Sabbath and keep it holy is generalized to a commandment to take time to rest and honor God. The Sabbath commandment doesn't have the continuing force in the era of the church that it did before Jesus. He is our rest. It's the rest and the holiness rather than the particular day that's important."

We went on to other commandments.

Hal related the command to honor father and mother to the reciprocal obligation of the parents to teach their children the things of God, an obligation we had seen in the last chapter and would see again several times in Deuteronomy.

Finally, he showed me how the commandments flowed in perfect logical order and spiritual priority. The first three—no other gods, no idolatry, no misuse of the name of the Lord—were directed exclusively at giving proper honor to God. The fourth—keeping Sabbath holiness—was transitional, honoring God but doing so by providing needful rest to people. The fifth was directed to proper relations in the family, the next priority after God. The sixth, seventh, eighth, and ninth commandments—against murder, adultery, theft, and false testimony—were directed to proper conduct or outward action toward others, the "neighbors" whom Jesus famously defined in the parable of the Good Samaritan. Finally, the tenth commandment against coveting addresses the state of the heart, teaching the need to internalize godly thinking so the mind is pure, as well as the outward actions. It is this thought that Jesus picks up and expands in the Sermon on the Mount when he teaches that, in God's eyes, our anger and lust are violations of the commandments against murder and adultery.

We turned to the follow-up on the commandments. Hal read verse twenty-nine: "Oh, that their hearts would be inclined to fear me and keep all my commands always, so that it might go well with them and their children *forever*!"

"I told you the other day that Deuteronomy is about life in this world, and not the next," Hal said. "But in that verse there is a hint of eternity—fearing God and always keeping his commands will lead to it going well for them *forever*. I think this is about more than just living successfully in the new land."

The coals were mere embers now. Hal prayed for me before we parted.

He prayed that I might ever know God's voice out of the fire and never lose my awe and reverence for him and his word. He prayed that I would be free of the idolatry into which everything in the culture around me cried out for me to fall. He prayed that my prayers would honor God and would not misuse God's name by asking for things out of idolatry or wrong desires of my heart. He prayed that my life would know God's Sabbath and that I would enter into God's eternal rest when my time in this "tent of flesh" was done. He prayed for right relations in my family, with my wife and children and grandchildren, that they would all know God and that I would be a suitable teacher of the things of God to them. He prayed that I would not let anger tempt me to the sin of wishing ill on any other person, and that I would love and pray for those who hate me; that I would look on every person as a precious soul in God's eyes and not be tempted to lustful thoughts about anyone, and that I would learn to pray for the souls of any who might tempt me. He prayed that I'd keep the purity of the relationship in my mind and heart as well as body; that I'd keep an honest measure in my business and personal life, taking advantage of no one; that I would be straight in all things to all people and never lie to take an advantage for myself or disadvantage others. Finally, he prayed that I would be content with what God, in his infinite wisdom and concern for my well being, had provided, and would not seek or yearn for that which he had not given me.

Proverbs says, "The Lord hears the prayer of the righteous." As I drove home that evening, I prayed my own weak prayer of thanksgiving for Hal's prayers on my behalf.

CHAPTER SIX

It was one of those rare Sundays when everything about church was right. If I was made for worship, to love God and enjoy him forever as the Confession taught, too often that worship proved elusive, even during the worship hour. Sunday morning services were full of announcements of the busyness of congregational life. People buzzed irreverently in the sanctuary before the service and applauded like a theater audience to music performed by untrained voices singing to tapes. Prayer consisted of asking God to do things for this or that person in the body, or for their relatives, with little attention to adoration, confession, or thanksgiving. The pastor entertained with jokes and gave a humdrum message that never brought people to a deep confrontation with their sin, the awesome majesty and perfect holiness of God, or the power of Jesus Christ in bridging that unbridgeable gap.

However, this Sunday it all came together. The pastor began with a prayer that invoked familiar Scripture to immerse us in the confession of personal sin. "Lord, have mercy on me, a sinner." The choir sang with a power that lifted the spirit from the pit of human need and evil until we seemed almost lifted bodily from the pews. Then the soloist sang the "Our Father" with a cathedral voice that began in the low ranges and moved up the scale until it soared beyond our presence and into heaven itself: "For thine is the kingdom, and the power, and the glory, forever and ever, Amen."

The pastor preached on Matthew 7:13–14: "Enter through the narrow gate. For wide is the gate and broad is the road that leads to destruction, and many enter through it. But small is the gate and narrow the road that leads to life, and only a few find it."

By the time he finished, every soul in the church was convicted that he or she was on the broad road that leads to destruction and had resolved to change his or her life and take the narrow path.

As the service progressed, I was carried back in time as well as upward in spirit. In another church, thirty years before, I had stood beside my parents and among their friends, our neighbors, Sunday school teachers, and people I'd known and who had known me since my birth, and sang and learned and loved the great hymns: "Holy, Holy, Holy," "The Church's One Foundation," "Be Thou My Vision," and "How Great Thou Art." And I had listened to the pastor who first taught me—and made me memorize—John 3:16, as the heart of the Christian faith: "For God so loved the world that he gave his only begotten son that whosoever believeth in him shall not perish but have eternal life."

I traveled in time that morning, and the journey didn't end when Anna and I left the sanctuary to find the children in their classrooms. Somehow I knew it wasn't just a coincidence; this Sunday was different for a reason. God doesn't deal in coincidences, Anna told me once. It didn't surprise me when Hal called midweek to tell me to get a babysitter for Friday evening. Anna and I had to talk about chapter six together.

> These are the commands, decrees and laws the LORD your God directed me to teach you to observe in the land that you are crossing the Jordan to possess, so that you, your children and their children after them may fear the LORD your God as long as you live by keeping all his decrees and commands that I give you, and so that you may enjoy long life. Hear, O Israel, and be careful to obey so that it may go well with you and that you may increase greatly in a land flowing with milk and honey, just as the LORD, the God of your fathers, promised you.
>
> Hear, O Israel: The LORD our God, the LORD is one. Love the LORD your God with all your heart and with all your soul and with all your strength. These commandments that I give you today are to be upon your hearts. Impress them on your children. Talk about them when you sit at home and when you walk along the road, when you lie down and when you get up. Tie them as symbols on your hands and bind them on your foreheads. Write them on the doorframes of your houses and on your gates.
>
> —Deut. 6:1–9

"Shema, Yisrael, Hashem Elokeinu, Hashem Echad!" Hal greeted us with cups of decaf as he entered the study after we had settled down.

We looked at him expectantly.

"Hear, O Israel: The Lord our God, the Lord is one," he said. "It's Deuteronomy six-four, in Hebrew. I thought you should hear it in the original because the language has some lessons."

These were, he told us, the opening words of what has become known simply as the "Shema"—literally "hear"—the central creed of Jewish monotheism. The full Shema includes, in order, Deuteronomy 6:4–9, 11:13–21, and Numbers 15:37–41. The Shema is worthy of memorization, especially this first section—like the Lord's Prayer. Faithful Jews recite it twice a day, in the morning and evening, at the time of circumcision of a baby boy, and before death. It introduces the core thought of Deuteronomy 6.

"Then 'Hashem' must mean 'Lord,'" Anna said.

Hal smiled. "Not exactly. 'Hashem' literally means 'the name.' The personal name of God that appears in the text of the Shema is 'YHWH.' Theologians sometimes refer to it as the Tetragrammaton, or four letters. In traditional Judaism it's considered too holy to be said, or even written."

As Hal spoke, I was carried back to the sense of awe and holiness I had experienced the previous Sunday. He and I had spoken the previous week about the holiness of God's name and the commandment not to misuse it. Now, I learned, the people to whom the command had originally been given would not even use the name.

"The tradition," he said, "is not only from the sense of God's holiness but the desire to avoid unintentional blasphemy. In Leviticus chapter twenty-four, death by stoning is the punishment for an individual who blasphemed 'the Name' with a curse. During prayer, blessings, or the reading of Torah, YHWH is spoken as 'Adonai' or 'Lord.' Elsewhere, and in writing, 'hashem,' is substituted."

"Does 'YHWH' have a meaning?" Anna asked. "You called it God's personal name. Where does it come from?"

"God gave Moses 'the name' when God appeared to him in the burning bush in Exodus chapter three. 'YHWH' is usually given in English transliteration in commentaries and scholarly texts as 'Jahweh' and indicated by custom in English Bibles by the term LORD, with the last three letters written in subscript capitals.

"As to the meaning, the translation of YHWH has challenged scholars, theologians, and spiritual leaders for millennia. It comes from the Hebrew root of the word for being or existence, and is sometimes translated as 'I Am' or 'I Am Who I Am.' It has a combination of tenses and can be understood as 'He Is-He Was-He Will Be.' Variants of the word mean 'being' and 'let there be.' The term is used that way in the creation narrative of the first chapter of Genesis. It captures—perhaps as much as human language can in one word—God's infinite being and existence."

I thought, *For thine is the kingdom, and the power, and the glory forever. . . .*

"How do you say it?" Anna asked.

"In Hebrew," Hal said, "there are no vowels, although a system of 'pointing' the Hebrew consonants—making little marks over, under, or beside them—was developed to show proper pronunciation. If one pronounces the name of God, YHWH, the consonants themselves, Y, W, and H, are not hard sounds but soft, the blowing of air through the mouth, like the spiritual nature of God.[7] 'Spirit gives birth to spirit,' as Jesus teaches in John chapter three."

"What does it mean when it says that 'the Lord is one'?" I asked.

"You are swimming in deep water here," Hal replied. "It's not only the name Jahweh that challenges translation, as the infinite should when addressed in human terms. The phrase as a whole, which your Bible translates, 'The Lord our God, the Lord is one,' also challenges translation. It can have a number of meanings, such as 'The Lord is our God, the Lord alone.' The question is whether the phrase describes a *relationship* with God, as in 'the Lord alone is our God,' or the *nature* of God, as in 'the Lord is one.' Both are correct, of course, and Jewish teachers and commentators have taught both. There is some temptation among Jewish writers to use the monotheistic sense of the phrase as a proof text against the Christian understanding of the Trinity—God as Father, Son, and Holy Spirit."

"How do we understand that?" I asked. "God as three in one can seem like three gods instead of one."

"Yes," Hal replied. "But Jesus taught that 'I and the Father are one,' although he prayed to the Father and interacted with him in his earthly existence. It took several centuries of Christian thought and meditation on the life, teachings, and resurrection of Jesus—and what the Scriptures teach about him—to formulate exactly how the Trinity is understood. God is of one substance or essence—one God and not three, but coexisting in three persons of Father, Son, and Holy Spirit."

"Is that what's new in the New Testament?" Anna asked.

"Not entirely," Hal said. "The Old Testament contains many hints of this fundamental truth about God's nature. The opening words of the Bible, 'In the beginning, God created,' use a plural noun for God, but use it with a singular verb. The word is *Elohim*. And there are innumerable references in the Old Testament to God the Spirit, starting in the second verse of Genesis, where the 'Spirit of God was hovering over the waters.' Other passages refer to the Messiah in divine terms. Human beings are created in God's image. Theologians from Augustine in late antiquity to contemporary times have recognized that the plurality in what the early creeds called the 'Godhead' is in turn reflected in the nature of human beings created in God's image. Communication and relationship in perfect love are the nature of the persons of the Godhead. And this is part of what we're made for and what we would be if we reflected God as we should."

My mind raced back to the memories of the oneness of the church family—or at least what I had perceived to be oneness—in my childhood. Was this what God was all about? And then my thoughts raced forward to the fractiousness of my experience among Christians as an adult. What a mess we make of it! And then those thoughts moved back to Anna: At least two of us could strive for that perfection of love and communication that would reflect the image of God.

Hal brought me back to the present. "Now read the next verse."

The next verse—"Love the Lord your God with all your heart and with all your soul and with all your strength"—was familiar to me from the New Testament teaching of Jesus. It was, he said, the first and greatest commandment.

"But I thought it said with all your mind," I said.

"Jesus adds mind to heart, soul, and strength," Hal replied. "Loving God includes the intellect in the faculties that Deuteronomy describes as heart, soul, and strength. He wanted to be sure we understood that. All truth is God's truth. Believers need never be afraid of knowledge or learning. Paul teaches this also, in Philippians." He turned to it and read: "'And this is my prayer: that your love may abound more and more in knowledge and depth of insight.' This is about intellectual knowledge. It's part of the foundation of Christian understanding, even if it isn't sufficient for the Christian life all by itself."

Hal then showed us how the next verse, "These commandments that I give you today are to be upon your hearts," along with the commandment to love God with all our heart and soul and strength, meant that the practice of faith was not to be a matter of outward observance but of inward mindset. Jesus was following Deuteronomy when he taught that the commandments were broken by those whose state of mind was a desire to act disobediently, even when they did not do so; it was the inner state of a person that counted, not the outward acts of compliance.

"Now," Hal said, sitting back and relaxing from his teaching mode, "show me pictures of your children."

We both reached for our wallets. I had the school pictures: Elizabeth (Lily) in her ponytail and school jumper, smiling shyly; and Willy, her little brother, exuberant, mischievous grin, hair askew.

Anna had an accordion of photos. She moved over and sat on the arm of Hal's chair and went over them one by one. The first was of both kids posing under the Christmas tree, and then there was Lily flying a kite at the beach, Willy jumping in the waves, pictures in highchairs and in beds and family groups, baby pictures, birthday pictures—the memories preserved, even as they outgrew them faster than July corn. Hal studied them, laughed at them, and asked questions about them, until the subject was exhausted and Anna left the arm of Hal's chair and returned to her own chair.

"You know why I wanted you to be here tonight, don't you?" he asked her.

She nodded slightly, a faint smile of recognition struggling with anticipation of where we were going now.

"Nothing you will do in your lifetime," Hal said, looking at both of us, "nothing is as important as bringing these children up to know and love their God. It's even more important than your own salvation because it's the salvation of someone else, not just anyone but the particular souls God himself has put in your care—not that you're likely to do a good job teaching your children if you don't believe it yourself."

He turned back to the text.

"'Impress them on your children,' the text goes on. Teaching God's laws to the children is one of the most frequently repeated teachings of Deuteronomy. We saw it in chapter four, when Moses told them to teach the children both the words and the deeds—the history."

He continued, "I can't tell you how many times I saw families drive up to drop children off at the church for Sunday school, and then drive off. The parents wanted the children to have the benefit of church teaching but wouldn't receive any themselves. We had them for an hour a week. Someone else had them for the other one hundred and sixty-seven hours. We had less than one percent of their time. It's better than nothing, of course. We did a lot with those kids in that hour, and some of them turned out better than their parents had any right to hope they would. But children learn much more from how they observe adults behaving around them, especially their parents, than they ever will from lectures or classes."

Hal went on to show us that the next few verses expressed the comprehensiveness of how we were to impress God's commands on our children:

- *"Talk about them when you sit at home and when you walk along the road."* The teaching fills the space we occupy, whether at home or away from home.
- *"When you lie down and when you get up."* The teaching fills the time we occupy, resting or up and about.
- *"Tie them as symbols on your hands and bind them on your foreheads."* The location of the symbols, on hands and foreheads, represents the physical and mental aspects of human life. Observant Jewish males, he told us, bind a literal box, called a *tefillin*, to their arms and heads, but usually only during morning prayers.
- *"Write them on the doorframes of your houses and on your gates."* The house is the home, where the family lives. The gate is the city gate, where community functions occur. In Moses' time, most cities were walled for protection, and occupants entered through

gates. The town or city gate was the center of public life in the community. This verse teaches embedding the word of God in family and in community life.

"Together," Hal said, "these verses of the Shema admonish us to teach or model God's word everywhere we are, at all times, in our physical and intellectual lives, and in our families and communities. They embrace the totality of life, all of which belongs to God. And it's the totality of life in which we are to impress an understanding of God on our children."

Anna clung to her fistful of pictures as Hal talked. "But can we really do this?" I asked Hal. "Even in the best Christian homes, after age five the child is off to school all day and out with friends a lot of the rest of the time. How do we teach our children God's word and his ways in every part of life?"

"Every mom and dad has to make a judgment for each child," Hal said. "The right way for one isn't necessarily the right way for all. But this I know: The Christian school and home school movements in this country have been a direct response to this teaching. Millions of children today are spending those learning hours in a Christian environment, either in school or in the home. And they are outperforming their counterparts in public schools and other private schools—except for the elite boarding schools at least—by a wide margin on every standardized test. To achieve this, parents are making large financial sacrifices, either by giving up a job to do home schooling, or paying tuition to a religious school when they are already supporting the public schools by their tax dollars. It's one of the things that gives me hope for our country. Our public schools and other public institutions are less and less the conveyors of the positive parts of our heritage. Some of that is because courts won't let them include anything religious and hence deprive them of the ability to teach or model the basis for morality and godly conduct. Some is because the people in charge are so steeped in moral relativism and so devoid of belief themselves that they don't have anything else to offer. But as the public part of society declines, the private rises to the challenge. Every Christian parent in this time of our history should at least think about Christian schooling or home schooling for their children."

Anna and I looked at each other. Another discussion lay ahead. Lily and Willy were in public school. We liked their teachers and thought they were having a good experience, but they were in the early years, and more challenging times lay ahead. Already they were coming home with language and ideas that needed correcting in the home. The idea of paying for school when the public schools were available for free was against my intuition and our budget. Still, if Hal was right that the most important thing we would do in our lives was the transmission of the knowledge of God's ways to our children, then perhaps our priorities needed revisiting.

"You know, Hal," Anna said, "all the articles I read say that kids raised in Christian families—I mean, evangelical families where people go to church and believe the Bible—are only a little ahead of their peers in Christian social behavior. Most of them become sexually active before marriage, just a little later than other kids. They know the right language, but what they really believe is almost as relative as everyone else. And the divorce rate among Christians isn't much better than the rest of the world either."

"All true," Hal said. "And every pastor can affirm it. There is a massive failure of the church to ground its children—and its adults—in understanding of godly living and thinking, what it is and why it's important. And to give people an understanding of God's holiness—his awesome majesty and power. And how he's part of their life, the source of every good thing they have—their creator, redeemer, sustainer, and friend. And that's what Moses is talking about here."

I was back in the last Sunday service. For that hour, I had understood. I had understood as a child, washed in the music and words by which a community expressed its relationship with its Creator. It's amazing, I thought, how much theology you can learn as a child, just from the hymns.

"And when we do learn," Anna's voice broke into my reverie, "we forget so quickly."

"Another lesson from Moses," Hal said. "Let's read on."

> When the LORD your God brings you into the land he swore
> to your fathers, to Abraham, Isaac, and Jacob, to give you—a
> land with large, flourishing cities you did not build, houses
> filled with all kinds of good things you did not provide, wells

you did not dig, and vineyards and olive groves you did not plant—then when you eat and are satisfied, be careful that you do not forget the LORD, who brought you out of Egypt, out of the land of slavery.

—Deut. 6:10–12

"Did you ever hear the question 'What have you done for me lately?'" Hal asked. "Fallen human beings have a great tendency to forget the good things that have been given to them—by their parents, teachers, church leaders, and those who built the community and nation in which they live. We are all the beneficiaries of good things we did not provide."

"Cities we didn't build," I said, echoing the Scripture. "Wells we didn't dig, vineyards and olive groves we didn't plant."

"Take yourself," Hal said to me. "You have a good education, but where did you get the mind to absorb it? You had to study and work to get where you are, but you didn't give yourself the ability to succeed. And good athletes . . . they have to train and practice and develop their skill, but the body and coordination that enables them to be successful if they apply themselves is God-given. Never forget that most of the good things in life come to you from the Lord and are not of your own provision."

"And that tendency to forget the Lord and what he's done for us is why it's important to teach our children the ways of the Lord in every aspect of life," Anna added.

Her voice barely registered. I was absorbing Hal's reminder that the credit for the things the world valued most about me had little to do with me but were gifts from God. My pride was slipping out of my hands, falling down around me like a poorly pitched tent struck by a gust of uncooperative wind. I heard Hal reading on:

Fear the LORD your God, serve him only and take your oaths in his name. Do not follow other gods, the gods of the peoples around you; for the LORD your God, who is among you, is a jealous God and his anger will burn against you, and he will destroy you from the face of the land. Do not test the LORD your God as you did at Massah. Be sure to keep the commands of the LORD your God and the stipulations and

decrees he has given you. Do what is right and good in the
LORD's sight, so that it may go well with you and you may
go in and take over the good land that the LORD promised
on oath to your forefathers, thrusting out all your enemies
before you, as the LORD said.

—Deut. 6:13–19

"Do you recognize anything in here from the New Testament?" Hal asked after reading these verses. When neither Anna nor I replied, he went on. "You will remember it from what we call the temptation of Jesus. At the beginning of his ministry, following his baptism by John the Baptist, he went into the desert and fasted for forty days and nights. During his time in the desert, the devil took him to a high mountain, showed him all the kingdoms of the world and their splendor, and promised him all of it if he would worship the devil. Jesus resisted this Faustian bargain, quoting these words from verse thirteen of this passage of Deuteronomy: 'Worship the Lord your God, and serve him only.'"

"I never knew he was quoting Deuteronomy," Anna said.

"All of the Scripture he used to resist Satan came from Deuteronomy. In another part of the same episode, the devil took him to the highest point of the temple and invited him to throw himself down to demonstrate his power by being miraculously saved. Jesus answered with words from verse sixteen of this passage: 'Do not put the Lord your God to the test.' The third temptation Satan presented to Jesus was to challenge him to feed his hunger and prove that he is the Son of God by turning stones into bread. Jesus responds with a passage from Deuteronomy 8: 'Man does not live on bread alone, but on every word that comes from the mouth of God.'"

"That one I remember," Anna said.

"Jesus knew the words of Deuteronomy and used them to refute Satan's temptations at every turn. It's a good lesson on the significance of the Scriptures we are studying. People who don't think the Old Testament is worth studying aren't following Jesus' model. There's good reason to know the Scriptures well enough to draw on them when we are challenged by our own temptations."

I thought, *Like the temptation to think what a smart guy I am, or what a great lawyer, or what great things I can do, and not give all the glory to God.*

"Now," Hal said, "at the end of the chapter, God ties it all together. In this chapter, Moses has taught the most important commandment: Love God with all of your being. He has taught that it must be inward love, in the heart, not just outward compliance. He has taught how it needs to be impressed on your children and transmitted to them by living it in every aspect of your life, in time, in space, in thought and deed, in family, and in community. He has taught how easy it is to forget what God has done for us." He read on:

> In the future, when your son asks you, "What is the meaning of the stipulations, decrees and laws the LORD our God has commanded you?" tell him: "We were slaves of Pharaoh in Egypt, but the LORD brought us out of Egypt with a mighty hand. Before our eyes the LORD sent miraculous signs and wonders—great and terrible—upon Egypt and Pharaoh and his whole household. But he brought us out from there to bring us in and give us the land that he promised on oath to our forefathers. The LORD commanded us to obey all these decrees and to fear the LORD our God, so that we might always prosper and be kept alive, as is the case today. And if we are careful to obey all this law before the LORD our God, as he has commanded us, that will be our righteousness."
>
> —Deut. 6:20–25

"The meaning of the teachings of God," Anna paraphrased, "is found in what he has done for us, what he has given us—our life, our bodies, our minds, the world we live in."

"Our freedom from the bondage of sin is like Israel's freedom from bondage in Egypt," I said.

Hal nodded. "Every machine or appliance I have acquired—lawn-mower, chain saw, refrigerator, even an electric toothbrush—came with an owner's manual or manufacturer's handbook that told me how to use it. Usually it starts with a set of safety rules, many so basic one would think they hardly needed to be stated: 'Do not use your new Acme blow dryer while taking a bath.' Basic operating instructions follow, then maintenance procedures. Usually there's a trouble-shooting guide that tells me what to do to identify and fix common problems without seeking outside help. Finally, I find a list of repair centers or resources when I encounter a problem beyond my own ability to address. If I read and follow the directions, I can expect to get a long life of useful service out of my appliance. If I disregard them and plunge ahead on my own with the appliance, using it as I think fit and not as the manufacturer intended, neglecting the maintenance it needs, letting things that are broken on it go without repair, I will have problems."

"And the Scriptures are . . ." I said.

"The Manufacturer's Handbook," Hal said, completing the sentence. "They are the Owner's Manual for human life. It doesn't tell us how to brush our teeth and avoid cavities, or what kind of diet and exercise is best for us. But it does tell us what's most important: how to have a healthy spiritual life, how to prepare to enjoy eternity with God when our few years in this world are over, how to be in a right relationship with our Creator and his creation, especially our 'neighbors.'"

He opened the front of his Bible to show us. There on the for-merly blank first page inside the cover was written in a big scrawl, "The Manufacturer's Handbook."

"Let me see," Anna said, reaching out and taking the Bible from him.

Under the big scrawl was a longer writing, a cursive scribble that crossed the page for two lines. She squinted at it, and then read aloud: "The original and only perfect guide to the use and enjoyment of hu-man life. Given to Hal with infinite love by his Creator."

She handed it back to him with a warm smile.

Hal took the book back and closed it. "In these last verses Moses is still talking about teaching the children. Every child wants to know why. Why are the rules this way? Why do I have to do this? Why can't I do what I want? I know your children have asked you these questions."

We both nodded. It was all too familiar.

"Probably nearly every child has asked his or her parent these 'why' questions. And the answer is not 'because I say so.' God gives the parent the answer here, and the very reason to teach. God—who has proven his good intentions toward us by freeing us from bondage and bringing us into every good thing that we have—tells us how to live 'so that we might always prosper and be kept alive.' I actually prefer the Revised Standard Version of verse twenty-four, which says, 'For our good always.' God gave us his laws for our own good. That's why we teach them to our children. Just as the engine will fail if you run it without oil, our lives will fail if we run without the lubrication of living God's way. Teaching children the Bible and to live as God instructs us to live is as fundamental to their health and safety as teaching them not to touch a hot burner on a stove."

"There are a lot of laws," I said.

"Yes," Hal said. "The Jews count 613 in the Torah, the first five books of the Bible, only about 270 of which can be performed today. We'll talk later about how we are to understand the meaning and application of these laws as contemporary Christians. But Jesus simplified it for us. The command to love the Lord your God with all your heart, soul, strength, and mind is the first and greatest commandment. And the second, he says, is like it: 'Love your neighbor as yourself. All the Law and the Prophets hang on these two commandments.' But I want you to notice something else, and this is important."

Now Hal was going deeper. "The last verse of chapter six says that if we obey all the law, 'that will be our righteousness.' The first and greatest law is in verse five: to love God with all our heart and soul and strength. Loving God, *truly* loving him, is, in itself, obeying the law, and is righteousness. So the Scripture teaches, in Genesis and again in Romans, 'Abraham believed God and it was credited to him as righteousness.'"

We parted on that thought, that belief itself was obedience and righteousness. But throughout the next week I wondered how many of the people I encountered were parents—or had parents—who had decided to let their children make up their own minds about religion when they were old enough to study the matter and form independent opinions, or who thought they should be provided a sampler of the religions of the world so they could pick what was most attractive to them—or none at all. I wept for the children whose parents had failed them so. In God's eyes there was no place for parenting that cared so little for their children's temporal and eternal well-being.

CHAPTER SEVEN

"How odd
   Of God
   To choose
   The Jews."
—Ogden Nash

When the LORD your God brings you into the land you are entering to possess and drives out before you many nations—the Hittites, Girgashites, Amorites, Canaanites, Perizzites, Hivites, and Jebusites, seven nations larger and stronger than you—and when the LORD your God has delivered them over to you and you have defeated them, then you must destroy them totally. Make no treaty with them, and show them no mercy. Do not intermarry with them. Do not give your daughters to their sons or take their daughters for your sons, for they will turn your sons away from following me to serve other gods, and the LORD's anger will burn against you and will quickly destroy you. This is what you are to do to them: Break down their altars, smash their sacred stones, cut down their Asherah poles and burn their idols in the fire. For you are a people holy to the LORD your God. The LORD your God has chosen you out of all the peoples on the face of the earth to be his people, his treasured possession.

The LORD did not set his affection on you and choose you because you were more numerous than other peoples, for you were the fewest of all peoples. But it was because the LORD loved you and kept the oath he swore to your forefathers that he brought you out with a mighty hand and redeemed you from the land of slavery, from the power of Pharaoh king of Egypt. Know therefore that the LORD your God is God; he is the faithful God, keeping his covenant of love to a thousand generations of those who love him and keep his commands. But those who hate him he will repay to their face by destruction; he will not be slow to repay to their face those who hate him. Therefore, take care to follow the commands, decrees and laws I give you today.

If you pay attention to these laws and are careful to follow them, then the LORD your God will keep his covenant of love with you, as he swore to your forefathers. He will love you and bless you and increase your numbers. He will bless the fruit of your womb, the crops of your land—your grain, new wine and oil—the calves of your herds and the lambs of your flocks in the land that he swore to your forefathers to give you. You will be blessed more than any other people; none of your men or women will be childless, nor any of your livestock without young. The LORD will keep you free from every disease. He will not inflict on you the horrible diseases you knew in Egypt, but he will inflict them on all who hate you. You must destroy all the peoples the LORD your God gives over to you. Do not look on them with pity and do not serve their gods, for that will be a snare to you.

You may say to yourselves, "These nations are stronger than we are. How can we drive them out?" But do not be afraid of them; remember well what the LORD your God did to Pharaoh and to all Egypt. You saw with your own eyes the great trials, the miraculous signs and wonders, the mighty hand and outstretched arm, with which the LORD your God brought you out. The LORD your God will do the same to all the peoples you now fear. Moreover, the LORD your God will send the hornet among them until even the survivors who hide from you have perished. Do not be terrified by them, for the LORD your God, who is among you, is a great and awesome God. The LORD your God will drive out those nations before you, little by little. You will not be allowed to eliminate them all at once, or the wild animals will multiply around you. But the LORD your God will deliver them over to you, throwing them into great confusion until they are destroyed. He will give their kings into your hand, and you will wipe out their names from under heaven. No one will be able to stand up against you; you will destroy them. The images of their gods you are to burn in the fire. Do not covet the silver and gold on them, and do not take it for yourselves, or you will be ensnared by it, for it is detestable to the LORD your God. Do not bring a detestable thing into your house or you, like it, will be set apart for destruction. Utterly abhor and detest it, for it is set apart for destruction.

—Deut. 7:1–26

As I read chapter seven and prepared myself to discuss it with Hal, I became preoccupied with the subject of choice. The chapter dealt with a lot of other things—much of it repetitive of, and to some degree expanding on—that had gone before. The nations to be driven out of the land were to be totally destroyed, as the people of Heshbon and Bashan had been on the east side of the Jordan. It would not happen all at once, so the land would not go wild, but it would happen. There were to be no treaties and no intermarriage. The idols or images were to be destroyed, even if they had great value as silver or gold. The reasons are explained: The images would have turned God's holy people to worshipping other gods, and engaging in fertility rites and child sacrifice, and other abominable practices to which these people had degenerated. God would destroy those who hate him. But if Israel kept God's commandments, he would bless them with fruitfulness in their families, their crops, and their livestock. God's powerful acts for them in the past were evidence of what he would do for them in the future if they were faithful.

But it was the notion of choosing Israel that bothered me. Ogden Nash's little ditty kept going through my mind. The Scripture said God had chosen Israel "out of all the peoples on the face of the earth to be his people, his treasured possession." It was not because they were more numerous than other peoples; indeed they were the fewest. Rather it was because he loved them and kept the oath he had sworn to their forefathers. But why? Was there a reason for this love—for this choice?

When I got to Hal's, his house was dark except for a dim light somewhere deep inside. I wondered if he was hauling boards at the house-building project down the road again. As I crossed the old screen porch to knock on the door, I heard his voice. "I'm over here," he said. As my eyes adjusted to the darkness, I could make out his form nearby.

Hal was sitting in the dark, in a rocking chair on the porch. It was a clear, crisp October night. He had a blanket wrapped around his lap and legs. "I thought we should sit outside tonight," he said. "It's too beautiful a night to miss. But you can't see the sky well enough from here. Let's go out to the garden."

He retrieved another blanket inside for me and led me out to the rose garden, where we had had our first discussion back in August. There was no moon, but the sky was so clear and the stars so bright that we could make our way without a flashlight. The roses were wilted and faded now, the ground littered with fallen leaves and petals. We sat on the old wooden bench and looked up.

"I don't know much about the stars," he said. "But I know the dippers and the North Star."

We found the Big Dipper and the Little Dipper, pouring into each other in the northerly sky. The North Star at the end of the handle of the Little Dipper was posted as a standard around which all of the armies of heaven moved from east to west in a great circular ballet.

"You know, the real names for the dippers are Ursa Major and Ursa Minor, the Great Bear and the Little Bear," I said. "But they don't look like bears at all to me. It takes a lot of imagination to find a bear in either of them."

"I heard once from a man at the university who had studied such things that when the Europeans got over here and got to talking to the Indians, they showed them the dippers and told them that they called those constellations the Big Bear and the Little Bear. The Indians were pleased to hear it—'Those are our bear stars too,' they said. Two civilizations thousands of miles apart, separated by an ocean, and they both called the dippers 'bears.'"

"What do you make of that?" I asked. "It is a remarkable coincidence."

"Not a coincidence," Hal said. "I make of it that humanity has more common origins than people want to acknowledge. It was once all together, a single family or tribe that got bigger and bigger until it split up, or God split it up, as seen in the story of the Tower of Babel in Genesis. There are some things that are still remembered and passed down from that ancient time. One of them is pots they all call 'bears.' Probably there weren't any pots or dippers when people first began looking at the sky and giving names to the patterns of stars up there. If I were a detective, I would look for the traces—the remains—of human unity, of our common origin."

"Do you know of any others?" I asked.

"Well, I have heard that virtually all languages, no matter how different they are, use an 'm' sound for mother. Hebrew does, just like English—'eem' is mother in Hebrew, even though the two languages have no common roots. Eve is the 'eem' of all the living, and Deborah is the 'eem' of all Israel. That may be another clue."

The mention of Eve led to talk about the "Eve theory" in the science of genetics. Teams of geneticists had done studies, as we both had read, and concluded that all humanity could be traced back to a single woman who lived in Africa many millennia ago. Now they were working on showing the same thing for a male ancestor, an "Adam theory."

"The problem with the 'Eve theory,'" Hal said, "is that they have her on the wrong end of that Great Rift Valley that we talked about a few weeks ago. Otherwise, it's pretty much the story of Genesis. But what's a few thousand miles when science is coming that close to verifying what the Bible has been telling us all along? By and by they'll get it all straight.

"Take the 'Big Bang,'" he went on. "When I was growing up, most scientists thought the universe was in what they called a 'steady state.' Matter turned to energy and turned back to matter. The way it is is the way it always was. Then someone came along and proved that the whole universe has some sort of background radiation that can be detected and is the residue of the creation event. They call it the 'Big Bang,' when everything that is came out of one great explosive event. They have found that the universe is expanding, just as you would expect if that's how it started. They can measure speeds and distances and find that everything is moving away from one central point in time and space. It's fascinating stuff, but it's all been there in the Bible all the time."

We gazed silently at the vast universe above us for some time, the shimmering veil of the Milky Way brushed across the expanse of sky, the hundreds, perhaps thousands, of twinkling points of light, each representing a wonder of the creation we could hardly imagine. Finally Hal broke the silence. "What do you want to talk about in chapter seven?" he asked.

I told him about my issues with the choice of the Jews as God's special people. I asked Hal for help in understanding.

In response, he told me a story. "Once upon a time, Chris, there was no such thing as history. All that was was God—God the Father, God the Son, God the Holy Spirit, in eternal majesty and glory, occupying all space and time and existence. The triune God did not need anything else, but he decided to create the universe. He did so, in his infinite power speaking into existence the heavenly bodies, the earth with its waters and skies, and living things—plants, animals, and finally human beings, man and woman. He made them to exist in a linear dimension we call 'time,' although he himself was not bound to a linear existence.

"Adam and Eve knew their God. They communicated with him, and they understood his eternal power and divine nature from the creation around them. He endowed them with certain qualities that he himself had, including the quality of moral choice, free will, and the ability to choose to obey or disobey him—to do good or to do evil."

As he spoke, I felt as if we were in another time—a time thousands of years earlier—when an elder or priest would explain the origins of the world to the young around a campfire. Stories told and retold passed ancient verities from generation to generation. Embers from the mystery of fire shot red and orange sparks at the cold white sparks that blinked back at them from the canopy of the heavens.

Hal continued, "Men and women chose not to retain the good or the knowledge of God. They allowed foolish thinking to darken their hearts. They began to worship created things—animals, human beings, heavenly bodies—instead of their creator. They invented gods that thought and acted like people. They corrupted their worship into sexuality, making cults of fertility and prostitution to false gods. They exchanged the truth of God for a lie."

In the distance, a pack of coyotes yapped and howled under the moonlight.

Paying the distant pack little heed, Hal continued. "God desired to redeem his creation, to bring it back to himself, in understanding and right relationship, and worship of his eternal majesty—the real God, and not gods of wood and stone that are nothing but man-made idols. He could have simply wiped it all out and begun again—or forgotten the whole project—but he didn't. Instead, he had a plan as to how he would bring about his purpose."

He paused. As I gazed into the profusion of starlight, I saw a small, steady light moving in a straight line across the sky. There was no sound. It must have been a satellite.

As the light passed off to the west, Hal said, "He found a man in the caravan city of Haran, an Amorite town located in what is now southern Turkey. He told this man to leave his country and his family and go to another land that he would show him, and he promised to make him a great nation and to bless all peoples of the earth through him. The man did as God told him. Later, when this man had not had a son, he contemplated adopting a household servant to be his heir to fulfill God's promise in his own way, but God told him that he would have a natural heir and descendants as numerous as these stars in the sky that we see above us."

He raised his arm and swept it across the heavens. "The man believed him, even though it seemed unbelievable. God saw his belief as righteousness. You know what I mean; we talked about this last week with Anna. Later he repeated the promise to bless all the nations of the earth through this man so that he would direct his descendants to keep God's way by doing what is right and just."

I knew we were talking about Abraham.

"The man had the promised son, miraculously, when he was one hundred years old and his wife was well beyond normal childbearing age. The righteousness of his belief was rewarded. But God wasn't through with him yet. He directed him to take his son onto a mountain and sacrifice him, giving up what he loved the most, and with it the fulfillment of the promise God had made to him. In his love, reverence, awe, and fear of God, his Creator and the ruler of the universe, Abraham obeyed this latest and most-distressing command. Just as he was about to slay his son as a sacrifice, God intervened to save the boy and provided an animal to use as a sacrifice. The man's obedience and submission to God was complete. Because of his obedience, God confirmed the blessing on him and his descendants and that through his offspring, all the nations on earth would be blessed."

"It's the story of Abraham," I said.

"The man in my story," Hal confirmed, "is Abraham. Here, in the time of Moses, the promise to make his descendents 'as numerous as the stars in the sky' has been fulfilled, and the promise of possession of the land is about to be fulfilled. Much later, 'when the time had fully come,' as Paul says in Galatians, the rest of the promise will be fulfilled as all nations on earth are blessed in Christ through Abraham's descendants."

"And what about the choice?" I asked.

"I'm getting there. We talked earlier about why God would command the herem—the complete slaughter and destruction—of the people in the Promised Land. That command is given more expansively here in chapter seven. But some have said that the right question isn't why God told Israel to destroy the nations in the land it was entering, but rather why he didn't destroy Israel along with everyone else. They weren't free of sin anymore than we in the church are—sometimes of grievous sin.

"The answer is that God loved and chose Abraham and his descendants as the means of redeeming his wayward creation. Verse eight of this chapter says, 'It was because the Lord loved you and kept the oath he swore to your forefathers.' There is a history here, and if you don't understand the history, you can't understand why God chose the Jews. There may be a certain mystery to it—an element of grace or undeserved favor in theological terms—but ultimately it's a choice that is purposeful and not random, a choice that will lead to the redemption of a fallen race, or at least the part of it that's willing to be redeemed."

"So should I understand that Israel was chosen because it had some merit, at least in the form of believing God?"

"No," Hal replied. "Moses will deal with that notion a little later, but it's not because of Israel's merit. It was because of God's promise to Abraham. God keeps his promises. But this is the story of God's desire to save all humanity. Think of Israel as a theater, a stage in which God performs a play that tells the story of redemption or salvation, the way to enjoyment of eternal life with him. 'Trust and obey, for there's no other way,' as the old hymn goes. Abraham's trust and obedience allowed the fulfillment of God's promises to his descendants, and through them, all humanity. Their trust and obedience in turn will lead to their opportunity to receive the blessings."

"Are there other ways to understand this?" I asked.

"Over the centuries, the rabbis struggled with this issue too," Hal replied. "One theory they came up with is to set God's love and choice of Israel against the previous verse—verse seven—in which Moses taught that God did not choose Israel because it was the most numerous of people; in fact, it was the fewest of people. This got turned around into the idea that being the fewest and not the most numerous represented being humble before God and it was that humility that attracted his favor. It reminds me a little bit of a *Peanuts* comic strip in which Lucy is accused of not being humble and replies angrily, 'What do you mean I'm not humble? I'm the most humble person around here.' People who have true humility are usually not conscious of it and certainly don't take it as a source of merit."

A shooting star blazed across the sky, so bright it almost lit our faces. Hal gazed at it without wonder or comment. He seemed to take the marvels and beauties of creation as so embedded in his surroundings that the delight they provided was merely another confirmation of what needed no confirming.

"The rabbis' idea taps into a great truth about God, though. Jesus teaches that the first shall be last, and the last shall be first in the Kingdom of God." He opened his Bible and fumbled through some pages, then realized that the light was too dim to read. But for Hal, most of the Bible didn't need to be looked up. He gave up the effort and recited from 1 Corinthians 3 by memory: "But God chose the foolish things of the world to shame the wise; God chose the weak things of the world to shame the strong. He chose the lowly things of this world and the despised things—and the things that are not—to nullify the things that are, so that no one may boast before him."

He closed his eyes as if in prayer. "My grace is sufficient for you, for my power is made perfect in weakness."

Then, looking at me again, he continued: "You see, Chris, if God had chosen Egypt or Assyria or the great empires of China or India, people would think it was worldly human power that brought people into his favor. It is not. By choosing the weak things of the world in which to display his power and his kingdom, he shows his sovereignty over the whole world, his creation."

We went on to discuss how the notion of God's choice of a people related to us as Christians today. This brought us to one of the most enduring topics of theological controversy—the issue of predestination and free will. Did God predestine certain people for eternal salvation, leaving others out in the cold or consigned to eternal damnation without ever having a chance or a choice? Or did he somehow evaluate people on their merits, including the merit of belief?

"Begin your thinking on this subject with a clear understanding of God's sovereignty. Any other thinking is futile. As he is the creator, he *can* create us in any way he likes and for any purpose he likes. He *can* create people to be bad examples to teach others goodness. C.S. Lewis uses the example of the playwright and his play. Shakespeare wrote *Hamlet,* and he can write the script any way he chooses. Hamlet does not tell Shakespeare how the play will end.

"But God is not Shakespeare," Hal continued. "He created Hamlets who can think and talk back, who can choose to believe or disbelieve, to do good or to do evil. The Bible is full of exhortations to obey, to make the right choices, to choose good and not evil, to believe God. The Bible also is full of passages about God's choice and election—of the Jews as a people in the Old Testament and of certain people who are to experience salvation, the Israel of God, in the New."

"So how are we to think about this?" I asked.

"Christian thought about this falls into two camps. One, the predestination camp, says that God in his own will or pleasure chooses to save some sinners and not others. Human will is so corrupted that it cannot, on its own, seek salvation. Only through God's grace can man even have the prompting of faith to believe. 'It does not depend on man's effort or desire, but on God's mercy,' as Paul says in the ninth chapter of Romans. Or, in Ephesians two, eight through nine, 'For it is by grace you have been saved, through faith—and this not from yourselves, it is the gift of God—not by works, so that no one can boast.'"

"So God gives faith?" I asked. "And in doing so, chooses whom to save?"

"So some would say," Hal replied. "But the gift of God—the second 'it' in this verse—is in Greek grammar—in which the text was written—a neuter pronoun, and 'faith' is a feminine noun. It's pushing the meaning too far to say that this means faith is a gift from God. What it means is that the whole thing—the grace of salvation through faith—is a free gift of God, freely available to all. Salvation is not earned by 'works' or good behavior, although God certainly expects it of his people.

"The predestination camp is often associated with the thought of John Calvin, who was a major thinker in what is now known as Reformed theology, represented in particular by Presbyterianism. Calvin saw predestination as a doctrine of assurance—believers could be confident of their eternal destiny, since they are of the elect. To Calvin, predestination was an encouragement, but others saw it as arbitrary, harsh, and inconsistent with both God's justice and mercy."

A night bird flew overhead, distracting us momentarily. "And the other way of thinking about free will and predestination?" I asked.

"Jacobus Arminius," Hal replied, "was a seventeenth century Dutch theologian who took issue with Calvin's view of predestination. His thought, which represents the other way of looking at this issue, focuses on God's foreknowledge. Romans eight, twenty-nine says, 'For those God foreknew, he also predestined.' And Peter speaks of God's elect as those 'who have been chosen according to the foreknowledge of God the Father.' According to the thinking that is called Arminianism, God knows in advance who will respond to the offer of salvation, and that's what is meant by election. Methodist and

Roman Catholic thought is Arminian. Baptists have been on both sides of this issue."

"Which side are you on?" I asked.

Hal smiled. "No matter what position I took, someone in the churches I served would have been unhappy," he said. "But the Scripture teaches that God 'wants all men to be saved and to come to a knowledge of the truth' and that Jesus will draw all men to himself. I think the opportunity to make the right choice about God is one he offers to everyone. If I didn't believe that, my preaching, my whole ministry, my life, would have been in vain." He looked back up into the vastness of God's universe, the great picture window above us in which God makes the glory of what he has made visible. "The distances from us to the stars and galaxies up there are so great that they are measured in light years. Light travels around 180,000 miles per second. A light year is almost six trillion miles. The nearest star is four light years away, 24 trillion miles. The distance is unimaginable. Some of the lights we can see out there are thousands, even millions, of light years away."

"I can't imagine those distances," I said.

"What we see when we look up," Hal said, "is a picture of times past, not present. The sky is like an old movie. The images we are seeing began traveling toward us a long time ago. But we see a different point in time for every star, every galaxy, and every object, depending on how far away it is and how far the light from it has to travel to get to us. If we could move to some other point in the universe right now and look at the same objects, we would see them as they appeared at a different point in time. But wherever we are, we don't know what is actually happening up there right now. Some of the stars we see may no longer exist—they may have exploded into supernovas or been sucked into black holes, but we go on looking at them as though they are still there, and will until the light or radiation or whatever it is our astronomers detect shows up here at some time in the future. For all we know, the universe itself is collapsing or exploding all around us, and the end of time is already under way out there.

"In the same way, the light that goes out from the earth travels into the universe around it. If there is anyone or anything out there that can see us, they will see us as we were in the past. The image of everything that ever happened is carrying forward out into space somewhere. If someone had a big enough telescope, he could see it. Someone in one part of the universe could look at us and see Israel hearing God in the fire and cloud and smoke on Sinai, or listening on the Plains of Moab to Moses tell them the words that would be recorded in Deuteronomy. Someone else could see Israel being marched into exile—or returning— or Jesus' miracles, or the crucifixion. People who were nearer could see the Norman Conquest, the French Revolution, or the Second World War.

"God, of course, doesn't need to sit on some particular planet or star or in some galaxy in some neighborhood of the universe to observe what is going on in the cosmos. He is omnipresent, as the theologians say—everywhere at the same time. So he sees things that are happening at all times, simultaneously.

"Thinking about the universe helps me to think about foreknowledge. God doesn't need a crystal ball to predict the future; he's in the future, just as those stars and planets and galaxies a million light years away are in a future that we have no way of knowing. God knows how the story is going to end—not just the big story, but also each little story within it, before they ever happen from a human perspective. It's not that we lack the ability to choose, but he can see the choices before we have made them. His presence in all time at the same time makes it hang together. My analogy to the light from other parts of the universe is probably not very good when it comes to thinking about God's omnipresence, but it gives my feeble ability to understand these mysteries something to hang on to."

"You've given me a lot to hang on to, Hal."

The night chill had set in. We rose and walked slowly through the starlit darkness to my car. Perhaps, I thought, Ogden Nash was wrong. God needed a vessel to redeem his creation, and the Jewish people were that vessel, a vessel of belief, descended from Abraham who believed God, and it was credited to him as righteousness. The first thing that has to happen to be in a right relationship with God is to believe him.

We reached the car, and through the overhanging branches, I looked up once again at the splendor of the night sky above. "So the universe could be collapsing all around us," I said. "Could have been collapsing from the outer edges for millions of years, and we wouldn't even know it."

"At that time," Hal said, quoting Luke, "they will see the Son of Man coming in a cloud with power and great glory. When these things begin to take place, stand up and lift up your heads, because your redemption is drawing near."

Before we parted, I lifted my head and looked up one more time, almost afraid of what I might see.

CHAPTER EIGHT

W hat did you get out of this chapter?" Hal asked. A heavy autumn rain was audible outside his study window, the kind of rain that brought down what was left of the foliage. It was a rain that made me glad to be inside, to cling to the soft lamplight and think of reading a book I had read years before, a book that would lead me into old thoughts and roll them through the years to see how they had grown and changed.

"It seemed pretty repetitive," I said. "Mostly things he'd said before."

"Deuteronomy has a lot of repetition," Hal said. "That's part of how people learn. But let's read it aloud. Look for themes, and then relate those themes to your own life. It's all here for a purpose."

He read chapter eight:

> Be careful to follow every command I am giving you today, so that you may live and increase and may enter and possess the land that the Lord promised on oath to your forefathers. Remember how the Lord your God led you all the way in the desert these forty years, to humble you and to test you in order to know what was in your heart, whether or not you would keep his commands. He humbled you, causing you to hunger and then feeding you with manna, which neither you nor your fathers had known, to teach you that man does not live on bread alone but on every word that comes from the mouth of the Lord. Your clothes did not wear out and your feet did not swell during these forty years. Know then in your heart that as a man disciplines his son, so the Lord your God disciplines you.

Observe the commands of the LORD your God, walking in his ways and revering him. For the LORD your God is bringing you into a good land—a land with streams and pools of water, with springs flowing in the valleys and hills; a land with wheat and barley, vines and fig trees, pomegranates, olive oil and honey; a land where bread will not be scarce and you will lack nothing; a land where the rocks are iron and you can dig copper out of the hills.

When you have eaten and are satisfied, praise the LORD your God for the good land he has given you. Be careful that you do not forget the LORD your God, failing to observe his commands, his laws and his decrees that I am giving you this day. Otherwise, when you eat and are satisfied, when you build fine houses and settle down, and when your herds and flocks grow large and your silver and gold increase and all you have is multiplied, then your heart will become proud and you will forget the LORD your God, who brought you out of Egypt, out of the land of slavery. He led you through the vast and dreadful desert, that thirsty and waterless land, with its venomous snakes and scorpions. He brought you water out of hard rock. He gave you manna to eat in the desert, something your fathers had never known, to humble and to test you so that in the end it might go well with you. You may say to yourself, "My power and the strength of my hands have produced this wealth for me." But remember the LORD your God, for it is he who gives you the ability to produce wealth, and so confirms his covenant, which he swore to your forefathers, as it is today.

If you ever forget the LORD your God and follow other gods and worship and bow down to them, I testify against you today that you will surely be destroyed. Like the nations the LORD destroyed before you, so you will be destroyed for not obeying the LORD your God.

—Deut. 8:1–20

"There is a lot about remembering and forgetting," I observed. "There is," Hal said. "But remembering and forgetting what?"

"Their history," I said. "What had gone before."

"Not just history," Hal said. "Not just happenings, not just facts. This isn't about keeping track of where people went and what they did. Five times in the chapter, we're brought back to it. Verse four says, 'Remember how the LORD your God led you all the way in the desert these forty years.' Then verse eleven says, 'Be careful that you do not forget the LORD your God when you have eaten and are satisfied.' Verse fourteen comes back to the danger of forgetting God. Verse eighteen reminds us that we are to remember that it is the LORD our God who gives the ability to produce wealth. And in verse nineteen, we are admonished that if we forget the LORD our God, we will be destroyed."

"So it's about remembering God," I said, "and what he's done for us."

Hal got up and walked to his bookshelves, squinted at the titles, and pulled down an old volume.

"When I think of remembrances of God," he said, "I think of John Bunyan."

He sat and opened the book, talking as he thumbed it for a familiar passage.

"Bunyan was a Puritan pastor in seventeenth-century England. He spent twelve years in prison for his refusal to abandon his preaching and teaching the Puritan understanding of the Word of God. Bunyan and the Puritan preachers of his time were non-conformists; out of compliance or conformity with the policies of Queen Elizabeth and the Church of England, of which she was more than the titular head. She was the 'Defender of the Faith,' a title still held by the English monarch. Elizabeth believed church should be ceremonial, spiritually inspiring, and comforting to her people but not a source of preaching or teaching them how to live their lives or what the Scripture meant. Preachers who instructed the people were a potential source of sedition. Despite her good reputation in modern times for her strength of leadership and success in expanding British influence in the world, she was no friend of religious freedom."

"So she put Bunyan in jail?" I asked.

"She and her lackeys," Hal replied. "Bunyan's most famous work among his many writings is 'Pilgrim's Progress.' It's a spiritual classic, the complete title of which is . . ."

He flipped to the title page. "*The Pilgrim's Progress from This World to that Which is to Come; Delivered under the Similitude of a Dream.* It was written from prison. It's an allegory of the Christian life from conversion to entry into heaven. Bunyan wrote an autobiography to accompany it. He called it *Grace Abounding,* and in it he talks about chapter eight of Deuteronomy."

Hal had found the page for which he was looking: "'It is profitable for Christians to be often calling to mind the very beginnings of grace with their souls.'

"I always loved that line," he went on. "Then Bunyan tells about the remembrances of David and how Paul spoke of the manner of his conversion when he was put on trial. He also wrote about how Israel was to remember the events of its history, the delivery from Egypt, the miracles at Sinai, the wanderings in the desert wilderness. And then this: 'My dear children, call to mind the former days, and years of ancient times; remember also your songs in the night, and commune with your own heart. . . . Yea, look diligently, and leave no corner therein unsearched for that treasure hid, even the treasure of your first and second experience of the grace of God towards you.'"

"What was the beginning of grace in your soul, Hal?" I asked.

He thought for a time, then rose and replaced the volume of Bunyan on the shelf and returned to his place in the old red chair. The rain beat down outside, and the wind blew it against the window.

"Some things are too personal to speak about publicly," he said at last. "I have never told anyone else this story, not even when I have been asked to give my 'testimony' in church settings where people want to know how I became a Christian. But I guess someone should hear it, and if they don't soon, no one ever will."

I sensed I was entering a privileged sanctuary in Hal's soul.

"It happened when I was eleven years old. I had always gone to church and Sunday school, and I knew the basic Bible stories most young people know. I had been taught to pray at bedtime, and I knew the Lord's Prayer. But I had a problem that was deeply troubling to me as a young boy: I wet the bed, even at that late age, and did so not occasionally but regularly. My mother washed sheets day after day and must have been in despair that it would ever end. My despair was even greater. Imagine the shame of waking up in a pool of your own urine and going to school, knowing that you could smell it on yourself and hoping no one else could as well. In those days, no one had showers and you only took a bath twice a week. I prayed to God night after night to take that curse away, but he never did.

"Then a new family moved into our neighborhood, with a boy just my age. His name was Henry. They were from Canada, and I never knew why they moved here. Henry and I did everything together and were as close as two boys can be. One day my father came to talk to me about Henry. He wouldn't be able to play with me anymore, at least for a while. Henry's father had called my Dad and explained that doctors had discovered that Henry had a heart defect. It was a serious problem, and he was going to have surgery to try to correct it. He would be in the hospital for quite some time, and, even if things went well, for some time after he would not be able to run around with me as we always had. I was heartbroken.

"My bedroom looked toward the street. I could see Henry's house from my window. That evening, as I was going to bed, I looked out the window toward it. In the glow of the streetlight, I saw Henry with his father and mother come out of the house and get into the car. His father had a little traveling bag in hand. I knew they were going to the hospital.

"At that moment, my heart was overwhelmed with emotion. Love, sorrow, compassion, regret—I don't know how to describe it. The only thing on my mind was Henry and what he was going through. I dropped to my knees beside my bed and poured out my heart to the Lord. I prayed for Henry with all the power my eleven-your-old soul could muster. My prayer was no longer for myself, not even for being delivered from the shame and loathing of the bed-wetting I had prayed about so much before. It may have been the most selfless prayer I have ever prayed."

Hal was silent for a long time, his eyes closed as if reliving it. Eventually, I broke the silence softly: "What happened?"

He looked up. "I woke up the next morning in a dry bed. And I never wet the bed again. Not even once. Not ever. And I knew, even at eleven years old, I knew in a way that you know when you have an encounter with the Holy, that it was only by losing myself that I gained myself. It was the purity and unselfishness of my prayer for Henry that brought an answer to the prayer I didn't pray that night. 'Whoever finds his life will lose it, and whoever loses his life for my sake will find it,' says the Lord Jesus. I know that no doctor would say it was a miracle. Children wet the bed, although not usually at that late age. They get over it sooner or later. But for me, it was the touch of God on me, and still is."

"And what about Henry?" I asked. "What happened to him?"

"He survived the operation and came home. I saw him a few times while he was convalescing. Then his family moved back to Canada. We wrote to each other a few times, but we were eleven and lost track after a while. As far as I know, my prayer for Henry was answered. Let's talk about Deuteronomy."

"I think we were," I said.

"Of course," said Hal. "But let's look at the text."

He had shared something too personal to go further and escaped into the Scripture. "God tells Israel to remember how he led them in the desert for forty years. He humbled them, making them thirsty and hungry. The desert is described as vast and dreadful, without water, with venomous snakes and scorpions. He did that with purpose, to test them, to discipline them, to teach them, to humble them, to find out what was in their hearts."

I allowed him the escape, though my mind was full of Henry and Hal's prayer as an eleven-year-old. "God didn't make it easy for them, did he?"

"God's job description," Hal said, "is not to make our lives easy or pleasant, or to solve our problems. All through my pastoral ministry, I counseled people going through the desert of their lives. Illness, poverty, job loss, the grief of deaths in the family—sometimes of their children—divorce, spouses or children gone bad, it came into my little office in the back room of the church every day. And God had a purpose in it for them, although I couldn't always tell them what it was. Teaching, testing, disciplining, humbling, finding out what was in their hearts. The best of them were like Job, praising God in their misfortunes and still thinking more of others than themselves. They were like the man who had lost several daughters in a shipwreck and out of that experience wrote one of the great Christian hymns, 'It is Well with My Soul.' But others blamed God and even gave up their faith. If he wouldn't solve their problem, he was no good to them. They had no sense of the glories of the life to come and no appreciation for the sufferings of God himself on their behalf in the crucifixion of Christ for their salvation."

"I can't imagine what it must be like to cling to belief when God seems to have no answers for you."

"That," Hal said, "is what the saints called 'the dark night of the soul.' But God always provides for those who walk in his way. Sometimes he doesn't provide what they ask for or expect, or provide it when they want it, but he does provide. He sent Israel through the wilderness to teach them dependence on him and not themselves. In the desert he provided them with manna for food, water from a rock, clothes that didn't wear out, and feet that didn't swell. And he did that to teach them, and through them, all of us, the lesson that 'man does not live on bread alone but on every word that comes from the mouth of the Lord.'"

"The words of Jesus in the wilderness," I recalled.

"Just so," Hal said. "Jesus used these very words from right here in Deuteronomy to reply to Satan during his temptation in the wilderness, when Satan invited him to turn stones into bread to feed himself, as we discussed a few weeks ago. We need physical food, of course—our daily bread—but feeding ourselves with God's Word, living according to The Manufacturer's Handbook, is much more important."

Appreciating the theme, I said, "All part of the beginning of grace in the soul of Israel."

Hal went back to his shelf and retrieved another book. "What other themes do you see in this chapter, Chris?"

Our conversation turned to the subject of pride. In verse fourteen, God warns against the temptation to forget him when things are going well. "Then your heart will become proud."

"When Christians talk about sin," Hal said, "they usually mean sexual sin. They never mean gluttony. And almost never pride—certainly not in themselves, the one place where you can be sure they won't recognize it. Most people define sin in ways that confine it to things they're sure they aren't guilty of."

He opened the small book in his lap to a page with a turned down corner. I could read the title. It was one of the first and most precious Christian books I had read, C. S. Lewis's *Mere Christianity.* Hal read from the marked page:

> The vice I am talking of is Pride or Self-Conceit: and the virtue opposite to it, in Christian morals, is called Humility. You may remember, when I was talking about sexual morality, I warned you that the centre of Christian morals did not lie there. According to Christian teachers, the essential vice, the utmost evil, is Pride. Unchastity, anger, greed, drunkenness, and all that, are mere fleabites in comparison: it was through Pride that the devil became the devil: Pride leads to every other vice: it is the complete anti-God state of mind.[8]

"Pride," Hal said, "is what Moses warned about when he told the Israelites about what might happen to them when they become prosperous. They 'eat and are satisfied,' 'build fine houses and settle down,' their 'herds and flocks grow large,' and their 'silver and gold increase.' In short, prosperity. Then they congratulate themselves and think that their own power and strength brought about their blessings. It's what Jesus is talking about when he says it's easier for a camel to pass through the eye of a needle than for a rich man to enter the kingdom of heaven. Spiritual thinkers from Augustine to Lewis have always recognized pride as the central sin. It is the movement of idolatry from the worship of that which is not God to the worship of self."

He set Lewis aside and found another volume, small, red, hard-covered. "I've kept track of this business of pride," he said. "It's one of the most elusive elements of Christian life, but the most important. All the great Christian thinkers have written about pride. Abundant provision becomes an even greater temptation to sin than poverty."

He opened his volume of Luther and read: "'Luxury has invaded as an even greater foe.'"[9]

"What are you proud of, Chris?" he asked, closing the volume.

If he had asked me that question at the beginning of the evening, I might have spoken of my family, my education, or my professional achievements. There was little in which I wanted to claim pride at that moment. Hal didn't press me for a response.

"The hardest people to bring to a true relationship with Christ are the well off. They think it beneath their dignity to humble themselves before the Lord. They are doing just fine without religion, thank you. They're too busy or important to serve the Lord, and don't want to be associated with the more humble of his people. If they go to church, they choose one that the 'right sort of people' attend, people like themselves who are doing well and don't think they need God very much. They certainly don't want to be where spiritual matters are taken too seriously."

As I pondered whether I fit Hal's description, he went on. "These are the people who are in the most danger. They have forgotten that it was God who gave them the ability to produce wealth; he gave them their intellect, creativity, physical strength, indeed their very existence. They, like all of us, came into a world of wells we didn't dig and vineyards we didn't plant. It's the worst of sins to attribute our success to ourselves. That is the sin of pride. Yet it's the way of the world."

As we were winding down, Hal brought me back to where we started, asking me the question I had earlier asked him: "What about you, Chris? What do you call to mind when you think about the beginning of grace in your soul?"

I was glad he asked—not so much because I was eager to share the memory as because I knew it needed to be called to mind again. As the great hymn went:

"'Twas grace that taught my heart to fear
    and grace my fears relieved.
How precious did that grace appear
    the hour I first believed."[10]

"Like you, Hal," I said, "I was raised in a church environment, went to Sunday school, was even taught John three-sixteen as the heart of the faith when I was young. I drifted far away from that in later years, both in my heart and mind and in my behavior. My adult experience with grace came fairly recently. In our house we have a room we call the library. My father-in-law had built bookshelves there and even left a book to begin stocking it. The book he left was a New Testament in four versions—columns on each page with the different renditions of the text. One evening I went to the library for no particular reason—so I thought—and picked up that Bible for no conscious reason. When I opened it, it fell open to the beginning of the Gospel of Mark. I began to read, 'The beginning of the gospel about Jesus Christ, the Son of God.'"

"Take it and read, take it and read," Hal said, recalling the story of the conversion of Saint Augustine, told in the *Confessions.*

I knew the story. Augustine, like Lewis, had been among my early readings as an adult Christian. Augustine—unconverted but agonizing over the sinful life he had become conscious of—heard the singsong voice of a child calling, "Take it and read." He hurried back to where he had a copy of Paul's epistles, opened it and read the first passage on which his eyes fell. It was Romans 13:13–14, which told him, "Clothe yourself with the Lord Jesus Christ, and do not think about how to gratify the desires of the sinful nature."

"Instantly, in truth," Augustine wrote, "at the end of this sentence, as if before a peaceful light streaming into my heart, all the dark shadows of doubt fled away."[11]

"Yes," I went on, "it was my Augustinian moment. I took it and read. I read the whole gospel of Mark in one sitting that night. It was like I was hearing it for the first time—a new and wonderful story, gripping, thrilling, that had to be pursued. I didn't have an instant conversion that evening. I was much too rational for that. I was, after all, a lawyer, and lawyers deal with evidence and are well aware of how fragile human testimony can be."

"So what happened next?" Hal asked.

"I began a quest for the truth of the Gospel," I said. "I read it all, and everything I could get my hands on about it. To make a long story short, I put Matthew, Mark, Luke, and John, Peter, Paul, James, and Jude on trial, and the only one who got convicted was me."

"That's a great remembrance," Hal said. "But was it all from books, or was there more to it?"

"At the same time I was going through the head learning part of it," I said, "I had a series of experiences that I believe are very biblical, but almost no other Christian I have ever talked to has had anything similar. God spoke to me in dreams—not a dream but a series of dreams. They were vivid—I still remember them, even though I can rarely remember a dream a few minutes after I wake up. And they were progressive. They told me a story about myself."

"You're right that the Bible is full of God speaking to people in dreams, 'songs in the night,' in Bunyan's words. And I don't know anyone who has had any either. Tell me about yours."

"The first several were about the state of my soul. The images were so vile, and what they told me about myself was so frightening that I have never told anyone the details. Let's just say they impressed on me what a foul person I was and how hostile I was to the things of God. Once I came to terms with that, they got better. But I remember one in which Christ was brooding over his creation spread out before him. By that time I was beginning to be removed from the pit I had been in and could see more objectively the world I was leaving and how depraved it really was."

Hal nodded, as though he could see the image.

"Then I had a climactic dream, the one in which I finally came to God in my heart and soul. I was in a large room, like an institutional dining hall, with tables and chairs throughout. A lot of people were there with me. I knew only one person, and he was one of my best friends. I knew, somehow, that all of the people in that room, including me, were waiting for salvation, for the opportunity to go to heaven, but that only one person would actually be saved, and the rest would be condemned. I wanted in the worst way to be that one person. But then, gradually, I became conscious of my friend, and my selfish desire for my own salvation began to give way to a desire for his. The feeling for him welled up in me until it overcame me, and I prayed and cried out in my heart for God to save him, even though I knew I would be left behind if he saved my friend instead of me. It was a moment of total selflessness, something I can't say I often feel, and it was with no spiritual pride. All I wanted was what was best for him, whatever the cost to me. As that feeling overcame my selfish feelings and finally possessed me entirely and in purity, the room's ceiling parted. A beam of light came down from above and settled on my friend. I knew he had been selected for salvation instead of me, and I was glad. And then—when I experienced a genuine and overwhelming rejoicing at his salvation, even though I knew my own was lost as his was gained—the beam enlarged and took me in. I had found my own salvation only when I ceased to seek it and lost myself in prayer for someone else."

Neither of us spoke for minutes after I finished the story of my dream. As I told the story, I realized how similar my experience in the dream had been to Hal's, when he prayed for Henry.

Then Hal spoke Jesus' words for both of us: "No man has greater love than this; that he lay down his life for a friend."

Augustine, Luther, Bunyan, and Lewis seemed spectral presences as he spoke the words. I could almost imagine them sitting around the fireplace with us, sharing their remembrances of grace and divining the sin of pride.

"Have there been other dreams?" Hal asked.

"I have had other spiritual dreams since then," I said, "but they have been different, dreams of looking up to the Lord or being in heaven praising him. In one dream I was part of a heavenly choir. I was afraid to sing because my voice is so bad, and I can't carry a tune. But when I opened my mouth to sing praises to the Lord, the imperfect had passed away. My voice had become perfect. I was in tune and on key and in harmony with the other singers, and it was glorious and gloriously perfect. I hope heaven is really like that."

Our evening was over. Hal gripped my hand with both of his as I left. "Heaven will be all of your dreams and so much more, Chris," he said. "And grace isn't a once-in-a-lifetime event. Once you recognize it, you find it everywhere. And it's at its best when it's knocking down your pride and reminding you that he died for you, and you need to be living for him."

The rain had let up by the time I left. The night world smelled washed and clean, and the remaining leaves sprayed the pure water onto my face with a gust of wind as I made my way to the car.

CHAPTER NINE

Hal hadn't been in church for a time. He seemed to have somewhere else to go on weekends. But this Sunday he was there and we visited briefly on the way out.

"What is sin, Chris?" he asked as we made our way to the parking lot while Anna rounded up the children.

"Anything that is against God's will . . ." I answered, hesitatingly.

"Good enough for a working definition," Hal said. "Where does it come from?"

I hesitated again. From bad choices? Free will? Temptation by Satan, the tempter, the evil one? Inherited from Adam?

Hal didn't wait for my response. "Read chapter nine," he said. "Then read St. Augustine again, the *Confessions,* and let's talk."

Later that day I began reading Deuteronomy 9.

> Hear, O Israel. You are now about to cross the Jordan to go in and dispossess nations greater and stronger than you, with large cities that have walls up to the sky. The people are strong and tall—Anakites! You know about them and have heard it said: "Who can stand up against the Anakites?" But be assured today that the LORD your God is the one who goes across ahead of you like a devouring fire. He will destroy them; he will subdue them before you. And you will drive them out and annihilate them quickly, as the LORD has promised you.
>
> After the LORD your God has driven them out before you, do not say to yourself, "The LORD has brought me here to take possession of this land because of my righteousness." No, it is on account of the wickedness of these nations that

the LORD is going to drive them out before you. It is not because of your righteousness or your integrity that you are going in to take possession of their land; but on account of the wickedness of these nations, the LORD your God will drive them out before you, to accomplish what he swore to your fathers, to Abraham, Isaac and Jacob. Understand, then, that it is not because of your righteousness that the LORD your God is giving you this good land to possess, for you are a stiff-necked people.

—Deut. 9:1–6

Saint Augustine had come up in my remembrances the week before. As Hal had suggested, I reread Augustine's personal and spiritual autobiography, *Confessions,* before we met to discuss chapter nine. It is one of the spiritual classics, a story of one of the worst among sinners who became one of the best among saints. And I thought I understood why Hal had suggested I reread it. It seemed to me relevant to a major issue in chapter nine: whether there is righteousness and integrity in God's people, even those he has chosen as his "treasured possession."

Augustine is one of the giants of Christian history, a rich source of understanding for both Protestant and Catholic traditions. His life, from 354 to 430 in the late Roman Empire, is a classic story of a Christian life. He was brilliant and well educated. By his own account, his early life was filled with both fleshly and intellectual corruption. His Christian mother, Monica, prayed for him throughout his life, with eventual reward as he was converted in his mid-thirties. He became an intellectual and spiritual leader of the church and wrote prolifically. Some of his better-known contributions to Christian understanding include works on the subjects of original sin, the Trinity, just war, and the relationship between the church and secular society.

In his *Confessions,* Augustine relates an incident in his youth when he and others raided someone else's pear tree and stole a large quantity of fruit for no better reason than the desire to do wrong. He had no lack of fruit himself and did not eat most of what he stole, but threw it to pigs. Reflecting on this incident in later life, Augustine saw that he had been prompted to wrong for no purpose but the sheer love of doing the forbidden. It was the wrong itself that he desired. These insights into himself helped convince Augustine of the inherent sinfulness of human beings.

"What's the connection between chapter nine and Augustine?" Hal asked when we met next. I recalled the incident with the pear tree and guessed that it was connected to Moses' message about the lack of righteousness in Israel, his chosen people.

"In the previous chapter," Hal said, "God told Israel that he had not chosen them because of their power or position among the nations. Now he adds that it is also not because of their righteousness or their integrity that they are going to take possession of the land. There is no basis for any 'holier than thou' attitude among God's elect. They come before their Lord dripping with sin and evil, not in triumphant self-righteousness. The church is a hospital for sinners."

Hal had his own pear tree story. When he was an adolescent, a boy of his acquaintance fell out of favor with the "in crowd" of his junior high gang. There was no particular reason for this; the disfavored boy had done nothing to offend the group. Nevertheless, each of the others pooled a quarter (more money then than now) to pay one of their own to beat up the boy to whom they had taken a dislike. When he reflected on this incident later, Hal was horrified at himself for participating in the event. It was, he told me, gratuitous violence, without reason. In this he saw in himself—as Augustine had with the theft of pears—the love of evil for the sake of evil, even in a young man brought up in a Christian home.

"There is no one righteous, not even one," he said, quoting the Psalms and Ecclesiastes, "and the scripture is echoed in the New Testament. Paul repeats it in Romans four. 'The heart is deceitful above all things and beyond cure. Who can understand it?' Jeremiah lamented."

I was grateful that Hal did not ask me about the pear trees in my life. It wasn't hard to understand the experience of Augustine and of Hal—it was my own, in countless deceits and greeds and lusts and secret disobediences that had no need or purpose but my own love of the delicious nature of evil. "And yet," I voiced the thought, "was there not a difference in you or Augustine or me when we recognized with horror that ghoul of evil in ourselves compared with those whose 'glory is in their shame,' as Paul says in Philippians three-nineteen?"

"Don't dare to think it," Hal said. "Praise God for opening your eyes enough to see who you really are. The minute you start comparing yourself to others and thinking yourself better, the snare of pride has a loop around your foot and is pulling you down. That was God's warning to Israel in this passage."

"I take it you believe in 'original sin,'" I commented after this discourse. I meant the idea that Augustine articulated so well that sin is inherent in human beings, part of our fallen nature, so that even babies are not innocent.

"No one who has raised children thinks they're born innocent," Hal said. "The first words out of their mouths are 'no' and 'mine.' Their primal instincts are greed, fear, and jealousy. How much time do we spend as parents teaching children not to behave the way their nature tells them to? They have a lot of charms, to be sure, and their innocence can be captivating. Jesus loved them and called them to him, and so should we. But they need to be taught, and the learning is life-long."

"What about grownups?" I asked. "I mean, after we get taught properly, we do learn to be unselfish."

"To a point," Hal said. "But I don't think there are very many pastors—not those who have spent real time in pastoral ministry—who aren't painfully aware of the frailty and perverseness in those they shepherd. And if they have any self-understanding, they know that it infects them as well. People can and do act unselfishly and with great goodness, but the same people can astonish you at how contrary they are in other circumstances. There are a lot of doctrines and disagreements about how original sin came about or is transmitted, and how and in what sense we are Adam's heirs in the Fall. But the reality of it is what's important. I am convicted of original sin, not just because God's word teaches it, but also because it explains the human condition like nothing else can. This is empirical theology, one of the few things in the faith that we can test and verify. Human beings are not born good, only to be corrupted by their environment later. Others who were babes once themselves made that environment. No, we don't become sinners by sinning. Rather, we sin because we're sinners."

The Scripture also talked about the wickedness of the nations who were to be driven out "to accomplish what he swore to your fathers, to

Abraham, Isaac, and Jacob." We had talked before about that wickedness when we discussed the herem that required Israel to destroy the occupants completely. I asked Hal about the relationship between the wickedness of the nations and the promises to the forefathers: Which was the reason for the delivery of the land to Israel?

"They're tied together," he said. "You can't think of them separately." He showed me in Genesis 15:16 that God's promise of the land to Abraham would not be fulfilled in his lifetime, but "your descendants will come back here, for the sin of the Amorites has not yet reached its full measure."

"God tolerates a lot," Hal said. "But his tolerance is limited. He would fulfill the promise to Abraham when the time was right, and the time would be right when the sin of the people in the land 'had reached its full measure.' In the same way, life as we know it will end at some time in the future—just as it ended for those Amorite peoples when Israel invaded the land—when the cup of God's wrath overflows. Then there will be another invasion, this time of the whole earth. But that's a discussion for another day. Let's read on."

> Remember this and never forget how you provoked the LORD your God to anger in the desert. From the day you left Egypt until you arrived here, you have been rebellious against the LORD. At Horeb you aroused the LORD's wrath so that he was angry enough to destroy you. When I went up on the mountain to receive the tablets of stone, the tablets of the covenant that the LORD had made with you, I stayed on the mountain forty days and forty nights; I ate no bread and drank no water. The LORD gave me two stone tablets inscribed by the finger of God. On them were all the commandments the LORD proclaimed to you on the mountain out of the fire, on the day of the assembly.
>
> At the end of the forty days and forty nights, the LORD gave me the two stone tablets, the tablets of the covenant. Then the LORD told me, "Go down from here at once, because your people whom you brought out of Egypt have become corrupt. They have turned away quickly from what I commanded them and have made a cast idol for themselves."

And the LORD said to me, "I have seen this people, and they are a stiff-necked people indeed! Let me alone, so that I may destroy them and blot out their name from under heaven. And I will make you into a nation stronger and more numerous than they."

So I turned and went down from the mountain while it was ablaze with fire. And the two tablets of the covenant were in my hands. When I looked, I saw that you had sinned against the LORD your God; you had made for yourselves an idol cast in the shape of a calf. You had turned aside quickly from the way that the LORD had commanded you. So I took the two tablets and threw them out of my hands, breaking them to pieces before your eyes.

Then once again I fell prostrate before the LORD for forty days and forty nights; I ate no bread and drank no water, because of all the sin you had committed, doing what was evil in the LORD's sight and so provoking him to anger. I feared the anger and wrath of the LORD, for he was angry enough with you to destroy you. But again the LORD listened to me. And the LORD was angry enough with Aaron to destroy him, but at that time I prayed for Aaron too. Also I took that sinful thing of yours, the calf you had made, and burned it in the fire. Then I crushed it and ground it to powder as fine as dust and threw the dust into a stream that flowed down the mountain.

You also made the LORD angry at Taberah, at Massah and at Kibroth Hattaavah.

And when the LORD sent you out from Kadesh Barnea, he said, "Go up and take possession of the land I have given you." But you rebelled against the command of the LORD your God. You did not trust him or obey him. You have been rebellious against the LORD ever since I have known you.

I lay prostrate before the LORD those forty days and forty nights because the LORD had said he would destroy you. I prayed to the LORD and said, "O Sovereign LORD, do not destroy your people, your own inheritance that you redeemed by your great power and brought out of Egypt with a mighty hand. Remember your servants Abraham, Isaac, and Jacob. Overlook the stubbornness of this people, their wickedness and their sin. Otherwise, the country from which you brought us will say, 'Because the LORD was not able to take them into the land he had promised them, and because he hated them, he brought them out to put them to death in the desert.' But they are your people, your inheritance that you brought out by your great power and your outstretched arm."

—Deut. 9:7–29

"Where did they come up with the golden calf?" I asked.

"Oh, they didn't just make it up," Hal said. "The symbol of the bull or calf is well known as a religious icon of the ancient near-east. Bull or calf cults were present in Egypt in the time of the Exodus. In Canaan, these were also used as symbols of the Baals, who were often depicted as standing on the backs of such animals. The horns of the bull were a religious symbol in the ancient Mycenaean civilization on Crete. Bull and calf images represented fertility and physical strength to these people, and the worship of it was a worship of those attributes."

"Does this have anything to do with Satan being depicted as having horns?" I asked.

"I've never studied that, but I suspect it's not a coincidence. The resemblance of the horn to the evidence of arousal in the male wasn't missed, and is probably related to a contemporary term for that state."

"Small wonder Moses threw down the tablets when he came onto that scene—God's people worshipping the golden calf while he had been up on the mountain praying," I said.

"Breaking the tablets was a symbolic breaking of the covenant, like tearing up a will or legal document. The people knew the commandment against worshipping idols. That had been given to them verbally before Moses brought the tablets back from the mountain. But they fell into the sin almost as soon as the command had been given—like Adam in the garden."

"How could they?" I asked. "After all they had experienced in the escape from Egypt and at Sinai. It doesn't seem possible."

"I preached every Sunday of my ministry to people who professed to believe all of those things I taught, everything in the Bible," Hal said. "And they would walk out of the church and serve their own idols of sex and power and money as soon as they were gone. It goes back to the discussion we just had, the inherent sinfulness of humanity."

"The end of the chapter relates to the beginning," he went on. "It's the same subject. What Moses did here is to reinforce from their recent experience Israel's unrighteousness and the message that God's favor to them is not on account of their righteousness. He begins with the golden calf episode, and then, without describing the details, reminds them of three other episodes."

"What were those all about?" I asked.

"All instances of disobedience," Hal said. "At Taberah . . . ," he turned in his Bible, ". . . Numbers chapter eleven tells us the people, shortly after leaving Sinai, 'complained about their hardships in the hearing of the Lord.' And then 'fire from the Lord burned among them and consumed some of the outskirts of the camp,' but died down when Moses prayed to the Lord.

"The story of Massah or Meribah is told in Exodus seventeen. There the people complained about the lack of water and quarreled with Moses. Moses brought forth water from a rock by following the Lord's instructions to strike the rock with his staff.

"At Kibroth Hattaavah, the people complained about having to eat manna and not having meat, so the Lord sent a large volume of quails to feed them, but also sent a severe plague because they had craved other food and complained. That story is also in Numbers eleven.

"Moses then reminds them of the rebellion at Kadesh Barnea, when they refused to go up and take possession of the land the Lord had given them, the story he'd retold at the beginning of Deuteronomy.

"Each of these rebellions showed the people's lack of righteousness in the most fundamental way—their lack of faith or trust in God. They turned to the golden calf because Moses had been so long on the mountain. They complained about hardships, lack of water, and lack of meat because they didn't trust God to provide for them. They refused to go up and take possession of the land because they didn't believe God could defeat their enemies. It's the story of their nation and of every nation—and every person: 'You have been rebellious against the Lord ever since I have known you.' There is no basis for pride here."

"And Moses prays for them," I added. "It sounds like that happened a lot."

"Every time," Hal said. "But his intercessory prayer was particularly needed with the golden calf incident. Notice that before he prays, he acts—to destroy the calf idol. He burns it, crushes it, grinds it to powder like dust, and throws the dust into a stream. Now this is gold he's throwing away; the calf was made from their gold earrings. He didn't hesitate to discard what was of great value in worldly terms to protect their holiness. He didn't melt it down and make new earrings out of it."

I contemplated the reality of throwing away the things that have the most worldly value to us when they interfere with our relationship with God.

"I sometimes think," Hal mused, "that we pastors are too gentle with our flock. We need to spend more time grinding up the gold. The mission of the church, as has been said, is to 'comfort the afflicted and afflict the comfortable.' But we're afraid of how they'll react if we really confront them. Flee the church, go somewhere else that's more comfortable, fire the pastor and find someone they like better, I don't know what. We'll be thought of as judgmental, not letting people find their own way down a path we never really show them. We won't be user-friendly, and new people won't come in. There are a thousand excuses. Not many of us have broken up our congregations' golden calves."

We turned to Moses' prayer. After destroying the calf idol, Moses prayed. And not just a now-I-lay-me-down-to-sleep prayer. Moses fasted for forty days and forty nights, the same time period as Jesus' fasting and temptation in the wilderness, and the same period of time God sent the rains in the time of Noah.

"When is the last time anyone spent forty days and nights praying for anything?" Hal asked rhetorically.

"And Moses prayed for the Lord to forgive—not his own sins, but those of others," I observed.

"Good observation," Hal said. "He didn't lead the people in prayer for their own forgiveness; he took on himself the burden of pleading for them. In the Exodus telling of the story, Moses goes further, asking the Lord to blot his name out of the book if he would not forgive the people. In this sense, he is prefiguring Christ taking the sins of the world on himself. It's like your dream, Chris, of the light coming down on your friend in the great hall crowded with people, only one of whom can be saved."

We discussed Moses' prayer for Israel. Hal showed me that Moses, in speaking to the people, had called their unfaithfulness to mind in a recital of their recent history; but in speaking to God, he calls on God's faithfulness, remembering Abraham, Isaac, and Jacob, the ancestors to whom God made the promises. The contrast between the promise-breakers and the Promise-Keeper is clear.

"But what about Moses' last plea?" I asked. "He seemed to be saying that God needed to refrain from destroying the people because otherwise the Egyptians would get the wrong idea and think he really hated the Israelites and didn't have the power to deliver them after all."

Hal smiled.

"The Scripture reports that Moses argued this point to God; it doesn't say God responded to it. I hear this sort of prayer all the time, people asking God to give a sign to show his power to them or others, invariably one that will make them better off. God doesn't work that way. He chooses when and to whom he'll give those signs. I don't think you can pray it out of him, even to prove him to someone else. God responded to Moses' selfless prayer for the people, not to a clumsy attempt to embarrass him into it."

Hal reminded me that Moses' retelling of the story of the golden calf and the tablets on which the Ten Commandments were written continued in chapter ten. Since I had not studied it yet, we decided to save it for the following week.

I left Hal's home that night sobered by my own lack of prayer or concern for the unrighteous conduct of others. I had always thought I had enough to do to try to keep up with God in confessing and seeking forgiveness of my own sins. I knew enough of my own sinful nature to feel little right to be critical of anyone else. God's grace to me, as to Israel, was not premised on my righteousness or integrity. Others could take care of themselves on the matter of sin and confession and making things right with their Maker. If they didn't recognize the need to do so, who was I, the chief among sinners, as Paul described himself, to get involved? If I addressed them directly, they would probably react with hostility and think I was a self-righteous prig who should mind my own business.

But they were under God's judgment, just as I was, and needed him as much as I did. On the drive home, I began to think about the people I knew and to pray for each of them—family, friends, co-workers, and people in my church and community. I knew what some of their golden calves were, but for most I did not, as they did not know mine. But I prayed for them anyway, individually and by name, and put them before the Lord for their sins and idolatries—those sins and idolatries I knew and those I did not, those that even they themselves did not know or recognize. I prayed that they would come to know their Lord and know his will for them and would confess and seek forgiveness for those things in their lives that displeased him. And I asked him to forgive them, each one, individually, and to bring the precious soul in them—that he had created—to himself. I prayed they would know for themselves what Augustine wrote in the very first paragraph of the *Confessions*: "You made us for yourself and our hearts are restless until they find their rest in you."

My restless heart found rest in my newfound approach to prayer. As I slipped into the worldly rest of sleep, I thanked my God for a Moses who would spend forty days in prayer and caring for his people, and a Hal who would awaken my soul to the need to pray for the souls of others.

CHAPTER TEN

"D oes the Bible contradict itself?" I asked Hal when next we met. "Where did you get that?" Hal replied. "You sound like the village atheist."

"Well," I said, "just read the first part of chapter ten, and I'll tell you."

We read the first eleven verses:

> At that time the LORD said to me, "Chisel out two stone tablets like the first ones and come up to me on the mountain. Also make a wooden chest. I will write on the tablets the words that were on the first tablets, which you broke. Then you are to put them in the chest."
>
> So I made the ark out of acacia wood and chiseled out two stone tablets like the first ones, and I went up on the mountain with the two tablets in my hands. The LORD wrote on these tablets what he had written before, the Ten Commandments he had proclaimed to you on the mountain, out of the fire, on the day of the assembly. And the LORD gave them to me. Then I came back down the mountain and put the tablets in the ark I had made, as the LORD commanded me, and they are there now.
>
> (The Israelites traveled from the wells of the Jaakanites to Moserah. There Aaron died and was buried, and Eleazar his son succeeded him as priest. From there they traveled to Gudgodah and on to Jotbathah, a land with streams of water. At that time the LORD set apart the tribe of Levi to carry the ark of the covenant of the LORD, to stand before the LORD to minister and to pronounce blessings in his

name, as they still do today. That is why the Levites have no share or inheritance among their brothers; the LORD is their inheritance, as the LORD your God told them.)

Now I had stayed on the mountain forty days and nights, as I did the first time, and the LORD listened to me at this time also. It was not his will to destroy you. "Go," the LORD said to me, "and lead the people on their way, so that they may enter and possess the land that I swore to their fathers to give them."

—Deut. 10:1–11

"So where are the contradictions?" Hal asked.

"I want to believe the Scriptures," I said, "but sometimes God throws us curve balls. The first five verses seem to tell a different story about the events surrounding the golden calf than the same story in Exodus."

"How so?" Hal asked.

"In Deuteronomy, after Moses pleads for God to overlook the sin of the people in the incident, God tells him to chisel out two stone tablets like the one he had broken and come up on the mountain, and make a wooden chest to put the tablets in. Moses then says he makes the ark and the tablets, goes up on the mountain, the Lord writes the Ten Commandments on them as he did before, and Moses comes down and puts the tablets in the ark."

"What's the problem?" Hal asked.

"Well," I replied, "in Exodus, the story of the second set of tablets containing the Ten Commandments is told in chapter thirty-four, and the ark wasn't made, or even commanded to be made, until chapter thirty-seven, after Moses came down from his second trip to the mountain. And Moses didn't make it, as Deuteronomy says. Rather, a craftsman named Bezalel made it."

"I'm ashamed of you," Hal said. "A smart fellow like you shouldn't be taken in by something like that. In Deuteronomy, Moses gave a summary of recollections of events. Exact chronology of when he went up on the mountain and when he made the ark is not the point. It doesn't matter if the instruction to make the ark, and the making of it, came a little later. We're trying to read too much into the text if we expect precision in time sequence. If someone asks me what I did last weekend, I might say I went to church and went shopping, even though I went shopping on Saturday and went to church on Sunday. The Bible often tells things out of order. People don't always think or talk or write in exact time sequences. Don't let something like that intrude on your faith. Only people who want to find reasons to question the Scriptures or can't see in them the ordinary way people communicate get hung up on these things."

"What about who made the ark? Was it Moses or Bezalel?"

"As for who made the ark, we regularly speak of leaders doing things when someone else actually did it for them or at their direction. When we say Sir Francis Drake defeated the Spanish Armada or President Bush invaded Iraq, we don't mean they did it all by themselves. The Bible is written the way real people write and talk. There is nothing contradictory about Moses' saying he made the ark when he actually had Bezalel make it at his direction. Is there anything else that bothers you here?"

I plunged on. "The text in Deuteronomy goes on to say Aaron died in Moserah, but in Numbers twenty-seven it says he died on Mount Hor. Why isn't that a contradiction? He can't have died in two different places."

"The fact is," Hal answered, "that no one knows for sure where either Mount Hor or Moserah is. The most probable explanation is that they are two different names for the same place, or that one of them is a regional name and one a specific place. We see this all the time in the Bible."

"Such as?"

"Such as Horeb and Sinai for the name of the mountain where the law was given, or Pisgah and Nebo for the mountain from which Moses was to see the land before he died, or Meribah and Massah for the place where Israel sinned in the desert. It's how people talk. We have different names for the same place too, or older and newer names, or names for larger regions and specific places in the region.

"There is an explanation for every supposed contradiction that people find in the Bible, Chris. You just have to look for it. Faith seeks understanding, and will find it. 'Seek and you shall find,' as the Lord taught us."

"Then why are there so many people, and even churches, that won't believe the Bible?"

"Let's talk about that," Hal said. "You are into a topic that could be a college major or whole course of study in seminary, but we can summarize a little. Since we're talking about the Old Testament, did you ever hear of the 'documentary hypothesis'?"

In my study of Deuteronomy, I had become aware that many religious scholars did not accept the book as it was literally presented—Moses' words, speeches, and teachings, as well as repeating God's laws and commands to his people Israel on the Plains of Moab before crossing into the Promised Land. When we had studied the passage in chapter four that taught that we were not to add to or subtract from the Scriptures, Hal had warned me about the hazards in academic religion. But the documentary hypothesis was new to me.

"The documentary hypothesis" Hal explained, "is a theory—widely accepted in certain academic circles—that the first five books of the Old Testament are an integration of several strains or traditions of writing from separate sources. These sources are identified as J, E, P, and D. J and E refer to source writers known as the Jahwist and the Elohist, based on different names of God used in certain portions of these Scriptures. Use of the name Jahweh as the name of God—the Tetragrammaton we discussed when we studied chapter six—is characteristic of the J writer. Use of Elohim as the name of God identifies the E writer. P is the priestly source, supposedly more concerned with ceremonial matters such as are detailed extensively in Leviticus. D is the deuteronomist, the supposed author of Deuteronomy. The books of Joshua, Judges, First and Second Samuel, and First and Second Kings, are sometimes referred to as the deuteronomic history, for the idea that they follow closely on the teachings of Deuteronomy. The books of the deuteronomic history relate the subsequent history of Israel, its successes and failures, to its degree of obedience or disobedience to the laws of Deuteronomy."

"Can you give me any examples?" I asked.

"A classic example of applying the documentary hypothesis is the notion that the first and second chapters of Genesis are two different accounts of the creation, rather than a general account in chapter one, which then focuses on certain particulars in chapter two. Some scholars dissect scriptural writings even further, seeing layers of text from different sources and time periods, or integration of different texts, even within short sections of Scripture and inside single sentences. The characteristic of Deuteronomy to move from back and forth in the form of address between the second person singular and second person plural, the individual and the community—the 'numeruswechsel' we discussed back in chapter one—is an example of this. Other approaches to finding supposed layers—or varying sources—in the text are discerned through study of what are perceived as different uses of language, style, theological points, and versions of certain events. Scripture is full of contradictions, so the theory goes, and these can only be explained by this method of interpretation."

"And what's wrong with this?" I asked. "I mean, can we ignore scholarship altogether? Is there nothing to learn from it? Is it sufficient to just study the Scriptures literally and not think about where they came from?"

"If you take away the 'village atheist' stuff we talked about earlier—finding contradictions where there really aren't any—most people who don't have the benefit of academic training in religion can see the Scriptures as logical and consistent with the way people write or talk in everyday life. It was logical and consistent with God's purpose for Moses to address the Israelites individually and collectively in the same speech. We do the same in our normal patterns of speaking, especially in sermon types of speech such as what Moses gave in Deuteronomy. We use different names for God, like 'God' and 'the Lord,' interchangeably. I suspect that the writings of many a modern religious author could be shown to have come from a variety of sources if one applied the same kind of analysis as the documentary hypothesis does to the Bible. It's like 'proving' that various people wrote Shakespeare. Someone analyzing my own speech or writings over my adult lifetime could well conclude that I was four or five different people as well."

I followed Hal's thought with my own. "And every lawyer knows that different people can observe the same thing and remember different aspects of it. Like the famous tale of the blind men and the elephant. All may be true at the same time: The elephant may be like a wall, a tree trunk, a fan, and a hose simultaneously. And an individual may tell the story with a different perspective on different occasions, depending on his audience and purpose in the telling. So what may seem to be different versions of the same event are simply different perspectives or points of emphasis."

"Just so," Hal said. "Like whether Aaron died at Mount Hor or Moserah."

"Or whether Moses or Bezalel made the ark," I said. I recalled also Hal's observation at one of our earlier discussions that academic consensus was a moving target, like the scientific consensus about the steady state of the universe that we had discussed when we were gazing at the night sky in his rose garden and talking about chapter seven. My faith in the integrity of the Bible, I decided, had not suffered from the "contradictions" I had observed, nor would it from the documentary hypothesis or other academic dissections of the Scriptures.

"Of course," Hal added, "even if any particular theory about the origins of Scripture is correct, it doesn't take away from the role of the Holy Spirit in bringing it about. God can write the Scriptures through any combination of human authors and editors and time sequences he chooses. That's a point that's often overlooked."

We took a break from the discussion and moved into the kitchen. Hal had an espresso machine, which, he explained, he had just acquired in Boston and wanted to try out to make some decaf cappuccino. While he struggled with it, he ruminated on the things we had been discussing.

"The problem is that a lot of people hear about these theories of where Scripture came from and decide that the Scriptures are just a manmade invention and have no more value or authority than anything else that people write or think up. Then they're in trouble."

He spooned some coffee beans into a grinder. "Academic analysis is of no value in pastoral ministry. That's where a lot of churches, and even whole denominations, have gotten off the track. It began in the seminaries and divinity schools. They were so invested in pursuing the scholarship of the academic life that they lost the spiritual purpose for which they existed. Professors—pursuing the latest theory from some German university or liberal American seminary—trained the pastors, and the pastors carried that training into the church. Those whose business was to investigate and question the Bible became the source of opinions that got into the pews. Once the people lost their traditional and orthodox understanding of the Scriptures, they lost the moral compass that went with it. They may have retained a residual understanding of right and wrong, but they no longer understood why. When the foundation becomes rotten, the rest of the structure will stand for a while, but eventually it will fall."

He pressed the top of the grinder and held it for a long time, grinding the beans fine. When the whine of the grinder stopped, he went on.

"The academic world has its own orthodoxy. People who choose that career path are unlikely to advance unless they conform to it. We talked before about how they are under pressure to come up with some new theory or idea or research that no one has thought or done before. But once an idea gets established in academic circles because some prominent scholar has sold it to his peers, it can be hard to dislodge. People have a vested interest in sustaining it. New students get trained in it, the careers of those who control the university departments are built on it, and it gets ingrained and impervious to challenge. Sometimes that's because the evidence for it or the persuasive value of it is so strong. But sometimes it's just a new tradition replacing the old, and it winds up stifling creative thought or even rethinking whether the theory was sound in the first place."

He poured the fine powder that was left of the beans into a filter basket, juggling it to fit.

"But advancing in knowledge of the Lord comes in a very different way—through prayer, meditation, studying what the Scripture teaches rather than where it comes from, and losing oneself in obedience to it. It doesn't lie in coming up with new ideas about the sources of Scripture or the history of Israel or the church. There is an inherent contradiction in purpose between the church and the academy."

The rig was almost put together, with milk to be steamed into a froth to top off the thick coffee.

"There will always be the question of whether Scripture should have a privileged place in the world of literature, or whether it should be subject to the same kind of analysis that scholars devote to other types of literature. As a pastor, I find that study and analysis can add to my understanding as long as I keep it in perspective. Scripture is self-authenticating in the sense that the power of the Scriptures to inspire, to teach, to lead people to God, and to know God, is something that simply is—as God himself simply is. People who read and study and pray the Scriptures with the eyes of faith understand that. It has stood the test of centuries and millennia, and has inspired and guided and been believed by many of the greatest minds and best people who have ever lived. Through its many human authors, it is the product of the work of the Holy Spirit and is able, as Paul wrote to Timothy, 'to make you wise for salvation through faith in Christ Jesus.' That's what the people in the pew need, not the latest academic theory that, in the course of time, will become as irrelevant as last year's newspaper."

The cappuccino was ready. As Hal triumphantly poured us both cups and led me back into his study, I wondered vaguely what had led Hal to Boston to buy a specialty coffee machine. He pointed to the walls around us, filled with books—the learning and thinking of the ages about the things of the Lord.

"Some of these are great books—spiritual classics like Augustine's *Confessions*, Pascal's *Pensees,* or the writings of Luther, Calvin, Aquinas, or modern writers like C.S. Lewis or G.K. Chesterton. There is value to a pastor, and to any believer, in knowing how the church and the great thinkers in its history have thought about the Scriptures and their Author. I've spent my life reading and studying these things. But they don't replace the value of the Scriptures themselves, and simply being a person of faith and righteousness as they teach us to be. You don't need a university education to understand what they teach."

As Hal spoke, I recalled the legal concept called the "burden of proof." It tells the judge or jury which side has the obligation to prove its case. In civil cases, the burden of proof is on the plaintiff, the party who initiated the lawsuit. That party has to demonstrate that it is "more probable than not." In other words, there has to be more than fifty percent probability that the essential elements of the plaintiff's case are correct. Judges commonly illustrate the point when instructing juries by holding out their hands to simulate the scales of justice. If the evidence causes the scales to tip ever so slightly to the plaintiff's side, the plaintiff should prevail. If they remain evenly balanced or tip the other way, the defendant should prevail. In criminal cases, a different standard is used. The prosecution has the burden of proof and must prove its case "beyond a reasonable doubt," a much higher requirement than "more probable than not."

Those who attack the understanding of Scripture that "was once for all entrusted to the saints," as Jude writes, surely have the burden of proof. I was satisfied with Hal's defense of the consistency, integrity, and value of the Scriptures.

As we settled back into our chairs, I raised another issue I'd seen in chapter ten. "God is supposed to be the same yesterday, today, and forever, unchanging in his nature. Here he says he will destroy Israel in chapter nine, but in chapter ten, after Moses intercedes, God seems to change his mind. Does God change his mind about things? If you're lucky enough to have a holy or righteous person pray for you, will God forgive you, even though he may not forgive someone else who wasn't the beneficiary of such a prayer?"

"Your problem, Chris, is that you're looking at it from a human perspective. From that perspective, these are troubling questions indeed. We can't see it from God's perspective.

"Consider an ant that lives his whole life on what seems to be an infinitely large surface, like a tabletop. He can travel as far as his ability will allow in any direction of left or right, forward or back. But he is utterly unable to travel up or down. He lives in two dimensions. He may—or may not, since he is an ant—be able to imagine a creature that can travel up and down, but it's not him. It is utterly beyond his ability.

"In fact, there is such a creature, a human being, who isn't limited by the flat surface of the table top. The ant may make efforts to move up or down, and we can observe them and respond to them, but his efforts are helpless unless we intercede and move him where he can't move himself."

"What does this have to do with God changing his mind?"

Hal sipped his cappuccino. His pleasure in his achievement in mastering the machine was apparent. Then he went on.

"We understand now better than the ancients that time is a dimension, like the three dimensions of space. Remember our discussion of the universe the other night when we sat out under the stars? Time is a dimension we can't move around in, except linearly, and we don't have any control over that. We're like the ant, stuck in certain dimensions.

"How is it?" he asked, referring to the coffee, as I tried a few sips myself. The machine worked, I reassured him. I could have been sitting in a bookstore café in Boston or New York, Vienna or Paris, at that moment.

After I reassured Hal of his brewing success, he continued. "But God exists, and he moves in all dimensions simultaneously. He knows about our prayers before we pray them, in ways we can hardly understand, and his responses have to do with things he knows before they happen from our perspective. It's like our discussion of election and foreknowledge. When the Bible talks about God seeming to change his mind, it's only reflecting—in the dim light in which we see ultimate reality—the existence and the actions of God in his presence in the dimension of time. There he is omnipresent, just as he is in every other dimension."

"This is hard to understand," I said.

"There is a mystery to the interaction of God's love, grace, and mercy, as well as in the actions of human beings in prayer and intercession for others. I can't explain it; I can only tell you that it's real. Moses interceded in prayer for the people, and God responded to that prayer. There is one thing in this world that you should covet, Chris, and that is the prayers of a righteous man or woman. Nothing else anyone can give would mean more to me."

I contemplated the thought that prayer is a gift one person can give to another. The thought had never occurred to me before. Then Hal went on. "In the end, everything we've been reading for the last several chapters leads up to this fundamental New Testament teaching: There is no inherent or intrinsic merit in human beings; we are unwilling or unable to keep God's commands or covenants, and we are without hope absent God's gracious mercy. Only faith can lead us out of this dilemma. The righteous live by faith. Let's read on."

And now, O Israel, what does the LORD your God ask of you but to fear the LORD your God, to walk in all his ways, to love him, to serve the LORD your God with all your heart and with all your soul, and to observe the LORD's commands and decrees that I am giving you today for your own good?

To the LORD your God belong the heavens, even the highest heavens, the earth and everything in it. Yet the LORD set his affection on your forefathers and loved them, and he chose you, their descendants, above all the nations, as it is today. Circumcise your hearts, therefore, and do not be stiff-necked any longer. For the LORD your God is God of gods and Lord of lords, the great God, mighty and awesome, who shows no partiality and accepts no bribes. He defends the cause of the fatherless and the widow, and loves the alien, giving him food and clothing. And you are to love those who are aliens, for you yourselves were aliens in Egypt. Fear the LORD your God and serve him. Hold fast to him and take your oaths in his name. He is your praise; he is your God, who performed for you those great and awesome wonders you saw with your own eyes. Your forefathers who went down into Egypt were seventy in all, and now the LORD your God has made you as numerous as the stars in the sky.

—Deut. 9:12–22

"Let's do a little review," Hal said. "There is continuity here from what's gone before."

I tried my hand. "In chapter seven, Moses taught that God didn't choose these people because they were numerous. In chapter eight, he taught that they had no basis for pride and were not to attribute to themselves the good things they received. In chapter nine, he taught that God's choice of them was not based on their righteousness. To demonstrate the point, Moses reminded them in detail of the golden calf sin just after the revelations at Sinai, followed by reminders of a series of occasions when their faith failed them on their desert wanderings, and then the disobedience of refusing to go out of Kadesh Barnea. After Moses spent forty days and nights in fasting and prayer to seek forgiveness for the sins of the people in the golden calf incident,

God wrote the Ten Commandments on another set of tablets and sent Moses on his way to lead the people to the land again."

"Good," Hal said.

I continued. "In the last half of the chapter, Moses returned to God's requirements and the people's obligation. They are to love him, serve him, fear him, walk in all his ways, and observe his commands and decrees. God owns the highest heavens, the earth, and everything in it. Despite his sovereignty over the cosmos, he chose them for special favor. They were to circumcise their hearts. He is an impartial God who defends the powerless, and they were to do the same. He has demonstrated his power and worthiness for this devotion by his performance of great and awesome wonders done before their eyes."

"Do you understand circumcision?" Hal asked. "What do you think he means by circumcising the heart?"

When I struggled with the answer, Hal helped me out.

"Begin with the history," he said. "Circumcision appears first in Genesis fifteen, where God instructed Abraham that all males in his household who were eight days or older were to be circumcised. The circumcision served as an outward sign of the covenant between God and Abraham and his descendants. God promised to make Abraham the father of many nations and kings, to be his God and the God of his descendants, and to give them the whole land of Canaan as an everlasting possession. Abraham and his descendants were to keep the covenant, walking before God blamelessly.

"The covenant was often forgotten. Exodus chapter four says Moses' wife, Zipporah, had to intercede to perform the circumcision of one of their two sons—which Moses had apparently forgotten—to rescue Moses from God's wrath. And after crossing the Jordan, Joshua had the whole nation circumcised at Gilgal. The children born during the desert wanderings had not been circumcised."

"It must have another meaning," I said. "Like a metaphor."

"Yes, and not just with respect to the heart. In Exodus, chapter six, Moses used uncircumcision as a metaphor for imperfection, when he described himself as a man of uncircumcised lips."

He turned to it. "It's translated as 'faltering' lips in the NIV translation. Uncircumcision is used in Jeremiah six as a spiritual metaphor to refer to ears—'their ears are closed' in the NIV. But he referred to ears that cannot or will not hear the word of the Lord that Jeremiah is proclaiming."

"There are a lot of uncircumcised ears around these days."

Hal nodded his agreement. "Acts fifteen tells us the early church struggled with the issue of whether salvation required converts to follow the Jewish law, especially circumcision. Following Paul and Barnabas's investigative journey among the Gentile churches, the Council of Jerusalem—including Peter, Paul, Barnabas, and James—decided that circumcision and other particulars of the Mosaic Law were not required of Gentiles."

He turned his Bible to the Acts 15 passage: "'It seemed good to the Holy Spirit and to us not to burden you with anything beyond the following requirements: You are to abstain from food sacrificed to idols, from blood, from the meat of strangled animals and from sexual immorality.' That's what the council wrote to the Gentile believers."

"So circumcision of the body wasn't required for Christians."

"No," Hal said. "But circumcision for Jews is an outward sign of commitment to God, of being part of his people. 'Circumcision of the heart,' on the other hand, is a scriptural phrase that appears for the first time in this passage. We'll encounter it again in Deuteronomy, chapter thirty. The metaphor is clear: The heart represents the inner person, the reality of who people are rather than how they make themselves appear. Circumcising the heart means putting the commitment to God inside, in the reality of your thoughts and emotions and will, rather than in your outward appearance. Moses used it here to make the point he made throughout Deuteronomy: Following God is a matter involving the whole person—the heart, soul, and strength. Obedience to God's law is the result, the manifestation, of that love of and commitment to God. Jeremiah uses the metaphor in chapters four and nine: God will punish those who are circumcised only in the flesh—they are really uncircumcised unless they are circumcised in their hearts. Later he teaches that God himself will circumcise the hearts of his people. The New Testament picks up on this theme, especially in Paul's letters: Only inward circumcision counts."

"It's the first time I really understood what circumcising the heart means," I said.

"Now go back and look at the passage as a whole. It's practically a hymn, and much of it is echoed over and over in Scripture. Repetition is one of the most effective methods of teaching, and Moses repeats teachings here that get repeated—repeatedly—later. Verse twelve teaches that they are to 'fear God.' Scripture—Psalm one-eleven and Proverbs nine, for example—says this fear of God is the beginning of wisdom and Proverbs one says fear of God is the beginning of knowledge.

"Then it says they are to 'walk in all his ways.' That instruction is repeated many times in Deuteronomy alone. Then it says that they are to love the Lord with all their heart and soul. That's an abbreviated paraphrase of the first and greatest commandment, from the Shema in chapter six, also repeated over and over in Deuteronomy.

"Next it tells them to observe the Lord's commands and decrees. That command is repeated perhaps a dozen times in Deuteronomy.

"And it tells them that the laws and decrees are given to them 'for your own good.' This is 'The Manufacturer's Handbook' message— the laws are intended for their good, to enable them to live well and right, happily and successfully, in harmony with their creator and his creation.

"All of that is packed into two verses. Moses goes on to remind them that God owns 'the heavens, even the highest heavens, the earth and everything in it.' Some may have thought that the Lord was a tribal god—everyone has their own god, so who is to say that mine is better than yours? This kind of relativism fills the thinking of modern people and was a problem even then. But God is not relative and not tribal. He is the sovereign over all.

"Moses then reminded them that in the face of God's majesty and power over all things in heaven and in earth, he has chosen them for special favor and blessing. The instruction to circumcise their hearts follows from this. Their gratitude and inner commitment is called for within these circumstances. God is not partial and is not bribed—not even by legalisms such as circumcising the flesh but not the heart."

Hal paused and drained what was left of the cappuccino. Then he went on. "Moses had already given them a repetition of the first and greatest commandment. Now he comes to the second: loving one's neighbor. God loves the 'alien,' that is, the stranger—the person who is not part of your nation, community, or group. Therefore you, too, are to love the alien. How dare you reject what God loves? And as a practical illustration, Moses reminds them that they were aliens in Egypt, so they know what it's like to be aliens. The theme is the 'golden rule' that Jesus articulates in Matthew seven: 'So in everything, do to others what you would have them do to you, for this sums up the Law and the Prophets.' As we go through Deuteronomy, we'll come back to the theme of loving and caring for aliens, over and over." He rose and picked up our empty cups. I followed him into the kitchen.

"What about the phrase 'He is your praise' in verse twenty-one?" I asked. "I never understood exactly what that meant either."

"It could mean either of two things," Hal replied, rinsing the cups in the sink. "It may mean God is the object of their praise, or it may mean that anything others may praise them for is God's work, not theirs. Both fit the context and are theologically correct. The phrase is tied to what follows—the repetition of reminders that God performed 'great and awesome wonders' before them and enlarged them as a people, from the seventy who went down to Egypt in the time of Jacob to being 'as numerous as the stars in the sky.' Like other phrases in the Bible, when you see the depth of the picture, you understand that there are layers of meaning in them. What they were praised for was only from God—it wasn't their doing—and their proper response was to forward the praise to God. It's like the image in Revelation, where the twenty-four elders in heaven lay their crowns before the throne. The crowns are the symbols or rewards for their righteousness, but the righteous lay their righteousness before God in recognition of the fact that he alone is worthy of praise and is the source of all righteousness."

"This is a great passage," I said.

"This passage—verses eleven to twenty-two of chapter ten—is one where the whole message is summarized, condensed into a few verses. Like the Shema, it would be a great passage to memorize."

The evening was over. I went back to the study to pick up my Bible. Then I left Hal among his bookshelves filled with learning of the world about that which was not of the world. My own bookshelves were full of the same kind of learning, though not as full as Hal's. But in Hal I could see the ability to see through the volumes of human writing, thought, theories, and philosophies, to keep the spiritual vision; to remain grounded in the eternal truths and the Eternal Truth; to discern what was of value and discard what was not, and, through it all, to remain a child before his God. He was, I thought, a better book than any in his library.

CHAPTER ELEVEN

When Hal and I met again to discuss chapter eleven, the autumn spectacle of reds, oranges, and yellows painting the hills and valleys with the rich warmth of the foliage had passed. The world had turned brown, gray, and cold, and soon would turn white. A certain foreboding was in the air, held at bay by the anticipation of the holidays. Pumpkins still sat on doorsteps, but turkeys held center stage. And in the department stores, red and green were designed to accelerate the shopper's thought to the spending orgy that would begin as soon as the last forkful of squash and stuffing left the Thanksgiving table.

The year had a repetitive pattern. The enthusiastic pews from the Sunday after Labor Day in church were thinner now, the hymns and praise music a little weaker. It had all happened before, and it would happen next year and the year after and the year after that.

"Patterns," Hal said. "Think in patterns."

We reflected together on how the world is put together in patterns. Mathematics is patterns expressed in numbers. Music—good music—is patterns that are harmonic; chords composed of notes that go together to make a pleasing sound; melodic, structured, progressive patterns of composition that come together to make up the particular genre. Chorus and verse, movements, keys, the forms of a sonata or symphony, a fugue, a cantata, an opera or operetta. Art is similarly composed of patterns of form, shape, color, and style. Biology, the stuff of life itself, has patterns large and small, from the double helix of the DNA molecules that code life's building blocks to macro systems of biological functions. The world around us is a mélange of the same patterns of sound, shape, color, style, and organization.

"Most people miss the patterns in Scripture, and in missing it, miss both the beauty and something of the message," Hal said. "Let's look at some patterns in chapter eleven. Read with me." Hal read verse one: "Love the LORD your God and keep his requirements, his decrees, his laws, and his commands always."

He paused and nodded at me to continue:

> Remember today that your children were not the ones who saw and experienced the discipline of the LORD your God: his majesty, his mighty hand, his outstretched arm; the signs he performed and the things he did in the heart of Egypt, both to Pharaoh king of Egypt and to his whole country; what he did to the Egyptian army, to its horses and chariots, how he overwhelmed them with the waters of the Red Sea as they were pursuing you, and how the LORD brought lasting ruin on them. It was not your children who saw what he did for you in the desert until you arrived at this place, and what he did to Dathan and Abiram, sons of Eliab the Reubenite, when the earth opened its mouth right in the middle of all Israel and swallowed them up with their households, their tents and every living thing that belonged to them. But it was your own eyes that saw all these great things the LORD has done.
>
> —Deut. 11:2–7

He held up his hand to stop me. He picked up with verse eight: "Observe therefore all the commands I am giving you today."

Then he paused again and let me continue through verse twelve:

> . . . so that you may have the strength to go in and take over the land that you are crossing the Jordan to possess, and so that you may live long in the land that the LORD swore to your forefathers to give to them and their descendants, a land flowing with milk and honey.
>
> The land you are entering to take over is not like the land of Egypt, from which you have come, where you planted your seed and irrigated it by foot as in a vegetable garden. But the land you are crossing the Jordan to take possession of is a land of mountains and valleys that drinks rain from heaven. It is a land the LORD your God cares for; the eyes of

the LORD your God are continually on it from the beginning
of the year to its end.

—Deut. 11:8–12

"Do you see the pattern, Chris? Command and consequence, command and consequence. The verse I read is a command. The verses
you are reading are the consequences of obeying or disobeying the
command. It's not random language, but patterned, intentional, and
rhythmic, a teaching driven home by repetition with variation. Let's
keep going."

He read on in verse thirteen: "So if you faithfully obey the commands
I am giving you today—to love the LORD your God and to serve him
with all your heart and with all your soul . . ."

Seeing the pattern, I picked up in verses fourteen and fifteen:
". . . then I will send rain on your land in its season, both autumn and
spring rains, so that you may gather in your grain, new wine and oil. I
will provide grass in the fields for your cattle, and you will eat and be
satisfied."

Hal again: "Be careful, or you will be enticed to turn away and worship other gods and bow down to them."

And I read verse seventeen: "Then the LORD's anger will burn against
you, and he will shut the heavens so that it will not rain and the ground
will yield no produce, and you will soon perish from the good land the
LORD is giving you."

Then Hal read verses eighteen through twenty: "Fix these words of
mine in your hearts and minds; tie them as symbols on your hands
and bind them on your foreheads. Teach them to your children, talking about them when you sit at home and when you walk along the
road, when you lie down and when you get up. Write them on the
doorframes of your houses and on your gates . . ."

And I continued with twenty-one: ". . . so that your days and the
days of your children may be many in the land that the LORD swore to
give your forefathers, as many as the days that the heavens are above
the earth."

Then Hal: "If you carefully observe all these commands I am giving you to follow—to love the LORD your God, to walk in all his ways and to hold fast to him . . ."

And I finished with verses twenty-three through twenty-five: ". . . then the LORD will drive out all these nations before you, and you will dispossess nations larger and stronger than you. Every place where you set your foot will be yours: Your territory will extend from the desert to Lebanon, and from the Euphrates River to the western sea. No man will be able to stand against you. The LORD your God, as he promised you, will put the terror and fear of you on the whole land, wherever you go."

"Do you see?" Hal asked. "Act is followed by consequence, act by consequence, again and again, like waves rolling in to an eternal shore."

"Now as then," I said, "the waves still roll."

"Yes," Hal said. "And the other patterns are still the same too. Numbers, colors, music. The universe, like the teaching of its Creator, has structure. Once you understand it . . ."

He left the thought unfinished and turned to another pattern.

"How many repetitions did we do?" he asked.

I counted quickly. "Six."

"Look at the first and last," he said. "Do you see any similarity?"

I studied verses one through seven, and twenty-two through twenty-five. "They both tell about God's acts toward the enemies of his people, first against Egypt and the desert rebels, which is past, then against the nations in the land they are entering, which is future."

"Just so," Hal said. "Now look at the second and fifth set of commands and consequences."

I reviewed verses eight through twelve and eighteen through twenty-one. "They both promise long life in the land."

"Yes," he said. "Now look at the middle two."

I reread verses thirteen through seventeen. "They promise rain or lack of rain, with the result of fruitfulness or unfruitfulness of the land, depending on obedience or disobedience."

"Do you remember when we talked about chiasms at the beginning of our study?" he asked.

I remembered the word, but not the meaning.

"It's a pattern of thought," Hal reminded me. "You begin with a thought, progress to another, then a central thought, then reverse direction and come back to the original. Deuteronomy is full of chiastic patterns, and this is a good example. The consequences of obedience or disobedience are given in this pattern, which would have been familiar to the people:

- God's acts on their enemies in the past
- Long life in the land
- The blessing of rain for obedience
- The curse of lack of rain for disobedience
- Long life in the land
- God's acts on their enemies in the future

"Scholars call this pattern A-B-C-C-B-A."

"Pattern laid upon pattern," I said, gaining a new respect for the measured intentionality of the Scripture.

"And there's more," Hal said. "Did you notice the repetition, almost verbatim, of the introductory part of the Shema here in chapter eleven, as we had first seen it in chapter six?"

I reread verses eighteen through twenty aloud: "Fix these words of mine in your hearts and minds; tie them as symbols on your hands and bind them on your foreheads. Teach them to your children, talking about them when you sit at home and when you walk along the road, when you lie down and when you get up. Write them on the doorframes of your houses and on your gates."

"This too," Hal said, "is a pattern, not an accident. The teachings that lie between the Shema, the 'Hear, O Israel,' of chapter six and the Shema of chapter eleven, are some of the great scriptural truths that God has to teach Israel and to teach all people in all times. The principles of these last several chapters begin and end, in chapters six and eleven, with the same message: Teach them to your children, bind them on your hands and forehead, and write them on the doorframes of your houses and on your gates. This is a pattern, a literary frame to set around the general principles that are taught in between. The

Shema verses set off and surround the great scriptural truths that God has been teaching Israel."

The conversation paused as I reflected on the three layers of patterns that were embedded in chapter eleven.

"How do you like your cider?" Hal asked, interrupting my thoughts. "I mean, hot or cold. I have some in the fridge and some I've been simmering on the stove."

We made our way to the kitchen. The evening was chilly, and I opted for the hot cider, fragrant with the simmering spices Hal had added. The sweet aroma filled the kitchen. Hal pulled out a box of fresh doughnuts to go with the cider. Fall in New England!

Between sips of cider and bites of doughnut, I asked Hal, "Do you think we should take the command to bind the law on our hands and foreheads and write it on the doorframes of our houses and city gates a little more literally than we do?"

Answering indirectly, Hal said, "Some people get very exercised about posting the Ten Commandments or other Jewish or Christian symbols in public places like schoolrooms or courthouses. To do so would be very much in keeping with what Moses taught in Deuteronomy, but that raises another set of issues we need to get into at some point about the separation of church and state in the American Constitution and how we should understand the application of these commands to a modern secular society.

"I do observe, however," he added wryly, after sipping the cider from his mug and coming back to my question, "that the people who advocate public display of these religious words or symbols do not, so far as I am aware, comply with the Mosaic law in displaying them privately. I have never seen the Ten Commandments, or any other parts of the law, written on the doorframes of anyone's home. And, except for Orthodox Jews, I have never seen anyone bind them on their foreheads or hands. Even the Orthodox Jews don't usually wear them all the time, just symbolically during prayer. Some people seem to be more interested in imposing the law on others than on complying with this part of God's law themselves."

"Don't you think they're important, though, to our public life?" I asked. "I mean, they're symbols of what guides us, especially something like the Ten Commandments. And they're part of our heritage. We can't pretend that we didn't come from where we came from or don't believe what we believe just because a few people question it."

"You're the lawyer," Hal said. "And we should talk about these things more. But I do think we take too lightly—especially we Protestants—the value of symbols, things you can see, hear, touch, and smell in keeping us close to God. We're reminded of truth and goodness by those objects or words that represent them. We do it with music, of course, but we limit ourselves too much. Most of our music is either contemporary praise music or older hymns. There's nothing wrong with either one; they can be inspiring and worshipful. But much of the great music of history was written to glorify God, yet we confine ourselves to a couple of contemporary time periods."

"So what about writing the law on your house or gates?" I asked. "Or binding it on your forehead or on your hands? These are symbols that God commands."

"Writing God's word on your house would be a wonderful idea," Hal said. "I don't know why people don't do it. As for the city gates, that was appropriate at the time, but you couldn't do it now. The question is, 'What could we do to more effectively symbolize and communicate God's ways and his word?' We can't write it on the city gates, but we have the freedom of speech to present it in other ways. I think the church has overlooked the best means of broad-based public communications. We have a lot of Christian broadcasting, but most of it is only watched or listened to by Christians. The same for Christian literature and music. These are good things because they do strengthen the faithful, much as the symbols in the Shema would have done in a society where everyone was, or should have been, a believer. But we don't use the means of public communication very successfully as outreach. It all costs money, of course, and there's another issue. The church is too fragmented, and its funds are used too much for its own purposes—bricks and mortars, salaries, etc.—to get the funds together that would be necessary to do outreach well. People should be thinking about billboards, and ads in the print media and on television and radio. We could spend a lot of time talking about this."

"What about the phylacteries or tefillin that Jews bind on their hands and foreheads?" I asked, as we moved back to the study. "What's our equivalent of that?"

"These are very personal reminders," Hal said as he sank into his old red chair, "like a cross pendant, worn for the right reason. People wear crosses for a lot of reasons that have nothing to do with faith, but I always appreciate it when I see someone wearing a cross and I know it's being worn for the right reason. It's an outward sign, of course, like circumcision, and outward signs don't count for much if they have no inward effect. But we are such fickle creatures; we need these reminders of who we really are and what's really important."

I suggested to Hal that Scripture memorization served the purpose even better than wearing symbols because then God's word did get imprinted in the mind. "If you know the Scriptures by heart, it's easier to call them up when their teaching is needed for some situation you're facing."

Hal agreed. "Especially for children," he said. "They memorize and retain things much more easily than adults do. Most people who learned Scripture when they were young still know much of it, especially familiar passages that have had much repetition. But try to learn it at a much older age, and keep it in your head for any length of time." He shook his head.

We reopened our Bibles and moved on to the last few verses of the chapter:

> See, I am setting before you today a blessing and a curse—
> the blessing if you obey the commands of the LORD your
> God that I am giving you today; the curse if you disobey
> the commands of the LORD your God and turn from the
> way that I command you today by following other gods,
> which you have not known. When the LORD your God
> has brought you into the land you are entering to possess,
> you are to proclaim on Mount Gerizim the blessings, and
> on Mount Ebal the curses. As you know, these mountains
> are across the Jordan, west of the road, toward the setting
> sun, near the great trees of Moreh, in the territory of those
> Canaanites living in the Arabah in the vicinity of Gilgal. You

are about to cross the Jordan to enter and take possession of the land the LORD your God is giving you. When you have taken it over and are living there, be sure that you obey all the decrees and laws I am setting before you today.

—Deut. 11:26–32

"You wouldn't know this yet," Hal said, "because we haven't gotten to the other end of the book, but these verses about the blessings and the curses being proclaimed on Mount Gerizim and Mount Ebal are also part of a pattern, just like repeating the Shema here frames the general principles of the law we've been studying in chapters six through eleven."

"How so?"

"In chapters twelve through twenty-six, we'll be studying the specific details of the law. Chapter twenty-seven, which follows the law, sets out in more detail the ceremony of blessings and curses on these mountains. Between the reference to pronouncing the blessings and curses in chapter eleven and the details of the ceremony in chapter twenty-seven is the law. The specific rules of the core of Deuteronomy are both preceded and followed by the blessings and curses. The people are reminded on both ends that their response has consequences."

As we closed our Bibles, Hal told me we were at a transition point in our study of Deuteronomy. These chapters—five through eleven, the "general stipulations"—contain guiding principles like the Ten Commandments, the Shema, election, covenant, the consequences of faithfulness or unfaithfulness to God, the lack of human merit, and the failure of human beings to live in conformity to God's instructions. They are teaching and preaching, a long sermon on human nature, and on God's justice and mercy.

"The principles that we have studied so far," Hal said, "are familiar to most Christians who are biblically literate. What may surprise them is that they are all in the Old Testament. It shouldn't surprise them because Jesus said he came to fulfill the law and that his teachings summed up the law and the prophets."

"So what lies ahead, Hal?"

"Now we go into the details. Not just loving God and teaching children to do so, but a lot of very specific rules and cases of how this nation is to be governed. Christians bog down in the details, partly because they are—well, detailed. People will content themselves with generalities when they can get away with it. It's a lot easier to say we should love our neighbors, and think we do, than to actually do anything about it."

"And perhaps even easier," I added, "to say we love God, and think we do, than to do anything about it." Hal nodded and rose to walk me to the door. He reminded me to reclaim my jacket from his closet.

"So we are going to begin studying the details of the law," I said at the door. "But Christians aren't obligated to follow the Jewish law."

"A lot of the laws are laws that even Orthodox Jews acknowledge are no longer applicable since they simply can't be performed today. There are laws that were pertinent to the Israelite society of Deuteronomy but not to later and different societies."

"So why bother with them? And why are they even part of the Bible?"

"Why, indeed?" Hal echoed with a smile.

Hal asked me to think on these matters before we met again. Why should we study the law? And what application, if any, did it have to the modern Christian? We would spend the next fourteen sessions on the law. It was almost half of Deuteronomy.

Why bother?

INTERLUDE

You could feel the snow coming all day, with the gathering and lowering gray. Anna had invited Hal for dinner, and the large soft flakes began falling as we were finishing up. Willy and Lily spotted them first, seeing the flakes drifting through the sphere of luminescence thrown around our driveway by the outside light. They could hardly contain their excitement.

"Come on," Hal said, pushing back his chair and motioning to them. "Let's go for a walk. Maybe we can drag your mom and dad along."

Jackets and boots were hastily donned, and we set off down the driveway and along the road. The children dashed around us, sticking out their tongues to catch flakes and trying to scrape together enough of the thin cover gathering on the ground to make a snowball.

"What is law, Chris?" Hal asked as we ambled along.

"What do you mean?" I asked. "Law is a pretty general term. Can you be more specific?"

"No," Hal said. "I meant to be general. What do we mean when we use the term *law*?"

"Law," Anna offered, "is a job that keeps your husband away from home a lot more hours than he ought to be."

"Law is a jealous mistress," I said. "At least that's what they used to say in law school. I suppose a dictionary definition would be more like this: 'Rules that can be enforced by the government—if they're not obeyed.' Jail and fines for criminal laws, court orders enforceable by sheriffs or marshals for civil laws."

"Are there different types of law?" Hal asked.

"Sure," I replied. "Constitutional law is at the top. The United States Constitution is the 'supreme law of the land,' as they say. And every state has its own constitution, which is the supreme law in that state, as long as it doesn't contradict the federal constitution. Then there are the statutes, passed by Congress on the federal level, and state legislatures for each state. And ordinances passed by municipal governments, towns, and cities. And rules and regulations, adopted by administrative agencies to interpret and enforce the statutes they are in charge of administering."

"What's the difference between a rule and a regulation?" Hal asked.

"None, really," I said. "Two different words for the same thing. Sometimes we use *rule* more generically to refer to some principle of law, whatever the source, but administrative rules and regulations are the same thing."

"What about the courts?" Hal asked. "Do they make law?"

"Yes," I said, "for the 'common law.' Those are the rules that have evolved historically through court decisions to deal with rights or conflicts that aren't covered by constitutions or statutes. Most common-law principles are well established, but the common-law rules do change from time to time. Negligence law, for example, has been around a long time and hasn't changed much as far as the courts go, but the legislatures have passed statutes to tinker with it to some degree. On the other hand, the right of privacy is a common-law concept that has emerged mostly through court decisions over the last half-century or so."

"I sense that these questions have something to do with Deuteronomy," Anna said.

Before Hal could respond, Willy lobbed a small, soft snowball toward him.

"Willy!" Anna shouted. "You know better."

But Hal smiled and caught it with his hand. He repacked what was left of it and chucked it back toward Willy, who ran off ahead of us, laughing.

"This will get worse before it gets better," I said.

"The weather or his behavior?" Anna replied.

"His behavior is fine," Hal said. "He's just having fun. And so am I. And, yes, the questions have to do with Deuteronomy."

"How so?" I asked.

"Well, the reason I brought it up is that we are about to plunge into fifteen chapters of what, by anyone's definition, is 'law.' Chapters twelve through twenty-six are pure law chapters: statutes, ordinances, rules, and regulations about how God's people are to live. They're the center of the book and a large part of its content. You need to think about why you're studying these laws to make doing so meaningful."

"Help me out," I said. "I know it's important. If God put it in the Bible, it's worth studying. But why?"

"First," Hal said, "understand that the Bible uses a lot of terms for 'law,' just like we do. You spoke of constitutions, statutes, ordinances, rules, regulations, and court decisions. Deuteronomy uses a lot of different terms too, like laws, decrees, stipulations, commands or commandments, teachings, and requirements. In your legal terminology, most of the terms that are part of our law have a distinct meaning, usually referring to the source of the law: constitutions adopted by the whole people, statutes passed by a legislature, ordinances adopted by a municipality, regulations of administrative agencies, or courts' decisions, orders, or decrees. In Deuteronomy, the terms are not distinct. It isn't clear that Moses means something different by the different terms he uses. They are all part of the terms for talking about the whole thing. And here is a most important distinction: Your different types of law have different sources of authority—legislatures, courts, and so forth. But all law in Deuteronomy—and the rest of the Bible for that matter—has only one source."

"God?" Anna asked.

"God," Hal confirmed. "There are distinctions, of course. The Ten Commandments stand alone as being written by the hand of God on the mountain. Other laws, both the general principles we've been looking at in the last few chapters, and the very specific and detailed laws we'll be looking at in the next ones, came through Moses. But Moses was clear. He did not make these up—God gave them to him. He was the mediator who transmitted God's words to the people. This was not a man making up rules he thought God would approve of. This was God giving his chosen people rules through his chosen leader, Moses. If you don't understand that, you can't understand the text. And if you don't believe it, this all has no more meaning than studying some other ancient historical document from Egypt or Babylon to find out what people thought then. Purely historical interest."

"So when the New Testament refers to the 'law,'" I asked, "what does it mean? The whole thing?"

"There are a lot of references to law in the New Testament," Hal said. "They don't always mean the same thing. Sometimes it means the whole Old Testament, sometimes part of it, and sometimes just the Torah—the first five books. Sometimes it refers to the specific laws given by Moses. It can also be used to refer to all of God's will or revelation, as in 'the law of God,' or 'the law of Christ.'"

"How can we tell the difference?" Anna asked.

"Only by context," Hal answered.

Willy and Lily were back and dragging us off to the side of the road to stand under small trees they could shake and make the gathering snow fall down on our heads. In the distance I could hear a snowplow scraping along a neighboring street.

The snow was accumulating rapidly, and we turned back toward home. Our tracks were barely visible under the streetlights, the newer snow obscuring them quickly.

"If this is all God's word, Hal—his direct commands—then why shouldn't we follow all the Old Testament law now?" I asked.

"The Old Testament law was given to a particular people for a particular time. Jews count 613 laws in the Old Testament and acknowledge that only a little over two hundred can be followed today. It's pretty obvious that it isn't practical or even possible to do a lot of things, like gathering all of God's people in Jerusalem for certain festivals, sacrificing bulls and goats, or gathering around an ark that doesn't exist anymore."

"Then why follow any of it?" Anna asked. "Is there anything there that we really need to do?"

Hal replied, "Most people make a distinction between the moral, civil, and ceremonial laws. Jesus has set the ceremonial law aside. His sacrifice made the Old Testament sacrifices obsolete. It was once for all, not a sacrifice to be repeated again and again, year after year. The civil law was for the government of a people whose sovereign was God himself. We don't have that anymore, and Israel itself couldn't sustain that kind of obedience. There are a lot of good lessons in the civil law on how a society should be governed, and we can learn a lot from it. Some think it contains the essential components and teachings of Western democracy. But the moral law has ongoing force, just as it always did."

"Why the moral law?" I asked. "Why does it have any more validity today than the ceremonial or civil law?"

"First, the moral law is repeated almost in its entirety in the New Testament. You can't read the Gospels or the letters and think it doesn't apply anymore. Capital punishment may not be the necessary or appropriate punishment for adultery—that's a matter of civil law. But adultery is still wrong—that's a teaching of the moral law.

"Second, nothing about the moral law has changed. These are not rules that are unique to a particular time, place, people, or circumstance. The Ten Commandments are an overview of the moral law. The principles of loving God and loving your neighbor summarize the moral law. It's no different today than it was three thousand years ago."

We were back in the driveway. The snow was letting up already, but a couple of inches had accumulated on Hal's car. He pushed it off with a gloved hand as we talked. Willy and Lily were rolling on the lawn, making snow angels by lying on their backs and moving their arms up and down.

"Hal," Anna said, "if the moral law is all that really counts, and that's repeated in the New Testament, then why is it important to study these laws that you and Chris are going to study in the next part of Deuteronomy?"

"Think of it this way. We have only a certain amount of revelation from God. It's contained in this book we call the Bible. Deuteronomy reveals God's plans for that people and that time. And God doesn't change. Even if there are parts of it that don't apply to us directly, the principles are timeless. Read the law to read the mind of God."

I knew something of what lay ahead in my study, having read Deuteronomy through before Hal and I had started. I had been somewhat dreading getting into it, wondering if I could sustain my interest. Hal had piqued my curiosity and commitment to going forward.

The snow had stopped. Hal's taillights disappeared into the distance.

"What's the weather tomorrow?" I asked Anna as she herded Willy and Lily into the house.

"Rain," she said. "Then warm and sunny again."

CHAPTER TWELVE

Anna's weather forecast had been correct. The rain melted most of the snow, and what was left succumbed to the unseasonably warm sunshine that followed. Encouraged by our walk with Hal, I plunged into chapter twelve.

> These are the decrees and laws you must be careful to follow in the land that the LORD, the God of your fathers, has given you to possess—as long as you live in the land.

> Destroy completely all the places on the high mountains and on the hills and under every spreading tree where the nations you are dispossessing worship their gods. Break down their altars, smash their sacred stones and burn their Asherah poles in the fire; cut down the idols of their gods and wipe out their names from those places.

> You must not worship the LORD your God in their way. But you are to seek the place the LORD your God will choose from among all your tribes to put his Name there for his dwelling. To that place you must go; there bring your burnt offerings and sacrifices, your tithes and special gifts, what you have vowed to give and your freewill offerings, and the firstborn of your herds and flocks. There, in the presence of the LORD your God, you and your families shall eat and shall rejoice in everything you have put your hand to, because the LORD your God has blessed you.

> You are not to do as we do here today, everyone as he sees fit, since you have not yet reached the resting place and the inheritance the LORD your God is giving you. But you will cross the Jordan and settle in the land the LORD your God

is giving you as an inheritance, and he will give you rest from all your enemies around you so that you will live in safety. Then to the place the LORD your God will choose as a dwelling for his Name—there you are to bring everything I command you: your burnt offerings and sacrifices, your tithes and special gifts, and all the choice possessions you have vowed to the LORD. And there rejoice before the LORD your God, you, your sons and daughters, your menservants and maidservants, and the Levites from your towns, who have no allotment or inheritance of their own. Be careful not to sacrifice your burnt offerings anywhere you please. Offer them only at the place the LORD will choose in one of your tribes, and there observe everything I command you.

Nevertheless, you may slaughter your animals in any of your towns and eat as much of the meat as you want, as if it were gazelle or deer, according to the blessing the LORD your God gives you. Both the ceremonially unclean and the clean may eat it. But you must not eat the blood; pour it out on the ground like water. You must not eat in your own towns the tithe of your grain and new wine and oil, or the firstborn of your herds and flocks, or whatever you have vowed to give, or your freewill offerings or special gifts. Instead, you are to eat them in the presence of the LORD your God at the place the LORD your God will choose—you, your sons and daughters, your menservants and maidservants, and the Levites from your towns—and you are to rejoice before the LORD your God in everything you put your hand to. Be careful not to neglect the Levites as long as you live in your land.

When the LORD your God has enlarged your territory as he promised you, and you crave meat and say, "I would like some meat," then you may eat as much of it as you want. If the place where the LORD your God chooses to put his Name is too far away from you, you may slaughter animals from the herds and flocks the LORD has given you, as I have commanded you, and in your own towns you may eat as much of them as you want. Eat them as you would gazelle or deer. Both the ceremonially unclean and the clean may eat. But be sure you do not eat the blood, because the blood is the life, and you must not eat the life with the meat. You must not eat the blood; pour it out on the ground like water. Do not eat it, so that it may go well with you and your children after you, because you will be doing what is right in the eyes of the LORD.

But take your consecrated things and whatever you have vowed to give, and go to the place the LORD will choose. Present your burnt offerings on the altar of the LORD your God, both the meat and the blood. The blood of your sacrifices must be poured beside the altar of the LORD your God, but you may eat the meat. Be careful to obey all these regulations I am giving you, so that it may always go well with you and your children after you, because you will be doing what is good and right in the eyes of the LORD your God.

The LORD your God will cut off before you the nations you are about to invade and dispossess. But when you have driven them out and settled in their land, and after they have been destroyed before you, be careful not to be ensnared by inquiring about their gods, saying, "How do these nations serve their gods? We will do the same." You must not worship the LORD your God in their way, because in worshiping their gods, they do all kinds of detestable things the LORD hates. They even burn their sons and daughters in the fire as sacrifices to their gods.

See that you do all I command you; do not add to it or take away from it.

—Deut 12:1–32

I read in my commentaries that many Old Testament scholars see chapter twelve—in its seeming direction for the centralization of worship at "the place the Lord your God will choose as a dwelling for his Name"—as key to understanding the origin and purpose of Deuteronomy. Although Jerusalem is nowhere mentioned in

Deuteronomy and did not become an Israelite city until the time of David hundreds of years later, it was the eventual location of the temple built by Solomon in 960 B.C., where God chose to place his name, as told in the books of Kings and Chronicles.

By the time of King Josiah, who reigned over Judah from 631 to 609 B.C., there was a long history of idolatrous practices in the temple, going back to the time of Solomon himself. In 2 Kings 22–23, the story is told of the discovery of "the Book of the Law" in the temple. When the book was brought to young King Josiah, he tore his robes—a sign of great emotion and distress. He seemed to recognize the gravity of the situation, so he sought the counsel of the prophetess Huldah, and she confirmed the Lord's anger over the great disobedience in worshipping other gods; she warned of his intent to bring disaster on Jerusalem and its people. Because Josiah had a responsive heart and humbled himself, however, he was spared the disaster—it was postponed.

Josiah then embarked on an aggressive program of cleansing the land. He called together the elders of Judah and Jerusalem, the people of Jerusalem, the priests and the prophets, and all the people of the city, "from the least to the greatest." He read to them the "Book of the Covenant," which had been found in the temple, and renewed the covenant with the Lord. Then he removed from the temple the articles made for the false gods and burned them, executed the pagan priests, and tore down the quarters of male shrine prostitutes and women who wove articles for the goddess Asherah. The cleansing expanded out from Jerusalem and through the land. High places, altars, idols, and false gods were destroyed. Priests serving other gods were slaughtered. Shrines to idols were desecrated and defiled. Then the greatest Passover since the time of the judges was celebrated in Jerusalem.

Scripture does not tell us exactly what the "Book of the Law," or "Book of the Covenant," discovered in the temple was. But the similarity of the account—along with Huldah's prophecy in relationship to it, and especially the actions of Josiah in cleansing the land of false religion in response to it—has led many to conclude that it was the book of Deuteronomy, either entirely or in part. Others speculate that it might have been the entire law, consisting of the five "books of Moses"—the first five books of the Bible. Scholars with a low view of

Scripture go on to speculate that the book was not really discovered but was written or created in the time of Josiah to justify his actions in destroying competing religious factions and centralizing religious— hence political—power in Jerusalem. Deuteronomy is thus perceived as a political document, using Moses as authority, or cover, to advance the agenda of this king and those who supported him.

Those who do not share this cynical view of Deuteronomy and Josiah's fervor for the Lord point out that it is unlikely that a document with such a specific political purpose would fail to identify Jerusalem spe- cifically as the place the Lord would choose to place his name. In that respect, Deuteronomy is more logically identified as what it presents itself to be—a document from Moses' time, when the centralization of Jewish religious and political authority in Jerusalem was hundreds of years in the future. Before Jerusalem, there were other central places to which the people came for worship: Shechem, Bethel, and Gilgal, for example. One thought is that the place the Lord would choose for his name was movable, and that each central shrine in turn served this purpose for its own time until the temple in Jerusalem was built. Another thought is that the real meaning of the text is not to focus on a particular place but on the sovereignty of God in his choice of where and how he was to be worshipped. God will choose, and his choice will not be a copy of pagan religion. Focusing on particular points of geography is a misplaced approach to understanding what God is up to in this chapter.

These were the thoughts I brought to my next session with Hal. He had suggested that we meet on a Saturday, during the day, and somewhere different this time. We rendezvoused in a parking lot in my town, and Hal invited me to ride with him. He drove to a quiet neighborhood on the outskirts and turned into a drive marked "Carmelite Convent." We wound down a drive through well-groomed lawns and shade trees to a small parking area with a few other cars. Despite the lateness of the year, it was a sunny day, with a soft warm breeze. A few lingering piles of snow where they had been pushed by shovel or plowed, but not quite melted, were a reminder of the early storm the week before. Hal led me down a flagstone path to a small garden with benches around the edge of a circular central area. A statue of the Madonna and Child stood on one side, flanked by beds of flowers that wouldn't bloom again until spring. We sat together quietly, absorbing the tranquility and beauty of the setting.

I had lost my thoughts about chapter twelve, King Josiah, and the rationale given by some for the writing of Deuteronomy. The soft sights and sounds and smells of late autumn drifted by my senses, and I felt a oneness with the place. My reverie was interrupted by a voice from behind, where the path led into the garden near our bench seat. It was surprisingly familiar.

"Hi," Julie said. "Am I interrupting?"

I was surprised to see her and even more surprised to find that she knew Hal. Julie had worked in my office, and we had been acquaintances for years. I knew her as a believing Christian, a middle-age woman who'd had her own spiritual journey and quietly and firmly reflected what often seemed the best in the outward demeanor and practice of God's people. But we had never really spent time together. Our mutual respect grew from an unstated knowledge of common values and commitments, something we just knew and didn't have to talk about. Hal wanted us to talk about it. He had planned our meeting, in this time and place, to bring out what we had not brought out in the years we had been colleagues.

"Do you know that saying, 'Tomorrow is the first day of the rest of my life?'" Julie asked. "It so fits the believer. Meeting Hal was the most important day of my life, the day I found the path to God. It was the beginning of the rest of my life."

She was actually Jewish, she told me, from a family who celebrated the Jewish holidays and traditions but had no real spiritual convictions. They did not instill the love of God in their children because they didn't really believe in him themselves. They were good people, moral in their behavior and good neighbors in worldly terms, but without spiritual foundation for who they were. Their morality and worldly goodness survived on the echoes and traditions of teachings they no longer believed.

As is common in such families, soon after getting out from under their roof in early adulthood, Julie drifted far from behaviors her parents would have condoned. She experimented with the wrong things and spent time with people who a bad influence. Eventually she found herself pregnant and alone. One day, while sitting on a park bench in the center of the city and contemplating the alternatives of suicide or abortion, a "big man with a Bible," as she put it, sat down beside her. That man was Hal.

"Hal was an angel sent by God," she said. "He told me that my life had value, that there was a God who cared about me and was ready to forgive me and guide me and watch over me, that no sin was too great to be forgiven and no life too insignificant to be of value to him. It sounds corny to people who have never been there, but it was like the psalm: He lifted me out of a slimy pit and set my feet on a rock—not him, of course, but God in him.

"Hal was pastoring a church in a nearby town at the time," she continued. "He never pressed me to go to it, and I never did. It was never about his church or his ministry. He just kept in touch with me every day and gave me the spiritual counseling I needed to get onto solid ground. I eventually found my way into a charismatic fellowship that met in the city where I was living. They brought me to a pregnancy care center that helped me with the pregnancy, the birth, and getting started as a mother. I eventually married Jack—we met in the church—and my baby had a wonderful father, even if he wasn't the real father." She paused. "I never knew who the real father was," she went on. "Today you would probably have genetic testing and sue people and all that sort of thing, but you know, none of the candidates were men I really wanted to be doing the fathering . . . so, here I am."

Hal insisted she tell the rest of the story—what happened between the charismatic fellowship and where she was today.

"I loved that little fellowship," she said. "They had the Holy Spirit in them. There was a fervor there that I haven't seen anywhere else. It was a wonderful place to start my pilgrimage in Christ. But eventually, the passion wore thin and began to seem superficial. The fellowship became intrusive, insisting that everything between us and the Lord was the church's business. We needed something more, some space to grow in our own way and something that connected us to the church in a larger sense. We needed some gray hair around.

"We attended a large evangelical church for a while, but that too seemed too unconnected to the larger tradition. The music was all contemporary, and contemporary is good to a point, but the church has been making music since it was a church, and we wanted to worship with—if I can put it that way—those who had gone before."

"The democracy of the dead," I said, quoting G.K. Chesterton's famous description of Christian tradition.

"Yes," she said. "And it was all music and a message, and the message was teaching doctrine, not salvation. There was prayer, of course, but it seemed superficial, curing parishioners with health problems, etc. The high praise, adoration, and gratitude for the majesty of the Creator weren't there. And nobody ever thought about confessing anything. Somehow the power of my original time with Hal and the early days in the fellowship were missing.

"So we tried an Episcopal church. The liturgy was good and comforting, and the pastor was, well, pastoral. But we eventually realized that most of the people in the pews were there for different reasons than we were. They had no real conviction about Christ and his saving power. Church was a social setting for some, a place to bring children for others who thought their kids should be exposed to church, even though they had no real commitment to it themselves. Others did have some real interest in the things of the Lord, but they needed to be in a more socially acceptable setting than evangelical or charismatic churches. They had an aversion to commitment to anything that would bring into question the priority they had given to the business or professional commitments of their lives. Still others saw the church as a place for social or political action, where God had no place, but the platform of the more liberal politicians or political parties would be faithfully parroted. They were always jumping on the cause of the hour, and that became the focus of their life in church."

"And where are you now?" I asked, embarrassed that, long as I had known her, I didn't know.

"All roads lead to Rome." She smiled wryly. "We became Catholic. It seemed like coming home, even though we'd never been there before. We've been in the Catholic Church for ten years now, and we're very happy. The liturgy has a grace and beauty that brings out all the right thoughts and emotions about our relationship to God. We can be under a teaching authority that brings the wisdom of the millennia. We don't have to be our own interpreters of the Bible, or subject to teachers who are too often their own interpreters. The Catholic understanding of the oral tradition is very similar to Jewish understandings. So, by the way, is the liturgy. It seems like we have finally become part of the church."

"The one holy, catholic, apostolic church," Hal said, loosely echoing the words of the Apostles' Creed. "By the way," he added, as if reading my thoughts, "the Apostles' Creed dates to before all the church splits, in the early centuries. And it's still followed today in virtually all churches. It's part of the Catechism of the Catholic Church, and it's still found in the back of hymnbooks used in some of the most fundamentalist Protestant churches. The word *catholic* in the creed means 'universal,' of course, not Roman or any other kind of Catholic with a capital 'C.' And that's just the point," he added. "Let's go inside."

Hal and Julie led me on the path from the garden into a small chapel. There, about two dozen women, most dressed in a modern habit with a light bonnet for a head covering and a pale blue dress, were kneeling in prayer. A handful of others sat here and there in the small chapel, heads bowed. We entered as quietly as we could. Hal led me to near the front where the prayers of the women would be audible.

I was caught up in the gentle current of prayer that flowed from their lips. One after another, with no self-consciousness and no sense of rite or ritual or rehearsal, they spoke softly to their God and mine. Some of their words were words of adoration for his majesty and glory and awesome acts in their lives and throughout history. Sometimes they were words of confession, individually and corporately, for themselves, their religious community, the church, and then the local community, the nation, and all humanity. They prayed as if they had been personally responsible for every wrong done to every victim, and they prayed for forgiveness for the wrongdoers, even as Moses had for the golden calf worshippers. And they gave thanks—thanks for every provision made for them, thanks for the good land in which they lived, thanks for the wells they had not dug and the trees they had not planted, thanks for the flowers and the sky and the stars and the oceans and the mountains and all the beauty of the land. And then they prayed for God's help for those who needed help; for the poor, the sick, the prisoners—even the prisoner who was justly imprisoned—for those suffering persecution around the world, and specifically for those in areas where the righteous were subject to persecution. They prayed for God's kingdom to come, on earth as it is in heaven. Sometimes they broke into scriptural prayer, speaking the words of the psalms, the gospels, the prophets, and the letters. Sometimes they broke into gentle song, their high voices lilting out the melody of a Latin chant.

After an hour, Hal touched my sleeve, and we rose and left. Julie stayed behind. "They'll pray for another half hour or so," he said. "Julie usually stays until the end." It was obvious he had been there many times before.

"Tell me that God is not present in that chapel," he said as we walked back to his car, retracing our steps through the garden. We were passing the Madonna. I took his point.

Our next stop was a little Orthodox chapel on a side street near downtown. There was a small Greek community in our town, and a few others from countries—Russians, Ukrainians, Serbs—where the principal national church is Orthodox. The church was dark inside but richly decorated with icons, figures of the Lord Jesus and the apostles, of Mary the Mother of God, and of the saints of the church.

"In the year 1054," Hal said as we sat quietly in a pew while a black-robed priest set candles for the liturgy that would take place the next day, "the Pope and the Orthodox Patriarch of Constantinople—I don't remember either of their names—excommunicated each other. There were some theological issues between the Eastern and Western churches, but it was mostly about power. The Pope thought Rome was the center of Christian civilization, the place where God had chosen to place his name, so to speak, for the Christian era. It followed that the Pope was the leader of the whole church, that is, all Christians everywhere. The Orthodox were unwilling to concede that power and primacy to Rome, so they went their own ways, each believing the other to be heretics. Today it seems more difficult for Rome and Orthodoxy to come together than for Rome and the various Protestant traditions. The Orthodox still emphasize the seven 'ecumenical councils' that defined

Christian doctrine for the ages in the early centuries. Theirs are 'the ancient paths,' as the prophet said. They're not bad paths to be on."

We moved on. Hal drove me past the various Protestant churches in the community. Time did not permit us to go inside each, but I didn't really need to. I had been in most of them, and most were much the same.

He took me by the Lutheran church, the home church of many families of German and Scandinavian heritage. Luther, a Catholic monk, had given birth to the Reformation, rebelling against abuses that had crept into the Catholicism of his time. "Sola gratia, sola fide, sola scriptura" was the Reformation cry, bringing Christianity back to the Bible. Salvation by grace alone, through faith alone, taught by Scripture alone. Tradition outside of Scripture was rejected. Yet much of Catholic belief not shared by most Protestants was and remains part of the Lutheran church: liturgy, the role of baptism, and the "true presence" of Christ in the elements of communion. Older Lutheran churches in Europe often are indistinguishable from their Catholic counterparts.

We then passed the Episcopal Church, a part of the worldwide Anglican Communion, the origin of which was the rupture with Rome, when the Pope refused to approve King Henry the Eighth's divorce and remarriage. Many of its practices and beliefs remain close to Catholicism, prompting the term "Anglo-Catholic" for those who are closest to Rome in their views. The Anglican Communion worldwide is a biblical and conservative church, but it is kept so by the African, Asian, and Latin bishops. In the United States and England itself, many bishops and large portions of the church have abandoned much biblical teaching.

Our next stops were at the Presbyterian and Congregational churches. These were the heirs to the Reformed teachings of John Calvin, the Geneva lawyer-turned-preacher, whose convictions about the absolute sovereignty of God led to a doctrine of strict predestination, the choice of the "elect" for salvation based on God's pleasure alone, with the rest condemned to damnation. Historic differences between these churches were principally in forms of governance, the Congregational churches vesting all authority in the members of the local congregation, while the Presbyterian had a combination lay/ministerial hierarchy that gave more authority to a denominational eldership. The Westminster Confession and the Catechism, written in the 1600s by Presbyterian theologians in England, are among the great theological documents of church history. The Congregationalists, on the other hand, look to Pilgrim and Puritan settlers of early America who established their own "city on a hill" in the New England colonies. Congregationalism was virtually an established church in the New England states until the late 1700s, and even later in some states. Contemporary Congregationalism has become one of the most theologically liberal of the denominations, often seeming to have little regard for the divinity of Christ, which is the bedrock of Christian belief. Many churches left the denomination to pursue more biblically faithful understandings, and a rival Conservative Congregational Conference has brought some of these churches together again.

Presbyterianism, for years sustained by the great minds of American Reformed thought that prevailed in the Princeton Theological Seminary, split into the smaller Orthodox Presbyterian Church and Presbyterian Church in America, which have sustained biblical orthodoxy, and the larger Presbyterian Church USA, which has been torn apart by controversy on biblical and theological issues.

There was, of course, the Methodist church, founded in England by the brothers John and Charles Wesley in the 1700s and brought to America at the earliest stage by English preachers. Methodism was fiery and evangelical in its origins but today is a mixture of modernism and biblical orthodoxy; in the United States the southern and western churches tend to balance the theological liberalism of the northeast.

Hal then drove me past two Baptist churches. The first was very fundamentalist and following a literal understanding of most Scripture, a separatist philosophy, and a conservative dress and comportment requirement of its people. The other was more "mainstream" evangelical, user-friendly to those not already committed, biblically faithful but contemporary in its worship and other practices. Both followed a "dispensationalist" understanding of Scripture, attributing historical scriptural significance to current and future events in the Middle East and a literal understanding of most biblical descriptions of the time when current history would come to an end. Then we passed an independent charismatic church, where worship was free form, people spoke in tongues, and raised their hands and moved their bodies in worship music. These three churches had the highest attendance of any churches in the area, and all three had their own K-12 school systems. Only the Catholic Church offered an alternative religious school system.

Along the way, we passed perhaps twenty other churches, almost all relatively small, conservative evangelical, fundamentalist, or charismatic congregations. Some had split off from other churches; churches or denominations in other parts of the country had founded some; and others were products of a lone pastor or group of believers who wanted their own worship style and group. Many had their own building, others met in schools, and still others in public or nonprofit facilities around the city.

It was almost dinnertime, and we stopped at a small diner. "Bring your Bible," Hal said as we exited the car.

"It is the scandal of Protestantism," Hal continued after we settled into our booth and had given our order, "and it is the scandal of all Christianity. Not that there are so many different churches and worship styles—I think the Lord is pleased with that—but that so many of them don't recognize the validity of the others.

"When I was growing up, most evangelical Christians didn't think Catholics were Christians. And I was told that the Catholic priest taught his children they'd go to hell if they set foot in a Protestant church. We've come a long way since then, but most are still bound up in their own denomination, tradition, or church, and some still think people aren't saved who don't believe everything they do."

"Are we still studying chapter twelve?" I asked.

"Oh, yes, I have prayed over this chapter more than any other part of the law. Everyone who studies Deuteronomy thinks it is central to understanding the book. I agree. But it is not about geography, at least not now.

"You see, Chris, when God says he will place his name somewhere, he isn't talking about a name like yours and mine, like putting a nameplate on the door to your office or sewing a name onto a worker's uniform. In biblical terms, 'the name' signifies much more than the word or words that identify you. It means your reputation, your honor, your essential nature. For God to place his name somewhere means to disclose his essential nature there, to reveal it to people as an active force in their lives. In the end, it was not in a city or a building where God revealed himself in this way, but in a person, the person of God himself, Jesus Christ.

"He is the image of the invisible God, the one in whom God was pleased to have his fullness dwell, the radiance of God's glory and the exact representation of his being," Hal said, interspersing quotes from Colossians and Hebrews as he talked. "This chapter may have had a short-term meaning in centralizing the worship of Israel in one place—ultimately Jerusalem—but in the end it's about Jesus, the 'name that is above every name,' the name that will cause 'every knee to bow in heaven and on earth and under the earth.' Believing in Jesus' name means believing in who he is, in all of his fullness and glory and radiance—part of, and a representation of God himself.

"In chapter twelve we see God preserving the central teachings and understandings by keeping them in one place, so every village and tribe and family would not go off and invent their own understandings. That tendency is ever present in our fallen race."

He opened his Bible as the waitress brought our meal. "I pray also for those who will believe in me through their message, that all of them may be one. . . . May they be brought to complete unity to let the world know that you sent me and love them even as you have loved me," he read from John 17. He then turned to the first chapter of 1 Corinthians and read Paul's teaching on divisions in the church. "'Is Christ divided?'" was the rhetorical question Paul put to the quarreling believers.

"There is more disobedience to this passage of Scripture than anything I can think of." I had not seen Hal this roused about anything yet in our study.

"I rest my case," Hal said before he began eating. We shared the unity of fellowship of the meal and, as we did, we shared stories of friends and experiences we'd both had with believers outside our own churches and traditions. By the time coffee came, we had only scratched the surface.

"Some teach that it's only right doctrine that leads to salvation," Hal said. "I think that's heresy, if it goes beyond loving and trusting God, and loving and trusting and believing him in the person of Jesus. The only requirement the Scripture places on people is to believe in Jesus, believe on his name, believe with your heart and confess him with your mouth, however any particular passage puts it. I don't say the rest is not important, but that's all you need to have. When I was young, I preached through the Scriptures, taught doctrine, doctrine, doctrine, from this passage or that, or my version or understanding of the doctrine and why everyone else was wrong. As I grew older and matured, I didn't do that anymore. Love God and obey him, that is what Deuteronomy teaches, and that is what the New Testament writers taught also. I don't know how bad your theology can be and still be saved, but I don't think God gives theological achievement tests for people to get into heaven."

I had a momentary comic image of the recently deceased gathered in a heavenly classroom under the supervision of some angelic being or saint who had gone before. TAT booklets (Theological Achievement Tests) were passed out. Then came the multiple-choice score sheets and the number-two pencils. "If you don't know the answer, don't guess. Wrong answers are deducted from correct ones. Just go on to the next question," instructed the overseer. The clock started, and the gathered souls plunged in, hoping their score would be sufficient for admission.

I came out of my silly reverie. "Is there hope, Hal? Do you see anything going on that is positive?"

"Speaking broadly, the church is evolving into two groups: those who honor the teachings of the Bible—the historic and orthodox understandings of the faith—on the one hand, and on the other those who think that the core teachings of the Bible are untrue, or that it's not important, whether on the divinity, virgin birth, and resurrection of Christ, sexual morality, the inspiration of Scripture, or many other issues. Are the two groups really part of the same religion? If you don't share a common view of the nature of Christ or biblical morality, what do you share? Some denominations and individual congregations are being torn apart by this. And some people are surprised at who they find standing beside them.

"The Catholic and evangelical communities have discovered each other. A lot of thought is going into how they can share the proclamation of the faith and right living in the world. There is a group called ECT, Evangelicals and Catholics Together, comprised mostly of a small number of theologians, church leaders, and prominent thinkers on both sides who are exploring these things. There are a lot of inter-denominational groups springing up outside the organized church in which members of all denominations and traditions share a particular purpose or mission. And on the ground, in local communities, people are cooperating across church lines in things like the March for Jesus, supporting pregnancy care centers, food pantries, even Billy Graham crusades. It's only a beginning; we still have a long way to go."

Evening had fallen. We left the restaurant. As Hal drove me back to my car, I looked out over the silhouette of the skyline of our small city. It was broken by a number of steeples—steeples of the churches we had toured before our meal. How many, I wondered, marked places where the one whose name was above every name was honored and worshipped? How many had forsaken their first love, like the Ephesian church in the second chapter of Revelation? In how many of them— and in how many of the gathering places of all the other groups of believers who would come together the following morning—was there an understanding of Jesus' prayer in John 17 that they would all be one, that they would be "brought to complete unity to let the world know that you sent me and have loved them even as you have loved me"?

CHAPTER THIRTEEN

"Judge Orders Ten Commandments Removed from Courthouse"

The Chief Justice of the Alabama Supreme Court had installed a massive stone block with an engraving of the Ten Commandments in the rotunda of the state courthouse. Lawsuits followed. A federal judge ordered the exhibit removed. It was, the federal court opined, a violation of the provision of the United States Constitution that prohibited an "establishment of religion." It had to go. The federal appeals court agreed. And the federal courts had the last word in the American system. The federal constitution was the supreme law of the land. It trumped whatever the Alabama constitution said or whatever the state's chief justice thought the law ought to be. The public was outraged. National media descended on the scene. Protestors gathered. Polls showed nearly four out of five Americans disagreed with the decision. We had "under God" in our Pledge of Allegiance and "In God We Trust" on our money. Surely a people who acknowledged the sovereignty of God in these ways could do so by displaying the Ten Commandments in a public building. The commandments were the foundation of our morality—the central standards of right living in the Judeo-Christian tradition. Some claimed they were the foundation of our legal system. Conservative religious leaders deplored the orders of a federal judiciary that they viewed as unaccountable, arrogating powers to themselves in defiance of our history and the democratic will of the people, and tearing down the fabric of our society. Most counseled compliance with the law, however, even while asserting their disagreement with it. Local politicians agreed. No one wanted to be perceived as being against the Ten Commandments, their vitality in our culture, or the views of eighty percent of the voters.

I followed the news accounts with great interest. Here was a subject I knew something about—law and religion. Hal had asked me before to explain the church-state law to him. When the Ten Commandments exploded into the national news, he e-mailed to ask again. I composed my thoughts and e-mailed back. This is what I told him:

> The First Amendment to the Constitution of the United States provides for America's "First Freedom," freedom of religion: "Congress shall make no law respecting an establishment of religion or interfering with the free exercise thereof." These few words have been the subject of dozens of controversial and strongly contested decisions of the United States Supreme Court, most of them dating from the 1940s and escalating through the end of the last century and into the present one. Although it refers only to "Congress," later Constitutional amendments and court interpretations apply the religion clauses to government at every level. The "establishment clause" prevents government from imposing or endorsing any particular religious practice. It protects government, the "public square" and the public functions, which all citizens are entitled to enjoy equally, from the intrusion of religion. It has been the basis of controversial decisions banning prayer in public schools, prohibiting the teaching in public schools of creationism as an understanding of human and world origins, and addressing the extent to which religious symbols can be displayed or speech can occur in government institutions, events, and space. The "free exercise clause," on the other hand, protects the "garden of the church," as Rhode Island Baptist Roger Williams would have said, from interference by the state. It commonly has been invoked in cases involving some group or individual's desire to be exempted from some generally applicable law or regulation. Free exercise cases have involved such things as unemployment benefits for people who lose jobs due to their religious practice or beliefs, the requirement that people wear or refrain from wearing certain clothing or symbols such as head coverings, the right to speak in or have access to public facilities on the same basis as others, and the right to witness or evangelize in public places. In one illustrative free exercise

case, the Court struck down an ordinance of the City of Hialeah, Florida, that prevented a group called "Santeria" from practicing the sacrifice of chickens in the city.

Americans are justly proud of their heritage of religious liberty. People of all faiths and no faith have equal benefits and access to all government functions, and are equally entitled to practice their own faith freely as long as they do not unduly intrude on important government functions or the rights of others. Whether some establishment clause decisions make the government hostile to religion instead of neutral, or accommodate religious practices in government settings too much, will always be an issue. When, if ever, people of faith should be exempted from government requirements that everyone else has to follow will also always be controversial. Courts will be called on to referee these conflicting views and establish guidelines for what conduct is or is not permissible, by government and by the people.

Pre-Revolutionary War residents of the American colonies considered themselves Englishmen, not Americans, a term that was used in early days for the Native American population. The religion clauses of the American constitution grew out of a transplanted population of Europeans tired of a century of religious wars that had wracked Europe in the 1600s. Enlightenment philosophy in some quarters, and Baptist separatism in others, combined with recent European history to produce a new nation convicted with the necessity to separate government and religion. The established churches of England and Europe had led to nothing but persecutions and power struggles. In the new nation, no King or Parliament would tell people how to worship God. So convicted were citizens of the nascent republic on this issue, and others expressed in the Bill of Rights, the first ten amendments to the Constitution, that it is unlikely that the Constitution would have been adopted had not the adoption of these amendments been universally understood.

Not all of the founding fathers were Christians. Some, like Jefferson, were Unitarians or Deists who believed in the existence of a God, but an impersonal distant God, not the personal God of the Bible. They rejected miracles and did not believe in the divinity of Christ, or that God involved himself in the affairs of the world.

James Madison was one of the founders of our republic and its fourth president. Unlike his Virginia colleague and predecessor as president, Thomas Jefferson, he was a Christian. He shared with Jefferson, however, a deep distrust of mixing the affairs of government and religion. Individuals, he believed, had a duty to the "Universal Sovereign" that was higher than their duty to their nation, but that could only be determined by the conscience of every citizen. And if one conceded that the government could impose the Christian religion, it followed that it could impose any religion. Separating church and state, the principle represented by the establishment clause in the Constitution, protected Christians, as well as those who had not yet seen the wisdom and truth of that faith, from coercion and violation of conscience. Madison and Jefferson's views were embedded in the religion clauses of the Constitution, and their writings referenced in subsequent interpretation of them.

The courts—and ultimately the Supreme Court of the United States, which has the final authority in interpreting the United States Constitution—have long struggled with the specific applications of the religion clauses. Their decisions have not always been consistent. When it comes to something like the government display of as clear a religious symbol or message as the Ten Commandments, courts have generally prohibited it. Exceptions exist for situations where a religious symbol is embedded in a display that includes other religious and secular symbols, as, for example, a display of a variety of sources of law of which the Ten Commandments is only one. And some references to God have been allowed that are generic and historic and reflect more what the court has called "ceremonial deism" than a real endorsement of religion. "In God We Trust" on coins and "under God" in the Pledge of Allegiance are probably in this category.

As for the Ten Commandments in the courthouse in Alabama, they are not part of a display tracing the history or sources of law. And they go well beyond what could reasonably be called "ceremonial deism." However much most of us might like to see the Ten Commandments on public display in every government building, the federal judge was right. The establishment clause prohibits this display. The law on this subject has been settled for a long time. The United States of America may be a "Christian nation" in its history and culture, and its citizens are and should be free under its Constitution to exercise their Christianity without government interference. But its government, at every level, must be neutral in matters of religion, favoring no religion over another or over nonreligion. In our Constitution and laws, we are not a Christian nation.

My long discourse brought a short reply: "Go read chapter thirteen of Deuteronomy and tell me if you still believe all that."

I pulled my Bible from the shelf behind my desk and read the following:

> If a prophet, or one who foretells by dreams, appears among you and announces to you a miraculous sign or wonder, and if the sign or wonder of which he has spoken takes place, and he says, "Let us follow other gods" (gods you have not known) "and let us worship them," you must not listen to the words of that prophet or dreamer. The LORD your God is testing you to find out whether you love him with all your heart and with all your soul. It is the LORD your God you must follow, and him you must revere. Keep his commands and obey him; serve him and hold fast to him. That prophet or dreamer must be put to death, because he preached rebellion against the LORD your God, who brought you out of Egypt and redeemed you from the land of slavery; he has tried to turn you from the way the LORD your God commanded you to follow. You must purge the evil from among you.

If your very own brother, or your son or daughter, or the wife you love, or your closest friend secretly entices you, saying, "Let us go and worship other gods" (gods that neither you nor your fathers have known, gods of the peoples around you, whether near or far, from one end of the land to the other), do not yield to him or listen to him. Show him no pity. Do not spare him or shield him. You must certainly put him to death. Your hand must be the first in putting him to death, and then the hands of all the people. Stone him to death, because he tried to turn you away from the LORD your God, who brought you out of Egypt, out of the land of slavery. Then all Israel will hear and be afraid, and no one among you will do such an evil thing again.

If you hear it said about one of the towns the LORD your God is giving you to live in that wicked men have arisen among you and have led the people of their town astray, saying, "Let us go and worship other gods" (gods you have not known), then you must inquire, probe, and investigate it thoroughly. And if it is true and it has been proved that this detestable thing has been done among you, you must certainly put to the sword all who live in that town. Destroy it completely, both its people and its livestock. Gather all the plunder of the town into the middle of the public square and completely burn the town and all its plunder as a whole burnt offering to the LORD your God. It is to remain a ruin forever, never to be rebuilt. None of those condemned things shall be found in your hands, so that the LORD will turn from his fierce anger; he will show you mercy, have compassion on you, and increase your numbers, as he promised on oath to your forefathers, because you obey the LORD your God, keeping all his commands that I am giving you today and doing what is right in his eyes.

—Deut. 13:1–18

Chapter thirteen came as a shock to me; God commanded the execution of anyone who advocated false religion. The sentence did not fall only on false prophets who would lead the people astray. If your spouse or children or closest friend sought to entice you to worship other gods, you were to be the first in putting them to death. And if the departure from the faith occurred in a town, the whole town fell under the herem and was to be destroyed, people and even livestock. It was a far cry from the religion clauses of the First Amendment to the United States Constitution.

I pondered these matters as I drove to Hal's for our next meeting. I had long viewed the religious freedom we practiced in America as part of our greatest strengths. The European countries that shared our heritage most closely had followed our lead. Today, the established churches of Europe no longer prevent other faiths from being practiced, and religious freedom is almost universally respected there. But in many other countries, especially those with dominant Muslim or Hindu populations—or Communist countries with official state philosophies of atheism—the concept of religious freedom remains foreign and offensive. In atheistic states, religion is viewed as a threat to the dominance and control of the government. Many Muslims, on the other hand, view the proper role of the state as being to adopt and enforce religious law. Whether through official government actions or the violence inflicted by mobs or zealots, Christianity and other minority religions are actively persecuted in many parts of the world, even as the Christian faith was in its origins.

Chapter thirteen seemed to me quite at odds with everything I understood as a modern American Christian. Did God really teach that his people should slaughter those who deviated from religious correctness—even their wives and children? Weren't the fundamentalist Muslims, who imposed death penalties on apostate Muslims or anyone who "blasphemed the prophet," practicing a faith closer to God's teaching in Deuteronomy than we were with our religious freedom? Did this chapter provide justification for the execution of those who were perceived as heretics, as practiced by both Protestant and Catholic Christianity in the late Middle Ages and early Reformation times? If God demanded the death of the unfaithful, then what did he think of our religiously tolerant society?

Hal cross-examined.

"What is the definition of treason?"

"Betrayal of your country. Supporting your country's enemies."

"What is the penalty for treason?"

"Death."

Death has been the universal penalty for treason in almost all times and places. The United States hadn't executed anyone for treason, so far as I was aware, since Julius and Ethel Rosenberg, who gave atomic secrets to the Soviets in the 1950s. I could see how that would qualify for the death penalty. More recent spy scandals have resulted in the government trading life imprisonment as a sentence for the traitor's cooperation. The death penalty certainly seemed appropriate today to an American who cooperated with Al-Qaeda, for example, to allow something like the destruction of the World Trade Center towers to occur.

"Why is death the penalty for treason?"

"Because it puts the whole nation at risk of being overcome or destroyed by its enemies." The Rosenbergs had exposed the United States to an atomic attack by its principal enemy of the time.

"Who was the sovereign of Israel?"

"Moses, I guess."

"Wrong. Moses speaks for the real sovereign and transmits his laws and his message. The sovereign of Israel is God. The whole book of Deuteronomy is a sovereign-vassal covenant, the kind of covenant or contract that dominant kings in the ancient near-east made with subordinate states. Examples of these covenants in other nations are known from both the Hittite empire of Moses' time and the Assyrian empire of later times. But there is one difference, and it is all the difference: In Deuteronomy, the sovereign is God, not an earthly king. No other example is known of a nation making a sovereign-vassal covenant with a god. Israel in the time of Deuteronomy was unique in time and space—a nation that was 'under God' in the truest sense that it forgoes any other head of government and pledges allegiance to God as its head of state. Israel in Moses' time was like no other society that has ever been, even up to the present, or will be until Jesus returns to reclaim the world as his own. It was a theocracy, a society or nation in which God himself was King. Moses didn't make his own rules like other ancient near-eastern kings did, even if they claimed to rule by divine right or appointment. God is not only sovereign over his entire creation, as we understand today, but he has chosen this people as a model for the nations, and rules them directly.

"Now," Hal continued, "who are God's enemies?"

"The other nations in the Promised Land?" I guessed.

"Wrong again. Well, they were his enemies in that they followed practices he hates. But his real enemy was not the people but the one they served—the other gods or idols they followed."

"How can these false gods that don't really exist be the enemy of the real God who is sovereign over everything? That's like saying that the enemy of the United States is some imaginary country."

"Not so fast. Their idols of wood and stone are false, nonexistent gods. But what lies behind them is not false. It is real evil."

I was beginning get it. "The 'father of lies'?"

"Yes. Satan. A real being, ultimate evil, and the enemy of God. Following false gods amounts to following Satan, who lures and entices away from truth and the true God. This is treason, betrayal, moving into the enemy's camp. And what will happen to the people God has chosen if they turn away from him?"

"Disaster."

"Now, Chris, do you see why this is such a serious thing? Chapter thirteen is the law of treason. Deuteronomy is entirely in line with the practices of this country and every other country in this regard, at least until modern times, when some countries abandoned the death penalty entirely for any crime. It follows chapter twelve, where the people were taught to destroy all the vestiges of the old and false religions of the people before them. God was doing a new thing in this land. He was reclaiming it for himself. He was invading a little corner of his creation to redeem it from the evil that had taken over. To go over to that enemy is to betray God himself, and—because this was his chosen nation, in covenant with him—to betray their countrymen and bring disaster on them. They would lose the land, their fruitfulness and prosperity, and everything he had given them. And this was not just an idle threat on God's part; it was a description of what actually happened to Israel in the time of the exile. When we discuss the blessings and curses in chapters twenty-seven and twenty-eight, you will see more of the dire consequences that follow. That is why betrayal of God cannot be tolerated, even when it occurs among those closest to you. The consequences to the entire society are too grave to be overcome by personal relationships, including family and friends."

"So what about burning heretics at the stake in the Middle Ages? Was that justified by Deuteronomy?"

"At the time, the people involved thought it was," Hal responded. "This chapter did provide a scriptural justification, at least in their eyes. Salvation depended on faith in Christ. Those who threatened that faith by teaching heresy were threatening the eternal salvation of others who might be beguiled by these false teachings. There was some logic behind the Inquisition. Those involved in it at the time thought they were doing a good thing, not a bad thing."

"And what was wrong with their thinking?" I pressed.

"First, they overlooked the fact that they no longer lived in ancient Israel. In his sovereign wisdom, God had provided rules for that theocratic society, but Israel failed because fallen, sin-filled human beings could not sustain the commitment and faithfulness it required. When the church looked at the requirements of the law in the early years after Christ, it decided—under the Holy Spirit's guidance, as reported in Acts fifteen—that most of the requirements of the law were not binding on Christians. There is no scriptural mandate for Christians to persecute or kill anyone who does not share their beliefs. The message of Jesus is to go and make disciples of all nations, not kill them.

"These matters were important to Jews in Jesus' time. In fact, chapter thirteen—along with the prohibitions on blasphemy—provided the scriptural authority for the Jews to seek Jesus' execution." Hal opened his Bible to Mark 14 and read.

> "Again the high priest asked him, 'Are you the Christ, the Son of the Blessed One?'
>
> 'I am,' said Jesus. 'And you will see the Son of Man sitting at the right hand of the Mighty One and coming on the clouds of heaven.' The high priest tore his clothes. 'Why to we need any more witnesses?' he asked. 'You have heard the blasphemy. What do you think?'

"They all condemned him as worthy of death."

—Mark 14:61–64

"You see, Chris, they understood there was to be a 'Christ' or Messiah, 'the Son of the Blessed One,' who is God himself. They just didn't believe it was Jesus. By putting himself in that position, they viewed him as a blasphemer, teaching a false religion, leading the people to worship another god.

"Jesus, on the other hand, never claimed to be starting a new religion or teaching anything other than worshipping God as the Jews always had. Jesus and the early church were very mindful of the command that we looked at in chapter four, not to add to or subtract from the Scriptures. That command is repeated at the end of chapter twelve: 'See that you do all I command you; do not add to it or take away from it.' Jesus and the early church followed it. He grounded himself in the Hebrew Scriptures throughout, as did the apostles—including Paul—and the early church. Jesus was the fulfillment of the Scriptures, not a departure from it. We saw before that many view the New Testament as a commentary on the Old Testament. Remember Augustine's saying, 'The New Testament is in the Old Testament concealed, the Old Testament is in the New Testament revealed.' When Jesus taught on the road to Emmaus, he explained 'what was said in all the Scriptures concerning himself.' When Paul and his companions preached to the Jews, they taught about Jesus from the Old Testament. 'What God promised our fathers he has fulfilled for us, their children, by raising up Jesus.' In Jesus the mysteries of the Old Testament Scriptures are revealed.

"The Christian church, in its origins, was wholly and devotedly Jewish. Jesus, the apostles, Paul and his companions, all were faithful Jews. They did not violate Deuteronomy chapter thirteen."

"But Christianity is a different religion, isn't it?" I asked. "I mean, the Jews ultimately rejected Jesus."

"Some did and some didn't. According to the book of Acts, Paul and the Apostles preached first to the Jews. Some accepted their preaching, and some did not. It would be more accurate to say that the religion of Israel became inclusive, reaching out to the rest of the world through Jesus. This was the fulfillment of the promise to the patriarchs that through them and their seed all the nations of the world would be blessed. Old Testament Judaism was not evangelical except by example—it did not reach out to the rest of the world. There were occasional exceptions, as in the story of Jonah preaching to Nineveh, and there were always others who came to Israel and accepted its religion, like Ruth, or were attracted to it where there were groups of worshipping Jews. But the time had not yet come for the blessing being transmitted to the nations."

I went back to the notion of religious freedom. How should we think about Muslims who want to execute those who depart from their religion, or commit what they view as blasphemy?

"This forces us to think through our ideas of toleration and religious freedom. From their perspective, they are acting as Deuteronomy teaches. Like the Inquisition of the Middle Ages, they are protecting their society and the individuals in it from departing from God, with all that implies. There could be no greater service to God and humanity than that."

"And?" I continued expectantly.

"And they are wrong," Hal said. "Mohammed is a false prophet. Some say we have no right to judge, that one person's religion is as good as another's. From a civic perspective, we allow people that freedom, and that protects Christians as well as others. But from a religious perspective, we must judge, and we must judge them wrong. Mohammed is the sole author of the Koran and source of authority for their religion. Christianity has the authority of dozens of inspired writers of Scripture over a period of nearly two millennia, telling a developing and consistent story. Mohammed purported to honor the biblical writings, but he didn't really. He rejected Jesus' divinity and retold other stories in his own way. And as for the Koran being inspired, Mohammed's secretary left him when Mohammed adopted as part of the Koran some text that the secretary had made up to finish Mohammed's dictation. The secretary realized that it was not inspired, just Mohammed's own vision.

"The task of Christians is to use all practical and available means to bring to all peoples on earth the good news of God's salvation through Jesus. We are to live in peace and harmony—as far as it is up to us—with these people and be fair to them, just as Israel was to the nations it passed through on the way to the Promised Land. But that is very different from saying that their religious opinions are as good as ours. A lot of people are confused about that today.

"You know, what this whole chapter teaches is how serious it is to depart from God." He reached for a book on his shelf. "Let me read you a bit from a writer who catches the essence of it," he said, opening Wright's *Deuteronomy*:

> C.S. Lewis once said that if we no longer feel comfortable with the cursing psalms, for example, it is not because of our greater "Christian" sensitivity but because of our appalling moral apathy. We no longer feel the passion of the psalmist that God should deal with evil and evildoers and vindicate God's own moral order in the world. We respond to idolatrous, blasphemous evil not with a curse, but a shrug, and then have the gall to claim morally higher ground than ancient Israel. Similarly, if we can no longer identify with the scale of priorities and values that undergird Deuteronomy 13, it is manifestly not because we have acquired a greater appreciation of the value of human life, but because we have lost any sense of the awful majesty of God's reality. The western church, more than it cares to admit, has imbibed that dichotomized, privatized, cultural worldview in which God is no longer the ultimate governing reality and Lord of all human life and community, private and public, domestic and political, local and global. And having for all practical purposes accepted the box into which the surrounding culture has confined God, it is not surprising that we have difficulty with the concept of idolatry. For if the living God is little more than an idol, where do other idols fit? We lack the categories to define them and the tools to discern them. And thus, in reality, their power over us is infinitely enhanced because we don't even recognize them. We can't begin to work on the relevance of a chapter like Deuteronomy 13 when we don't know what it is talking about. We have long since failed the test of verse 3. For only those who know and love the living God "with all their heart (=understanding, mind, intellect) and soul (personal commitment)" know what idols are.[12]

Hal had turned me around. Now I was beginning to think the founding fathers got it wrong. Religious freedom means tolerating religious views that are not just non-Christian but may even be satanic. It allows people to be led into beliefs and practices that prevent their salvation and threaten God's favor on the nation. We have succumbed to a way of thinking, and even enshrined it in our Constitution, that is neutral on the most important issue in the universe, the issue on which everything else depends. No matter what we write on our coins or put in our Pledge of Allegiance, we are not a nation under God. And we should be. Those who would bring us in line with the requirements of Deuteronomy 13 are on target—we need to enshrine in our Constitution and laws and court decisions the absolute commitment and fidelity to our Lord that he requires.

"Come back," Hal said when I expressed these thoughts. "You were supposed to be teaching me about religious liberty, not vice versa."

He took me back over the ground. God's laws to Israel were the laws of a theocracy that lived under the direct rule of the sovereign God. That society disappeared with the exile of Israel in 586 B.C., and God in his providence had not brought it forth again. Theocratic government will return in the future millennial kingdom—that blessed future time when Christ will rule on earth for a thousand years. In the meantime, we live under the law of Christ, rather than the law of Moses. Christ taught us to share the good news, to evangelize and persuade, to make disciples of all men, Jews and gentiles, to the ends of the earth. Nowhere did he teach us to force people to convert or to execute God's enemies, even those who should be his people and had turned against him. The American republic, with its religious toleration and constitutional guarantee of religious freedom, was the ideal environment in which to carry out Christ's command—the "Great Commission" as it is sometimes called. Here Christianity can compete in the marketplace of religious ideas. It can be freely communicated to those who are lost and in darkness. Christianity's openness in seeking to bring people to God through voluntary persuasion rather than compulsion was a great strength in a free society. We had a Constitution that was providential for the time and place in which we lived. For that, we should be grateful to God.

CHAPTER FOURTEEN

N ot ordering the ham and cheese?" I asked.
I was behind Julie at the deli lunch counter. The noon rush of office workers flooded into the sandwich shops, a two-hour wave that would subside as people receded from their brief recess to resume the day's work.

"You know how it is with us Jews," she replied. "No ham, no pork. It's all those food laws. A pain in the neck. Sometimes I long for a little hoopoe, or fillet of bat."

"You still eat kosher?" I was surprised.

"Yeah . . . I know I don't have to."

She referred to Mark 7. I knew she was right, although I had to look up the reference later. Jesus had made all things clean when he taught that it was not what went into a person that made him unclean. Rather, it was what came out of the heart: "evil thoughts, sexual immorality, theft, murder, adultery, greed, malice, deceit, lewdness, envy, slander, arrogance, and folly." The imagery is carried forward in Acts 10, where Peter was shown clean and unclean foods in a vision. The Lord told him not to call anything impure that God has made clean, and showed him that he was not to regard Gentiles as unclean. At the Jerusalem Council, recorded in Acts 15, the church, under the guidance of the Holy Spirit, limited impure food to food sacrificed to idols, blood, and the meat of strangled animals. For the church, the Old Testament food laws had become history, although some honored them to avoid offending those who still felt bound by them.

"So why do it? Why not enjoy a roast pork?"

"It's part of my heritage," she said. "I like being part of something that goes back to the writing of the Torah. Tradition, respect for the past . . . all that stuff. We follow most of the Jewish customs in our house—Seder meal, high holy days. A lot of Jews who believe in Jesus do that."

The food laws—the central portion of Deuteronomy 14—puzzled me. They were among Orthodox Judaism's most distinctive practices. Food must be "kosher," acceptable in nature and preparation, and so certified by religious authority. So familiar is this requirement that the word *kosher* has gained the more generic meaning in the larger society of being approved, suitable, and proper. Muslim practice has its own food laws, much of it similar to the Old Testament and probably borrowed from it. And yet few requirements of the Old Testament law are more curious to moderns.

When our sandwiches arrived we sat together at a small, vacant table in the corner. It was an unplanned meeting but a serendipitous chance to get to know her a little better.

"What do you think the point of the food laws was?" I asked. "What was in God's mind when he made them?"

She thought for a moment. "Obedience. There doesn't have to be any other reason. It's enough that God says so, and God can say so just to discipline us by obedience. God has always told us that there are some appetites that we aren't supposed to indulge. Adam and Eve were allowed to eat the fruit of all the trees but one. When animals were given to people to eat after the flood, they could eat the meat but not the blood. Gluttony is still a sin, like drunkenness and sexual immorality. The food laws forced people to distinguish between what God permits and what he doesn't. It forced them to acknowledge him by obedience. There doesn't have to be any other reason."

She was silent for a bit as I digested her thoughts, along with my sandwich.

"And you know what?" she added. "If there is another reason, God doesn't have to tell us what it is. He doesn't owe us explanations. And we don't have to find them."

"I've got to think about that," I told her as we put our paper plates and drink cups in the trash and headed back to our desks.

After dinner that night, I read the first twenty-one verses of chapter fourteen to Anna.

You are the children of the LORD your God. Do not cut yourselves or shave the front of your heads for the dead, for you are a people holy to the LORD your God. Out of all the peoples on the face of the earth, the LORD has chosen you to be his treasured possession.

Do not eat any detestable thing. These are the animals you may eat: the ox, the sheep, the goat, the deer, the gazelle, the roe deer, the wild goat, the ibex, the antelope, and the mountain sheep. You may eat any animal that has a split hoof divided in two and that chews the cud. However, of those that chew the cud or that have a split hoof completely divided you may not eat the camel, the rabbit or the coney. Although they chew the cud, they do not have a split hoof; they are ceremonially unclean for you. The pig is also unclean; although it has a split hoof, it does not chew the cud. You are not to eat their meat or touch their carcasses.

Of all the creatures living in the water, you may eat any that has fins and scales.

But anything that does not have fins and scales you may not eat; for you it is unclean.

You may eat any clean bird. But these you may not eat: the eagle, the vulture, the black vulture, the red kite, the black kite, any kind of falcon, any kind of raven, the horned owl, the screech owl, the gull, any kind of hawk, the little owl, the great owl, the white owl, the desert owl, the osprey, the cormorant, the stork, any kind of heron, the hoopoe, and the bat.

All flying insects that swarm are unclean to you; do not eat them. But any winged creature that is clean you may eat.

Do not eat anything you find already dead. You may give it to an alien living in any of your towns, and he may eat it, or you may sell it to a foreigner. But you are a people holy to the LORD your God.

Do not cook a young goat in its mother's milk.

—Deut. 14:1–21

I shared with her Julie's view of the food laws.

"I don't agree," she said. "God doesn't work like that. There's always a reason for what he tells us to do. You like to call the Bible 'The Manufacturer's Handbook.' Great comparison. But manufacturers don't tell people to do things just for the sake of seeing if they'll do it."

"Then what is the reason for the food laws?"

"Health," she replied. "Pigs carry trichinosis. Other things that were prohibited were for other reasons. I know people have done studies to show that the prohibited foods weren't good for you. That's what this is all about."

She was right about the studies. Much effort had gone into showing that there was a health reason for the food laws. The danger of trichinosis in pork is well known, and health issues had been identified in some of the other foods as well. But I wasn't convinced.

"If this is about health, then why did Jesus and the church abandon it? There wasn't any refrigeration in Jesus' time either, and the local health inspector wasn't in business yet. I don't know any reason why these foods would have been any healthier then than when God gave the law to Moses."

"Maybe they did have better means of preservation or knew more about cooking meat thoroughly by the time of Jesus," she said tentatively. "I don't know enough about it. They must have."

I brought her back to Julie's point. "Why can't God test our obedience? Isn't that what it was all about when he told Abraham to sacrifice Isaac? God didn't want the sacrifice; he hated the sacrifice of children. But he wanted to know if Abraham loved him enough to obey, even when the obedience went against every fiber of Abraham's being. And just in the last chapter, Moses said that when false prophets give miraculous signs and wonders but try to lead the people into worshipping other gods, the Lord is testing them."

I turned back to Deuteronomy 13 and found the verse: "The Lord your God is testing you to find out whether you love him with all your heart and with all your soul."

"Those are all one-time things," she replied. "The food laws are for every day, all the time. I think it's different."

"Then why, according to verse twenty-one, is it all right to give dead animals to foreigners?" I pressed her. "Deuteronomy is full of God's concern for the foreigners. Back in chapter ten, he said he loves the alien. Are you saying that God allows the Jews to give unhealthy things to other people he loves and cares for? It's OK to give them diseases and harm their health as long as the Israelites are protected?"

She looked at the passage. "Verse twenty-one is just about dead animals," she replied. "Maybe there's another reason for that one."

"Maybe there's another reason for all of them," I said.

"Maybe. Why don't we call Hal and see what he thinks?"

We got on the phone to Hal. With two extensions, we could talk to him at the same time with our Bibles open.

"What do you see in this passage that says anything about health or God's concern for their well-being?" Hal asked.

After rereading it, we both acknowledged there was nothing.

"Text without context is pretext," Hal said, repeating the maxim he had given me before. "Put it in context. The last chapter was about apostasy, people who would lead Israel to worship idols or false gods. This is a continuation of the thought, only more specific.

"The first two verses of this chapter—prohibiting the people from cutting themselves or shaving their head in mourning for the dead—is a clear reference to pagan religious practices. In first Kings eighteen, twenty-eight, we see that the priests of Baal slashed themselves until their blood flowed—'as was their custom'—to awaken their unresponsive *nongod*. The instruction not to do this is accompanied by the reminder that the Israelites are 'children of the Lord your God, a people holy to the Lord,' the ones God had chosen as his treasured possession.

"The last instruction in this section, 'do not cook a young goat in its mother's milk,' is another reference to a pagan religious practice.

"Unclean food is described as 'detestable' and 'ceremonially unclean,' terms which suggest that there is an unholy aspect to consuming them, presumably based upon some pagan religious practices we're not familiar with. The specific laws close in verse twenty-one with a reminder that 'you are a people holy to the Lord your God.'

"Put it together and it looks to me like the underlying reason for the food laws is to distinguish holy religious practices in worship of the real God from unholy practices in worship of pagan gods. We don't have a lot of information to back that up, but it makes sense in the context of the Scripture that precedes and follows it—and from the specific language describing unclean foods as 'detestable' and 'ceremonially unclean.' It also explains why God would lay down these rules for their own good: It was part of avoiding the deviant religious practices that Deuteronomy repeatedly warns against. And it explains why Jesus, exercising his divine authority, rescinded these laws. By the time of Jesus, the Canaanite religions were ancient history. There was idol worship and food sacrificed to idols, but it was an entirely different thing—the Greek and Roman pantheon of gods with human personalities. Abstaining from food sacrificed to idols remained part of the food laws in the early church. The food laws have always been about holiness, separation of the things of God from the profane and unholy.

"They separate God's people from those around them. Like wearing tefillin, they are practices that say, 'These people are different' and invite others to ask why. 'What makes you different? Why don't you worship these gods or engage in these practices?'"

We were satisfied with our understanding of the food laws and let Hal go.

I read the rest of chapter fourteen before retiring that night. It seemed to change the subject and be unconnected to what had gone before.

> Be sure to set aside a tenth of all that your fields produce each year. Eat the tithe of your grain, new wine and oil, and the firstborn of your herds and flocks in the presence of the LORD your God at the place he will choose as a dwelling for his Name, so that you may learn to revere the LORD your God always. But if that place is too distant and you have been blessed by the LORD your God and cannot carry your tithe (because the place where the LORD will choose to put his Name is so far away), then exchange your tithe for

silver, and take the silver with you and go to the place the LORD your God will choose. Use the silver to buy whatever you like: cattle, sheep, wine, or other fermented drink, or anything you wish. Then you and your household shall eat there in the presence of the LORD your God and rejoice. And do not neglect the Levites living in your towns, for they have no allotment or inheritance of their own.

At the end of every three years, bring all the tithes of that year's produce and store it in your towns, so that the Levites (who have no allotment or inheritance of their own) and the aliens, the fatherless and the widows who live in your towns may come and eat and be satisfied, and so that the LORD your God may bless you in all the work of your hands.

—Deut. 14:22–29

We needed Hal to put the sections of the chapter about tithing together with the food laws. When I saw him next, we continued.

"The subject has only changed a little bit," said Hal. "This whole chapter, except for the first couple of verses, is about eating."

We talked about eating and its relationship to worship.

Hal showed me that the Bible is full of significant occasions of eating. The primal sin in the Garden of Eden was the sin of eating the forbidden fruit. The Passover meal was instituted as a ceremonial meal to remember the events of the Exodus from Egypt. Manna was provided in the desert to show the people that God would provide for them in seemingly impossible circumstances. Jesus ate with the outcasts, tax collectors, and prostitutes to show God's love and concern for all people and willingness to bring them into the kingdom. The kingdom of God is not just for "nice" people or those who enjoy the better things of this world. He fed the multitude through the miracle of loaves and fishes.

Food is a metaphor for spiritual life: "Man does not live by bread alone." Jesus described himself as the bread of life and as living water. In the Upper Room, the last supper was a Passover meal during which Jesus prepared his followers for his becoming the sacrificial lamb that took away the sins of the world. In the world to come, the "wedding supper of the Lamb" is an image of the joining of Christ and his church.

Then Hal tied the parts of the chapter together. "Notice that the tithe is expressed in terms of food and eating before the Lord.

"Food has two functions in life: nourishment and fellowship. In nourishment we get the metaphor of the communion meal as the body and blood of Christ. Whether you understand communion as symbolic, as I do, or believe as Catholics and some of the liturgical churches do that in a mystical way the elements are transformed into the body and blood of Christ, the sacrament represents our unity with Christ himself. That is the spiritual nourishment that sustains us—the bread of life, the living water, the Word that proceeds from the mouth of God."

As Hal spoke, I was in communion with the hundreds of communion meals I had shared. Tiny as those bits of wafer or cubes of bread were, and the thimbleful of grape juice that accompanied them, communion was always one of the holiest moments of worship. In a congregation of God's people bowing before him as the elements are passed and consumed, there is unity unlike any other experience. And the oneness is not only within the congregation. I was drawn closer to God in communion than almost any other experience. The words of Christ spoken by the pastor before the elements are consumed—"Do this in remembrance of me"—shut out the world and bring the mind, heart, and soul into the presence of the Lord himself. It was a shame, I thought, that most Protestant churches served communion only once a month, and some had moved it out of the regular Sunday morning service and into an evening service when participation was greatly diminished.

As I mused about communion, Hal continued. "The second function of food is the communal function, what churches like to call the 'fellowship' aspect. Meals are times of sharing with those you are closest to or that you want to share something with. One of the three things children remember from their childhood is what went on around the dinner table. (The other two are outdoor activities and vacations.) People invite their friends over for dinner, or go out for a meal together. The Passover meal, the last supper, and the wedding supper of the

Lamb are all fellowship events, times of togetherness, of celebrating, of remembering, or looking ahead."

"Moses used the first part of the chapter to teach about the holiness of food, about what foods were and were not consistent with the holy nature of God's covenant people. Here he taught about some particular things they are to do with the food they raise. The tithe is to be set aside each year, and the first instruction is to eat it 'in the presence of the Lord your God and rejoice.' Not to give it away, but to enjoy it themselves, in God's presence, with rejoicing, 'so that you may learn to revere the Lord your God always.' Whether they can travel to the place of worship or need to sell the tithe and travel there and buy more food when they get there, this is to be a festive occasion, an occasion of thanksgiving and an occasion of remembrance of the blessings God has given. The purpose of it is to induce reverence. God owns the earth and everything in it, and he has blessed them in their produce. They are to remember that it is the Lord, not they themselves, who is to be credited with bringing about the blessings.

"Of course, they are not to consume it all themselves, and how could they? One festive occasion is unlikely to consume a tenth of the harvest. If it did, they would be hard put to survive the rest of the year. So God tells them not to neglect the Levites who have 'no allotment or inheritance of their own.'"

I replied, "The Levites are, I assume, equivalent to pastors and religious workers today."

"Of course," Hal said. "They are the people who are dedicated to various levels of religious service—some as priests and some in other functions. The Levites were one of twelve tribes, and they did not receive land of their own. Instead, they were to lead and preserve the religious practices for those who worked the land. Now consider this: If the Levites were one of twelve tribes, we must assume that roughly one of twelve Israelite workers was dedicated to the service of the Lord."

I did some quick arithmetic in my head. There are more than 300 million people in the United States. One-twelfth is approximately 25 million people. If, say, 40 percent are too old or too young to be in active service, that is still nearly 15 million religious workers by the standards God designated for Israel. In my little state of New Hampshire, with a population of over 1,300,000, we should have about 65,000 religious workers. In my home city of Concord, with a population of 40,000, we should have at least 2,000. To support that would certainly take something like a real tithe from everybody.

"It shows the difference in priorities between the God-ordained society of Israel under Moses and a secular society in which a lot of people are religious," Hal said. "If everyone who went to church tithed—never mind the rest of the people—every church should be able to support one-twelfth of the number of adult workers as it has adults, or at least families, to contribute."

I thought of my own church. Although rural, it had perhaps 200 member or supporting families and perhaps three or four paid staff. It did support a number of missions and missionaries, of course, but that hardly made up the difference. How far we were from the Deuteronomic standard!

"But what about 'the aliens, the fatherless and the widows'? Every third year, the tithe was to support them as well," I added

Hal continued explaining. "This is the second time this phrase—the aliens, the fatherless, and the widows—has shown up in Deuteronomy. In chapter ten we learned that God loves and defends them. Here we are taught to share the third-year tithe with them. It will appear eight times before we are through with the book, and it refers to the other categories of people who have no means of support. When a man died, his widow and children were left without means to support themselves economically. And the aliens were by definition people who had no inheritance in the land.

"There is a religious obligation, structured into the basic rules of the society, to care for these classes of people—the religious workers, the widows, the fatherless, and the aliens. No one was to go hungry. Those who had the means to produce would dedicate enough of the produce to those who did not so they would be cared for. And this is to be done 'so that the Lord your God may bless you in all the work of your hands.' It is the sharing and unselfishness—not the hard work on one's own account—that brings the sharer prosperity.

"We talked about patterns in Scripture before. There is a pattern here too. The subject has moved. Chapter twelve was about the unity and centralization of worship and destruction of the forms and places of false worship. Chapter thirteen dealt with the great dangers of apostasy. Then chapter fourteen shows the distinction between foods associated with apostasy and foods that are clean or holy, the use of food as a means of worship, and the sharing of food with others in need. In chapter fifteen, the subject moves on to other means of assisting the needy. But the laws build on one another. This is not just a random collection of laws. Each layer stands on and is connected to what went before. It's like studying math. First you need to know the numbers, then to be able to add, subtract, multiply, and divide them. After that you can go on to other functions—algebra, geometry, trigonometry, calculus."

Hal had given me much on which to reflect. I thought about the food laws, as Hal had explained them. Had I set aside the unholy foods, the things in my life that nourished the worst in me, things that led me to paths of unrighteousness and to my idols? Did I keep a kosher kitchen in my soul? Did I understand that everything that I had was not mine but the Lord's property? Did I understand that when I gave to the church or other ministries it was not giving something of mine but returning what he had allowed me to use for a while? Did I rejoice in giving? Was I before him when I did so? Did I do what needed to be done for the religious workers and those who lacked the economic means that I possessed? And I thought about the patterns of life, from child to parent to grandparent, from student to worker to retiree, about the patterns of spiritual life, from conversion to learning to doing, and how each step built on what went before.

Where was I in God's pattern?

CHAPTER FIFTEEN

The little courtroom tucked into a corner of the fifth floor of the federal building was crowded with people. A man sat at a table in the front, with the judicial bench behind him, the table where lawyers and parties sat when court was in session. He was in his fifties, with dark straight hair swept back along his skull, and horn-rimmed glasses. In front of him was a stack of folders. From time to time, a door to the left of the judge's bench opened, and a thin, officious-looking woman came out to deliver some more folders and pick up the ones he had finished.

It was the Bankruptcy Court. The man with the dark hair was a lawyer who served part time as the bankruptcy referee. He looked tired and bored as he called out the name of one of the people or couples before him. When the name was called, the person addressed came forward and sat at the table across from him. A few had a lawyer who came up and sat with them. Before the referee was a set of schedules, papers listing the assets and debts of the applicant for bankruptcy. The referee walked through his routine of questions in a monotone, rarely looking up at the people in front of him.

"Are these all of your assets?"

"Have you listed all of your debts?"

"Does anyone owe you money that isn't on the schedule?"

"Are you the beneficiary of any trusts?"

Occasionally something out of the ordinary would pique his curiosity, and he would ask about it. But in the end, after five or ten minutes of the routine, he would sign at the bottom and put them in the pile for the clerk. The applicants, looking relieved at the end of their brief ordeal, would stand and move out. The next name was called and the ritual repeated.

I had to visit the Bankruptcy Court for a client that morning, but I wasn't alone. I had invited Hal to join me to see how our society discharges the debt of those who are unable to pay.

The Bankruptcy Court is federal, separate from the court system that administers other federal laws. It is a place to which individuals and businesses can have recourse when their economic situation becomes too dire for them to meet their obligations. Restructuring plans can be devised that defer or reduce certain debts and cancel some contracts, but allow the debtor to continue a normal economic life and emerge intact. Or one can opt for a "straight bankruptcy" in which the debtor's assets, with certain exceptions, are liquidated and applied to the debt, in exchange for all of the debt being forgiven (also with exceptions, such as fraud). Most individuals who go through bankruptcy go through straight bankruptcy. Usually, by the time they get there, they have no assets left. Every business day, the bankruptcy courts of America process the debt relief of thousands of citizens and allow them a new start in their economic life. Over a million cases are processed in some years.

When I had done my business and we had watched for a while, we rose and left. Hal had his Bible under his arm as usual. In the little coffee shop on a lower floor, he read from Deuteronomy 15.

> At the end of every seven years you must cancel debts. This is how it is to be done: Every creditor shall cancel the loan he has made to his fellow Israelite. He shall not require payment from his fellow Israelite or brother, because the LORD's time for canceling debts has been proclaimed. You may require payment from a foreigner, but you must cancel any debt your brother owes you. However, there should be no poor among you, for in the land the LORD your God is giving you to possess as your inheritance, he will richly bless you, if only you fully obey the LORD your God and are careful to follow all these commands I am giving you today. For the LORD your God will bless you as he has promised, and you will lend to many nations but will borrow from none. You will rule over many nations but none will rule over you.
>
> If there is a poor man among your brothers in any of the towns of the land that the LORD your God is giving you, do

not be hardhearted or tightfisted toward your poor brother. Rather be openhanded and freely lend him whatever he needs. Be careful not to harbor this wicked thought: "The seventh year, the year for canceling debts, is near," so that you do not show ill will toward your needy brother and give him nothing. He may then appeal to the LORD against you, and you will be found guilty of sin. Give generously to him and do so without a grudging heart; then because of this the LORD your God will bless you in all your work and in everything you put your hand to. There will always be poor people in the land. Therefore I command you to be openhanded toward your brothers and toward the poor and needy in your land.

—Deut. 15:1–11

"Bankruptcy law is actually in the Constitution," I said, feeling didactic in my lawyerly role. "Congress has authority over it. That's why it's a federal court."

"Interesting," Hal replied, "and quite biblical. I think God would approve of the bankruptcy law. Do you think the authors of the Constitution were thinking of him when they put that in?"

"More likely they were thinking about the need to have the law be the same everywhere in the country," I said. "Otherwise people would run around from state to state looking for the most favorable law."

"Of course. I was probably too naive in thinking that the Bible might have something to do with how the law handles matters involving money."

"Well, it might," I said. "Most of the founders were pretty familiar with it. I just don't know the history."

"Anyway, the Bible is much too radical for most people to deal with on this issue. Let's take a look at it."

Deuteronomy 15 mandates the *shemitah,* the cancellation of all debts on a seven-year cycle. The cancellation applies to all debt, not just those of debtors in distress or who ask for it. And it applies only to loans to fellow Israelites, not to foreigners.

"The loan," Hal said, "is based on the borrower's need. It's a loan made to 'the poor and needy in your land,' the very people who would be unable to get a loan in commercial society. It's not part of a system of commerce but of a welfare system. It's a command from God to care for the poor and needy. Just like the tithes we studied in the last chapter are to go to the Levites, the widows and fatherless, and the aliens."

"It sounds like a command that would get a lot of resistance," I said. "I can't imagine applying it in the church today."

"Oh, yes," he replied. "The Jews have struggled with this one since it was given to them. You can't imagine the ways they have thought of to get around it. The Philadelphia lawyers have been busy devising evasions for centuries."

"Like what?" My Philadelphia lawyer's curiosity was piqued.

"Well, try this. One idea is that the command is not to cancel the debt but just defer it for the sabbatical year. This is tied to the command in other scriptures to let the land lie fallow every seventh year. Since the debtor would have no income from the land that year, he would have no ability to make payment. This would also explain the exemption of the debt of a foreigner from the requirement of cancellation: the foreigner would not be obligated to let the land lie fallow and would be able to pay his debts."

"What's wrong with that?" I asked.

"If deferral is all God requires," Hal replied, "then it isn't clear why Moses went to such lengths to exhort Israel not to avoid loans to the poor as the sabbatical year approaches. Certainly a lender can calculate the effect of a one-year deferral. If payment is to be deferred only for a year, it should not be the deterrent to lending that the text anticipates."

"OK, I see that," I said. "Were there other evasions?"

"Yes, several. Another one is to take the requirement literally, as a cancellation of the debt, but to add that the borrower still has a moral obligation to repay. Thus, if you pick your borrower well, you will be assured of repayment despite the law mandating forgiveness. The criteria for lending would shift to assessing the good character of the borrower to make sure he would honor the obligation despite the law."

"And that's not what the Scripture says," I observed. "The loan is supposed to go to the poor and needy."

"Right," Hal said. "The text gives no hint that the borrower continues to be under a moral obligation to repay; the moral obligations it addresses are entirely those of the lender."

"What else?" I asked.

"Another approach commonly followed in Jewish interpretation is to limit the application of the law to agricultural communities in 'Erets Yisrael,' that is, the land of Israel. This made it conveniently inapplicable to most Jews in most times and places until the widespread return of Jews to the land in the twentieth century and the reestablishment of agricultural communities there."

"And the Scripture doesn't make that limitation either," I said.

"It does not," Hal said. "Although the command is given to a community that's about to become an agricultural society, there is again nothing in the text itself to limit it in this way."

"Quite a list. I see what you mean about the Philadelphia lawyers."

"I've got one more. Around the time of Jesus, the Jewish sage Hillel came up with a device to avoid the effect of the remittance of debt. It's called the 'prosbul,' and it consists of the creditor turning the debt over to a court for collection. The 'prosbul' may be used to protect a creditor against an unscrupulous debtor, and the court can do what the individual cannot do under the shemitah."

"So the creditor washes his hands of the matter but lets the court go after the debtor for him?" I asked. "It sounds like the kind of technical compliance that avoids acting out of right motivation of the heart— just what Jesus preached against. But, Hal, really, how do you keep lazy people from taking advantage of something like this? It sounds like Hillel may have been dealing with a practical problem. People run up debt knowing they won't have to pay it, and don't do the work that other people do to be able to support themselves. It's like the welfare dependency that we've been struggling with in this country. It becomes a way of life for some people to just live off others."

"I think the community could figure out who is in real need and who is trying to live off the system," Hal said. "In Israel, where the tribes had territories and people lived in extended families and agricultural communities, the poor and needy could be separated from the lazy and the cunning. But there is a danger here, and the larger the society and the greater the population, the more of a problem it can be.

"You notice that it says in verse four that, because of the blessings of the land, there should be no poor people. In a perfect society, that would be true. But God is realistic, and a few verses later the passage says there will always be poor people among you. Jesus quoted this verse when the disciples complained about the woman who wasted a bottle of expensive perfume on him instead of selling it and giving the proceeds to the poor. All of our giving—or lending in this case—is not supposed to go to the poor. Some should be used to glorify God in other ways."

We had finished our coffee, so we donned our coats, pulled on our gloves, and started for the car. It was December; a light snow covered the ground. The wind was from the north; it stung my cheeks and even blew through my heavy overcoat. I began to wish we had parked closer but was glad I had heeded Anna's advice to wear a scarf and a hat.

The courthouse was on the edge of a rundown neighborhood. As we approached the car, a small woman wearing a thin, worn coat hurried by us. She had what looked like a threadbare summer dress underneath. She was pulling a small boy by the hand, almost dragging him in her hurry to get through the winter air to whatever warmth lay ahead of them. He was dressed as lightly as she was, with a sweatshirt instead of a jacket for outerwear. Neither had gloves, mittens, or head covering.

As they passed, the woman glanced sidelong at us, the kind of cold look the poor give the rich. I wondered briefly what thoughts lay behind that look. Was it envy? Hatred? Perhaps she was thinking, "Shame on you, secure in your warmth, while my child and I can't afford the clothing to keep warm."

Hal saw the look too. As we came to the car, he paused before getting in. "We talked earlier," he said, "about the different kinds of law in the Old Testament, and whether it made any difference in our thinking about how they apply today. Do you think the law of lending freely to the poor and forgiving the debt in the seventh year is a ceremonial, judicial, or moral law?"

I paused, hand on the door handle, eager to get in and start the engine and enjoy the flood of warmth that would soon follow. "It has to be moral," I said. Hal didn't need to remind me that almost everyone thought the moral laws of the Old Testament still applied. "But, Hal," I went on, "we live in a very different world. Now the government takes care of the poor. We pay taxes—more than a tithe—and meet these moral obligations by welfare, food stamps, homeless shelters, and all the things the government does."

"But doesn't do very well," Hal replied. "If you think the government is doing everything needed, go ask your city welfare director. Or ask some of the people involved in the agencies that provide services to these people. You can ask the pastors, too. Most of them know how bad things are for some of their people. And most of the people who are in the greatest need probably never see the inside of a church."

I started the car. We drove in silence for a few minutes. The welcome warmth of engine heat began to flood the passenger compartment.

Hal finally spoke. "I tried to do something about it once. I used to keep track of my people, not just preach to them. When someone gets burned out in a fire or has a major health problem, you can get people to help. But for plain old poverty, it's a different story.

"We had a family that had been out of work for some time. I could see them going downhill. The husband got unemployment checks for a while, but then it ran out. The wife was in poor health and had never been able to work much. They had a slew of kids, and she needed to be at home anyway. I went to see them and find out how bad it was. They were getting food stamps and keeping the kids fed, sort of. But they couldn't meet their house payments or their car payments. They were months behind on both and were about to lose their home and means of transportation. They had nowhere to go, and without a car it would be almost impossible for him to find work."

"What did you do?"

"I went to my elder board, but the cupboard was bare. We were behind on collections and weren't making the budget. They were worried about paying for oil to heat the church and that kind of thing. So I went to some prominent families in the church to ask for help for this family. The first four refused me. They were upset that I asked. They didn't think they were a welfare system or that it was any business of the church. Call the town or some agency, they said. They made their pledge to the church and that was that. I struck pay dirt with the fifth family. They couldn't really afford it, but they borrowed from their pension fund and got up enough money to tide the folks over—to catch up on the house and car payments—until he finally found work again. And they thanked me for telling them about the need."

"Great story; did they ever get repaid?"

"Not entirely a great story," Hal replied. "I don't know if they got repaid or not. The elders and the other families I had asked to help said I wasn't doing my job right. I was spending my time worrying about people making car payments, and my preaching was suffering. They were paying me to lead a worship service and oversee the programs of the church, not run a welfare society. Basically, they got me fired. I heard the family that had the needs and the family that helped them left the church after I did. But my next pastorate was quite a distance away, and I didn't stay in touch. I got Christmas cards for awhile, but you know how it is."

I shook my head. I was beginning to understand the time in the coffee shop months before, when Hal said he had been a failure, when he didn't want to talk about it. Glancing over at him, I could see the sadness back in his eyes. He opened his ever-present Bible and retreated into his knowledge of it to keep up the conversation as we drove back.

"The notion of the shemitah—the release of debts—is one of the most radical notions in the Bible, one of the least honored, and one of the commands that is most contrary to human instinct," he said. "The first requirement of releasing debt, of course, is that there be debt to be released. Those who have the means are not to be 'hardhearted or tightfisted' toward the poor, but rather be 'open-handed' and 'freely' lending, 'giving generously.' They are to remember that their blessings come from the Lord, and that what they 'own' is not really theirs but is held for God, who owns the heavens and the earth, and that they are not to be invested in the temporary things of the world.

"God sees the heart, and grudging obedience doesn't honor him. It's a great sin to withhold generosity because the time of remission is near and the lender may not get repaid. The lender's thought and motive should be to honor God and love his fellows by helping the poor and needy. The obligation of forgiving should not lead to the sin of unforgiveness. 'There should be no poor among you' says verse four. And this would be so if the law was followed. In Acts chapter four, the early church was a community that shared possessions and distributed to those who had need, so that 'there were no needy persons among them.'

"Jesus teaches the forgiveness of debt in the Lord's Prayer: 'Forgive us our debts as we forgive our debtors.' I don't know if Jesus was thinking of this passage in Deuteronomy or not when he taught the Lord's Prayer—or that part of it—but that teaches the real meaning of this passage. Our generosity to those in need is like God's generosity to us. We are paupers in his kingdom, poor and in need of his grace for salvation. Our debt of sin to him is not repayable. We are at his mercy, but he doesn't withhold his generous grace from those who believe. How dare we not forgive the debts of others when he has freely forgiven us?"

I pondered these matters the rest of the day. Our economic system of capitalism works by its appeal to human nature. Its success is due to the fact that it rewards those who are hard working, creative, and strong contributors to the overall success of the economy. People want to be rewarded for what they do, and have a sense of the justness of the reward. They have earned it; they took the risk; they did the work; they had the idea. And when they achieve substantial material well-being as a result, many see it only as something to be expended on themselves. Yet God says that no matter how talented we are or how hard we work, everything we have is a gift from him. We are obligated to be openhanded and generous to the poor and needy among us, without regard to repayment. Our generosity will be rewarded by more blessings from God. We have nothing to give away that is not already God's, and our reward for openhanded generosity will surely be given. "Lay up your treasures in heaven," Jesus taught.

Where had I laid up my treasures? My sleep was troubled that night. I went to sleep resolving to discuss with Anna in the morning how we could do more for those in need.

It was the following evening before we got to have the discussion. Anna read chapter fifteen for herself before we talked about it.

"Helping the poor and needy," she said, "is one of the most consistent teachings of the Bible. I think you and I are disobedient about this, and it doesn't give me much comfort that just about every other believer is as well. But I think you're getting a little hung up on the matter of lending and forgiving. That may have been the way to do it then, but that was a very different world. Who are you going to lend to anyway? And how are you going to find them? What's that phrase Hal taught you? 'Text without context is pretext'? Look at the rest of the chapter; it's about slavery. How do you apply that today?"

We read the next section of the chapter.

> If a fellow Hebrew, a man or a woman, sells himself to you and serves you six years, in the seventh year you must let him go free. And when you release him, do not send him away empty-handed. Supply him liberally from your flock, your threshing floor and your winepress. Give to him as the LORD your God has blessed you. Remember that you were slaves in Egypt and the LORD your God redeemed you. That is why I give you this command today.
>
> But if your servant says to you, "I do not want to leave you," because he loves you and your family and is well off with you, then take an awl and push it through his ear lobe into the door, and he will become your servant for life. Do the same for your maidservant.
>
> Do not consider it a hardship to set your servant free, because his service to you these six years has been worth twice as much as that of a hired hand. And the LORD your God will bless you in everything you do.
>
> —Deut. 15:12–18

Together, Anna and I concluded that the passage is not really about slavery but what people used to call indentured servitude, a concept that persisted until relatively recent times. People became servants for a period of time to learn a profession or skill from a master, to pay for passage to a new land, or to provide for themselves in cases of poverty.

In patriarchal times, Jacob served Laban for seven years and got Leah for a bride because she was the older sister. But he really wanted Rachel, so he served another seven years for her.

In modern American law, the right to compel service from a human being disappeared with the thirteenth amendment to the constitution, forbidding slavery or involuntary servitude. Court decisions have made it clear that regardless of any contract, an employer cannot compel a person to continue to work for him, though he may be able to recover damages if he suffers harm from the employee's refusal to honor an employment contract. In a famous English case, *Lumley v. Guy*, where a singer refused to give a performance to which she had agreed, the court found she could not be compelled to sing but would have to compensate the other party for losses due to her refusal.

In Deuteronomy, servitude among Israelites was the product of poverty. A way of dealing with adverse economic circumstances was to sell oneself. This was not slavery in the sense of compulsory servitude—the ownership of one human being by another—but rather a way of using one's ability to provide services to buy security or pay debts. The release of the servant in the seventh year followed the same thought as the release of debts in the seventh year. The cycle of release of the servant appeared to be related to the years of servitude rather than the seventh year, regardless of when the obligation began, as with the forgiveness of debt in the earlier part of the chapter, but the principle was the same. No member of the covenant community was to be deprived of personal or economic liberty indefinitely, no matter what circumstances brought them into the situation.

We thought it understandable that some servants might refuse the opportunity of liberty when the seventh year came. The reality of supporting themselves independently may be more than they want to undertake; they may be better off in their service than outside of it. The ceremony of pushing the awl through the earlobe into the door was curious, though. When we came to that, we decided to call Hal.

"It is curious to us," he said, "but probably was well understood by people at the time. It may have symbolized the requirement that the servant hear the master. It may have been the binding of the servant to the household. Or, perhaps it was for the placement of an earring or other symbol of servanthood not mentioned in the text. In any event, the servant was bound only for the master's life, not the servant's, and the obligation could not be transmitted to the master's heirs. And even in such cases, the servant was to be freed in the year of Jubilee, the fiftieth year, as set forth in the twenty-fifth chapter of Leviticus."

Hal agreed with Anna that the release of servants was part of the same thought as the forgiveness of debt. "And notice," he said, "the fact that the servant may choose to stay with the master when offered freedom presumes that the master will treat the servant benignly. There is no warrant for a master being a Simon Legree."

He also told us that verse fourteen had a wonderful imagery in the Hebrew. The words *supply him* were, literally, "put upon his neck" (make a necklace for him of those things that he needed to start out again, from the flock, the threshing floor, and the winepress).

"The central thought again," Hal said, "is generosity. The servant is not just to be released but to be released with generous provision to sustain himself. And the master is not to be resentful of the obligation of release or consider it a hardship. He has gotten his money's worth.

"God calls to their attention again that they are to do this in memory of the fact that they were slaves in Egypt, and the Lord redeemed them. Always the Golden Rule. God did for them, so how dare they not do as much for others? Just as God in his grace and mercy has saved us from the bondage of sin and provided eternal life. How dare we not be generous with others?"

After we hung up, Anna and I returned to our discussion. She suggested that this passage gave a biblical mandate for employers to be fair, and even generous, with their employees. Owners might have the legal right to keep all of the business profit for themselves, but the Bible taught a more generous attitude. I was one of a number of lawyers who owned my law firm. She suggested that I ought to think about this when we determine wages and benefits for our staff. It wasn't a favor to people to pay or promote those who haven't earned it, or to employ those who aren't able to meet the job requirements and pretend they are OK when they aren't, or to pay people more than the value of their service. But employers need to think about more than the bottom line of profits. Christian employers should have a very different attitude toward employees than others might. Employee welfare should be as much a concern to the enterprise as is churning out profits.

We went back to the matter of lending to the poor and forgiving debts, and we resolved to review our budget to see what more we could allocate to the needy, and to investigate how we could most effectively use our resources. Finally, we decided to approach the pastor and elders of our church and ask them to establish a fund to help needy people within the church and the community. We agreed that setting aside a little money from time to time in case a need came up was not sufficient. The fund should be substantial, enough to be meaningfully helpful. There should be a way of making people aware that the fund existed, and a solid administrative system for it within the congregation. Based on Deuteronomy, chapter fifteen, we thought the church should have its own welfare system—for its members and its neighbors. There should be no poor among us.

Then we read the remainder of chapter fifteen together.

> Set apart for the LORD your God every firstborn male of your herds and flocks. Do not put the firstborn of your oxen to work, and do not shear the firstborn of your sheep. Each year you and your family are to eat them in the presence of the LORD your God at the place he will choose. If an animal has a defect, is lame or blind, or has any serious flaw, you must not sacrifice it to the LORD your God. You are to eat it in your own towns. Both the ceremonially unclean and the clean may eat it, as if it were gazelle or deer. But you must not eat the blood; pour it out on the ground like water.
> —Deut. 15:19–23

The sacrifice of the firstborn of the herds and flocks in the Lord's presence "at the place he will choose" repeats a command given in chapters twelve and fourteen. It was the third time I had encountered it in my study of Deuteronomy.

"But," Anna pointed out, "I notice that they're not to sacrifice an animal with a defect, that is lame or blind, or has a serious flaw. It's not a sacrifice to give God your junk. We are to give him our best, not what we would cast aside anyway. I think this applies to everything we give him—our time, our praise, our service, our money. God doesn't want our throwaways. He wants the things that are most valuable and meaningful to us; that's what we should be giving him."

"How do we do that?" I asked her. "Put some flesh on it."

"OK . . . our gifts of money should not be extras, the leftover. They should be built into our obligations, like the mortgage. Our time with the Lord in prayer, studying the Scriptures, the time we devote to him, should not be when we don't have anything else to do. We should be in some kind of service to him, whatever it is. It may be different for everyone. But again, it should be something that is a real and continuing commitment, not the occasional project when we can spare the time. If we have a heart of faith, we will want to make this kind of gift to God, and God knows our hearts."

I was thankful for her heart, and thought how wise, or fortunate, I was when I married her. And, I thought, Hal would have approved of Anna's summary.

I added my own thoughts: "Jesus is, of course, the perfect sacrifice, the one without sin. When God sacrificed himself for us, he gave perfection, the offer of the only unblemished one to cleanse us."

"It's funny," she said with a smile. "For a minute, I thought I was listening to Hal. Then I looked up and it was you."

Hal would have been smiling too.

I was beginning to get it.

CHAPTER SIXTEEN

Holiday season had arrived. Department stores were crammed with shoppers checking off their family members' request lists. Bing Crosby crooned "White Christmas" and "Frosty the Snowman" over their sound systems, and it seemed somehow appropriate that most of the music now came from satellites raining their pulses of electromagnetic radiation down from the heavens. Musicians of every genre—most of whom hadn't entered a church, even for any of their several weddings—recorded their own Christmas albums celebrating the Savior's birth. People who were normally grumpy warmly greeted others they hardly knew. Jews invited themselves to the party with Hanukkah, while Christians fretted about the commercialization of the birth of Christ. Newspaper editors dug up old stories from astronomers speculating that a nova or conjunction of planets provided a natural explanation of the star of Bethlehem. Online and phone vendors warned that they could not guarantee delivery before December 25 unless orders were placed by a certain date.

It seemed like a good time to visit with Hal. Actually, it was Anna's idea. We should invite him for dinner, she said, before Christmas. We should find out what he was doing for Christmas; people who lived alone got depressed around the holidays when everyone else was with family. If he didn't have other plans, he could spend Christmas Day with us. Besides, chapter sixteen of Deuteronomy is all about holidays, isn't it? The guys could talk about it; it would bore her to tears, but maybe she'd listen in.

Hal readily accepted.

The ham and sweet potatoes were a preview of the Christmas dinner we would enjoy as a family in a few days. Hal got on warmly with the kids, regaling them with tales from his childhood. He told them about naughty things he had done and spankings he had deservedly received; about sneaking into a pasture with a friend to provoke a bull and scrambling over the fence just in time to avoid disaster; about building rafts to pole across little ponds; and about a time before electric refrigerators, when he followed the ice man to get scraps of ice to suck on in the summer heat. When he had them eating out of his hand, he asked if they knew that Jesus especially loved children and always wanted them around him. Then he told the kids that Jesus said we should be like children to get into heaven because God was like a father who loved us and protected us and wanted everyone, even grownups, to be his children. Then, just before they went to bed, he told them to be sure to thank God for what they had, for their mother and father and home and the things that Santa would bring them for Christmas. He said they should be sure to tell God about all the naughty things they had done and that they were sorry so he would forgive them. Finally, he told them to tell God they loved him, just like he loved them, and that they would try their best to be as kind as they could to everybody and to be the sort of children he wants them to be.

How fortunate a child would be, I thought, to have Hal for a father.

After the kids were in bed, our talk turned to holidays. Hal advised us not to trouble our consciences about the commercial part of Christmas. People need holidays; that's why God gave them in Scripture. As long as we kept the holy aspects before us, there was nothing wrong with the rest of it. The gift giving, goodwill, and many reminders of miraculous events surrounding the birth of Christ and the saving purpose of his advent were good reminders to everyone of our culture's Christian foundations. When we asked about his Christmas plans, he told us he would be traveling to see his daughter and her family in the Boston area. We didn't press him more about family, remembering Julie's story about the death of his wife and two sons.

Then we opened our Bibles and read the first eight verses in chapter sixteen, about the three Jewish holidays, the "pilgrimage festivals" that were to be celebrated in the place the Lord would choose as a dwelling for his Name.

Observe the month of Abib and celebrate the Passover of the LORD your God, because in the month of Abib he brought you out of Egypt by night. Sacrifice as the Passover to the LORD your God an animal from your flock or herd at the place the LORD will choose as a dwelling for his Name. Do not eat it with bread made with yeast, but for seven days eat unleavened bread, the bread of affliction, because you left Egypt in haste—so that all the days of your life you may remember the time of your departure from Egypt. Let no yeast be found in your possession in all your land for seven days. Do not let any of the meat you sacrifice on the evening of the first day remain until morning.

You must not sacrifice the Passover in any town the LORD your God gives you except in the place he will choose as a dwelling for his Name. There you must sacrifice the Passover in the evening, when the sun goes down, on the anniversary of your departure from Egypt. Roast it and eat it at the place the LORD your God will choose. Then in the morning return to your tents. For six days eat unleavened bread and on the seventh day hold an assembly to the LORD your God and do no work.

—Deut. 16:1–8

"The Jewish festivals are hopelessly confusing to most Christians," Hal said. "Passover is called 'pesakh' in Hebrew and is combined with the Festival of Unleavened Bread that follows it. But you know what this is in Christian holidays, don't you?"

We did. Passover is Easter, we told him. The last supper that Jesus shared with the disciples was a Passover meal.

"It's a 'movable feast,'" Hal said. "Did you know that term means a holiday or festival that doesn't always happen on the same day, not a meal that moves around?"

We did not, so Hal explained further.

"The date of Passover varies from year to year, depending on the cycle of the moon in the Jewish month of Abib. Later, after the exile, they used the Babylonian name *Nisan*. It falls in March or April in the modern calendar. Julie invited me to share Passover with her family in New York once."

He told us about the elaborate custom and ritual surrounding the Seder (Passover) meal that is eaten the Thursday evening before Good Friday. It is a memorial celebration commemorating the exodus from Egypt, the night God brought Israel out of its captivity there. The last plague the Lord sent on Pharaoh and the Egyptians—and the one that caused Pharaoh to let them depart—was the death of the firstborn. The Israelites were instructed to slaughter the Passover lamb. Then they were to take a bunch of hyssop, dip it in the blood, and put some on the top and both sides of the door frames of their houses. The Lord struck down the firstborn of the Egyptians but passed over the Israelites' homes, which had the lamb's blood on them.

The Feast of Unleavened Bread immediately follows the Passover. For seven days the people eat no bread made with yeast, but rather matzah—unleavened bread, "the bread of affliction." It is unleavened because the Israelites left Egypt in such haste that they didn't have time to allow the bread to rise with the yeast and so took unleavened bread for the journey. The reference to matzah as the bread of affliction is variously understood as referring to their slavery in Egypt, to the hardships of the journey, or to the bread of the poor or humble. The leaven or yeast is often understood as symbolizing corruption, pride, and egotism. The meat that is sacrificed must be eaten before morning so it will not spoil or corrupt.

"Not only did they not eat bread," Hal said of his visit with Julie's family, "but they would not even possess it. They threw out or gave away everything in the house that contained leaven. They boiled any utensils that might have had contact with it. Then they took ten pieces of leavened bread that had been set aside and hid them in the house. The lights were turned out, and the children got to search for them by candlelight. When each piece was found, they swept it into a bag with a feather and burned it. After that, they had the Seder meal."

"I know the Last Supper was a Passover meal," I said, "but is there more to it as far as the Christian significance goes?"

Hal replied, "The church, coming as it did from the Jewish people, recognized immediately the significance of the Passover and Feast of Unleavened Bread and all those holy days represented in Christ.

"Jesus used yeast as a symbol of sin and evil. In Mark eight and Matthew sixteen, we see that he warned against the yeast of the Pharisees and Herod, and in Luke twelve he equated yeast with hypocrisy. Paul urged Christian believers to keep the Festival, not with the old yeast of malice and wickedness but with the unleavened bread of sincerity and truth.

"Isaiah had prophesied that the suffering servant, who was led like a lamb to the slaughter, had the iniquity of us all laid on him. John the Baptist saw in Jesus 'the Lamb of God, who takes away the sin of the world!' John's Gospel connects Jesus directly to the Passover lamb. Exodus says none of the lamb's bones are to be broken. In crucifixion, it was normal to break the legs of the crucified man to hasten death. But when the soldiers were ready to do this to Jesus, they found he was already dead and refrained from doing so.

"In First Corinthians five, Paul described Jesus as the Passover lamb. In Revelation, Jesus is described as a lamb, looking as if it had been slain: 'Worthy is the Lamb, who was slain, to receive power and wealth and wisdom and strength and honor and glory and praise.'" He recited from Revelation 5 the great heavenly hymn of praise to Jesus, sung by ten thousand times ten thousand.

"For Christians, the Passover meal is the sacrament of communion, the partaking of the bread and wine, which represent the body and blood of the sacrificial lamb. Jesus introduced the sacrament of communion at the Passover meal of the Last Supper. His death has the same liberating effect for Christian believers—in freeing them from the burden of sin—that the Passover had for Jews in freeing them from the bondage of Egypt."

A sound from outside interrupted us. We went to the window to find a group of carolers on the sidewalk, singing several old carols. Hal opened the door and walked out into the cold. "Sing 'Silent Night,'" he called. Anna and I joined him, coatless, on the steps, as the little choir rendered the soft strains of the familiar hymn. I could hear Hal's off-key voice joining them. The stars shone down on our pastoral scene, and one almost could imagine the angels descending on us, little flock that we were, with Hal, our shepherd, to announce the Savior's birth. When the carolers left, we left Passover and went on to the Feast of Weeks.

> Count off seven weeks from the time you begin to put the sickle to the standing grain. Then celebrate the Feast of Weeks to the LORD your God by giving a freewill offering in proportion to the blessings the LORD your God has given you. And rejoice before the LORD your God at the place he will choose as a dwelling for his Name—you, your sons and daughters, your menservants and maidservants, the Levites in your towns, and the aliens, the fatherless and the widows living among you. Remember that you were slaves in Egypt, and follow carefully these decrees.
>
> —Deut. 16:9–12

"Shavuot, first fruits, harvest, Pentecost: They have so many names for it; no wonder people get confused," Hal said. "The Feast of Weeks is held—as the passage says—'seven weeks from the time you begin to put the sickle to the standing grain.' The time is counted from the second night of the Passover. The term *Pentecost* means fifty days and refers to the days from the Passover to the Feast of Weeks. It celebrates the spring harvest, but someone figured out that the Feast of Weeks is the time that the law was given at Sinai, so that's the traditional understanding. The time between Passover and Weeks is the bridge from the celebration of freedom to the celebration of law, two equally important poles for God's people."

"What is the significance to Christians?" Anna asked.

"This feast is Pentecost, and the Christian significance is told in the first two chapters of the Book of Acts," Hal said. "Jesus had told the disciples to wait in Jerusalem until they were baptized by the Holy Spirit. On the day of Pentecost, a time of gathering of pilgrims in Jerusalem, the disciples were together among Jews from all lands. The Holy Spirit descended on them with tongues of fire, and they were able to speak the gospel in the languages of people from many different countries. In a sense, it was the time of the founding of the church, when the believers were endowed with power to be witnesses for Christ throughout the world. As God gave the law at Sinai, he gave the church at Pentecost as a means to draw men to him through Christ."

We went on to the Feast of Tabernacles, beginning at verse thirteen:

> Celebrate the Feast of Tabernacles for seven days after you have gathered the produce of your threshing floor and your winepress. Be joyful at your Feast—you, your sons and daughters, your menservants and maidservants, and the Levites, the aliens, the fatherless and the widows who live in your towns. For seven days celebrate the Feast to the LORD your God at the place the LORD will choose. For the LORD your God will bless you in all your harvest and in all the work of your hands, and your joy will be complete.
>
> Three times a year all your men must appear before the LORD your God at the place he will choose: at the Feast of Unleavened Bread, the Feast of Weeks, and the Feast of Tabernacles. No man should appear before the LORD empty-handed: Each of you must bring a gift in proportion to the way the LORD your God has blessed you.
>
> —Deut. 16:13–17

"Tabernacles, Booths, Ingathering, Sukkot," Hal said. "Again, many names. As the Feast of Weeks celebrates the spring harvest, so does the Feast of Tabernacles celebrate the fall harvest."

Anticipating our question, he went on. "There is no Christian counterpart to the Feast of Tabernacles. Both Weeks and Tabernacles are much like our Thanksgiving, harvest celebrations that presume there is not only something to be thankful for, but Someone who is worthy of thanks. You cannot escape the religious nature of Thanksgiving.

"They do add other elements: Weeks is also a celebration of the giving of the law, and Tabernacles is celebrated five days after the Jewish high holy days. The holy days begin with Rosh Hashanah, the Jewish New Year. There are ten days of repentance, ending with Yom Kippur, the Day of Atonement. The booths, or tabernacles, recall the time of hardship in the desert and God's provision for them during this time.

"But notice a couple of things: Both the Feast of Weeks and the Feast of Tabernacles are inclusive of everyone—sons and daughters, menservants and maidservants, Levites, aliens, widows, and the father-less. God's blessings through the harvest are to fall on all, and all are to be thankful for it and participate in the celebration.

"Notice also that these are to be joyous occasions. Three times in this passage, some form of the word *joy* is used: rejoice, be joyful, your joy will be complete. God's people are to enjoy the fruits of his blessing, and their time of praise for this is to be a time of joy."

We discussed how the phrase *your joy may be complete* is carried forward in the New Testament. Jesus used it in John 15 to describe how the believers will feel if they remain in his love and bear fruit for him. Paul used the phrase in Philippians to describe how he would feel when the believers love one another as Christ has loved them and have a unity of spirit and purpose. John used the phrase in his letters to describe his feeling on writing of his experience with Jesus, the Word of Life, and how he will feel when he can see the people to whom he is writing face to face. Joy before the Lord is completed in believers' submission to him and fellowship in him, just as in the unity of the believing community in its festivals of thanksgiving and remembrance in the Old Testament. Once again, Jesus and the New Testament writers carried forward God's language and thinking from the Old Testament.

Finally, we discussed the requirement, in connection with the feasts, that "No man should appear before the Lord empty-handed."

"This command is given twice in Exodus as well," Hal said. "The obvious meaning is the literal, and tied in to the next verse. Each is to bring an offering in proportion to how the Lord has blessed him. Luther viewed the meaning in its application to his time to be more spiritual, but still applied it in this life—giving thanks and bringing praise before the Lord.

"But my favorite is Paterius. He was a disciple of Gregory the Great from the sixth and seventh century. Paterius saw the ultimate spiritual meaning of coming before the Lord empty-handed. The empty-handed are those who come before the Lord at the judgment bringing none of the fruits of their labor with them. They are the ones who pursue only the things they have to leave behind at death—earthly praise and power. Having a meritorious life of acting well brings the believer before the Lord as he wants and needs to be. It is the man who does not plan for the reward of a meritorious life that appears empty-handed before the Lord."

After Hal left, Anna and I held out our hands and joined them together. As our children slept the innocent sleep of childhood upstairs, we looked at the loss of innocence that we shared with each other and everyone else.

"What do you think?" she asked. "Are we empty-handed?"

I couldn't answer. From our discussion of the ancient harvest holidays in the midst of the modern carnival of Christmas, Hal had somehow led us back to the fire. *Paterius*, I thought, *someone who won't even know who you are will have reason to thank you.*

CHAPTER SEVENTEEN

The holidays had passed. The routine busyness that follows the turn of the year had set in. Other holidays were ahead—Martin Luther King Day, Presidents' Day—but it would be summer before another change of mood like the holiday season would visit us.

"It's time to talk about government," Hal had said when I called to arrange our next date. "Let's meet in your office."

My office is in the center of the capital city of our state. From my window, the State House dominates the view. Its gold dome rises above the surroundings, over the spacious plaza with statues of New Hampshire's most famous son, Daniel Webster; its only President, Franklin Pierce; and its Revolutionary War hero, John Stark. It is visible for miles and marks the center and the dignity of government in our postage-stamp state. The legislative chambers of the House and Senate are within. The governor sits in a second-floor corner office, a short walk down the hall from each. Legislative and state office buildings consume most of several surrounding blocks. A short walk away, other agencies occupy a former state mental institution renovated into an office park. Other agencies are in a complex of new buildings across town to the east, and rented space tucked here and there among the commercial sprawl of car dealerships and fast food restaurants along major arteries into the city.

Hal came over on a Saturday morning. A warm and welcome sunshine took the chill from the January air. Snow banks were melting, spreading a sheen of water over streets and sidewalks. It was a day to wear a lighter coat or unbutton heavier ones and look forward to the more enduring warmth that was still several months away.

"Remember, we skipped the government part of chapter one way back when," Hal said when he had settled down. "You were going to tell me about it."

We opened our Bibles and read Deuteronomy 1:9 to 1:18, the verses we had skipped before. Hal reminded me that Moses spoke here about what happened at Sinai, just after the Israelites had left Egypt, almost forty years before they gathered on the Plains of Moab to cross over the Jordan into the Promised Land.

> At that time I said to you, "You are too heavy a burden for me to carry alone. The LORD your God has increased your numbers so that today you are as many as the stars in the sky. May the LORD, the God of your fathers, increase you a thousand times and bless you as he has promised! But how can I bear your problems and your burdens and your disputes all by myself? Choose some wise, understanding and respected men from each of your tribes, and I will set them over you."

> You answered me, "What you propose to do is good."

> So I took the leading men of your tribes, wise and respected men, and appointed them to have authority over you—as commanders of thousands, of hundreds, of fifties, and of tens and as tribal officials. And I charged your judges at that time: Hear the disputes between your brothers and judge fairly, whether the case is between brother Israelites or between one of them and an alien. Do not show partiality in judging; hear both small and great alike. Do not be afraid of any man, for judgment belongs to God. Bring me any case too hard for you, and I will hear it. And at that time I told you everything you were to do.

Studying these verses made sense now. They addressed issues of governance, as did the end of chapter sixteen and all of chapter seventeen. They explained how God's chosen nation was to handle the matters of daily life that required the oversight or decision of some higher authority. Moses apparently had served that function alone at first, but the people were only in the third month out of Egypt. They had become as many as "the stars in the sky," an expression that was obviously figurative but in fulfillment of the promises to the patriarchs hundreds of years earlier. Moses needed help to govern and lead such a numerous people, with all of their problems and burdens and disputes.

"How do you understand this passage as a model for government?" Hal asked me.

"First of all," I replied, "government is necessary. This is no longer a family or a tribe, where one person can deal with all the problems. They are 'as many as the stars in the sky' and 'too heavy a burden' for Moses to carry alone. I suppose all human government reflects this. When people lived in small groups, they didn't need organization. Now they do."

"Good start," Hal said. "Regardless of how much some people may dislike government, it is necessary."

I continued. "The leaders—wise, understanding, and respected men—were to be chosen by the people, but the passage also says that Moses was to 'set them over you.' There is democracy in the choice, but Moses retains the authority to appoint. That part works only if you have a Moses, someone designated by God to give leadership, who can exercise that control. Presumably the appointment was not automatic, or it would have been meaningless."

"And we don't have a Moses to oversee and approve our choices," Hal said. "I wonder how many of our elected officials would hold their offices if Moses were here to veto the choices we make."

"Appointment versus election," I mused. "It sounds more like issues of church government than civil government."

"Remember that in Moses' time Israel was both a church and a state," Hal said. "Churches have to have government too. Let's take a walk."

We walked out into the winter brightness and strolled around the town. The churches, whose silhouetted steeples had pierced and formed the evening skyline when we were leaving the restaurant after discussing chapter twelve, now assumed more familiar shapes. Old brick, new brick, granite gray, yellow stone, wooden churches, brick or stone churches with wood additions, back rooms and upper rooms where start-up groups were meeting—a potpourri of church architecture and worship spaces each briefly caught our attention as we wandered the streets.

The potpourri of churches was not just *in* their buildings. Church governance, how each body of believers organized itself and assigned roles of authority, was just as mixed. As we passed one church and another, Hal talked about the mix of election and appointment in each—about the two poles of leadership selection in Deuteronomy, chapter one.

"Church governance, or polity," he said, "is an issue that every church and denomination must resolve. It comes down to a matter of authority—who can make decisions, and about what. The Israel of Moses was both a church and a nation. It had to have a way of making decisions that were in keeping with God's law and will—a way that resolved disputes and issues that may or may not have had direct religious relevance. Christians have generally looked to New Testament models for church governance, and have reached very different conclusions."

We were passing a Catholic church. A large parking lot and adjacent parish hall and parochial school attested to the size and health of the church. Nearby was a rectory where the clergy resided. It was one of four Catholic parishes in the city.

"On the one hand," Hal said as we passed by, "there is hierarchical church governance. This is the appointive understanding of church government that comes from Matthew sixteen, but also would follow the appointment authority that Moses exercises in this passage. In Matthew, Jesus says to his disciple Simon Peter, 'You are Peter and on this rock I will build my church.' The name 'Peter' means rock in Greek, so it is obvious Jesus is talking about Peter when he refers to the rock. Jesus goes on to tell Peter that he will give him the keys of the kingdom of heaven, and that whatever he binds on earth will be bound in heaven, and whatever he looses on earth will be loosed in heaven. Catholic understanding is that the authority given to Peter passed by apostolic succession. Peter is said to have been the first Christian leader in Rome. The claim of Rome to be the one true church and the Pope as the Vicar of Rome to govern the whole church is based on the authority given by Jesus to Peter and transmitted to his successors. The Pope is, of course, chosen by the College of Cardinals and not self-appointed or a hereditary successor like a king, so there is some element of democracy at the higher level, although it does not extend to the laity, or even the lower level of clergy. The Pope appoints the cardinals, and the cardinals elect the Pope."

The Catholic complex lay behind us. We passed a Baptist church, with a Congregational church a block ahead. "Baptists, Congregationalists, and other 'low church' Protestants," Hal said, "take the opposite view, based on the notion of the 'priesthood of believers.' Peter himself taught in First Peter two that all believers are 'a holy priesthood,' or 'a royal priesthood.' The language goes back to Exodus, where God said his people are to be 'a kingdom of priests and a holy nation.' All believers are part of the 'nation of priests' and equally entitled to participate in church governance. Denominations are more like trade groups, providing counsel, support, and assistance, but having no actual authority over the local congregation. All authority comes from the bottom. This is the congregational model of church governance. It would correspond to the choice of leaders by the people in Deuteronomy chapter one."

We turned back in to our office complex, with the old brick of the Episcopal Church visible across the State House plaza.

"Other denominations," Hal continued, "fall somewhere between the hierarchical and the congregational model. They retain some authority in a hierarchical structure but share it with the laity in other aspects. The laity, for example, elects Episcopalian bishops, but they require approval from the rest of the bishops to assume office. Presbyterians have a system of governance by approved elders that moves through a hierarchy of authority.

"In many independent evangelical churches, there is a trend to governance by elders who are appointed by the pastor, based on New Testament models. In Paul's letter to Titus, for example, he tells Titus to appoint elders in each town where he is starting churches on the island of Crete. This instruction occurs in the context of mission churches, where the New Testament missionaries are founding churches among people who were nonbelievers and have become new Christians. That model may have been appropriate in its original context and may still be appropriate for mission churches today. But it is less clear that it is appropriate for established churches with a membership of believers.

"What pastors and elders of churches with strong local governance from the top often fail to see is that they have recreated a hierarchical governance style on the local level. The pastor becomes, in effect, the Pope of the local church, and the elders become the College of Cardinals, or bishops. The scriptural basis for it may be different than for the Catholic governance model, but the result is the same."

I was well familiar with the issues that arise in church governance, especially with start-up churches, as I had counseled many of them as a lawyer. One of the most common causes of litigation involving churches, I told Hal, arises when churches split and someone must decide who owns the real estate or other church assets—that is, which group is the "real" church. A variant on the theme is when divisions in the congregation lead to disputes over firing pastors or other significant congregational actions. American courts have generally abstained from deciding cases that require resolving doctrinal issues. If a church dispute cannot be resolved by the application of neutral principles of law, it remains unresolved, at least by the courts. They will, however, honor decisions of religious tribunals established by the church or denomination itself. Since hierarchical denominations tend to have such tribunals and dispute resolution mechanisms built into the denominational structure, they have fewer tendencies to bring their fractiousness to secular courts, and courts have been more deferential to them than to congregations with governance authority resting in the laity. Every church, even the most local and independent, is well advised to have a dispute resolution mechanism consistent with its theology built into its governance documents.

Our tour of church governance was over. We returned to the more secular aspects of the text. "The authority of the people who are selected and appointed," Hal said, "is secular in the sense that they are not the priests or Levites, but are to give leadership and decision-making to the people in their everyday lives. The term *commanders* suggests they had military and possibly administrative responsibility. But the only function described more specifically in this passage is judging. This subject comes up again in chapters sixteen and seventeen."

The instructions to the judges, I observed, would be suitable for a modern American court. The judge was to be impartial, not only in disputes among Israelites but also in disputes between Israelites and foreigners. Everyone, regardless of national origin, whether they were or were not part of the covenant community, was entitled to impartial justice before the judges of Israel.

"There is a concept in the federal judicial system in America that echoes this," I said. "One basis for access to a federal, as opposed to a state, court is called 'diversity jurisdiction.' It allows a litigant to have a lawsuit tried in the federal court system if the suit involves citizens of different states. The dispute has to be significant in amount, currently one in which $75,000 or more is at stake. But the origins of diversity jurisdiction are a notion, embedded in our constitution, that local courts may not always be impartial when the dispute involves a local litigant against a party from another state. Federal courts are presumed to be more likely to give justice to diverse parties."

Hal appreciated the insight. "The other requirement of judges is that their impartiality extend to small and great alike," he noted. "The judge is not to be afraid of any man."

"But what does he mean when, after telling them to judge impartially, he says, 'Judgment belongs to God'?" I asked. "Who is making the judgment, the judge or God?"

"Moses was reminding them that in judging they are about the Lord's work," Hal answered. "Administering justice is carrying out divine work. That's why they should have no fear of human beings in doing so. In fact, to corrupt justice would be a violation of God's will and law, and far more dangerous to the judge than to act out of fear or partiality among men."

There was a final idea in this passage. Cases "too hard for you" were to be taken to Moses. It was not exactly a court of appeal, but reserved to the wisdom of God's chosen leader the most difficult cases, a protection against the fallibility of the human judges administering the system.

Hal asked me to summarize.

"The people selected wise, understanding, and respected men to exercise leadership, but they were subject to appointment by Moses. As part of their authority, they were to judge disputes impartially, even when the case was between an Israelite and a foreigner, or an important or wealthy person and someone who is unknown or poor. Cases that were too difficult for them were to be brought to Moses—as God's chosen leader—for decision. Justice is God's province, not just a secular system to enable people to get along. Those involved in the administration of justice are doing the Lord's work."

"Good," Hal said. "And I'll bet they didn't teach all of that in law school. Now let's look at the latter part of chapter sixteen and the first part of chapter seventeen."

> Appoint judges and officials for each of your tribes in every town the LORD your God is giving you, and they shall judge the people fairly. Do not pervert justice or show partiality. Do not accept a bribe, for a bribe blinds the eyes of the wise and twists the words of the righteous. Follow justice and justice alone, so that you may live and possess the land the LORD your God is giving you.
>
> Do not set up any wooden Asherah pole beside the altar you build to the LORD your God, and do not erect a sacred stone, for these the LORD your God hates.
>
> Do not sacrifice to the LORD your God an ox or a sheep that has any defect or flaw in it, for that would be detestable to him.
>
> If a man or woman living among you in one of the towns the LORD gives you is found doing evil in the eyes of the LORD your God in violation of his covenant, and contrary to my command has worshiped other gods, bowing down to them or to the sun or the moon or the stars of the sky, and this has been brought to your attention, then you must investigate it thoroughly. If it is true and it has been proved that this detestable thing has been done in Israel, take the man or woman who has done this evil deed to your city gate and stone that person to death. On the testimony of two or three witnesses a man shall be put to death, but no one shall be put to death on the testimony of only one witness. The hands of the witnesses must be the first in putting him to death, and then the hands of all the people. You must purge the evil from among you.

If cases come before your courts that are too difficult for you to judge—whether bloodshed, lawsuits or assaults—take them to the place the LORD your God will choose. Go to the priests, who are Levites, and to the judge who is in office at that time. Inquire of them and they will give you the verdict. You must act according to the decisions they give you at the place the LORD will choose. Be careful to do everything they direct you to do. Act according to the law they teach you and the decisions they give you. Do not turn aside from what they tell you, to the right or to the left. The man who shows contempt for the judge or for the priest who stands ministering there to the LORD your God must be put to death. You must purge the evil from Israel. All the people will hear and be afraid, and will not be contemptuous again.

—Deut. 16:18–17:13

"What happened to Moses' role in appointing judges?" I asked. "Did the rules change since chapter one?"

"The rules did change," Hal said. "At this point Moses was giving instructions for life in the land, and he wouldn't be there. So he instructed the people to appoint judges and officials for each of the tribes in every town the Lord would give them. Chapter one was for the journey to the land under Moses. Chapters sixteen and seventeen are for life in the land *after Moses*.

"It's the same with the difficult cases, which were to be brought to him while he was alive. But in chapter seventeen, the cases that were too difficult for them were then to be taken to the priests, who were Levites, and the judge who was in office at the time. Moses would no longer be available to hear such cases."

We noted the repetition of the command to follow "justice and justice alone." Hal showed me that in the Hebrew this is an emphatic phrase, the effect of which is somewhat lost in this translation. "'Justice, justice shalt thou pursue,' is an older but stronger translation," Hal said. "God's heart for justice is what the 'judging' passages are all about. Here he adds the prohibition against taking a bribe. The effect of bribery in perverting justice is obvious. Wisdom and righteousness go out the window, and money and corruption rule."

I asked Hal why the passages about worshipping other gods—at the end of chapter sixteen and beginning of chapter seventeen—were there in the middle of the teachings about judges and the law courts.

"Moses probably inserted these here because they are about the most important laws that will be administered. The first and most important priority is to keep the nation right with God, and there are a series of three laws here about that.

"At the end of chapter sixteen, in verses twenty-one and twenty-two, God told them not to put wooden Asherah poles or sacred stones beside altars to the Lord. He was referring to mixing worship of God with worship of false gods. Mixing of religions is called 'syncretism.' This was a great temptation in Israel, because the peoples all around them worshiped other gods. The Ten Commandments begin with the instruction to have no other gods and make no graven images to worship. The mixing of asherah poles and sacred stones dedicated to other deities is a violation of both."

"Not much of an issue for us," I observed.

"Don't be too sure," Hal responded. "We are surrounded by false religions, just like Israel was. I don't mean just the idolatry of greed, lust, and so forth that we talked about earlier—putting other things ahead of God. But eastern religions—Buddhism, Hinduism, and ideas based on them—are all around us. And the New Age people promote another whole idea of religion: man is God, God is a woman, the earth is God, and everything is God. Go look at the religion section of almost any bookstore; books on New Age and eastern religions get much more shelf space than anything Christian. That's not because the bookstore owners are trying to sell a bill of goods on religion—it's because that's what people are buying! You'd be amazed at how much these ideas have penetrated the pews. Millions of people think they are Christians but believe things totally contrary to the Bible."

I hadn't measured the shelf space devoted to different faiths or religious concepts in bookstores. But I had noticed that our little community had one Christian bookstore but four or five stores that catered to New Age spirituality. Another reason, I thought, why Christians needed to be more thoughtful about the zeal some of them had to restore prayer to public schools and religious displays to public places.

It was no longer clear what the nature of the prayer might be or whose religious symbols would symbolize the government.

Hal continued, "Chapter seventeen goes on to repeat the prohibition we saw in chapter fifteen of giving God your junk—in essence, phony worship, going through the forms but not really sacrificing anything.

"Finally we see the worst evil of all, worshipping other gods, or the sun, moon, and stars. Remember our discussion in chapter thirteen? This is treason against the ruler—God—and endangers the whole nation by provoking God's wrath. It is not just a betrayal of God and putting his people in jeopardy; it's following his enemies, who worship such things.

"This brings Moses back to the punishment for treason: death. We discussed this in chapter thirteen, but here he taught about the law, courts, and justice, and added an important qualifier."

I saw where Hal was going. "The requirement of two or three witnesses," I said. "And the witnesses themselves are the first in the stoning of the accused."

"Yes," Hal said. "This is a protection against false accusations. By requiring two or three witnesses, the court protects not only against people who are acting with improper motives, but it also protects against wrong perceptions, simply making a mistake. It may not be a guarantee against bad motives or error, but it goes a long way. And by requiring that the witnesses be the first to engage in stoning the person to death, it requires them to take the blood of the accused on their own head. If they have testified falsely, they are guilty of murder as well as bearing false witness. They are now subject to the death penalty. There is a lot of wisdom in this system to prevent injustice."

"Does this have any New Testament equivalent?"

Hal directed me to the account in John 8 of the woman caught in adultery. The woman was brought before Jesus. Her accusers reminded Jesus that Moses taught death by stoning for adultery, and they asked for his opinion. Jesus' famous answer calls directly on this passage in Deuteronomy: "If any one of you is without sin, let him be the first to throw a stone at her."

When the crowd of accusers melted away, Jesus told the woman that he didn't condemn her either, and then told her to go and leave her life of sin.

Hal directed me to other New Testament passages where the Deuteronomy 17 requirement of two witnesses comes into play. In Matthew 26, Jesus is seen being arrested and brought before the Sanhedrin for trial. Verse sixty recites the evidence that justifies them in finding him worthy of death. Two witnesses come forward to testify that Jesus said he could tear down the temple and rebuild it in three days. The two witnesses technically complied with this requirement, at least according to the Sanhedrin.

In the story of Stephen's execution, in Acts 7, the witnesses laid their clothes before Saul. They took off their cloaks to lead the stoning, again based on Deuteronomy 17.

I was amused by the imposition of the death penalty for those who showed contempt for the judge's or priest's verdicts. "Every judge in America would like this," I said. "It would gain a lot of instant respect for their orders."

"The judges and priests administered God's justice," Hal said. "Defiance of them is defiance of God himself. That's why there was a death penalty involved here. It's essentially like worshipping other gods."

"But what if the judge or priest was wrong or corrupt," I asked. "Does this give them absolute authority? Judges do make mistakes."

"That is a question that troubled the Jewish sages over the ages," Hal replied. "The Jewish religious court is known as the Beis Din. In Jesus' time, the Sanhedrin represented the court's authority for the most difficult cases. It certainly made a mistake in Jesus' trial. The conclusion most of the sages reached was that the answer to your question is yes, the court was to be obeyed, even if it was clear to the individual that the court was in error. Otherwise, schisms would have developed and fragmented and corrupted the unity of the faith. It was better to live with a wrong decision from time to time—which presumably was corrected by a wiser body in the future—than to abandon the unity of the law and its people."

"It never got corrected with respect to Jesus," I observed. "I guess in capital punishment cases, it's kind of hard to correct an error."

"True, but there is another chapter to the story. In Acts 5, we see Peter and the apostles arrested and brought before the Sanhedrin, just as Jesus was. They were charged with teaching in the name of Jesus and claiming that God exalted him to his own right hand as Prince and Savior. The Sanhedrin was concerned not only about what they saw as blasphemy and false worship, but that the apostles were making the Sanhedrin guilty of Jesus' blood. Essentially, they said, 'You are telling people we made the wrong decision.'

"There was a standoff in ideas here, and both ideas are from Deuteronomy. The guilt of the false accusation and execution of Jesus was a capital offense. So was blasphemy, false worship, and defiance of the orders of the highest judicial and religious authority. The apostles said they must obey God rather than men. They said, in essence, that God commanded them to teach and preach, and that command superseded the court's law.

"The Sanhedrin had the authority to execute the apostles, or at least to ask the Roman governor to do so, as they did with Jesus. But there must have been some doubt—'reasonable doubt,' as you lawyers would say—about the matter. A wise man named Gamaliel solved the problem. He had the accused apostles put outside and then talked to his colleagues on the court. He reminded them of a couple of other leaders who rose up with some followers, each of whom was killed and his followers scattered. These little movements amounted to nothing. Therefore, he advised them to let the men go: 'For if their purpose or activity is of human origin, it will fail. But if it is from God, you will not be able to stop these men; you will only find yourselves fighting against God.'

"Gamaliel's speech was persuasive. Instead of executing Peter and the apostles, they flogged them and gave them a vain order not to speak in the name of Jesus and let them go."

"So the later Sanhedrin reversed itself," I said, "and left the success or failure of Christianity to God. I never connected that up before. I guess we know how the story came out."

"And is still coming out," Hal said. "The verdict of history—or of God acting in history—is in as far as Gamaliel's advice is concerned.

The apostles' teaching, which some on the Sanhedrin wanted to stamp out, has endured for two thousand years and spread throughout the world. But the verdict still has to be given by every person who hears the Gospel. It is the most important question they will ever be asked. *Is Jesus Lord?* Will you believe him in your heart and confess him with your mouth?"

"It sounds like Gamaliel was an advocate of religious freedom," I observed. "I think he would have been comfortable with the separation of church and state."

"In those days," Hal said, "the state was Rome. Both Jews and Christians had trouble living with the state religion of Rome—that pantheon of human-like gods. The Romans left the Jews alone with their faith as long as they didn't defy Roman government. But Christians got in trouble because they were all over the Empire and in Rome itself. Gamaliel had the right idea—everyone may not accept God, but God can't be defeated by any human effort."

"When I first started practicing law," I recalled, "a wise older attorney told me he had concluded it was more important that disputes be re-solved than that they be resolved correctly. I guess what we are talking about is somewhat the same idea. If the matter is important enough to come up later, there will be opportunities to correct it."

We discussed the application of this principle in our own country and times. It had been a source of great controversy in the days before the Civil War, when the United States Supreme Court ruled in the *Dred Scott* case that a slave was the property of his master and had to be returned. Many Northerners treated the decision—and the fugitive slave laws that Congress enacted in an attempt to prevent the secession of the southern states—with contempt and disobedience. Daniel Webster, whose statue we could see out my window, was a vigorous opponent of slavery. But he advocated obedience to the fugitive slave laws. He believed that a wrong law, lawfully enacted, was to be obeyed by all, even on as momentous an issue as slavery. Pursuing justice required changing the law, not disobeying it. On this, Webster's thought was in line with God's instruction in Deuteronomy, chapter seventeen.

"In our own time," Hal said, "the Dred Scott decision and the fugi-tive slave laws are found in *Roe v. Wade* and the decisions and laws that followed it, protecting the right to kill unborn persons. We slid over this issue at the end of chapter twelve. There, in talking about the detestable things the Canaanite people do, it says, 'They even burn their sons and daughters in the fire as sacrifices to their gods.' This is, in God's eyes, one of the most profound evils and corruptions that can exist. Archaeological evidence has shown that this was real. Sites have been found with the bones of children burned in the fires in religious sacrifices."

"I'm not in favor of abortion," I said, "but it isn't conducted as a religious sacrifice."

"Don't be too sure of that," Hal replied. "Ask yourself what the real reason is for abortion, and for the passion that many have in defending it. It's justified by the euphemism of the woman's right to choose, but no one claims any other right to choose to kill another human being except in self-defense, capital punishment, or war. And the idea that the fetus is not a human being is nonsense in late-term and partial-birth abortions, which 'pro-choice' people defend vigorously. The baby is viable outside the mother's womb for most or all of the last trimester, and maybe the late part of the second trimester of a pregnancy."

"So what is the religious significance of abortion?" I asked. "I still don't see how you can say it's a religious sacrifice, like the Canaanites slaughtering kids on an altar to some satanic god."

"My point," Hal said, "is that we are an idolatrous society, and abortion is a direct product of the idolatry. Remember, idolatry is anything that you put ahead of God. It doesn't just mean bowing down at an altar to some phony idol. Everyone worships something, even if they don't think of it as worship. The underlying motivation for abortion is that people want a society in which they can have sex without consequences. Pregnancy is a natural consequence of sex. Except in the handful of cases involving rape, pregnancy is the result of choice. Abortion is the ability to undo the choice, to have an escape when it doesn't turn out the way you wanted. But when men and women engage in sexual relations, they are making the most intimate commitments to each other for the responsibility for the outcome. We'll be talking about that later when we come to the laws of marriage and sex. But that's why the most vigorous advocates for pregnant women to have an abortion are usually the boyfriends who don't want to be responsible, financially or otherwise, to the woman or the child.

"Pregnancy ruins the fun of sex. That's what abortion is really about. Our idolatry is to sex—unrestricted and without consequences. Nothing else can explain the commitment we as a society have carried into the legal system in making abortion a constitutional right."

The passion of Hal's condemnation of abortion surprised me. My mind raced across the arguments. Women will have back-alley abortions or use coat hangers on themselves if it isn't legal—all the horror stories of the predictably tragic results. But how many really did that compared to the tens and tens of millions of American children who had been killed by abortion since *Roe v. Wade*? Where was the greater evil in the comparison? Only if you assumed that the death of the babies was not an evil at all could you be persuaded by this argument. Another line of reasoning said that women should be able to control their own bodies, and pregnancy only affected a woman's body. But when the life of another human being is involved, you can hardly claim that control of one's body—the inconvenience of pregnancy—supersedes the life of another. I mentioned these arguments to Hal.

"Yes," he said. "Another one is that abortions are more prevalent among poor black women. That is supposed to make it a good thing. Some even justify abortion by claiming that it's responsible for lowering the crime rate. More abortions among poor black people are good for us, I guess. Get rid of all the riffraff and criminals. Like the Mafia killing each other off in gang wars. Make the world more like us good well-to-do white folks. It is the most racist defense of abortion you can think of, and mostly from people who would be horrified at the idea of racism."

He laughed. "Edith was speaking to a bunch of college kids at an expensive private school about abortion once," he said. "One girl, whose parents could probably write a check for her tuition off the top of their checking account, told Edith that if she knew what life was like in the inner city neighborhoods, she wouldn't be opposed to abortion. If it's that bad, I guess we would be doing them a favor by just killing them all."

I imagined the scene: College students, whose parents were paying tens of thousands of dollars a year for their education, thinking they were friends of the poor by advocating their extinction. But I made a mental note to find out more about Edith; I couldn't picture her in front of this upscale audience. And I wasn't sure if the irony Hal saw in the scene had anything to do with her.

My eyes drifted up to my bookshelf. There, spread across several feet of shelf space, were the volumes containing our state statutes. At the beginning of the first volume was the United States Constitution, the source of the right to abortion, according to the Supreme Court. I had my own ideas about what the Constitution required on this matter.

The United States Constitution is the nation's most fundamental governing document. The fourteenth amendment to the Constitution says that no person shall be deprived of life, liberty, or property, without due process of law. Many court decisions are devoted to determining the scope and content of the due process that the Constitution requires. The most obvious constitutional argument in the abortion debate is that the unborn are "persons," whose lives are protected by the specific language the founding fathers wrote into the Constitution. But the idea that the fourteenth amendment protects the life of the unborn child has received little attention. The 1973 *Roe v. Wade* decision finding a constitutional right to abort a child brushed the issue aside, finding that the unborn were not "persons" within the meaning of the Constitution. The court paid little heed to the long legal history of treating the unborn as persons with legal rights in other areas of law such as inheritance, property, and tort law—a willful disregard that continues to this day. The obvious and literal language of the Constitution was disregarded in favor of the court finding a right of privacy in the "umbras and penumbras" of the Constitution, imagined shaded or shadowy areas in which the court surmised its decision on abortion could be justified, although the Constitution was nowhere actually expressed to justify it in any apparent way. Thus the choice of death received Constitutional blessing from the highest arbiters of our law in what one dissenting judge called an exercise of raw judicial power.

In the more recent *Casey* decision, affirming and extending the right to kill the unborn, the court used the euphemism of "potential life" to describe a child in the womb. The term constitutes a judgment by the court regarding fetal development on which religious, moral, and medical authorities do not agree. Whether the soul is present in the human body from the moment of conception, when all of the necessary biological constituents for a human being are present, or enters at some later stage of development such as when the baby "quickens," can be debated. But it is not disputable that the baby's heart begins beating at about three weeks, has detectable brain waves at six weeks, and can feel pain by twelve weeks. The baby is viable outside the womb by twenty-one to twenty-two weeks, before the end of the second trimester. Yet the court has even given constitutional protection to the gruesome procedure of "partial birth abortion," a late-term abortive method in which the baby's skull is penetrated and the brain scooped out while the baby is in the birth canal and partially emerged. Partial birth abortion is performed as late as twenty weeks, an age when the baby can recognize its mother's voice.

To call the young victims of such abortion methods "potential life" is an Orwellian exercise in linguistic deception. For the purpose of constitutional law, it is a small step to extend to some indeterminate time after birth the constitutional definition of babies as nonpersons. Some of the more aggressive abortion advocates have gone this far, and the practice of killing babies who somehow survive abortion or letting them die by inattention is sufficiently widespread to bring about legislation to prevent it.

Another principle seemed to me relevant to the legal debate. One of the outworkings of the due process of law, which the Constitution requires before life, liberty, or property are taken, is that persons accused of crime must be found guilty "beyond a reasonable doubt." While the taking of life by abortion is not the result of an accusation of crime against the baby, the "beyond a reasonable doubt" standard seems applicable. If we set such a high barrier before the punishment for crimes can be applied, should we not set a similarly high barrier to the taking of unborn lives? No fair-minded person could claim that there isn't reasonable doubt as to when life begins in the womb. The constitutional principles of due process established in our criminal law would argue that in matters as serious as the taking of life, where there is reasonable doubt, the matter should always be resolved in favor of the one who will suffer the penalty. Such has not been the development of abortion laws. There is no presumption of innocence and no reasonable-doubt standard applied to the decision to kill. Tens of millions of American babies have died in the womb since *Roe v. Wade,* and the slaughter of the innocents continues.

I shared these thoughts with Hal.

"I'm glad to hear that everyone in the legal system doesn't think abortion is a good thing or that the Constitution really does require it," he said. "I hope it's a decision that will be corrected with time and greater wisdom."

His comment brought me back to the reason we were discussing abortion in the first place.

"Abortion," he continued, "is one of the most profoundly offensive practices to God—and to Christians—that exists in our society. Yet, like slavery, it is protected by court decisions interpreting the Constitution, and by congressionally enacted laws. Just as the Jewish sages wrestled with how God's people should react to an unjust law, and Daniel Webster and nineteenth-century Americans struggled with the proper reaction to laws and court decisions protecting slavery, so the church and Christian people in our time have had to decide how to deal with abortion. And the consensus, however reluctant, has been that it is better in a society in which change is possible to live with the law and work for change than to challenge it violently. I don't want to be presumptuous about people of other faiths or no faith who oppose abortion, and there are a lot of them. But the peacefulness of the reactions to the holocaust of abortion is due largely to the fact that the opposition to it is heavily grounded in Christian people and the Christian faith."

Our discussion and our walk had consumed the morning. We made our way to a local restaurant for lunch. With a window seat, you could just see the governor's office on the side of the State House. Hal and I read the rest of chapter seventeen, the "law of the King."

When you enter the land the LORD your God is giving you and have taken possession of it and settled in it, and you say, "Let us set a king over us like all the nations around us," be sure to appoint over you the king the LORD your God chooses. He must be from among your own brothers. Do not place a foreigner over you, one who is not a brother Israelite.

The king, moreover, must not acquire great numbers of horses for himself or make the people return to Egypt to get more of them, for the LORD has told you, "You are not to go back that way again." He must not take many wives, or his heart will be led astray. He must not accumulate large amounts of silver and gold.

When he takes the throne of his kingdom, he is to write for himself on a scroll a copy of this law, taken from that of the priests, who are Levites. It is to be with him, and he is to read it all the days of his life so that he may learn to revere the LORD his God and follow carefully all the words of this law and these decrees and not consider himself better than his brothers and turn from the law to the right or to the left. Then he and his descendants will reign a long time over his kingdom in Israel.

—Deut. 17:14–20

"Power, sex, and money," Hal said. "These are the three great temptations and corrupters of those who can acquire them."

The "law of the King," as seen in the last part of chapter seventeen, prohibited Israel's king from acquiring great numbers of horses for himself. The horses, and returning to Egypt to get them, represented power, Hal explained. The king of God's people was not to emulate Pharaoh or other worldly emperors.

The temptation to multiply wives, freely engaged in even by David and Solomon, was a temptation to sin by sexual excess and to the possibility of being led astray. David's sinfulness led him to adultery with Bathsheba and taking another man's wife. Late in his life, Solomon was led astray by wives who followed other gods. Israel's history gave ample warning against the dangers of misusing authority for sexual appetites.

And the temptation to accumulate large amounts of silver and gold was the temptation to use power to enrich oneself. One need only look around the modern world to see this in play. In almost every nondemocratic country, those in power enrich themselves. National resources are milked and the people taxed while the rulers live in luxury and stash vast fortunes in foreign bank accounts.

"These are all negative commands—what the king is not to do," Hal said. "Now look at what he is to do. He is to write for himself, on a scroll, a copy of the law, taken from the Levite priests, and read it all the days of his life. And that's all! No other direction is given as to what the king is to do—there's nothing about making laws, leading armies, building monuments, or enlarging the kingdom. By writing down and reading the law, he would learn to revere God, to follow his commands, and to maintain the humility of not thinking himself better than others. Imagine a world in which these were the ways of the leaders!"

Imagine, indeed! I looked up at the governor's office and imagined the men and woman who had occupied it writing a copy of the Bible—or the parts of it pertinent to governing, or a book of it, any book—by night, when the day's duties were done. The copy would have to be made from one given to the governor by the religious leader of his or her church or denomination—the pastor or priest or bishop would share the Scriptures with the political leader. Every day the Scripture would be read, and every day the people's chosen leader would be reminded to revere God, to follow his laws, and imbue himself or herself with the humility of understanding that the position of leadership did not make the person occupying it better than other citizens.

"This is the biblical command for political leaders," Hal said. "Nothing else. He or she should be a servant leader who does not seek or use the position to gain power, wealth, or sexual gratification; one who lives by the Scriptures in awe of God, humbly following his laws. That is God's governor or president or king."

I wondered how one might run for office on that platform. People would be outraged. The candidate would be castigated as a religious fanatic. Panic about the separation of church and state would grip those who see as offensive the least mention of God in public life. And the people, the voters, would almost certainly choose someone more pragmatic, someone who could be relied on to leave God in the closet when considering matters of public import. We could not, after all, *really* trust God, or someone who was forthright enough to acknowledge him as a guide in civic affairs, could we?

But what a world it would be if we did.

As we paid the tab and donned our coats, I remembered Hal's story about Edith and the college students and reminded myself to find out more about Edith from Julie.

CHAPTER EIGHTEEN

Monday morning came, and I was into the workweek again. It was Tuesday before I ran into Julie. She was in the coffee room, indulging our mutual daily start-up ritual of caffeine addiction.

"Tell me more about Hal," I asked. "He doesn't talk about his family. I haven't asked—I just have a sense there's something there he doesn't want to share."

"You're right," she said. "There's a lot of pain. The only time he really shared it with me was the first time we met. I told you the story: I was somewhere between suicide and abortion when he just sort of descended from nowhere into my life. He told me about it then. His wife died, of breast cancer when she was forty-five. It was long and painful and devastating to him. They had two boys in their teens. After his wife died, he raised them alone. They were both good boys and meant everything to him. They looked like their mother. He told me they made him think of that old folk song 'Foggy, Foggy Dew' that Burl Ives used to sing about how every time he looked into his son's eyes, it reminded him of a fair young maid.

"Anyway, one of the boys went into the service and died in Vietnam. The other was in college when he was killed in an auto accident a few years later; I think the driver was drunk. It took Hal years to get over the grief; it was his 'dark night of the soul.' God didn't seem to be there anymore. For a long while, he tortured himself, thinking that God had taken them away from him because he loved them too much. They had become idols to him; he'd placed them ahead of God in his devotion. Then another pastor came alongside and showed him that he had not neglected God, and that God did not put limits on our love of others, not the right kind of love at least. Gradually, he got back into the Scriptures and got perspective and realized that the shortness of this life and the glories of heaven made his sons' deaths—young as they were—an incidental thing in eternity, and that maybe God had more work for him to do.

"His story showed me how precious the life was that was growing inside me. I was feeling sorry for myself and thinking I had to destroy my child to save myself, but Hal had lost his entire family. He was just as lonely as I was, but he was reaching out to help me instead of thinking about himself. That's when I knew I was going to keep my baby and that everything was going to be all right. I didn't know how, but I knew it."

"That's a wonderful story," I said. "I didn't know how Edith died."

"Oh, that was his first wife," Julie said, "not Edith. Edith came into his life later."

It was the first I knew that Hal had been married twice. Julie couldn't tell me much more about Hal's first family. They had passed on before she came to know him. I told Julie the story of Edith and the college students that Hal had shared with me.

"How typical," she laughed. "He never told me that one."

"But I had the sense that there was more to it," I said, "that it wasn't just the irony of the well-to-do college students thinking they were doing a good thing by advocating abortion as a service to the poor."

Julie looked at me with surprise. "Didn't you know that Edith was black? She grew up in the ghetto. Her father was the pastor of an inner city church."

The next time I sat with Hal, I was full of Julie's revelations about his life. As he was looking down to read the scriptures we were to discuss, I was looking at his face. Faces tell a lot to those who are sensitive enough to read them. I have never been skilled or sensitive in such matters and relied on Anna for insights into people—insights I often missed. But I could see in the lines and creases and deepset eyes a man of sorrows, whose counsel came from where he had been and what he had lived, as well as the words he had read and prayed over and engraved in his mind and heart. Then my attention drew near to the words he was reading.

The priests, who are Levites—indeed the whole tribe of Levi—are to have no allotment or inheritance with Israel. They shall live on the offerings made to the LORD by fire, for that is their inheritance. They shall have no inheritance among their brothers; the LORD is their inheritance, as he promised them.

This is the share due the priests from the people who sacrifice a bull or a sheep: the shoulder, the jowls, and the inner parts. You are to give them the firstfruits of your grain, new wine and oil, and the first wool from the shearing of your sheep, for the LORD your God has chosen them and their descendants out of all your tribes to stand and minister in the LORD's name always.

If a Levite moves from one of your towns anywhere in Israel where he is living, and comes in all earnestness to the place the LORD will choose, he may minister in the name of the LORD his God like all his fellow Levites who serve there in the presence of the LORD. He is to share equally in their benefits, even though he has received money from the sale of family possessions.

—Deut. 18:1–8

As Hal read, the words came to life for me in the man himself. Here was one who had no allotment or inheritance, whom God had chosen to spend his life ministering before him. The Lord, I thought, is indeed Hal's inheritance. He is to be provided for by the people, but he is entirely dependent on their faithfulness. As his voice shifted from reading the word to discussing it, I came back to listen.

"This passage," Hal said, "stands at the structural and theological center of Moses' teaching in Deuteronomy." He showed me that chapters sixteen through eighteen are about government of the people in the land. The office and functions of judges and law courts—the king, priests, Levites, and prophets—were addressed in turn. Together they constituted a government with separation of powers that was remarkable in its time and in stark contrast to the autocratic powers of other kings in the ancient near-east. Judges were to hear and decide disputes guided by the standard of impartial justice. The king was to preside in humility, a first among equals who renounces potentates' usual penchant for acquiring wealth, power, and sexual gratification. The priests and Levites were to stand and minister before the Lord, at the center of the society, leading the people in religious functions. And the prophet was to bring any further word the Lord commanded. All were to live under the Torah, the law, as the guiding principle: God himself had been their legislator.

As he talked, I imagined a wheel, with three spokes dividing it into thirds. In one sector were the judges and law courts, administering justice. In another was the king, who was the chief executive officer and servant leader. The last sector belonged to the prophets. God himself was the supreme legislator and had provided the law, but they would bring any additional word from him that was needed.

And in the center, the hub of the wheel, were the priests and Levites, leading the worship and religious functions. In my image, Hal was at the hub, kneeling before his God and ours, leading the judges and executive-king and legislator-prophets in worship and submission to him. The wheel of the society turned around this man and others like him who were at the center of the life of the land. How unlike the world we lived in—or is it?

In designing our government, the founding fathers of the United States had been mindful of humanity's sinful tendencies. "All power corrupts, and absolute power corrupts absolutely"—a saying attributed to Lord Acton and consistent with their biblical awareness of the evil of the human heart—influenced their thoughts. The careful balancing of government's legislative, executive, and judicial functions in the American Constitution is more than coincidentally related to the biblical teaching on the nature of man, as well as biblical structures of government.

"God chose the levitical priests," Hal said. "They didn't choose to be ministers of the word; God chose them. There are all too many people in ministry who chose it as a profession, like someone else might choose to go into business or law or engineering, because they like it or thought they had some aptitude for it. I once heard a fellow say that he became a minister because he was opposed to the Vietnam War, and after the war was over it seemed like a sort of consistent thing to do. That's not God's way of choosing those who serve in ministry."

"How did you get into ministry?" I asked.

"I can only tell you that I went into the pastoral ministry because I had no choice. There was nothing else I could do. In the old days, people thought of ministers as being 'called.' You don't hear that much anymore. But anyone who has been called knows what it means. As surely as Moses was called at the burning bush, those whom God wants in the ministry of his word are called into it. They know who they are. They did not choose it for themselves.

"I knew a fellow once who had been a minister for ten years before, as he said, he was born again. For those first ten years, he had a job. After that, he was called and he had a ministry. There is no comparison."

We had talked about the tithes for the Lord before. Hal pointed out that parts of the sacrificed bull or sheep due to the priests were what were considered the better parts. "It's another example of the principle of not giving God your junk," Hal said. "Those who minister before the Lord should get the best, not castoffs.

"At the same time, they are entirely dependent on the obedience of the people to receive this. They have no inheritance or allotment with Israel; the Lord is their inheritance. God is to be all-sufficient for them, and they are to have no concern or grasping for the things of this world."

We recalled together some of the scandals in the 1980s and more recently, when financial and sexual misconduct destroyed the ministries of some prominent televangelists. "These were less isolated events than one might hope," Hal said. "At the local level, sexual misconduct is much more common than financial. But anyone who is using his ministry for his own gain—whether financial or gratification of the flesh—is abusing it and is not chosen or carrying out a calling from God. Ministers should be well provided for, but that is the responsibility of the congregation. Ministers should not covet worldly gain."

I asked Hal about verses six through eight.

He replied, "The Scripture here teaches that Levites who move from an outlying area to the area of the central sanctuary are to have a place in the ministry there, including the provision for their support. Ministry is not a matter of competition. The priests and Levites in the central sanctuary are not to exclude others who may come there from outlying districts. There is to be no selfishness in God's work. I never felt badly when people left my church if they were going to another one where the word of God was taught and believed. If they found themselves closer to God in a Catholic or charismatic or fundamentalist church where some teachings and practices might differ from mine, but Christ is believed and taught, I was happy for them. We want our churches to grow because there are so many people out there who need to come to Christ and be nurtured in his word; we don't want them to grow just so we can pat ourselves on the back about how great our ministry is."

I told Hal about a book I had read once called *The Keys of the Kingdom* by A.J. Cronin. It tells a story of a Catholic priest, humble and unsuccessful by worldly standards—and even by his supervisors' standards—who was sent to China as a missionary. His mission had little success, and after some time he heard that a Methodist missionary was coming to the same city. At first he was jealous and afraid that the new missionary would compete with him for converts, bring in people who should have been his, and show him up for the lack of success he'd had in his mission. But then he had another thought and went, hesitantly, to meet the Methodist pastor. To his surprise, he found a colleague in Christ rather than a rival, a man whose humble heart and work for God were close to his own. Together—and largely neglected by their ecclesiastical superiors—they supported each other in their gospel work in that distant land.

"That," Hal said, "is more or less what verses six through eight are about."

As always in Deuteronomy, subject moves to subject in logical sequence. After addressing the central role of the priests and Levites, there is a warning about their opposite numbers, the servants of the dark powers.

We read on through verse thirteen:

> When you enter the land the LORD your God is giving you, do not learn to imitate the detestable ways of the nations there. Let no one be found among you who sacrifices his son or daughter in the fire, who practices divination or sorcery,

interprets omens, engages in witchcraft, or casts spells, or who is a medium or spiritist or who consults the dead.

Anyone who does these things is detestable to the LORD, and because of these detestable practices the LORD your God will drive out those nations before you. You must be blameless before the LORD your God.

—Deut. 18:9–13

We had discussed the "detestable practice" of child sacrifice, represented in the American culture by the extraordinary and passionate commitment to abortion as a means of assuring sexual freedom without consequences. Hal reminded me that it is a form of idolatry, a choice of another God, a false and manmade God.

"Notice," Hal said, "that these other occult practices are all in the same category: divination, sorcery, omens, witchcraft, casting spells, being a medium or spiritist, or consulting the dead. The issue here is religious: Follow God or avoid him and invent your own; choose to follow a spiritual being, Satan, who is opposed to God. These are the kinds of practices that caused God to drive out the Canaanite peoples before Israel. Here he warns them that he will drive them out of the land too if they follow these practices. It is remarkable in this time and country, when the truth of the Christian faith is proclaimed all around us and is accessible to virtually everyone, that people are still drawn to occult practices. Even under God's nose, so to speak, the 'father of lies' has his harvest, for the time being."

I asked Hal what he made of the widespread presence of abortion and occult practices in our society.

"I tremble," he said. "I tremble. I have held young Christian women who were sobbing at the very thought of the horror of abortion, even though they have never dealt with it personally. And I have counseled others who have had abortions and were so overwhelmed at the guilt of the realization that they killed their baby that they were near taking their own life. I have felt the presence of the Evil One when people in service to him have been in my church or my presence. It is a palpable presence to the spiritually discerning; if you have experienced it, you know what I mean."

I did not know what he meant at the time. It may be that I had been blessedly free of the presence of evil. More likely, I would not have sensed it when it was there. Later, when my time with Hal was through and my spiritual journey had taken me to more mature levels, I came to know what he was talking about.

San Francisco is one of the most beautiful cities in the world, and one with wonderful memories to Anna and me. We had our courtship there when I was in law school and she was working in the city. There are places in that town that are engraved in our hearts forever. But one time, on a visit, we went into a bookstore that was touted as representing much of the offbeat history of San Francisco: the beatniks, the drugs, the flower children, and the adoption of the city as the gay capital of the world. There was one token book on Christianity in the religious section of the bookstore. The rest of the section, and much of the rest of the inventory of the store, represented the dark side of life and faith. We both felt the cold, oppressive presence of Evil there. I came to know what Hal meant.

Next, Moses conveyed God's promise about where the people would find guidance.

> The nations you will dispossess listen to those who practice sorcery or divination. But as for you, the LORD your God has not permitted you to do so.

> The LORD your God will raise up for you a prophet like me from among your own brothers. You must listen to him. For this is what you asked of the LORD your God at Horeb on the day of the assembly when you said, "Let us not hear the voice of the LORD our God nor see this great fire anymore, or we will die."

> The LORD said to me: "What they say is good. I will raise up for them a prophet like you from among their brothers; I will put my words in his mouth, and he will tell them everything I command him. If anyone does not listen to my words that the prophet speaks in my name, I myself will call him to account.

But a prophet who presumes to speak in my name anything I have not commanded him to say, or a prophet who speaks in the name of other gods, must be put to death."

You may say to yourselves, "How can we know when a message has not been spoken by the LORD?" If what a prophet proclaims in the name of the LORD does not take place or come true, that is a message the LORD has not spoken. That prophet has spoken presumptuously. Do not be afraid of him.

—Deut. 18:14–22

"Moses was leaving," Hal said. "Deuteronomy was his last address to his people. Joshua had been appointed to succeed him, but he wouldn't live forever either. So Moses gave God's promise that the people would not be left without access to God. Beyond the priests and Levites—who would be the ministers and teachers of God's word—God would raise up a prophet from among them, one like Moses. There is no need for them to resort to false or satanic means of communicating with the other world.

"The prophet was a necessary intermediary," Hal went on. "Remember, this is what the people wanted Moses to be. They couldn't bear direct confrontation or communication with God."

"What does he mean by a 'prophet like me'?" I asked.

"Moses interceded and suffered for this people," Hal said. "A true prophet will do the same. And there are two other tests given for true and false prophets. If the prophet prophesies things that do not come true, then he is not a real prophet. That's sort of self-evident. The other test is in chapter thirteen. If he seeks to lead them astray, into worshipping other gods, that's a sure sign of his false nature, even if his prophesies do come true. Chapter thirteen teaches that signs and wonders—miracles, if you will—are sometimes provided by phonies."

"The prophet sounds a lot like Jesus," I said. "Is he?"

"Yes, this is the most specifically Christ-centered section in Deuteronomy. The reference, of course, is to the succession of prophets who spoke God's word over the centuries. But it culminates in Jesus, who is the final prophet and Moses-like figure. 'In the past God spoke to our forefathers through the prophets at many times and in various ways, but in these last days he has spoken to us by his Son, whom he appointed heir of all things and through whom he made the universe,' as it says in the beginning of Hebrews."

Hal led me through some of the New Testament references to the prophet. In John one, twenty-one, John the Baptist tells inquirers that he is not the prophet. In John one, forty-five, we see that Philip told Nathaniel, "We have found the one Moses wrote about in the law." That was a clear reference to Deuteronomy eighteen. In John five, forty-six, Jesus said Moses wrote about him, another clear reference. In John six, fourteen, after the miracle of feeding the five thousand, the people recognized him as the prophet. In Matthew seventeen, on the Mount of Transfiguration, God told Peter, James, and John to "listen to him," just as Deuteronomy instructed regarding the prophet. In Acts three, twenty-two, Peter quoted Deuteronomy eighteen in identifying Jesus to the crowd as the prophet. And in speaking of Jesus to the Sanhedrin, in Acts seven, thirty-seven, Stephen quoted Deuteronomy eighteen about the prophet.

"Through Jesus Christ, our Lord," Hal concluded, "we have the very words of God, placed in his mouth, as Moses promised. We also have the promise that if anyone does not listen to him, God himself will call that person to account. The need for obedience to Christ could not be clearer."

We had concluded the sections of Deuteronomy in which God taught what government should be like. When we first approached the subject in chapter one, when leaders were designated, we deferred discussing it until we came to the more complete discussion in chapters sixteen through eighteen. The reason was not just the convenience of keeping the subject matter together. Hal had told me at the time that I was not ready for the discussion.

I had been ready to talk about methods of designating leaders: election versus appointment, the virtues of democracy, and the hierarchical versus congregational approaches to organization, to put it in terms of church polity. And I understood separation of powers: the executive, legislative, and judicial functions of the government and how they interacted with each other. What I did not understand was that worship and obedience to God were central in a properly governed society or nation. Steeped in American constitutional thought about separation of church and state, I would have missed the heart of God for government.

The king—the chief executive officer of the nation—is to write a copy of God's law for himself and to read it and be guided by it. He is to use his office for no personal benefit, whether financial, sexual, or power over others. He is to lead and rule in humility, not thinking himself better than others. Nothing in the Constitution would prevent us electing such a president.

The law is to be God's law. The legislative function of adding to the law is to be fulfilled by those who look to God to determine what the law of the land should be. We do not have the office of prophet in our time, but we do have the final prophet, Jesus, and the Holy Spirit who will lead us into all truth. Legislators dealing with the thorny issues of our day can look to them for the guidance that is needed for a godly society.

Judges were to administer justice without partiality, between great and small, rich and poor, native and alien. They were to understand that justice is in God's heart, and they were his arm in carrying it out. All the functions of the government and society were to revolve around the worship of God, led by the religious leaders whom God had called to their position. They are to have no part in the material benefits others enjoy, but the people are voluntarily to bring them the best of everything.

As I went about the affairs of the week, I wondered how God views the United States of America. The question—I understood now as I would not have when Hal and I began our study—is not "How *would* God think about our country, as in 'What would Jesus do?'" Our Father and Creator God sees us and knows us as a people, a nation, a society, and a culture—collectively—just as he sees and knows each one of us individually. How do we measure up?

In my imagination, I saw the people of the United States—all 300 million of them—assembled on a great plain before the mountain, like Israel of old. The cloud and fire and smoke of the Lord's presence strikes awe into their hearts. Their hearts and deeds, blended together as one, are brought before him for judgment. It is, as they say, a mixed bag.

In every branch of government there are devoted men and women seeking God's wisdom for the tasks before them, the policies they must develop, and the decisions they must make. They search the Scriptures and pray for guidance. Millions of other Americans pray for them and for the nation as well, some in an occasional and perfunctory manner in church, others with passion and conviction as part of their daily prayer life. And there is much that is good and right in the nation and the world as a result. America has been generous in providing for poor and needy nations and peoples. Its wars have been fought for the good of others, as well as self-defense, but never for conquest or the aggrandizement of the nation or a political leader. Its military has provided food, health care, and other assistance to people in areas it occupies. Our government cares for our own people as well, taxing the wealthy at heavier and heavier levels as their income increases, to provide for the common good and those less well off. There will always be debates and differences of opinion over the best way to care for those who need care. Some believe direct support through government programs is best, while others argue that the poor benefit more from a healthy economy that promotes job growth and better conditions for everyone, best cultivated by leaving more room for private initiative and limiting government action. These are honest if sometimes intemperate debates; the goals of each side are, in the end, the same.

And we sustain an economy that gives us the highest, and, some would say, most wasteful standard of living on earth. People flock to our shores from all parts of the world, many illegally, seeking the opportunity to build a better life that America has always offered.

We are said to be the most religious country, at least among the nations that share the heritage of Western civilization. The percentage of participation in church and religious activities is far higher than almost anywhere in Europe. There is a residue of social and personal morality, even among those who do not share an ongoing commitment to the Jewish or Christian faiths, that sustains a basic goodness among us. Most people pay their taxes honestly, obey the law, help their neighbors, volunteer and give to church and charities, and are offended at some level by immoral conduct and want it kept off their streets and away from their children.

On the other hand, there is a widespread secularism and moral relativism that tolerates and condones behavior that only a few decades ago would have been unthinkable. The people and their institutions lack self-discipline. Students insult teachers in the public schools. Violence rages in the schoolyard and the streets. Family life has collapsed, with soaring divorce rates and children born out of wedlock. Drugs devastate inner city neighborhoods. Outrages of various sorts are engaged in and then defended under constitutional doctrines of freedom of expression. Art museums display pornography and blasphemy and claim the right to be supported by tax dollars in doing so. Speech and dress are coarsened at every level. Media, entertainment, and marketing thrive on shameless sensuality. Religious denominations abandon, or seriously consider abandoning, the moral teachings of the Bible that have been the foundation of their faiths and the civilization in which they exist. Politicians posture as people of faith while prostituting themselves for votes with the claim that they can't allow their religious convictions to affect their position on public issues: "I am personally opposed, but . . .", as if faith and obedience to God could somehow be divorced from right government. Greed holds sway in boardrooms and offices of the corporate culture that controls much of the commerce of the society. The powerful of the business world enrich themselves at obscene levels, leaving employees bereft of pensions and shareholders holding shares of nothing. Citizens resist taxation to provide education and health care for those who don't have the advantages of most.

Our cup is half full and half empty. And the battle goes on.

CHAPTER NINETEEN

A few days later I asked one of my professional colleagues, "Did
you know that a lot of our basic concepts of government and law
come from the Bible?" I suspected he knew no such thing.

"I'm not an expert on what the Bible says," he replied, "but I'm not
surprised. It's just a matter of natural law. It's not that one comes from
the other; it's just the way it is."

He hurried off to his appointment and I to mine. But his comment
surprised me. What did he mean by natural law? And what did it have
to do with the Bible? Or with our law? I resolved to read up on natural
law as I read chapter nineteen and got ready to meet with Hal again.

> When the LORD your God has destroyed the nations whose
> land he is giving you, and when you have driven them out
> and settled in their towns and houses, then set aside for
> yourselves three cities centrally located in the land the LORD
> your God is giving you to possess. Build roads to them and
> divide into three parts the land the LORD your God is giving
> you as an inheritance, so that anyone who kills a man may
> flee there.
>
> This is the rule concerning the man who kills another and
> flees there to save his life—one who kills his neighbor un-
> intentionally, without malice aforethought. For instance, a
> man may go into the forest with his neighbor to cut wood,
> and as he swings his ax to fell a tree, the head may fly off and
> hit his neighbor and kill him. That man may flee to one of
> these cities and save his life. Otherwise, the avenger of blood
> might pursue him in a rage, overtake him if the distance
> is too great, and kill him even though he is not deserving
> of death, since he did it to his neighbor without malice

aforethought. This is why I command you to set aside for yourselves three cities.

If the LORD your God enlarges your territory, as he promised on oath to your forefathers, and gives you the whole land he promised them, because you carefully follow all these laws I command you today—to love the LORD your God and to walk always in his ways—then you are to set aside three more cities. Do this so that innocent blood will not be shed in your land, which the LORD your God is giving you as your inheritance, and so that you will not be guilty of bloodshed.

But if a man hates his neighbor and lies in wait for him, assaults and kills him, and then flees to one of these cities, the elders of his town shall send for him, bring him back from the city, and hand him over to the avenger of blood to die. Show him no pity. You must purge from Israel the guilt of shedding innocent blood, so that it may go well with you.

Do not move your neighbor's boundary stone set up by your predecessors in the inheritance you receive in the land the LORD your God is giving you to possess.

One witness is not enough to convict a man accused of any crime or offense he may have committed. A matter must be established by the testimony of two or three witnesses.

If a malicious witness takes the stand to accuse a man of a crime, the two men involved in the dispute must stand in the presence of the LORD before the priests and the judges who are in office at the time. The judges must make a thorough investigation, and if the witness proves to be a liar, giving false testimony against his brother, then do to him as he intended to do to his brother. You must purge the evil from among you. The rest of the people will hear of this and be afraid, and never again will such an evil thing be done among you. Show no pity: life for life, eye for eye, tooth for tooth, hand for hand, foot for foot.

—Deut. 19:1–21

"Natural Law," I learned, is the body of law that is, as the dictionary definition says, "derived from nature." It is law that is inherent in the nature of things and doesn't need human legislation to enact it. It is based on a higher law than law made by human beings. Natural law would operate in conjunction with human law, provide a guide to its interpretation, or even supersede it in particular cases where human law contradicts the law of nature.

The Declaration of Independence is a natural-law document. It justifies the American Revolution based on the "laws of nature and of nature's God," and finds in this natural law the basis for the universal right of humanity to "life, liberty and the pursuit of happiness." The Declaration of Independence is a political, not a legal, document. However, it expresses a belief and philosophy that guided and grounded the founding fathers of the United States, including the authors of the Constitution, and it led to the "shot heard 'round the world" and established what President Lincoln would later call "a new nation, conceived in liberty, and dedicated to the proposition that all men are created equal." That belief and philosophy to which George Washington, Thomas Jefferson, John Adams, James Madison, Alexander Hamilton, Benjamin Franklin, and their colleagues found sufficient to pledge their "lives, their fortunes, their sacred honor" has fallen on hard times in American jurisprudence.

Discussions of natural law have arisen in some of the confirmation hearings for Supreme Court nominees before the United States Senate, which has the right to "advise and consent" to the appointments. Conservative nominees of conservative presidents have been accused of believing in natural law, as if such a belief were the equivalent of treason to the judicial oath to follow the Constitution. The idea that a contemporary Supreme Court justice might have recourse to the thinking of the men who wrote the Constitution for guidance in interpreting it is anathema to many moderns. Rather than looking to the authors' original intent, they prefer a Constitution that is malleable, a "living document," to be interpreted to mean whatever the majority of the court chooses in the cases that come before them. That approach allows the justices to adopt a judicial philosophy that finds rights in the "umbras and penumbras" of the Constitution, imagined shaded or shadowy areas in which the court surmised its decision on abortion could be justified though nowhere actually expressed to justify it in any apparent way. Such a right insulates from social control conduct that no serious natural-law thinker would find in natural law and that would horrify most, if not all, of the authors of the Constitution. Much of that conduct is sexual, or related to sexuality.

I reflected on natural law and my colleague's comment as I read chapter nineteen. Here was a collection of legal concepts for the ages. The cities of refuge, which we had first encountered in chapter four—when God had Moses set aside three such cities in the land east of the Jordan—provided protection of the innocent (though perhaps negligent) harm-doer from vigilante justice. In Joshua 20, we see that Joshua implemented the command by setting aside the cities of refuge west of the Jordan. Verse 10 of chapter nineteen of Deuteronomy teaches that there would be a communal sharing of guilt if God's people tolerated a legal system that would allow innocent blood to be shed. The punishment of intentional wrongdoing, perjury, and the attempt to commit the crime as well as the crime itself; the protection of land ownership from the theft of moved boundaries; the necessity of punishing perjury; sufficient evidence to convict a person of a crime; and the equitable nature of justice in making the punishment fit the crime, all seemed consistent with natural law. Every issue here was one I had encountered in law school. Coming, as these laws did, from God himself, it was a good primer in the outworking of natural law. It remained for Hal to put a theological cast on it.

"In Christian understanding," he said, "natural law is derived from God but should be knowable to all. In the second chapter of Romans, verse fifteen, Paul gives a classical statement of natural law. He refers to Gentiles who do not have the law as given by Moses: 'The requirements of the law are written on their hearts, their consciences also bearing witness, and their thoughts now accusing, now even defending them.' The law written on their hearts, the law that is known to their hearts and consciences, is natural law.

"Most of the content of the Ten Commandments is based on natural law. We talked before about how some people see all the law chapters—twelve through twenty-six—in Deuteronomy as a commentary or outworking of the Ten Commandments. This chapter is a good illustration. It presents laws concerning murder, theft, and false witnesses. It follows the order as well as the substance of the sixth, eighth, and ninth commandments.

"It also shows a dramatic contrast to both ancient and modern totalitarian states in the value it places on human life and on justice. The innocent slayer is protected from vengeance by the ability to flee to the cities of refuge. The guilty slayer is forbidden such refuge and is punished. The testimony of two or three witnesses is required to convict of a crime and to protect against individual malicious accusations. And the witnesses are subject to the same punishment as the accused would have been if they testify falsely. Justice is fair and equitable. Priests, judges, and elders administer the system; no autocratic or arbitrary king or dictator is allowed to serve his own interests or agenda."

"How would you preach on this chapter?" I asked. "Have you ever?"

"There are some great messages here about how God thinks," Hal said. "And, yes, I have preached it. Take the illustration in verse five of the man who goes into the forest to cut wood, and as he swings his axe the head flies off and his neighbor is unintentionally killed. As a lawyer, I'm sure you see this as a negligence case, 'wrongful death,' as you lawyers call it. It's not a crime, but compensation may be due to the man's estate or his survivors. You hire experts to find out why the axe head came off. Was the axe defective? Should you sue the maker or the store that sold it? Or was the axe misused or not properly maintained, so that the owner should have known it and not used it? Who was negligent here? Axe heads are not supposed to just fly around and kill people; the axe is made for swinging and cutting. Someone is responsible for this tragedy, and it isn't the deceased. How am I doing?"

"You're making my closing argument to the jury," I said. "But what's the theological point?"

"The point is the fragility of life," Hal said. "It doesn't matter to the deceased what happens in your lawsuit. He has crossed over, suddenly and unexpectedly, to eternity—in the midst of what may have been the health and happiness of youth or midlife. He wasn't ill or fighting a war. He was just cutting wood with a neighbor. He has no further chance to repent, to seek forgiveness, to accept Christ if he hasn't already—no chance to get right with God. It illustrates the urgency of evangelism and of believers keeping their own lives straight."

"Keeping short lists with God," I said, quoting Hal back to Hal. "I had a boyhood friend whose family had a wall hanging that said, 'Do nothing today you would not want to be doing when Jesus comes. Go nowhere today you would not want to be when Jesus comes. Say nothing today you would not want to be saying when Jesus comes.'"

"I like that," Hal said. "And now consider the man whose axe head flew off. He's still alive, but in one swing of the tool his life has changed forever. In our society, a more likely scenario would be an auto accident. One wrong move, one mistake, and someone else is dead or terribly injured. The event is final, irretrievable, and the consequences then flow. The matter is plunged into the legal system: Lawyers, insurance companies, courts, judges, and juries argue and decide the issues of negligence and responsibility. But the man whose act caused the accident has a lifetime to live with the fact that his act destroyed the life of another and devastated the lives of the deceased's family and friends. He needs the opportunity to confront, confess, and receive forgiveness. Otherwise, his legal problems may be the smallest part of his difficulty."

I could hear the counselor's voice as Hal described the agony and guilt that often follows people involved in such tragedies. Here was a sermon indeed. I pressed him for more.

"Look at the description of the true evildoer in verse eleven," he said. "This is the anatomy of evil, the pathology. First comes the thought and motivation—the man 'hates his neighbor.' Then the preparation for evil—he 'lies in wait for him.' Finally, he commits the act—he 'assaults and kills him.' The evil begins with thinking about it, with the hatred. That's why Jesus taught us to love our enemies and pray for those who persecute us. *That* is perfection—overcoming the hatred in favor of love so things never progress to preparation and acts of evil. There's another whole sermon."

Hal talked about the allegorical interpretations that many had seen in the down-to-earth laws in this chapter. The cities of refuge have been seen as an allegory for Christ, our refuge from the sin and evil that beset us. Moving the boundary has been seen as the changing of revealed truth. God owns the land, as he is the author and revealer of truth. To move the boundary is to change by human act what God has given. It is not just the crime of theft but a rebellion against God.

"What about the eye-for-an-eye concept?" I asked. "That seems to me pretty primitive justice. Didn't Jesus supersede this when he taught love of enemies and turning the other cheek?"

Hal read the last verse: "'Show no pity: life for life, eye for eye, tooth for tooth, hand for hand, foot for foot.'

"From the beginning," he said, "Jewish sages as well as Christian scholars have understood this as a metaphor for balanced justice, not something that is to be applied literally. It is summed up by the idea of making the punishment fit the crime. There is no evidence, other than capital punishment for murder, that it was ever understood or applied literally. It served as a restraint on feuds and the desire for retaliation or revenge, and kept justice just."

"So did Jesus teach injustice when he taught us to turn the other cheek and all that?" I pursued the issue.

"When Jesus taught about it in the Sermon on the Mount, he was bringing people to an inner morality and rightness with God, beyond what is achieved by outer obedience to the law. Although murder is forbidden, the anger that leads to murder—the inner thought—is not hidden from God and is subject to judgment. Although adultery is forbidden, the lustful view of another person is not hidden from God and is subject to judgment. When he talked about turning the other cheek instead of following the 'eye for eye' and 'tooth for tooth' Scripture, he was also bringing people to a higher morality. He wasn't teaching that we should accept evil. The 'eye for eye' idea of balanced justice is right for a civil justice system—it was in Moses' time and it still is. But Jesus taught a personal morality that went beyond that, not placing value on things of this world and not getting even or achieving personal justice with those who would wrong us or have wronged us. Rather than competing with evildoers, we are to surround them with good and let the good in us overcome the evil in them. Turning the other cheek, giving your cloak as well as your tunic and walking the extra mile with someone who forces you to go with him are examples of this. They reflect an inner attitude of the heart, like a heart that isn't consumed with anger or lust."

The next time I saw my colleague, I pursued our previous discussion of natural law. "Which of these," I asked, "do you think would be derived from natural law? Determination of guilt or innocence by an independent tribunal, rather than by vigilante justice or revenge seekers; the guilt of a society that allows the innocent to be killed; punishment of intentional killers; the wrongfulness of moving boundaries; requiring a sufficient amount of evidence to convict of a crime; punishment of perjurers, proportional to the damage their perjury would have done; or punishment proportionate to the crime."

He thought a moment. "All of the above."

"They're all in the Bible," I said. "Deuteronomy, chapter nineteen."

"I'm not surprised," he said. "Like I said before, some ideas are just the way things are. You don't need the Bible to figure it out. It's just natural . . . natural law. You get it from the Bible; I get it from my head."

Written in his heart, his conscience bearing witness, I thought, just like Paul said. Then I asked, "So what if people don't agree on what natural law is?"

"It doesn't matter," he said. "We don't go by natural law. We just go by the Constitution and the statutes the Congress and legislature have passed."

"If natural law is the way things are, then why can't we follow it?"

"Like you said, people won't agree on what it is."

"Maybe not everyone, but if it really is natural, won't most people agree?"

"You need a standard, something to hold onto. You can't have a legal system run by polls."

"If the law in the Bible is natural law, then that should be a pretty good standard. Why don't we look to the Bible for what it is?"

"You can't do that. Separation of church and state. Besides, if you allow that, next thing you know, someone else will want to look to the Koran, and who knows what."

"What if they all agree? I mean, some things are different, but there are basic ideas that will be the same all over."

"Then those will be in our laws. Everyone is against murder and stealing, but we don't need the Bible or the Koran to tell us those things are wrong; it's already in the law," he replied.

"What about the close cases? The interpretations? Especially of the Constitution? Can a Supreme Court Justice consider natural law in figuring out what terms like equal protection of the law and due process of law mean?"

"I'll have to think about that one," he said.

CHAPTER TWENTY

"Y ou've got mail." My computer, that black box that can write and speak and deliver the words of others, came to life. The message was from Hal: "Apologetics 101, first class. How do you know Deuteronomy is really from God?"

"Because it says so—six times just in chapter one, it says it is a message from God," I replied.

"True," he replied. "And we can't begin to understand it if we don't acknowledge that. From beginning to end, it presents itself as God's word. If it isn't God's word, it's a fraud, or at least a type of literature that doesn't attempt to be truthful and only uses stories to make a point. But anyone can claim to have a message from God.

"Apologetics 101, second class. What else gives us confidence in the assertion that it is God's word?"

"It talks about miraculous events and powerful acts of God that these people or their parents witnessed firsthand: the plagues in Egypt, the Passover, the destruction of the Egyptian army in the sea, the giving of the law at Sinai, the protection in the wilderness, manna, and the victories over Sihon and Og," I typed into the box and clicked "send."

"Eyewitness testimony," came the response. "Just like with Jesus. You lawyers should like that. Got anything else?"

I didn't. We were, I knew, about to read Deuteronomy 20, a chapter about the conduct of war. I couldn't fit it into Hal's distance-learning class on apologetics. When I acknowledged as much, Hal flashed back: "Read Judges seven and Joshua nine before we meet."

My homework was fresh in my mind when we met and read the first nine verses of chapter twenty:

When you go to war against your enemies and see horses and chariots and an army greater than yours, do not be afraid of them, because the LORD your God, who brought you up out of Egypt, will be with you. When you are about to go into battle, the priest shall come forward and address the army. He shall say: "Hear, O Israel, today you are going into battle against your enemies. Do not be fainthearted or afraid; do not be terrified or give way to panic before them. For the LORD your God is the one who goes with you to fight for you against your enemies to give you victory."

The officers shall say to the army: "Has anyone built a new house and not dedicated it? Let him go home, or he may die in battle and someone else may dedicate it. Has anyone planted a vineyard and not begun to enjoy it? Let him go home, or he may die in battle and someone else enjoy it. Has anyone become pledged to a woman and not married her? Let him go home, or he may die in battle and someone else marry her." Then the officers shall add, "Is any man afraid or fainthearted? Let him go home so that his brothers will not become disheartened too." When the officers have finished speaking to the army, they shall appoint commanders over it.

—Deut. 20:1–9

Hal asked, "How many military commanders have you heard of who complained that they had too many forces for the battle?"

I couldn't think of any except Gideon.

"Tell me the story of Gideon," Hal said.

I recited the story of Gideon's battle with the Midianites from Judges 7. The Lord had allowed Midian to oppress Israel for seven years because of Israel's disobedience. When Israel cried out to the Lord, he sent Gideon, a "mighty warrior," to free Israel from the oppression. Gideon assembled an army of 32,000 men for the battle. God, however, told Gideon he was overstaffed: "You have too many men for me to deliver Midian into their hands. In order that Israel may not boast against me that her own strength has saved her, announce now to the people, 'Anyone who trembles with fear may turn back and leave Mount Gilead.'" Twenty-two thousand men departed, leaving ten thousand. The army was further reduced to a mere three hundred men before confronting the Midianite army. With this minor force, less than 1 percent of the army that started out, Gideon struck fear into the Midianites who fled, freeing Israel for forty years.

"Whose idea was it to reduce the size of the army?" Hal asked.

"I guess it wasn't really Gideon's. He was carrying out the Lord's direction."

"And what does the account of Gideon's confrontation with the Midianites have to do with chapter twenty?"

God sent men home before the big battle. Twenty-two thousand men, over two-thirds of the army, left because they "trembled with fear." It is just as in Deuteronomy 20, when men were sent home because they were afraid or fainthearted.

"Apologetics 101, class three," Hal said. "We have seen that Deuteronomy claims, directly and forthrightly, to be a record of the words and commands of God himself as given to Moses. That was class one.

"We have also seen that its validity relies on the eyewitness testimony of the people to whom it was originally addressed—they'd seen these things with their own eyes. If they hadn't seen these things, you would expect to find a competing story, one that says, 'It ain't so.' Or, more likely, something like Deuteronomy would wind up getting the 'deep six,' being thrown into the circular file of pottery where the ancients kept their fire-starting materials. Instead, they treated it with reverence, and it became part of the Holy Scriptures. That attests to the historic validity that the people closest to the time it was written believed it had. That was class two.

"Now I want you to see a third thing, here in class three. Many other parts of the Bible make sense if you understand Deuteronomy; if you don't, they're just isolated stories. The story of Gideon follows exactly the rule of war in Deuteronomy 20. The fearful are sent home, and there are a lot of them. This is holy war. The Lord himself will fight for them and give them the victory. What they need in order to achieve it is faith that he will do as he says. It's not the size of the army but God's faithfulness that counts. The story of Gideon is the story of the first nine verses of chapter twenty put to real life. The Bible is not a series of unconnected writings. It is one book, one story—a story that's consistent but progressive. God acts as he said he would act. The rules of war are given, and they work when put to the test. A story like that must have a single author. The author of the Bible—the one who inspired the human writers—is God the Holy Spirit."

We moved on from the apologetics lesson.

"Why is the priest involved in this?" I asked. "You don't usually have religious leaders exhorting soldiers before a battle."

"Notice in verse one," Hal said, "that this is a battle against Israel's enemies, that is, the enemies of God's chosen. This is truly God's war. It's a religious event, a part of his reclaiming his land that evil forces had taken over. Those forces were real and well-armed, with horses and chariots, like the army that pursued Israel out of Egypt. There is an enemy, and the enemy is not nice.

"But if God's people rely on their own strength to defeat the enemy, they will fail. The religious leaders need to remind them that it is the Lord's strength that will bring the victory, and they need not fear. Even God's people need to be constantly reminded that they can't succeed in their own strength. '"Not by might nor by power, but by my Spirit," says the Lord.'"

Hal's phone rang. While he was talking, I reread the passage. There were other exemptions from military service besides faintheartedness. Men were sent home who had built a new house and not dedicated it, planted a vineyard and not begun to enjoy it, or become pledged to a woman and not married her. These men had not been sent home in the Gideon story. I asked Hal about them when he got off the phone.

"Don't be concerned that they aren't mentioned in the Gideon story. Just because it doesn't say they were sent home doesn't mean it didn't happen. They may have been sent home before the fearful were. More likely, since everyone knew the rules, they weren't expected to report for duty in the first place.

"Exempting these men from military service makes two points. First is what we have already seen, and the theme that's consistent through-out Deuteronomy: God's strength, not man's strength or righteousness, brings success in battle. God doesn't need a bigger army to win a battle or a war. Second, the whole purpose of bringing Israel into the land is to enjoy the fruits of life in it. Building homes, planting vineyards, and starting families fulfilled that promise; these things had priority, even over the needs of war."

Silence fell between us, as it sometimes does when people know each other well enough that they don't need to fill all spaces between them with sound. It came to me in our silence that these verses were not about military wars and battles. They were about wars and battles of quite another sort. Then the question arose in me from a spiritual center deep within: "Am I one of the ones who will get to fight, Hal," I asked, "or will I be sent home?"

My voice must have betrayed the uncertainty my soul felt as I gave voice to the thought. It was a thought that had appeared many times before in different guises, that midnight horror of realization of how far I really was from God—that look into the soul that revealed, as C.S. Lewis had put it, a nursery of fears, a zoo of lusts, a bedlam of ambitions, and a harem of fondled hatreds. Hal rose and walked behind my chair. I felt the reassurance of his hands, strong and firm despite his age and arthritis, on both my shoulders. He took as much time to formulate his answer as I had taken to discern my question.

"You won't be sent home for fear or faintheartedness, Chris," he said. "You are in the Lord's army, and you can't resign. But the hard work in God's service is not work for a novice. It takes a depth of faith that is only built with time and a lot of experience in the things of God. When the men were sent home who were just beginning in life—building a home, planting, starting a family—they didn't leave the field of battle forever. They would be back another day when they had matured. In the meantime, God had other work for them to do. You have a lot of years to be in this army."

He released his strong grip on my shoulders. As he moved back to his chair, he assumed a lighter tone. "Think of it as a football game," he said. "Thousands of spectators cheer on the players, but only a handful are out on the field banging heads with the other side, blocking and tackling, running and throwing, getting hurt and dirty. Between the spectators and the players are a lot of people supporting the team: coaches, trainers, cheerleaders, the band, and the water boys. And the bench has two or three layers of players training to go in when they're needed, when the first team needs relief, when special teams work the kickoffs and point after, and when the team is so far ahead that you can let the second and third string play for the experience.

"Some people will always be spectators, but the players will never get too old to be in the game. You're not just a spectator anymore, Chris. But you haven't made the first team yet.

"Let's read the rest of chapter twenty."

> When you march up to attack a city, make its people an offer of peace. If they accept and open their gates, all the people in it shall be subject to forced labor and shall work for you. If they refuse to make peace and they engage you in battle, lay siege to that city. When the LORD your God delivers it into your hand, put to the sword all the men in it. As for the women, the children, the livestock, and everything else in the city, you may take these as plunder for yourselves. And you may use the plunder the LORD your God gives you from your enemies. This is how you are to treat all the cities that are at a distance from you and do not belong to the nations nearby.
>
> However, in the cities of the nations the LORD your God is giving you as an inheritance, do not leave alive anything that breathes. Completely destroy them—the Hittites, Amorites, Canaanites, Perizzites, Hivites, and Jebusites—as the LORD your God has commanded you. Otherwise, they will teach you to follow all the detestable things they do in worshiping their gods, and you will sin against the LORD your God.
>
> When you lay siege to a city for a long time, fighting against it to capture it, do not destroy its trees by putting an ax to them, because you can eat their fruit. Do not cut them down. Are the trees of the field people, that you should besiege them? However, you may cut down trees that you know are not fruit trees and use them to build siege works until the city at war with you falls.
>
> —Deut. 20:10–20

"Tell me another story," Hal said after we had read the passage. "What happened with the Gibeonites?"

I reviewed the story from the ninth chapter of Joshua. The Gibeonites—a people who lived in the land and were to be completely destroyed—deceived Israel into thinking they were from a distant place. They loaded their donkeys with worn-out sacks and wineskins, wore old clothes and patched sandals, and had dry and moldy bread. They volunteered for a servant's role and made a treaty with Israel.

"Another example of apologetics, class three," Hal said. "Just as the story of Gideon makes sense because of the rules of war in the first part of chapter twenty, the story of the Gibeonites makes sense because of the rules in the second part of the chapter. These people understood they would be killed if the Israelites knew they were inhabitants of the land, so they disguised themselves as being from a distant place to get Israel to believe they fell into the category of those who would be spared if they submitted. Not only were they spared in violation of the command, but also they were able to make a treaty with Israel, which also violated the command back in chapter seven not to make treaties with the people of the land. When the ruse was discovered, it was too late. Now Israel had made a commitment. But the knowledge of God's command to allow distant cities to submit to save themselves is the key to understanding what is going on in this story. And that command is here in chapter twenty. One book, one story, one author."

We had talked earlier about the reasons for the lack of mercy to the inhabitants of the land. Hal reminded me of the reasons for the destruction that Israel brought on them. "There is a strain of Jewish teaching," he added, "that is reluctant to accept the literalness of this and other passages that command the 'herem' slaughter of people in the land. The sinner should not be punished unless he has been given the knowledge of the sin and chance to repent. But remember our discussion of natural law. Paul teaches that people are without excuse. At some level, they do have knowledge of God and of good and evil, even if they haven't had the specific revelation of the Scriptures. Love and mercy sometimes require hard decisions. 'The sin of the Amorites had reached its full measure.' Sparing them would perpetuate a culture of evil, ungodliness, and disobedience that would let such conduct go unpunished in the face of God's justice, as well as allow the example that would corrupt God's own people."

I was reminded of the military analogy of the submarine commander who has to order the sealing off of a section of the vessel—even though he knows some sailors are trapped there—in order to save the ship from sinking with the rest of the crew. The analogy was imperfect—the doomed sailors were not deserving of their fate in a way different from the rest of the crew—but the decision that was for the greatest good left some people behind.

We talked about the three categories of cities: the ones in the land, the distant ones that submitted, and the distant ones that resisted. But why, I asked Hal, subject distant cities that surrendered to servitude and then kill only the men in the cities that resisted?

"The depth of wickedness is centered in the land God is giving to Israel," Hal said. "The more distant cities are still enemies of God, but not beyond conversion. To put it in terms of God's message to Abraham in Genesis, their sin has not yet reached its full measure. Those that submit become part of God's people and in servanthood to God's purposes, and are spared. If they resist, those that carried out the resistance are not spared, but the rest are taken into the kingdom. There is a logic here that is consistent with God's purposes."

I was still reaching for personal meaning beyond the history in the passage. I could see that the inhabitants who were to be destroyed represent the sin that should be completely wiped out of our lives. But what about the distant cities; what do they represent?

"There is deep allegory and spiritual meaning here," Hal said. "The believer has all three of these cities within. The cities that submit represent our subjection to Christ in all things. Paul refers to becoming slaves for Christ. Being a servant to God is not a bad thing. And the cities that resist but are conquered—with the slaying of the adult males but sparing of the women and children—represent the destruction of the godlessness in our center so that our more malleable parts, even though still fleshly, can grow in grace."

He reached up to his bookshelf and pulled down a well-thumbed copy of Luther's Works. Finding the section on chapter twenty of the *Lectures on Deuteronomy*, he read from page 206: "When the godlessness of the heart is killed, the weakness of the flesh does no harm; for sin in the members is no longer imputed after the head of that serpent, that is, the will and the delusion of godlessness, has been cut off."

The hour was late. Chapter twenty had grown in my understanding from a short account of archaic war practices to a profound account of the Christian life and one that brought a "ring of truth" to other passages and the Bible as a whole.

Hal put his Luther away and opened his Bible. "The church has no armies," he said, "and the Crusaders—and others in the Middle Ages—who thought it should have armies were wrong. But from the beginning, the church has used the language of war to describe the experience of life in Christ."

He led me through some of the New Testament passages:

> For though we live in the world, we do not wage war as the world does. The weapons we fight with are not the weapons of the world. On the contrary, they have divine power to demolish strongholds. We demolish arguments and every pretension that sets itself up against the knowledge of God, and we take captive every thought to make it obedient to Christ.
>
> —2 Cor. 10:3–5

> And having disarmed the powers and authorities, he made a public spectacle of them, triumphing over them by the cross.
>
> —Col. 2:15

> Endure hardship with us like a good soldier of Christ Jesus. No one serving as a soldier gets involved in civilian affairs— he wants to please his commanding officer.
>
> —2 Tim. 2:3–4

> Dear friends, I urge you, as aliens and strangers in the world, to abstain from sinful desires which war against your soul.
>
> —1 Peter 2:11

And, of course, he read the familiar passage in Ephesians 6:11–17:

> Put on the full armor of God so that you can take your stand against the devil's schemes. For our struggle is not against flesh and blood, but against the rulers, against the authorities, against the powers of this dark world and against the spiritual forces of evil in the heavenly realms. Therefore put on the full armor of God, so that when the day of evil comes, you may be able to stand your ground, and after you have done everything, to stand. Stand firm then, with the belt of truth buckled around your waist, with the breastplate of righteousness in place, and with your feet fitted with the readiness that comes from the gospel of peace. In addition to all this, take up the shield of faith, with which you can extinguish all the flaming arrows of the evil one. Take the helmet of salvation and the sword of the Spirit which is the word of God.

"The Christian life," Hal said, "is a life of peace because we know our Savior lives and he has won the victory. But it is a life that is still in this world and filled with struggle—against our own tendencies to sin and the temptations of the world, the temptations of money, sex, and power . . . and against the forces of evil that are very real and that dominate the world. We can't demonize everything and everyone that is not Christian. A spiritually discerning person knows real evil from foolish and deluded humanity. Everyone we disagree with is not under Satan's influence, and we're all wrong about some things. But these Scriptures are not just metaphors. Spiritual warfare is real. Some people are 'people of the lie,' as one book describes them. We can't close our eyes to the spiritual evils we live among. Truth, righteousness, the gospel of peace, faith, salvation, and the word of God—these are our weapons."

We closed our Bibles and prayed together for a time. As we walked to the door, I recalled to Hal the last two verses of the chapter, teaching that the fruit trees of the city were not to be cut in a siege, although other trees could be cut to make siege works.

"The literal message is simple and practical," Hal said. "Cutting the fruit trees is self-defeating. They will yield their fruit to the conqueror as they did to the conquered. The rage and rampage of war should be controlled to avoid unnecessary destruction.

"The moral message is one that makes every believer an environmentalist at some level. Humanity is entrusted with caring for the garden of the earth. Destroying its fruitfulness is a spiritual failing in God's eyes.

"The allegorical meaning of the passage takes us to the fifteenth chapter of the Gospel of John. There Jesus, using a vine rather than a tree as an example, describes himself as the true vine and the Father as the gardener who cuts off the branches that bear no fruit, while pruning the branches that do bear fruit so they'll be even more fruitful. Remaining in Christ is essential to bearing fruit."

He paused and continued, "The allegorical meaning of the passage is probably close to the deeper spiritual meaning. It is God's will that his creation be fruitful, both in the natural and the spiritual sense. To destroy the fruit tree is to destroy the very things that sustain us spiritually."

The book was closed, along with the day and the door, and I was left to the night.

One book, one story, one author, one God. One army, trimming out the novices and those weak of faith, preparing to battle the spiritual forces of evil in the heavenly realms. One believer, wondering if he would be sent home from the war, unfit for service, powerful centers of sin within himself still needing to be sacrificed. One tree standing in the plain before the army, its fate depending on whether or not it bore fruit for them.

"Lord Jesus Christ, have mercy on me."

CHAPTER TWENTY-ONE

"I have a question about the law," Hal said, opening his brown bag in the chair across from my desk. It was a weekday, not when we usually met. But he had to be in town, and I was free for lunch. I had offered to take him out, but Hal said he would bring his own and something for me. Lunch turned out to be a hefty slice of cheddar cheese and an apple turnover that a neighbor had dropped off for him. He passed a plastic plate with the treasure, wrapped securely in plastic, across the desk.

"Do we have any laws in this state that are archaic?" he went on between bites. "Anything out of date?"

I knew we did, but I didn't usually encounter them. Lawyers deal with current laws, not ancient history that is still on the books because no one thought to repeal it. I wracked my brain. "Well, there is the attachment law. There are some pretty old exceptions. I was just looking at that the other day."

"What's an attachment, and what's an exception?"

I explained the basics of attachments. They are a legal process that someone bringing a lawsuit can use to put a lien—like a mortgage on a house—on some property of the person who is being sued. The purpose was to secure the judgment that the plaintiff or creditor hoped to receive at the end of the litigation. Otherwise, a person might get to the end of the line and find that the other party had nothing left with which to pay the debt. Courts supervised attachments so they could not be used abusively. You had to show that there was a reasonable prospect you would recover a judgment, and the other party could avoid the attachment by showing that there were plenty of assets to meet any obligations that came out of the lawsuit.

The law provided that not everything could be attached. These were the exceptions; for example, the property a debtor was permitted to own that could not be attached to secure his debts.

"What's archaic about that?" Hal asked. "It sounds like plain vanilla lawyer stuff to me."

"It's the exceptions," I said. "Some are really ancient." I pulled the attachment statute down from a shelf behind my desk and read Hal some of the exceptions: One hog and one pig, and the pork of the same when slaughtered; six sheep and fleeces of the same; the debtor's interest in one pew in any meetinghouse in which the debtor or the debtor's family usually worships.

"I see what you mean," Hal said. "Not too many people around here own pigs and sheep any more."

"And how many churches do you know where people still own their pews?"

"That one must go back to colonial times," Hal said. "Why do you suppose these exceptions were part of the law in the first place?"

"I suppose they didn't want to deprive people of the livestock they needed for survival. And as for the pews, if you had to own a pew or a part of one to worship in the church, well—no one would want to keep a person from going to church, no matter how much in debt he got to be. I did know some people—actually represented them—who built their own church. It was a small town, very rural. But they still didn't own the pews, and I'm sure anyone could come to it."

"So there was a purpose in the legislation. Those laws served a valid purpose in their time."

"I'm sure they did. Usually you can see it, even if it doesn't apply to us any longer."

Hal had finished his apple turnover and cheese, so he fished a napkin out of his bag, wiped his mouth, and brushed the crumbs off his lap. "I think we're ready to read chapter twenty-one," he said. "You'll find some laws here that may seem archaic. We may need to work a little to discern what was in the mind of the legislator. Let's take it a section at a time." We read the first nine verses.

> If a man is found slain, lying in a field in the land the LORD
> your God is giving you to possess, and it is not known who

killed him, your elders and judges shall go out and measure the distance from the body to the neighboring towns. Then the elders of the town nearest the body shall take a heifer that has never been worked and has never worn a yoke and lead her down to a valley that has not been plowed or planted and where there is a flowing stream. There in the valley they are to break the heifer's neck. The priests, the sons of Levi, shall step forward, for the LORD your God has chosen them to minister and to pronounce blessings in the name of the LORD and to decide all cases of dispute and assault. Then all the elders of the town nearest the body shall wash their hands over the heifer whose neck was broken in the valley, and they shall declare: "Our hands did not shed this blood, nor did our eyes see it done. Accept this atonement for your people Israel, whom you have redeemed, O LORD, and do not hold your people guilty of the blood of an innocent man." And the bloodshed will be atoned for. So you will purge from yourselves the guilt of shedding innocent blood, since you have done what is right in the eyes of the LORD.

—Deut. 21:1–9

"OK, Hal," I said after we read it, "what's going on here? That's a curious, primitive ritual . . . and performed by the judges, priests, and elders. God surely knew who the real culprit was, even if they didn't. And the real culprit surely would face judgment in eternity for his act, even if he escaped judgment in this life. The act of atonement was by the wrong people, those who were innocent of the crime. And God surely knew this as well. I mean, Hal, this one is not only archaic, it doesn't really make sense."

"You are a child of your times, Chris. You see everything in individual terms. God sees things in individual terms too; who you are and how you act as a child of faith is important to him. The real culprit in this unsolved murder surely will face judgment in eternity. But what the modern world has forgotten, even the church, is that God holds communities and nations accountable as well as individuals. That's not a welcome message these days, and people have trouble getting their arms around it, really understanding it, and taking it in like you take in the assumptions of the culture you live in. All the cultural assumptions that bathe you every day are individualistic. It's what *you* do, who *you* are, that counts. If the culture goes to hell in a handbasket, well, don't blame me, I voted for the other guy.

"The whole history of the land of Israel in the Old Testament is the story of the accountability of a people, not a person, to their God. God gave Israel the land on the condition of obedience—national obedience, the collective obedience of all the people. When there is collective national disobedience to his law, he isn't going to take the land away from only the Israelites that are disobedient but rather the whole nation. As Jesus said, the rain falls on the just and the unjust alike. In this world, at least, you're in the same boat as your town, your state, and your country—even when you're trying to row it in a different direction than it's going. The story of Israel in the Old Testament is the story of cycles of disobedience, punishment, repentance, and restoration—until the disobedience builds up to the breaking point. To put it in the biblical metaphor, the cup of God's wrath overflows. That's when the nation is destroyed and removed to exile in Babylon. National fortune does, in the long run, have everything to do with how closely a nation follows God's way."

I reshelved my law book about attachments while I thought about Hal's points. Did I feel responsible for what other people did—for policies or actions of the society, the community, and the nation, even if I disagreed with them? And what could I do about it anyway, other than advocate different laws and policies or vote for different leaders?

I was torn and confused. There was a troubling godlessness permeating much of our society and culture, and it seemed to be growing. And yet we were, we thought, the best nation on earth—the most free, the place with the most economic opportunity, even one of the most religious. "United we stand," as the bumper sticker declared.

Hal brought me back to the text of chapter twenty-one.

"This law of atonement for the unsolved murder acknowledges that the community cannot simply ignore evil, even if you don't know who's responsible for it. This is a ceremony of community action to address a wrong when it hasn't been able to right the wrong through civil justice—public officials take public responsibility for keeping the land right with God. The ceremony shows the solemn and significant nature of the situation when an evil act has been committed and there has been no justice and no accountability for it."

"I understand the first part, measuring to the nearest town. That's what we lawyers call jurisdiction: Whose territory does it fall in, and who needs to do whatever needs to be done? But what about the un-worked heifer, the unplowed valley, and the flowing stream? How do they fit into bringing the community right with God?"

"Some of the symbolism of the ceremony may be lost on us," Hal answered. "The text doesn't tell us what it is, and Bible scholars haven't all agreed. But here's my take: The slaying of the heifer is a symbolic slaying of the unknown criminal. The slaying of the symbolic murderer takes place in a valley that hasn't been plowed or planted, signifying that it's barren or defiled by the murder. In Jewish tradition, the area was never plowed or planted after the act, unless the murderer was later caught and punished. And the flowing stream is to carry the sin away. The importance of the event isn't the specific symbolism. It's the community leaders' acceptance of public responsibility before the Lord—on behalf of the community—for wrongdoing in the land. Even if they don't have personal responsibility for it and don't know who does, it's important to cleanse the community before God."

The handwashing seemed to me an easier symbol to understand. When community responsibility is accepted, the cleansing of the com-munity from guilt is the necessary next step.

Hal quoted Psalms 26 and 73: "I wash my hands in innocence." Then he elaborated: "The hand-washing symbol of innocence has endured. The most infamous hand-washing is Pilate's when he declared himself innocent of Jesus' blood before the crucifixion. We still use the term in common speech to refer to removing ourselves from responsibility for an event controlled by others. It all goes back to Deuteronomy, and no one even knows it."

"I don't suppose this is one of the laws Jews still follow," I said, "even in Israel."

"The ceremony was abandoned as impractical after the Exile. There were apparently too many murders for the authorities to keep it up, and they accepted that the literal performance of it was limited to a smaller and holier society."

I looked out my window and across the square to the state Capitol building. Over it, a large American flag snapped briskly in the wind. Nearby, and slightly lower and to its left, flew the flag of the state of New Hampshire. I imagined for a moment the political, judicial, and religious leaders of our state—hundreds, perhaps thousands, of them—assembling together in front of the Capitol. There they would join to beseech God to forgive them and their people for all the wrongs that had been done in the land—the corner of creation that we held in tenancy from the Owner and Landlord—that human justice had not righted. There they would, as Deuteronomy says, "do what is right in the eyes of the Lord." Then the cynicism welled up in me. *Fat chance*, I thought. If anyone suggested it, someone would sue because it would violate church and state separation. Media personalities and editorial writers would sneer and claim that it was meaningless unless the leaders they didn't like sought forgiveness for the policies they didn't like. Many of the leaders would refuse to participate, either because they didn't believe in it or because they wouldn't join in a community effort with those of other political parties or denominations or traditions within the church. The whole thing would dissolve in acrimony and hostility. So much for our biblical fidelity.

I turned back to Hal: "What can we do, Hal?" I asked. "If God holds us accountable together for all the wrongs of the land, how do we respond?"

"Our old friend Matthew Henry perhaps said it best," Hal said, recalling the English preacher of the late 1600s and early 1700s whose comments so often seemed to penetrate to the spiritual heart of the Scriptures: "'We must empty the measure by our prayers which others are filling by their sins.'"

"Translate for me, Hal."

"In other words, the prayers of the faithful for forgiveness of the evil in our community, nation, and society need to exceed the evil around us. God will preserve the nation from punishment if the righteous within it can be more faithful in atoning—even for the sins of others—on its behalf, than the faithfulness of evil people to their wickedness. There is the greatest merit in our prayers for our communities and nation, especially for forgiveness of them."

"And what about the evil that goes unpunished because it's simply tolerated? Can we atone for that by our prayers as well?"

"In this passage, which seems so culturally remote from us," Hal said, "we see that the significance of a single human death is so great that the judicial, civil, and religious leaders need to respond in a significant way. But in our society, death is so common that we become inured to it. Hear about it in the news, that's too bad, we go on with our lives. Abortions by the millions, people shooting each other in the streets, road deaths . . . too much is tolerated, and when it comes to abortion, it's even legitimized by court rulings on the Constitution. I tremble for our nation when I contemplate these things in the light of God's word. Mighty prayer is needed, but the prayers of a few cannot, I fear, save an unrepentant nation. Let's read the next section of chapter twenty-one."

> When you go to war against your enemies and the LORD your God delivers them into your hands and you take captives, if you notice among the captives a beautiful woman and are attracted to her, you may take her as your wife. Bring her into your home and have her shave her head, trim her nails, and put aside the clothes she was wearing when captured. After she has lived in your house and mourned her father and mother for a full month, then you may go to her and be her husband and she shall be your wife. If you are not pleased with her, let her go wherever she wishes. You must not sell her or treat her as a slave, since you have dishonored her.
>
> —Deut. 21:10–14

"I don't expect to have the opportunity to select a captive woman for myself," I kidded Hal lightly after we read this passage. "Can we skip over it?"

"Not a chance," he replied. "This is the beginning of a series of laws we will be studying that tell us how God thinks about marriage and sexuality. You will never be in the situation of the Israelite soldier who takes a fancy to a woman who has been captured in war, but you and every male alive will deal with women, and with a particular woman he will marry or has married. Let's dig into this one."

Hal pointed out that, from the beginning of history, conquering armies have abused and raped women at will. It still goes on in nations where undisciplined armies act outside the international agreements established by, for example, the Geneva Convention. In recent times we've learned of rape rooms in Saddam Hussein's Iraq, where women who were not in favor with the regime were brutally raped, and the ravaging of Muslim women in Kosovo by their Serbian persecutors.

War is usually a brutal business for noncombatants as well as combatants, and brutal regimes impose warlike brutality on dissenters among their own people.

"This is an extraordinary passage in the context of the assumptions that have governed soldiers throughout history. The captured woman is a human being with dignity; she should be treated with honor and respect. God does not tolerate the abuse of the powerless by the powerful. God pays special attention to the weak—in this case, captured women."

"But in the example we just read about it sounds like her parents had been killed or she'd been torn away from them," I added. "And she'd been taken in what amounted to a forced marriage. If the guy decides he doesn't like her, he can dump her."

"What happened to her parents happened," Hal said. "We're talking about a captive. The usual fate of captives in those days was death or slavery. Not so here. Look at the consideration she receives. She's given a month to mourn the loss of her parents. She is to set aside the clothing of her former life. She is to shave her head and trim her nails, removing the external signs of beauty that attracted the man to her. During this time of mourning and plainness, she is to live in the man's home, but not as his wife. Only after a month of this is he permitted to take her as a wife."

"What's the point?" I asked.

"The point is to prevent marriages motivated by lust. The man must see the woman in her least attractive state, and to see her that way for a full month. He must be able to love her, even when she is unlovable. The passage of time is necessary for the attractions of the flesh to balance themselves out. On the woman's part, she must show the willingness to give up her former life and look to the future with her husband. And, by the way, nothing here says she doesn't have a choice about the matter. If she refuses to go through this transition, she doesn't qualify to be his wife. Every marriage would benefit by applying these principles—a demonstrated willingness to love the other in his or her most unlovable moments, a willingness to give up the past in commitment to a future with the other person. These are the foundations of a marriage that will endure."

"And what about faith?" I asked. "Must she share his faith?"

"The woman in this passage is a captive outside the land where the herem ban is in effect," Hal said. "She is not one of those irrevocably committed to the religious evils that caused the land to vomit out its inhabitants. The passage does not explicitly say she must follow the God of Israel, but I think it's implied. God is quite clear in a number of places that for his people to marry people who do not share their faith is a great wrong. 'Do not be yoked together with unbelievers,' as Paul wrote in Second Corinthians. It's not likely that God would tolerate his people marrying captives who remained unbelievers."

We discussed the end of the passage in which the man could, in effect, divorce the woman if he wasn't pleased with her. If he did, however, he must allow her to go wherever she wished, and not sell her or treat her as a slave, "because you have dishonored her."

"Sexual relations," Hal said, "like all other acts, right or wrong, occur under God's watchful eyes. And in God's eyes, they don't occur without responsibility. In this particular case, the responsibility of the man is to elevate the woman's status to his own. She is no longer a captive, and she is not his property. She isn't a slave or a servant. Jesus taught that divorce was only allowed at this time in history because of hard hearts—even among God's people—and that hasn't changed, as any pastor or marriage counselor can attest. True divorce, in God's eyes, can only occur for adultery. But if there is a divorce, the man can't control the woman after they part. She is free and equal."

"I don't do a lot of divorce work as a lawyer," I said. "But I have done enough over the years to recognize the evil that God was addressing in this passage. It's a familiar pattern. The husband, usually a dominating man who expects his wife to jump to his bidding, achieves some material success. He controls his family, and he controls his business. With time, his wife loses the attractiveness of her youth and he is drawn to other women, inevitably younger and more attractive. Then he decides to divorce and marry his new girlfriend. But he won't let his wife go; he thinks he should still be able to run her life like he always has—give her what he wants to give her and control her as though they were still married. Usually it takes lawyers and judges and a lot of expensive lessons before he lets her go her own way."

"I've met a few of those men myself," Hal said. "Pastoral counseling usually doesn't touch them. They need to have their ears boxed by their wife's lawyer a few times before they get the message. But God's instruction is that the woman, even if she came into the marriage as a war captive from an enemy city, is entitled to her freedom and dignity if there is a divorce. This passage is a remarkable statement of sexual equality.

"Let's read the next three verses."

> If a man has two wives, and he loves one but not the other, and both bear him sons but the firstborn is the son of the wife he does not love, when he wills his property to his sons, he must not give the rights of the firstborn to the son of the wife he loves in preference to his actual firstborn, the son of the wife he does not love. He must acknowledge the son of his unloved wife as the firstborn by giving him a double share of all he has. That son is the first sign of his father's strength. The right of the firstborn belongs to him.
>
> —Deut. 21:15–17

"So the Mormons are right," I remarked. "Or at least the original Mormons. I guess the Mormon Church doesn't officially approve of polygamy any longer."

"No," Hal said, "though there are a few people out in rural parts of Utah and Arizona who still practice the old Mormon way of polygamy. And yes, polygamy—the practice of a man having more than one wife—occurred in the Old Testament, even among some of God's greatest men. And if there was only one wife, or sometimes if there was more than one, the men often had concubines or had relations with the wife's servants. Abraham, Jacob, David, and Solomon all had multiple wives or had sexual relations with their wives' servants."

CHAPTER TWENTY-ONE

"So this is all right with God?"

Hal replied, "Nowhere in Scripture does God say polygamy is OK. The Old Testament reveals that God *tolerated* divorce, even though he said he hates it. Likewise, he tolerated polygamy. He didn't sanction it; it just isn't explicitly forbidden. God didn't bring his people to perfection all at once."

Hal pointed out that the creation ideal of one man and one woman, joined for life as one flesh, is the way marriage is supposed to be. God created Eve—one woman, not two women, or many women—for Adam. Through the prophet Malachi, God taught that a man should keep faith with the wife of his youth, which he can only do by not abandoning her for another. And in the New Testament, one of the qualifications for a church leader is to be the husband of one wife, variously understood as disqualifying polygamous, divorced, or promiscuous men as church leaders.

"When polygamy occurred," Hal said, "it always caused problems. There may have been some social or cultural reasons for it. For example, a lot of men were killed in war, and women may have preferred to share a husband rather than to have no husband. But jealousy, rivalry, and bad feelings are built into the situation. There will always be a preferred wife, and the preference may change. This law prevented one of the natural evils resulting from one man marrying more than one woman."

We looked at the well-known story of Jacob with Leah and Rachel in Genesis, as well as the story of Elkanah with Hannah and Peninah in the beginning of 1 Samuel.

"These are actual instances of a polygamous marriage with one wife being more loved than the other," Hal said. "The best thing a man can do for his children is to love their mother. In polygamous marriages, that love is always uneven. The purpose of this law is to prevent that unevenness from poisoning the next generation. There is nothing so injurious to relationships among siblings as rivalry for the parent's affection, or the perception that the parent loves one child more than another."

"I've seen that as a lawyer," I said. "Some of the most bitter litigation is between siblings when a parent shows preference in a will. I can see the wisdom in this law that prevents a parent from changing the expectation of inheritance. But why should the firstborn get a double share?"

"In most agricultural societies the firstborn gets preferential treatment in the inheritance. There are practical reasons for this. First, if the estate is divided equally, it will get smaller and smaller with each generation unless the average family has no more than two children. Pretty soon, it won't support anyone. Some societies gave the eldest son the entire estate, as in medieval England. The younger sons are expected to find other means of support, perhaps the army or religious service.

"Second, defining the expectations, whatever they are, prevents fighting and jealousy among the children. Everyone knows how succession is going to work.

"Third, the eldest probably grew up taking some responsibility for the younger children and family affairs, at least more responsibility than the younger children. It's a fact that most older children, even in our society, assume more responsibility for the family than younger children. Giving the eldest a greater portion gives him more resources to deal with, for example, the unmarried sister whom he may need to support, or other responsibilities.

"In the end, this law is about the integrity of families, preventing rivalry, and fighting over who is going to get what. God is giving them a common-sense provision to keep greed and jealousy from destroying families.

"The last section about the captive woman who becomes a wife was about the honor and integrity of marriage. This section was about the honor and integrity of families in the father's following the rules and not playing favorites. Marriage and family is a big deal to God, and he has a lot to say about it. In the next section, he'll say something that may shock you."

> If a man has a stubborn and rebellious son who does not obey his father and mother and will not listen to them when they discipline him, his father and mother shall take hold of him and bring him to the elders at the gate of his town. They shall say to the elders, "This son of ours is stubborn and rebellious. He will not obey us. He is a profligate and a drunkard." Then all the men of his town shall stone him to

death. You must purge the evil from among you. All Israel
will hear of it and be afraid.

—Deut. 21:18–21

I said, "In our society a mom who spanks a rebellious child in public
is likely to get investigated for child abuse. In this state, the authorities
have taken children away from their parents for disciplining them in
ways that were considered routine, if not commendable, a generation
or two ago. Imagine a society where a rebellious child can be put to
death!"

"This law," Hal said, "is based on the fifth commandment to honor
father and mother. If you want to know God's heart, you must understand from this how serious God is about that commandment. It's
almost inconceivable in our times that such a law would exist or be
carried out."

"Was it ever carried out?"

"There isn't much evidence that it ever was," Hal answered. "It's one
of those laws like forgiving your debtors that everyone wants to avoid.
Even in ancient times, the Jewish sages surrounded it with so many
conditions and qualifications that it was almost impossible for it to
happen. They added a barrel of qualifications."

"Like what?"

"Such as that it applied only during the three months after a son's
thirteenth birthday, and that the mother and father had to swear they
had no fault in the child's upbringing, and a number of other conditions.
But listen: God views rebellion against parents—not just disobedience
and the kind of independence every child shows, but persistent, incorrigible, corrupt behavior in defiance of parental authority—as serious
enough to warrant the death penalty. Dishonoring one's mother and
father is dishonoring God.

"Notice also that both mother and father were involved in this. The
mother had an equal say. But, unlike the accusing witnesses who were
expected to cast the first stone in other cases, the mother and father were
not involved in the act of punishment or execution. That was the task
of the men of the town after judgment had occurred at the city gate.
As in the case of the injustice of the unsolved murder, the community

had responsibility. The community had to pass judgment and carry it out. Rebelliousness in the family was equivalent to rebelliousness in the community. Good family members make good citizens."

"Why just the son?" I asked. "Why aren't rebellious daughters punished as well?"

Hal assured me that we would get to the daughters. "You're getting ahead of the text," he said. "Daughters are dealt with in the next chapter."

"Another ancient law," I said. "But anyone reading it would go away with a whole new understanding of how they should be thinking about their parents. Does this one have any deeper application?"

"In the Bible, Israel's relationship with God often is described as rebellious. Since Israel is described as God's son or firstborn, we can see that death is the scriptural penalty for its rebellions. In chapter thirteen, we saw that death is the appropriate penalty for individual rebellion against God. And it's the same for all of us. Our rebelliousness against our heavenly father deserves death. If death is the proper penalty for rebelliousness against our human parents, how much more so for rebelliousness against God?"

As Hal spoke, a scene from the Clint Eastwood western *The Unforgiven* came to my mind. In the movie, Eastwood is a former gunman struggling to raise two children on a failing farm after his wife dies. A young "wannabe" gunfighter tempts him to join a quest to get a $1,000 reward posted by brothel residents to kill two men who have cruelly cut and scarred one of their own. Eastwood and the younger man track them down, and the young tough shoots one of them in an outhouse. It's his first killing. Later, reflecting on it with Eastwood's character, the troubled killer asks, "Well, he had it coming, didn't he?"

"Son," Eastwood replies, "we all have it coming."

It was beginning to dawn on me as Hal talked that I, too, "had it coming." This short passage shocks modern ears by suggesting that parents should have a rebellious child executed. But it represented the truth about my relationship with my God. My own sin was persistent, stubborn, profligate, and incorrigible. I was that rebel child. If I restrained myself because of law or convention, or to avoid unpleasant consequences that would follow, the sin surely lay in my heart, ready to spring forth when the ties no longer bound or when darkness would cover the deed. I deserve to be handed over for execution, even by my own parents. I had a feeling, then a growing conviction, that I am the rebellious son who should be condemned at the city gate.

Hal must have read my thoughts from my silence and the troubled look on my face.

"Fortunately, Chris," he said, "we have a savior, and Moses is about to talk about him."

> If a man guilty of a capital offense is put to death and his body is hung on a tree, you must not leave his body on the tree overnight. Be sure to bury him that same day, because anyone who is hung on a tree is under God's curse. You must not desecrate the land the LORD your God is giving you as an inheritance.
>
> —Deut. 21:22–23

There was a soft knock on the open door of my office. My assistant intruded briefly and apologetically on our sacred space. "I'm sorry to interrupt, but your one-thirty appointment is here."

"I've overstayed," Hal said, getting up and starting for the elevator.

"You can't leave me here, Hal," I said walking with him. "Give me a clue. I'll return to this passage later."

"The original law in Deuteronomy," Hal said as we walked, "was a restraint on vengeance and a preservation of dignity for the body of the executed criminal. It almost certainly did not refer to execution by hanging, which was invented in much later times, or even to crucifixion. The hanging of the criminal's body on the tree would be a reminder to all of the consequences of crime. In England in the 1600s and 1700s, they used to hang the bodies of executed pirates on posts along the Thames so all the ships coming and going could see them. It was a warning of what would happen to the sailors if they turned to piracy.

"But, like the law of the unsolved murder that began the chapter, preservation of the holiness of the land requires that the act of warning not be prolonged in an excess of vengeance or humiliation of the body.

The warning is given. Then, even a criminal's body is to be respected. It's to be removed before sundown and buried the same day."

"Why does the hanging on the tree make the person cursed?"

"It isn't the hanging on the tree that brings a man under God's curse; it's the act that caused him to be punished. Being cursed means being condemned to suffer the just consequence of sin or disobedience to God."

We had reached the elevator, but I clung to Hal for a few more moments. The rebellious son wanted the fatherly reassurance that all was not lost. "You said Moses was about to talk about a savior," I said. "Where is a savior in this?"

"In God's plan and providence, Chris, he brings the sacred forth from the profane and glory from shame. This law becomes a building block in the story of salvation. When Christ was crucified, Joseph of Arimathea and Nicodemus got permission from Pilate to bury the body and not let it hang overnight. They were not just good men who wanted to give Jesus a decent burial—they were that, of course—but they were also observant Jews who were acting in compliance with this law in Deuteronomy. And it is their action that leads to Jesus' being, as he prophesies in Matthew chapter twelve, three days and three nights in the heart of the earth."

Once again, Hal had connected the Gospel story to an obscure Old Testament law. One book, one author, one message—as surely as if a literary giant had planted a seed in some early chapter of his work and brought it forth to emerge in significance later. But Hal wasn't through. The elevator door opened and he stepped in, and then held it open with one hand.

"But the more important thing, Chris," he said as the door pushed against his arm, "is that this passage prefigures the whole message of Christ. 'Anyone who is hung on a tree is under God's curse,' says God's law in Deuteronomy. So Christ is hung on a tree and is under God's curse. God becoming a curse! And for what? Jesus' crucifixion is his taking on God's curse for our sins. This passage explodes into meaning in the New Testament. Second Corinthians five-thirteen says, 'God made him who had no sin to be sin for us, so that in him we might become the righteousness of God.' And in Galatians . . ."

Hal deftly flipped his small Bible with his other hand until he found the passage: "Paul quotes this verse in Deuteronomy directly in explaining the significance of the crucifixion: 'Christ redeemed us from the curse of the law by becoming a curse for us, for it is written: "Cursed is everyone who is hung on a tree."'"

"Go take care of your client, Chris," he said, releasing the impatient door that quickly cocooned him from my sight and whisked him away.

There are moments in my life when I believe that I have a guardian angel who can sing, or that the Holy Spirit surrounds me with a heavenly choir. As I stood alone before the metal closure, another sound replaced that of the receding elevator. Softly at first, and then growing and surrounding me, I heard the music of the holy choir in a hymn of the redeemed titled "And Can It Be?".[13]

> And can it be that I should gain
>
> An int'rest in the Savior's blood?
>
> Died He for me, who caused His pain?
>
> For me, who Him to death pursued?
>
> Amazing love! How can it be
>
> That Thou, my God shouldst die for me?

As the music faded, I struggled to regain the day. Business awaited. But a more important business would echo in my consciousness for days to come.

CHAPTER TWENTY-TWO

"Give me the first word that comes to your mind when you think of Deuteronomy," Hal said. "Or, if you don't know enough about it to think of anything, then think of the Old Testament."

He sat at a dark-stained oval table in a conference room in my law office. Our last study had convinced me he was too good a secret to keep, so I invited some of my professional colleagues to join us when he returned for another lunch meeting. Brown bags with leftovers from home or sandwiches from local delis were spread out in front of half a dozen of the curious but skeptical lawyers.

There was embarrassed silence for a few moments. Then Kevin broke it with a single word:

"Irrelevant."

Then the others gradually joined in:

"Archaic."

"Harsh."

"Ignorant."

"Unforgiving."

"Misogynous." When Hal raised his eyebrows at this, Joan quickly added, "Male-oriented; hostile to women."

Hal looked around at his little class. "This is a law firm of some size and substance," he said. "Do any of you practice property law?"

Jerry acknowledged it: "Well, real estate."

"How about trial practice?" he asked. "Who goes to court and tries cases?" Kevin, Paula, and Tom raised their hands.

"And family law," Hal went on. "Divorce and all that stuff. Anyone do that?"

"Guilty," said Joan. "It's probably not your favorite area of law practice."

"Me, too," Tom said.

"Well, we're all guilty, aren't we?" Hal said, reminding me of the Clint Eastwood line. "But you judge God harshly. When he gave his people laws, he had to deal with a lot of the same issues you deal with. People, after all, get into the same problems over the same things today as they did then. I don't suppose you all brought a Bible?"

No one had but me.

"That's OK," Hal said. "Follow me while I read a little." And he opened to Deuteronomy 22 and read the first four verses.

> If you see your brother's ox or sheep straying, do not ignore it but be sure to take it back to him. If the brother does not live near you or if you do not know who he is, take it home with you and keep it until he comes looking for it. Then give it back to him. Do the same if you find your brother's donkey or his cloak or anything he loses. Do not ignore it.
>
> If you see your brother's donkey or his ox fallen on the road, do not ignore it. Help him get it to its feet.
>
> —Deut. 22:1–4

The group dug into the text. There is no "good Samaritan" obligation in American law, they agreed. One had no legal obligation to protect or care for or expend one's own resources on the property, or even person, of another.

"So you know the 'good Samaritan' story," Hal observed. "Most people do. And it is not our law. But this passage is God's law, and it is the Good Samaritan story, only it's told about animals, which were perhaps the most important property people owned in those days. Jesus just adapted it to people, and in the process taught an important lesson about prejudice by showing that the one who honors God the most may not be the one who appears most outwardly holy. It's also the Golden Rule: 'Do unto others as you would have them do unto you.' Tell me, do you think God's law here is harsher or more archaic than the law you learned and apply as lawyers when you tell people what their obligation is for others or their property?"

The question was largely rhetorical, but Hal had scored. I could see the softening demeanor in my colleagues' faces, with a little embarrassment at how condemning they had been in their "first thought" descriptions of Deuteronomy. It formed the basis of Jesus' thought and teaching, and, as the little gathering clearly recognized, taught a higher morality than our law.

I didn't press the Jesus lesson, but I thought the principle of these verses was also a specific application of what Jesus called the second "greatest commandment": to love your neighbor as yourself, another Old Testament principle often applied in Deuteronomy. I had experienced the effects of such neighborly behavior many times and hoped I had extended the same assistance to others. The neighbors I'd helped were not always, or perhaps even usually, Christians. These rules seemed simple expressions of God's will, embodied in the more positive elements of humanity made in his image: Be helpful to others in need. They expressed the best in human instincts and linked them to God's laws for human conduct.

Hal then took the group a little deeper: "Helping a person who has a flat tire or car breakdown, or returning a lost object to someone, is one thing," he said. "Of course we should do these things, and most people do. Going to the aid of someone in obvious need is still a fairly easy case. But what would you do if you got the wrong change, more than you are entitled to, at the store? Or if you have an opportunity to acquire something for much less than it's worth, say an antique or precious stone, because the owner doesn't know the value of it? I'm not talking about a bargain—we all look for bargains, and sellers always want us to think we're getting one, whether it's true or not. But suppose someone offers to sell you a Stradivarius violin worth tens of thousands of dollars for a few hundred dollars because she thinks it's just an old violin but doesn't know the unique value of it?"

"I don't see the analogy," Jerry, the property lawyer, said. "When you receive too much change at the store, I suppose you can say the extra change is 'lost.' But the violin isn't lost. It isn't our responsibility to make up for the seller's ignorance. That's not the way it works when we negotiate business contracts or real estate deals in the legal profession, and I think our clients would fire us if we did."

Paula chipped in. "I had one case where my client, even though she had a legitimate claim, told me she would not go through a trial even if it meant giving up the claim entirely. She just couldn't handle it emotionally. If the other side had known that, the value of the claim in settlement negotiations would have been zero. Since we concealed her real feelings, we were able to get her a reasonable settlement. Were we wrong?"

"There's quite a difference in a business or professional situation like that," Hal said. "Maybe an insurance adjuster who knows what a claim is worth and tries to get a person to settle for a lot less because he doesn't have a lawyer has a problem. But where there is real value to a claim and both sides are represented, I don't think there's a problem in negotiating the best deal you can. Perhaps if the person owning the Stradivarius had an appraisal and you thought the appraisal was wrong, you would be justified in buying it at the low price. But if you're just taking advantage of your superior knowledge to enrich yourself at the expense of someone who lacks your knowledge, I think God thinks you have a greater obligation to your neighbor."

I could see a hundred variations on this theme that would challenge our ethical analysis. But Hal went on to deeper meanings.

"What," he asked, "is a person's most important possession?"

"His good name or reputation," Tom replied readily, echoing popular wisdom.

"Let's think about that," Hal said. "Your reputation refers to what people think of you, not what God thinks of you. It's a worldly notion. To be concerned only with how other people think of you is to be invested in the things of this world, not the things of God. I'm not at all saying it's not a good thing to be respected for having godly qualities or being of good character, to have a good name, and to be regarded as honorable. But a desire for approval by others is what drives many people to do a lot of things that aren't based on good character. Peer pressure, the desire for approval, drives many an adolescent to unhealthy behavior to be part of the group, to be in the in-crowd. And for most people, that desire doesn't diminish with age. People are driven to acquire things, to change their appearance, to join groups that have no positive qualities, to stay seated when they should stand up, and stand up just because someone expects them to when the cause is all wrong, or to have and profess opinions that are ungodly or make no sense, all because they want approval from others. And just as people behave in unhealthy ways to make an impression, so can some people's unhealthy conduct unjustly deprive others of their reputation. There is no guarantee that what the world thinks of a person is accurate. Reputation can be shaped by malicious gossip or slander, by false impressions, or by dwelling on a single mistake rather than the character of the whole person."

Paula brought up laws about defamation, libel, and slander—spoken or written falsehoods that injure reputations and sometimes economic positions, such as the ability to earn a living. "The law has always allowed for recovery for such injuries to reputation," she observed.

"Good point," Hal said. "I agree that these are things that may become lost—to put it in terms of our Deuteronomy passage—or that a person may be having difficulty with and need help. The Bible forbids gossip and slander for good reason. It can deprive others of something that belongs to them, a good name. It's a Christian duty to uphold people's reputation, not to besmirch them. It falls directly within the law Moses gave here. And the ancient rabbis always recognized that this law is not just about oxen or sheep or donkeys or cloaks. It's about 'anything he loses,' and that certainly includes reputation. But reputation is still not our most precious possession."

"So what is our most precious possession, Hal?" I asked.

"You should not have to ask, Chris" Hal said. "It's your soul. Jesus said, 'What good will it be for a man if he gains the whole world, yet forfeits his soul.' Our most profound responsibility to others, far beyond the responsibility to return lost property or help people in need, is to help people gain possession of their soul. If God is as concerned for the care of our neighbor's property, how much more is he surely concerned for his soul?" He read the last sentence of this Scripture: "'Do not ignore it.' The care of lost souls is surely our most important responsibility."

Suddenly, a Scripture that seemed easy and obvious, and a law that everyone in the assembled group probably felt sure he or she had complied with—in fact and in intent—condemned us. I could see the discomfort levels beginning to rise again, but now not with resistance to the Scripture but the discovery that it said something they were not prepared to deal with, that pulled them out of their complacent good neighborliness. It was almost a relief to go on to discuss transvestism.

> A woman must not wear men's clothing, nor a man wear women's clothing, for the LORD your God detests anyone who does this.
>
> —Deut. 22:5

"I suppose this is one of the passages you people lean on to put down people with a different sexual orientation than your own," Tom opened.

This Scripture puzzled me, and I hoped Hal could help. At first blush, it seemed to be related to homosexuality. But this prohibition in the law went only to clothing, not to sexual conduct, which was treated extensively elsewhere. Some commentators I had read said that the Hebrew meaning of the words of prohibition on the woman were broader than wearing men's clothing and included male implements such as, for example, weapons of war.

"How would you apply this passage?" Hal asked.

The group agreed that we live in a unisex society. While style, cut, and decoration may differ to a degree, a great deal of men and women's clothing is quite similar. It is, of course, culturally easier for women to wear pants and shirts, and feminine-style business suits, than for men to wear skirts or dresses, which would still look quite abnormal. But men have long hair, and wear earrings and other jewelry that would have been viewed as effeminate in the recent past. And what do you do with the Scots and their kilts? Clothing and other adornments seemed culturally determined. So does the Bible set a dress code? Were we supposed to freeze clothing customs in Moses' time? We were on a roll, and the questions kept pouring out.

What about acting and comedy? A number of plays and movies that did not have any improper sexual themes were based on cross-dressing, usually with men dressed as women, which seemed to come across as unusually comic if well done. *Some Like it Hot*, of an earlier era, starred

Jack Lemmon and Tony Curtis masquerading as women. Dustin Hoffmann's *Tootsie*, of more recent vintage, and television comedy with top-rated comedians, such as Carol Burnett and Jonathan Winters, also featured heavy doses of cross-dressing.

In my own Christian family, we had done plays around the campfire and in family gatherings in which comic cross-dressing was part of the fun. Did this Scripture teach that God detested us—and those comedians and actors and actresses? And what about the actors of an earlier era who portrayed women at a time when women themselves were not allowed to be on stage? The questions slowed, and we looked to Hal.

"We are about to discuss some laws," Hal said, "the original meaning of which is obscure to us several thousand years later. We must remain open to alternative explanations. The Jewish sages discussing some of these laws over the centuries acknowledged that the reasons for them, like the food laws, were not always clear. But it was important, they taught, not to judge our responsibility to the law by whether or not we can discern the reason for it, but rather by whether or not God commands it. We don't have to understand God's reason to be obedient. Otherwise we are placing ourselves in the role of God, and that is the greatest sin of all. We do need to remind ourselves that the Old Testament law does not bind us, except as specific teachings in the New Testament reaffirm it.

"As to the law against transvestism, the Scripture doesn't give a reason for it. There is an assumption that there is a difference in men's clothing or implements and women's clothing, though basic clothing in Moses' time differed between men and women more in decoration than style. Still, one could presumably put on what gave the appearance of the opposite sex. It certainly does not tie us to a clothing style that existed in some earlier millennium. Nothing in the text suggests that it requires a particular style of clothing, only that one avoid cross-dressing. I would not worry, and few people have, about Scots wearing kilts or modern American women wearing jeans.

"Some relate this prohibition to the time period and think it had to do with men of the tribes whose territory lay east of the Jordan seeking to avoid ongoing military duty by disguising themselves as women, and militant women who wanted to join the fighting disguising themselves as men. I think that unlikely, as the disguise would be too easily detected and the people likely were known well enough that they couldn't have gotten away with it, especially in such a tribal and family-oriented society.

"The Scripture states that God detests those who cross-dress, whatever that means in context. This indicates we're dealing with something serious, not a minor or incidental rule. I think there are two explanations that are consistent with this. Both are consistent with the rest of Scripture, and it may be impossible this side of heaven to know which God had in mind; maybe he had both in mind, when he gave this law."

All eyes were on Hal as we awaited his explanation. After a sip from his soda, he went on.

"First, we do know that in ancient times some pagan religious rituals involved priests or others dressing as members of the opposite sex. Usually these involved cults of female deities. It is quite consistent with the instructions to avoid the false and evil religions of Canaan to give this instruction, though the text does not specifically tie it to a religious practice. If this is what it means, it's a specific of the repeated instruction to destroy and avoid the false Canaanite religions.

"The other possibility is that it's teaching avoidance of practices often associated with homosexual behavior."

He looked at Tom. "Yes, that behavior is specifically condemned in both the Old and New Testaments and is undoubtedly within the sphere of immoral sexual behavior that remained unlawful in New Testament times. Not all cross-dressing involves homosexual behavior, and not all homosexual behavior involves cross-dressing. But outside the context of acting or comedy, cross-dressing usually occurs in a context that involves homosexuality or sexual stimulation."

"As far as I'm concerned," Tom said, "people are either born that way or they're not. And if they are, who am I to tell them they can't have a sex life when everyone else can? If they aren't hurting anyone, I don't see what the big deal is that Christians make about homosexuals."

Hal was gentle and careful in his response. "It's not just Christians, Tom. Most religions and cultures everywhere at all times have perceived homosexual behavior as a problem."

"I think we know more about it now," Tom said. "People didn't understand it was genetic. They thought people just chose it, and condemned the choice because they felt threatened or were uncomfortable with it."

"I've counseled a lot of people," Hal said, "who got involved in homosexual behavior or had strong urges to do so. Some were people I knew very well, people in my church whom I saw several times a week for years. All of them were Christians and were uncomfortable or worse with it—that's why they came to see me. You'd be surprised at how many people wrestle with these kinds of issues at some level. I've read a lot of medical and psychological literature on it, as well as Christian perspectives, and I can tell you that the jury is still out on the degree to which it is genetic."

"What do you think, Hal?" I asked. "I mean about the genetic issue."

"I do think there's a genetic component for a lot of people," Hal said, "and it differs from person to person. Most of us, whether we want to admit it or can even recognize it, are combinations of male and female traits and personalities, if you can sort out which is which. They occur in different mixes, and people who have more than the usual mix of the opposite sex are more easily drawn into or attracted to homosexual behavior. Very few, in my experience, are completely unable to enjoy heterosexual behavior. Some get into a homosexual lifestyle until a person of the opposite sex takes an interest in them, and then they fall out of it easily. Obviously they are not genetically stuck in that orientation. Others get married and have children and are obviously able to be in a normal heterosexual relationship, but then let the contrary urges get the better of them and go off to discover their 'real self.' When they do, they're usually leaving a part of their real self behind and making a choice.

"But even if the homosexual orientation is entirely genetic, that really doesn't resolve the matter as easily as people think. There are all kinds of orientations that may be partly or entirely genetic but that are unhealthy and we have no inhibition about suppressing, even by criminal penalties if necessary."

"Such as?" Tom asked.

"Such as rape and assault," Hal said. "I suspect there are a lot of criminals who have a genetic disposition to these behaviors, but that doesn't make the behavior acceptable. Even behaviors we call sexual harassment—usually men touching women or acting inappropriately toward them—could be defended as genetically natural."

"Sure," Tom said, "but these are behaviors that hurt other people. Rape and assault should be crimes because they hurt people, even if homosexuals commit them on each other. And sexual harassment is behavior that offends the harassed person. It's totally different than consensual relationships between people of the same sex."

"God doesn't condone consensual relations between people of different sexes outside of marriage, Tom. Even Christians have lost sight of the holiness of sexuality to a large degree," Hal said.

"So it comes down to marriage," Tom said. "And heterosexuals can marry with God's blessing, but homosexuals can't in most states—or even with the society's blessing unless the laws get changed."

Hal replied, "Many people are not able or allowed to marry for reasons that have nothing to do with sexual orientation: the disabled, people who can't find a partner, people who have lost partners. Inability to marry is not as discriminatory as you may think. But marriage creates family, which is society's central social unit. Marriage contains the wild beast of sexuality. When the beast escapes, it can wreck everyone around. In marriage, it leads to a lot of good things: pleasure, contentment, freedom of the spouses to pursue other things, and children made in God's image and educated in God's ways."

"Sounds like a good argument for gay marriage," Tom said. "Gay people can get all those things out of marriage, and even adopt children and raise them better than a lot of other people do."

"No doubt that's true of some," Hal replied. "But the price of approving it is to cheapen real marriage, which has enough troubles as it is. That's too high a price to pay, Tom. Anyway, God says no to this behavior, and we are way off the passage we started out with, which was just about cross-dressing. Whether it teaches avoidance of pagan religious rituals or prohibited sexual practice, it is a gloss on teachings that were explicit and well-understood from elsewhere in Scripture and just adds a detail to them that's not stated anywhere else but that should follow from the other teachings."

"What about the idea," I asked, "that there's a created order—men and women are separate and have different functions, and people shouldn't confuse them? Could that be what God is talking about here—women in the home, not the military; men doing manly things, not housework—that sort of thing?"

"A lot of people have read that into it," Hal said, "along with other Scriptures like the New Testament teachings about the role of women in the church. I don't see it. First, the strength of the condemnation—that God detests people who do this, or are an abomination in some translations—suggests more than role-modeling of differences. Second, there are too many approving Scriptures of women in what seem like masculine roles to take a firm stand on this. Deborah was a judge and military leader of Israel; Huldah was a prophetess, consulted by King Josiah; and there are other women as religious leaders. The wife of great virtue in Proverbs 31 is a woman who has her own earnings and economic life. There are obvious differences between men and women, and gender roles have a place in a God-ordered society. But I don't think that's what this passage is all about."

"I'm glad of that," Paula said. "But you've given me, at least, a few things to think about on this whole thing. I used to think the answers were obvious. Now I'm not so sure."

The lunch hour was passing, so we moved on to the law of the bird's nest.

> If you come across a bird's nest beside the road, either in a tree or on the ground, and the mother is sitting on the young or on the eggs, do not take the mother with the young. You may take the young, but be sure to let the mother go, so that it may go well with you and you may have a long life.
>
> —Deut. 22:6–7

The obvious message of the passage was one of environmental preservation: good husbandry of wild birds by not destroying the source of more life. It was, in this respect, similar to the law of preservation of the fruit trees in times of siege of an enemy city in chapter twenty. This was an easy lesson for my colleagues to take as they all prided themselves in varying degrees in their environmental sensitivity.

Hal added a biblical perspective to the environmental teaching: "The law of the bird's nest was called the 'least of the commandments' in rabbinical teaching," he said. "Jesus may have had it in mind when he used the phrase in Matthew five-nineteen, or when he taught that a sparrow would not fall to the ground apart from the will of the Father, in Matthew ten. Others have seen in it solicitude for the animal kingdom, a certain sensitivity to the idea that animals, although lacking a soul, have feelings that are entitled to some protection. Similar ideas have been seen in the prohibition against cooking a kid in its mother's milk, or killing a cow or sheep and its young on the same day."

I suspected Hal might have some deeper insights from the passage and pressed him to go further.

"I agree that the obvious principle here is good conservation of the wild. People should never take what cannot be replaced. The fruitful female bird is the source of more, and killing her destroys the food source. It is a basic principle of all good agriculture, silviculture, or wildlife management.

"But there are some interesting applications that have been made of the law of the bird's nest from rabbinical sources. One that is relevant to the abortion debate is what to do when a situation arises in childbirth in which both mother and child cannot be saved. That situation occurs much less frequently in our time of modern medicine than it did in earlier times. But when it occurred, the rabbis taught that the law of the bird's nest required that the mother's life be preserved, rather than the child's life. It is rare that an abortion is required to truly save the life of a pregnant woman, but when that is really the case, this principle would teach that the abortion is morally justified. It is really the only exception that Scripture would allow with respect to abortion."

I had not expected abortion to come up in this chapter. Hal did not pause on it but plunged into another difficult subject. "A more remote but interesting teaching the rabbis derived from the law of the bird's nest," he said, "has to do with how we should think about creation. This is a subject of great controversy in education, and court cases prohibit the teaching of creationism in public schools on the ground that it's religion, though the naturalistic religion of the theory of evolution is freely taught. The rabbis thought about these matters long before

Darwin and creationism. They saw the mother bird as the metaphor for creation or origins and derived the lesson that we should not delve into the source but content ourselves with the world we find ourselves in, represented by the young. I don't say that's what God had in mind here, but it is intriguing."

He looked around. "I suppose we could spend a lot of time on abortion and creation if we had it," he said. "But the next verse is one you lawyers will like."

> When you build a new house, make a parapet around your roof so that you may not bring the guilt of bloodshed on your house if someone falls from the roof.
> —Deut. 22:8

"The parapet on the roof represents a principle of Jewish law that has always been recognized as the general principle of protecting life, and the guilt of failure to take such steps whenever we have the opportunity to do so. In the ancient Middle East, and even today in that area, roofs were generally flat and used as living space. It's easy to say that anyone who falls off a roof, even a flat roof intended for living space, has only himself to blame. The Bible says otherwise. The person who fails to make his house safe in this obvious way is guilty of the resulting injury."

The passage pushed a button for the group of attorneys. Trial lawyers have gotten bad press for seeking compensation for victims of preventable accidents: the injured, the burned, the paraplegic, the disabled, and their families. The perception of "rich" lawyers milking insurance companies and the public through frivolous lawsuits is endemic. Most media reports that lead to the public perception of unjustified litigation focus on the rare silly lawsuit, or the even rarer runaway jury that awards more damages than most people think reasonable. It isn't deemed newsworthy that most injury lawsuits are won by defendants, that most settlements and jury verdicts are modest, and that the occasional silly suit or outrageous verdict is almost always thrown out or greatly reduced before the case exits the legal system. Most safety improvements in products that people use in their everyday lives— and in the workplace and all the ways that we encounter manmade hazards—are the direct result of lawyers representing injured people, and juries made up of random members of the community, calling others to account who profit from imposing hazards on others. And the average income of members of the "rich" legal profession is less than the average income of public school administrators.

All these facts, familiar to attorneys but mysteriously unknown to the rest of the world, passed back and forth across the table.

"You're right," Hal affirmed after listening to our frustration at the misunderstood role of the legal profession in our society. "The role of lawyers and the justice system in holding people accountable for injuries they cause to others is biblical. And the church does not understand it—not even the clergy. It's in God's heart that people do what they can to prevent injury to others and be held accountable when they fail." He went on to read the laws against mixing.

> Do not plant two kinds of seed in your vineyard; if you do, not only the crops you plant but also the fruit of the vineyard will be defiled. Do not plow with an ox and a donkey yoked together. Do not wear clothes of wool and linen woven together.
>
> —Deut. 22:9–11

"Are we archaic yet?" Jerry asked. "Surely you don't think people shouldn't plant two kinds of seed in the same field? What do these laws mean anyway? I mean, they're sort of obvious on their face, but what was the point?"

"These are the laws against mixing," Hal said. "The law against cross-dressing is sometimes included as representing the same principle. Some have seen these laws as prohibiting some cultic religious practices, though no specific practices of this sort have been clearly identified. Others see these laws as teaching that man should not disturb the created order, though it isn't clear how the created order would be disturbed by violating them. Still others see the laws as representing the separation of the holy from the unholy. The vineyard is a symbol for Israel in Scripture, so the planting of other seeds in the vineyard would represent the mixing of the unholy with the holy nation. The ox is a clean animal, the donkey unclean. Again, the symbolism is that of mixing the holy and the unholy. And the clothes of wool and linen are the clothing of the priests, so the teaching may be that others should not don garments of the material reserved for the holiness of the priest."

"So it's metaphorical?" I asked. "It isn't really about planting seeds?"

"There's still another level of symbolism here," Hal said. "These laws are just before a series of laws on sexuality—marriage, adultery, and rape. Each of the laws against mixing is loaded with sexual symbols. I think they're presenting metaphors that the original hearers would have understood perfectly well. In the Song of Songs, the vineyard is a symbol of the female body. Not planting other crops in the vineyard is a metaphor against adultery. The vineyard is to be planted with only the right form of fruitfulness.

"Plowing, like planting, is a symbol for sexual intercourse. Plowing with an ox and a donkey together represents marriage outside the faith, a metaphor Paul picks up in Second Corinthians when he teaches that believers should not be unequally yoked.

"The prohibition of wearing garments of linen and wool is less obvious, but the sexual symbolism is there as well. Covering with a garment is a symbol of sexual contact or joinder. When Ruth says to Boaz in the third chapter of Ruth, 'Spread the corner of your garment over me,' it's an invitation for him to take her in marriage. Wool is the material of the garments of ordinary people. Linen is a garment of beauty or richness—what a woman might adorn herself with to make herself attractive. Some think it was used by prostitutes or that prostitutes wove garments that mixed wool and linen. Thus the prohibition against wearing clothes of wool and linen woven together is seen as a metaphor against prostitution.

"Taking these three laws against mixing together, they lead into the laws about marriage, adultery, and rape, with the foundational principles that one's body or sexuality is not to be polluted through use by more than one; that the one to whom the vineyard is given, or by whom it is plowed, is to be a believer, one with whom there is spiritual as well as physical union; and that intercourse with prostitutes is not allowed. Metaphors that may be obscure to us were probably clear to Israelites of Moses' time. Having made these points, now God is ready to talk more explicitly about sexuality."

CHAPTER TWENTY-TWO

"If that's what they mean, I guess they're not so archaic," Jerry said.

"Before we go on to other laws on the subject," I said, "what do tassels on the garments have to do with sexuality?"

Hal read the next verse:

> Make tassels on the four corners of the cloak you wear.
> —Deut. 22:12

"In Numbers fifteen," he said, "the command to make tassels on the corners of the garments is given in more detail." He turned to the passage. "They're there as reminders of God's commands so the people will not prostitute themselves 'by going after the lusts of our own hearts and eyes.' The emphasis of the tassels has to do with sexuality—they are to prevent the lust of heart and eye. This ties in to another practical reason for the tassels—they were part of modesty in dress, giving weight to the bottom of the clothing. We could paraphrase these last four laws this way: Reserve your sexuality for your spouse alone; marry someone who shares your faith; don't be a prostitute or consort with prostitutes; remind yourself of God's laws on proper sexual conduct; and dress modestly."

The rest of the chapter, on marriage and sexuality, was lengthy but tied together. Hal read the first section:

> If a man takes a wife and, after lying with her, dislikes her and slanders her and gives her a bad name, saying, "I married this woman, but when I approached her, I did not find proof of her virginity," then the girl's father and mother shall bring proof that she was a virgin to the town elders at the gate. The girl's father will say to the elders, "I gave my daughter in marriage to this man, but he dislikes her. Now he has slandered her and said, 'I did not find your daughter to be a virgin.' But here is the proof of my daughter's virginity." Then her parents shall display the cloth before the elders of the town, and the elders shall take the man and punish him. They shall fine him a hundred shekels of silver and give them to the girl's father, because this man has given an Israelite virgin a bad name. She shall continue to be his wife; he must not divorce her as long as he lives.

If, however, the charge is true and no proof of the girl's virginity can be found, she shall be brought to the door of her father's house, and there the men of her town shall stone her to death. She has done a disgraceful thing in Israel by being promiscuous while still in her father's house. You must purge the evil from among you.

—Deut. 22:13–21

Most of the concepts in this passage were foreign, if not offensive, to my colleagues. To the family lawyers, they were bizarre and entirely unfair to the woman. Hal sat back in his chair and reflected on the passage. Here is the background he gave us.

God meets people where they are. The culture and society of Israel and the ancient near-east was in a very different place than the culture and society of twenty-first-century America. Ancient Israel was a patriarchal society in which the father was a much stronger authority figure than in most contemporary American families. In the time of the entry into the Promised Land—the time of the giving of the laws of Deuteronomy—things were about to shift from a nomadic, tribal life to a settled, agricultural life, surrounding towns that would be centers of civic activity. In both the nomadic and the agricultural lifestyles—in Israel and its neighbors—marriages usually were arranged, and betrothal was the equivalent of marriage in the commitment of the parties to an exclusive sexual relationship with one another.

When it came time for Isaac to marry, Abraham arranged the marriage by sending his servant back to his people to find a wife. When the servant had identified Rebekah as the woman of choice, he addressed his request to her father and brother, who approved the marriage.

When Isaac, as an old man, wanted Jacob to marry, he sent him back to Rebekah's family, where Jacob addresses his request for Rachel to her father, Laban. Laban promised Rachel to Jacob, but made him take Leah as well before he could have Rachel, the real object of his affection. The father was looking out for the older daughter by making sure she was provided for. It did not occur to Jacob or Rachel to act without the consent of her father. Although these patriarchal marriages occurred more than four hundred years before Moses' time, the traditions had not changed. Indeed, in that part of the world even today the traditions are much the same.

The expectation that a new bride would be a virgin was universal. The family was responsible for the children's moral and religious education, as well as their behavior while part of the patriarchal home. The matter of a girl's chastity before marriage went to the honor of the family as well as herself. An unchaste young woman disgraced her family and demonstrated the failure of the moral and religious climate of the home. While divorce and remarriage were permitted, a girl who had lost her virginity, whether voluntarily or involuntarily, before marriage had lost her ability to secure a suitable husband.

Women in Moses' time had little or no means of self-support. They lived in their father's home until marriage. The lack of a husband to provide was a serious threat to a woman's economic well-being. Her father would not live forever. While a brother would assume responsibility for her if she was unmarried when the father died, if she lacked a male relative who would support her, she would join the ranks of the widows and orphans that are so much the concern of the social teaching of Deuteronomy. Absent support from the community, she might be forced into prostitution to support herself. Ruth and Naomi's destitution after the death of Naomi's husband and sons, one of whom was Ruth's husband, illustrates these social realities. So does their turning to Boaz as their "kinsman-redeemer" to marry Ruth and rescue them from poverty.

God did not impose this social system, many elements of which persisted even into the nineteenth century in Western Europe, as many familiar stories in English literature illustrate. In other parts of the world, elements of this system are prevalent today.

It is difficult for modern Americans to grasp the reality of these unfamiliar social conditions. Today, young people fall in love and get married, usually with little or no input from their parents' wisdom. Sexual activity is common in mid- to late-teen years, and nearly universal before marriage. High percentages of junior-high-age children have been exposed to hard-core pornography. Popular entertainment treats premarital sex as normal, rarely raising any moral issues with participants. Advertising and music videos shamelessly exploit sexuality for commercial purposes. Even young people who resist peer pressures or cultural expectations for earlier sexual activity frequently drop their resistance on becoming engaged or entering relationships in which they expect marriage to be the outcome. Polls show children from families of evangelical Christians are only slightly more likely than others to resist the temptations of premarital sex.

At the same time, women are less dependent than ever on parents or family for economic support. Education and job opportunities are as available to women as men, and most women work outside the home after marriage and childbearing. Indeed the horror of abortion, the most profound moral and legal issue of our times, is driven by women's desire to be free of the consequences of sexual activity in pursuing education and careers, as well as men's desire to be free of the economic and emotional commitments of fatherhood that result from sexual activity.

Despite the differences between our society and the one to whom these laws were addressed, God has desires for us in the arena of marriage, family, and sexuality. We can discover eternal principles from culturally driven assumptions and conduct. God's principles are discernable through the cultural fog, and they are more relevant than ever. These Scriptures have much to teach us. They are not arbitrary; they have a purpose. Obeying God's laws is beneficial.

"Begin thinking about these laws with the larger perspective of Deuteronomy," Hal said. "God's principles do not occur in a vacuum.

"Let's begin with one of Moses' most frequently repeated instructions in Deuteronomy: *Teach your children.* Human society is like a conveyer belt, with new people being constantly added at the beginning and old people dropping off at the end. The belt is always moving. Society has continuity only if those further along on the belt transmit their knowledge to those who have more recently come onto it. That's what education is all about, not just academic and practical learning from school or job training, but moral and religious education; teaching children what it means to be a human being, where the world came from, what the purpose of life is, how to live it right, how to relate to God and others, and the qualities of love, sympathy, forgiveness, compassion, justice, mercy, grace, and courage. These qualities are learned, or not learned, or learned badly or wrongly, primarily in the home.

"The foundation of the home is a mother and father, two very different human beings who become, as God teaches in Genesis, one flesh. Children should be born into homes in which there is a mother and a father, and in which they are loved, wanted, and valued. And in which they are taught, not just by words but by example, what it means to be a man or woman created in the image of God, the divine creator, and to live in harmony with the universal principles of his creation. Children will learn far more about these things by what they see and experience around them than by what they are told or read in books. And the home and family is what is around them most of the time."

Hal paused. He got up from his chair and went to the window, gazing across a city of courts and judges and lawmakers. Then he turned back to his audience of young lawyers. "You may not understand or agree with this," he said, "but these are not matters of exclusively private concern. In finding that sexuality is inherently private and not a suitable subject of community concern enforceable by the civil or criminal law, the United States Supreme Court is wrong and has made rulings in profound contradiction to God's truth. Nothing could be more central to the larger community's welfare—its health, welfare, and morals— than its citizens' sexual behavior.

"God also has a profound concern for the protection of the weak within the community. Much of the teaching in Deuteronomy is about this. In Moses' time, women lacked power to protect themselves, economically and otherwise; hence the repeated concern for widows and orphans. The death of a husband and father was a threat to the economic wellbeing of his family in a way that the death of the wife and mother was not.

"Now look at these laws in the rest of Deuteronomy chapter twenty-two with these underlying principles in mind: protecting the weak and protecting the proper continuity of a God-honoring society through the proper teaching of children.

"In the law of the bride who is accused of not being a virgin, you see these principles at work. The woman and her family were protected against the possibility of a false accusation by showing 'the cloth' to the town elders. The reference is presumably to the bleeding that accompanies the loss of virginity, though some have thought it refers to a menstrual cloth, demonstrating that the girl is not pregnant. The price of a husband's false accusation was high: He was punished—some translations say flogged—hence publicly humiliated, as he would have humiliated his bride. He was fined, and the fine was paid to the father: double the normal amount he would have paid the father for the bride. This compensates the family of the accused for the ordeal and humiliation. And, finally, he forfeits forever the right of divorce. This guarantees the woman economic security for her life, or at least her husband's life. All of this is to protect the woman, the weaker partner, in her vulnerability.

"If the charge was accurate, however, the men of the town executed her at the door of her father's house. The death penalty shows the severity with which God views sexual promiscuity. The execution at the door of her father's house shows the family's shame and failure because of her conduct. And involvement of the men of the town shows that these matters are of the utmost concern to the wellbeing of the whole community.

"This law is the female counterpart to the law of the rebellious son. Chris and I studied that law in the last chapter, and it was very similar. When parents had an incorrigibly disobedient and profligate son, they were to present him to the elders, and he was subject to the death penalty. When the parents had failed, the community took responsibility. Disobedience to parents, whether manifested in profligacy, drunkenness, and rebelliousness of a son, or in the promiscuity of a daughter, is an offense of the most serious order, equivalent to idolatry or murder, and brings community action."

"Why," I asked, "wasn't the man executed for the slander against the bride if she was innocent? In the law of the false witness that we studied, the accuser received the same punishment as the person would have that he accused."

"Probably," Hal replied, "because his death would revictimize the woman by depriving her of economic support. She was no longer a virgin, even if she had been before. Hence she was no longer marriageable. While hardly the foundation of a happy marriage, requiring the man to support her for life, along with the other punishments, was a better option than executing him and leaving her without that support. The security of the woman is the paramount concern; no one else was likely to marry her.

"This law, like the law of the rebellious son, was probably instructional and not practical. There is no record of it actually having been applied. The penalties were so severe that it seems unlikely the girl, or the family, would allow the situation to occur. There is a custom in some parts of the Middle East of older women examining a girl before her wedding night to assure her virginity. The ancient rabbis understood that all women did not bleed on loss of virginity; hence independent witnesses settled the issue of virginity before the wedding bed. The woman's character, and the honor of all concerned, was at stake."

"I understand," I said, "that the bride's virginity was an expectation in the culture of the time. I suppose part of the reason for that was the danger of pregnancy."

"Of course," Hal said. "And that is consistent with God's desire for stable families that love and teach and train their children. Natural affection is strongest, by far, for one's own children. For the woman to be at risk of being pregnant with someone else's child would threaten that stability. The husband is unlikely to have the same affection or give the same attention to a child that's not his own."

The group had been absorbing Hal's lecture with silent interest. Now Joan broke in: "Apply this to our time. Birth control is readily available. Sexual activity doesn't have to lead to pregnancy and usually doesn't. It's readily preventable. Should we conclude that 'safe sex' is OK, given our ability to control the possibility of an adverse outcome?"

"There is no such thing as totally safe sex," Hal replied. "Every method of birth control or protection has a failure rate. Birth control and methods of safe sex may be an alternative for those who won't be guided by God's laws, but God doesn't make exceptions for safe sex.

"But there is another point here. You notice in this passage that the man's slander of his bride is said to give 'an *Israelite* virgin a bad name.' And the promiscuous girl is said to have 'done a disgraceful thing in *Israel*.' Israel is the holy nation. In the holy nation, sexual promiscuity and sexual slander are great evils. This is a set-apart people who are to live in accordance with God's holiness, not in the evil ways of the nations around them."

Joan had another question. "There seems to be a double standard here. The woman is executed for her premarital promiscuity. There is no comparable standard for the man. Why?"

"It is not just the promiscuity that brings her the death penalty," Hal said. "It's the attempt to deceive her husband about her real sexual status on top of the promiscuity. There is an element of fraud added to the underlying evil, so he would be dishonored by marrying a promiscuous woman he assumed was a virgin, who might even be pregnant with someone else's child. This is not a rule of capital punishment for any unmarried woman who has sex. There is no rule of capital punishment—or, for that matter, any sort of punishment—for prostitutes, even though the Scripture speaks clearly against the practice.

"And it isn't really a double standard. The book of Proverbs is full of admonitions against young men being tempted into sexual folly by loose women. And the profligacy of the rebellious son that can lead to death certainly includes such irresponsible behavior. While the principles are put differently and in different parts of Scripture, God's expectations for men and women's sexual behavior is not different."

We went on to discuss the laws of adultery and rape in the next eight verses.

> If a man is found sleeping with another man's wife, both the man who slept with her and the woman must die. You must purge the evil from Israel.
>
> If a man happens to meet in a town a virgin pledged to be married and he sleeps with her, you shall take both of them to the gate of that town and stone them to death—the girl because she was in a town and did not scream for help, and the man because he violated another man's wife. You must purge the evil from among you.
>
> But if out in the country a man happens to meet a girl pledged to be married and rapes her, only the man who has

done this shall die. Do nothing to the girl; she has committed no sin deserving death. This case is like that of someone who attacks and murders his neighbor, for the man found the girl out in the country, and though the betrothed girl screamed, there was no one to rescue her.

If a man happens to meet a virgin who is not pledged to be married and rapes her and they are discovered, he shall pay the girl's father fifty shekels of silver. He must marry the girl, for he has violated her. He can never divorce her as long as he lives.

—Deut. 22:22–29

Hal showed us that these were paradigm laws—that is, laws that were stated generally and that left room for the authorities to apply them in particular cases. The laws were straightforward. Sleeping with another man's wife is a capital offense for both parties. The same rule applies if the woman is engaged, when the offense occurs in town where she could summon help: Her failure to do so leads to the presumption that she was a willing participant. If the act occurs "out in the country," where help is not available, however, the presumption is reversed. The act is assumed to be rape, and only the man is to be executed. While the distinction between the sexual act in town and in the country is only given specifically with respect to betrothed women, it logically applies as well if the marriage has been consummated. If the man forces his will on a virgin who is not betrothed, however, the man is required to pay the woman's father and to honor the girl by marrying her and forfeiting the right to divorce. As with the falsely accused bride, the priority of protecting the weaker party by assuring her of economic support after she loses her marriagability takes precedence over the punishment of the assailant.

"The marriage relation," Hal said, "is used throughout Scripture as an analogy for the relationship between God and Israel, or God and his people. It's a holy relationship, going back to the joining of Adam and Eve as one flesh. In Moses' time, God tolerated men having more than one wife, though it was never presented as a source of anything but problems, and never approvingly. But both parties were expected to live within the boundaries of marriage in their sexual life. Violations were serious, in the same category as murder. The whole community had an interest in this.

"The lack of guilt on the part of the woman who was forced to have sex states a general principle: Acts that are otherwise wrong are not punishable if done under compulsion. Rabbinical teaching extends this principle to Jews who, in their view, violated the Torah under the duress of the Inquisition in the Middle Ages. We might reflect on that principle. Christian history is full of martyrs who accepted death rather than betray their faith. But in periods following times of persecution of early Christianity, the church had to deal with the same issue with believers who succumbed to the pressures of the authorities and denied Christ, even if they never gave up their belief.

"We could summarize the rules of this section in this way." He rose and went to a chalkboard on one conference room wall and began to write, speaking the words as he scrawled them out:

"God's expectation of his people is that they will reserve their sexual relations for their spouse. The responsibility for the moral education and behavior of children rests with the parents, and the children's failure to act honorably in matters of sexual morality reflects on the family. Sexual relations and marriage are a legitimate concern of the whole community. According to God, there is no such thing as a sphere of privacy in sex. Adultery is an offense of the most serious order, deserving of the death penalty. A woman is to be given the benefit of the doubt, or presumption of innocence, when the sex occurs in circumstances in which she is unable to prevent the occurrence. Sexual relations bring with them a responsibility to protect the weaker party."

Then he picked up his Bible and read verse 30, the last verse in the chapter: "'A man is not to marry his father's wife; he must not dishonor his father's bed.'

"Most commentators assume," Hal explained, "that the reference is to a stepmother, not a man's birth mother, and to a time after the father's death. A man could not marry his father's wife while the father was alive and could not marry his mother because of the laws against incest. The law is, in a sexual context, an outworking of the fifth commandment to honor one's parents. This offense appears in the

New Testament as the basis of excommunicating a church member in First Corinthians, chapter five. It's a behavior that, as Paul says, does not occur even among the pagans. And it is another example of how grounded the New Testament is in Deuteronomy.

"This rule," Hal said, "also shows respect for the woman by keeping a man from any notion that he might inherit his father's wife as if she were property." With that he closed his Bible and our time together. He looked around. "Before I leave," he said, "give me the first word that comes to your mind about these laws we've just looked at."

We went around the table, and the words flowed easily and freely.

"Relevant."

"Protective."

"Accountable."

"Thought-provoking."

"Demanding."

"Profound."

It was my turn. I closed my eyes: "Holy."

Hal rose and walked slowly around the table. His gnarled old hands rested lightly on each of the young lawyers in turn as he prayed our session to a close. He asked God, the One who Is, to lift each of them from where they were and bring them to himself, and to surround them with the Word of the Scriptures and make their revelation alive to them. He asked the Lord to show them how to see the world through God's eyes instead of trying to see God through the world's eyes, and to make their marriages rich with blessings and their children wise with the wisdom of the ages. He asked God to give them clarity and holiness of mind in the face of the assaults and assumptions of their surroundings, and to make their work into His work as they counseled the troubled and the lost, the mundane, and the ordinary, and the well-known and the well-to-do in their professional lives. Finally, he asked the Lord to bless the work of their hands, the words of their mouths, and the thoughts of their hearts in all that they did and all that they were.

As they rose to leave, some hugged Hal, and others shook his hand. All expressed appreciation.

Paula was the last one out the door. "It was like going to church," I heard her say to him. "I'd like to come to your church and learn more."

"My church is every church that's faithful to the Scriptures," Hal replied. "And God is everywhere. You don't need me to find him. If you want him, he won't be hidden from you."

She hugged him a second time, and tears on both their cheeks met and mixed for a moment. "No one has ever prayed for me before," she said softly. "Thank you." And she hurried off.

CHAPTER TWENTY-THREE

W hat do you think when you hear the term *sacred space?*" Hal asked. We were back in his book-lined study, that cocoon of teaching and thought and prayer where I had learned so much. His question provoked a cascade of thoughts. All space was sacred space, I thought, since God is everywhere. The heavens declare the glory of God, and nature at its best can seem sacred. But some spaces seemed sacred when something holy was happening there, like the closing moments of Hal's time with my partners in our conference room the previous week or the times I spent with Hal in this very room. And then there were places the Bible called sacred, at least for the occasion, like the sacred ground on which Moses found himself standing when he was confronted by God at the burning bush, as seen in Exodus 3, or the ground on which Joshua stood when he met the commander of the Lord's army, as seen in Joshua 5. More permanent were the sacred spaces created by Israel at God's direction, like the tabernacle in the desert or the temple, and the holy of holies within it in later years. These seemed more like the great cathedrals of Europe I had visited.

I shared all these thoughts with Hal.

"What made you think of the great cathedrals as sacred space?" he asked.

I reflected on the question. The architecture was designed to make a person feel small and direct one's thoughts upward, sweepingly, to the grandeur and strength and enduring nature of the setting. The images in the stained glass windows of the sanctuary or artworks in the side chapels—in the statuary and stone or woodcarvings in the structure itself—all brought the biblical stories of the history of salvation to mind. And the understanding that they were built to glorify God and designed to lift human thoughts to heavenly things surely was part of what made them sacred.

"What detracts from your sense of the sacred there?" Hal continued his quiz.

"Probably the presence of people who don't think of the space as sacred and have no sense of why they were built or what they really mean," I responded.

"Now you're ready to think about the next chapter," Hal said. "Read the first eight verses of chapter twenty-three."

> No one who has been emasculated by crushing or cutting may enter the assembly of the LORD.
>
> No one born of a forbidden marriage nor any of his descendants may enter the assembly of the LORD, even down to the tenth generation.
>
> No Ammonite or Moabite or any of his descendants may enter the assembly of the LORD, even down to the tenth generation. For they did not come to meet you with bread and water on your way when you came out of Egypt, and they hired Balaam son of Beor from Pethor in Aram Naharaim to pronounce a curse on you. However, the LORD your God would not listen to Balaam but turned the curse into a blessing for you, because the LORD your God loves you. Do not seek a treaty of friendship with them as long as you live. Do not abhor an Edomite, for he is your brother. Do not abhor an Egyptian, because you lived as an alien in his country. The third generation of children born to them may enter the assembly of the LORD.
>
> —Deut. 23:1–8

The collection of people excluded from "the assembly of the Lord" seemed curious. What was the "assembly of the Lord"? Why should people be excluded because they had suffered some genital mutilation, or because of parentage for which they had no responsibility, whether through a "forbidden marriage" or a national heritage that was disapproved for a longer or shorter term? The passage was troubling, and I was unable to relate it to the questions Hal asked before we read it.

"God referred to sacred space here, Chris," Hal explained. "Remember what God says of Israel in Exodus chapter nineteen: 'Although the whole earth is mine, you will be for me a kingdom of priests and a holy nation.' God used Israel to teach his human creation something about his holiness and the meaning of the sacred. When this chosen people modeling holiness came before him in what he calls 'the assembly of the Lord,' at the tabernacle—or the temple in later times—as a worshipping community, there were to be no distractions. It is just like the great cathedrals you're describing, Chris. Everything about the assembly was to direct the participants' thoughts to God's greatness and majesty. Those who don't share such thoughts were not to be there."

"It seems disconnected to me," I said. "Why should we assume that these categories of people don't or can't share the thoughts—or are excluded from salvation?"

"We don't assume that," Hal said. "Keep this passage in context. It isn't about salvation. It's about a time in history when one nation was being taught how to model holiness and worship for all people. That nation—that 'assembly'—had to be kept pure until it gained the strength to absorb others and expand into something more universal, and until the world around it was ready to hear the lesson it was designed to teach. It's a little like our immigration laws: If we open the borders to everyone in the world who wants to come, without any limitations, we would be flooded with immigrants and lose the things that make our country distinctive and attractive to those who do come, and a model for others."

"So what is it about these categories of people that exclude them? Why would an emasculated person pollute the holiness of the assembly?"

"We can't have absolute certainty about that," Hal said. "But there are several schools of thought. As with some other passages in Deuteronomy, meanings that may have been obvious to the original hearers are obscure to us in a different time and place and culture. Some think it has to do with the inability to reproduce, a duty given to humanity in Genesis. Others think it has to do with the perfection of those who come before the Lord, similar to offering blemished animals, which we saw earlier. But the best thinking, in my view, is that it refers to men who have voluntarily been sexually mutilated in service of a false god; such persons existed in some ancient near-eastern religions."

"Why do you favor that theory?"

Hal replied, "It explains why God would take the trouble to single out a category of people that, in general, is extremely rare and would have been rare then as well. It wasn't about people who were naturally unable to reproduce but about males who had been made so by crushing or cutting. And it's very consistent with the rest of Deuteronomy, where God shows such abhorrence of worshipping false gods and religious practices that are perverted to involve sexuality in some form. It doesn't mean these people can't repent and become worshippers of God; it just means that preservation of the holiness of the assembly requires that those who had been servants of false religion, even to the point of being sexually mutilated for the enemy, not be allowed in."

"OK," I said. "I'll buy that one. But what about the children of forbidden marriages? They did nothing to bring about their own exclusion."

"True," Hal said. "And remember again that exclusion from the assembly is not about their fate in eternity but about preserving a model of holiness before God. As with the emasculated male, we can't be certain as to exactly what marriages God referred to here, although it's likely the people to whom this passage was addressed understood completely. Some think it applied to all marriages that are unlawful, while others think it applies only to children of marriages with the peoples of the land with whom intermarriage is forbidden, or to children borne of prostitutes, incest, or adultery. Any of these is an act of the parent removing their family line from the holiness expected of God's people. That holiness is what's at stake here."

We went on to the rules banning various foreigners from the assembly. "These rules," Hal said, "address the neighboring nations but don't include the Canaanite nations, which were to be destroyed completely. They were based on the relatively recent harassment from Moab, Ammon, and Egypt. Moab and Ammon were the products of the incestuous relations of Lot and his daughters, told about in Genesis chapter nineteen. That gives two reasons to exclude Moabites and

Ammonites from the assembly, as children of forbidden marriages and as people who were hostile to God's people in a time of need.

"Edom, here as in chapter two, is given greater honor as a brother since it is the descendants of Esau, Jacob's brother. Edomites are only excluded to the third generation, not the tenth, as with the children of forbidden marriages and the Ammonites and Moabites.

"These were rules for the time of Deuteronomy. Foreigners, even the 'alien among you,' were entitled to be treated well and cared for in Israel, whether or not they could be admitted to the assembly. We have seen that over and over in Deuteronomy. They are among those whom God treats with special concern, like widows and orphans. Later, God taught in Isaiah fifty-six that eunuchs and foreigners who bind themselves to the Lord and hold fast to his covenant would be accepted. The time of modeling a holy people by exclusion from the assembly had passed. Now, God says, 'My house will be called a house of prayer for all nations.'"

Hal paused, and I pondered. It seemed that over time God had expanded the circle of those who could appear before him in the sacred space. In time, they would share the holiness of Israel and not be a distraction to those who were before their God.

"These laws," Hal said, "like all of the purity laws and rituals, are to teach us something about God's perfection and holiness. God is so holy and so perfect that the imperfect cannot approach him. Jesus said in Matthew chapter five, 'Be perfect, therefore, as your heavenly Father is perfect,' a near quote from Leviticus chapter nineteen, where God says, 'Be holy because I, the Lord your God, am holy.' But we are not perfect, and we are not holy, nor were the Jews perfect in Moses' time or later."

"That's for sure," I said, thinking more of myself than the ancient Israelites.

"And that," Hal continued, "is what Jesus is all about. We become perfect only through him. It is in Jesus that these laws have their final meaning, the breaking down of the barriers and making the access to God equally available to all without distinction. The New Testament is all about bringing the knowledge of God to everyone in the world. One of the people who received that knowledge was an Ethiopian eunuch, a man who would have been excluded from the assembly under the law as given by God in Deuteronomy. But in Acts chapter eight, Philip explained the gospel of Jesus to him and baptized him."

He opened his Bible to Ephesians 2 and read.

> Therefore, remember that formerly you who are Gentiles by birth and called 'uncircumcised' by those who call themselves 'the circumcision' (that done in the body by the hands of men)—remember that at that time you were separate from Christ, excluded from citizenship in Israel and foreigners to the covenants of the promise, without hope, and without God in the world. But now in Christ Jesus you who once were far away have been brought near through the blood of Christ.
>
> For he himself is our peace, who has made the two one and has destroyed the barrier, the dividing wall of hostility, by abolishing in his flesh the law with its commandments and regulations. His purpose was to create in himself one new man out of the two, thus making peace, and in this one body to reconcile both of them to God through the cross by which he put to death their hostility. He came and preached peace to you who were far away and peace to those who were near. For through him we both have access to the Father by one Spirit.
>
> Consequently, you are no longer foreigners and aliens, but fellow citizens with God's people and members of God's household, built on the foundation of the apostles and prophets, with Christ Jesus himself as the chief cornerstone.
>
> —Eph. 2:11–20

"Hal," I asked, "why didn't God just send Jesus with Moses and teach all those things then?"

"Paul taught that Jesus had to come in 'the fullness of time.' The experience of Israel in the Old Testament era had to happen before the world was ready to receive him. That includes the experience of having a holy assembly of people as a worshipping body that respected, modeled, and taught God's holiness by excluding those who had in their bodies the signs of unholy religions or were the products of unholy marriages or were from nations that had been hostile at some level to God and his people. That assembly had to know what God's requirements of holiness were and had to experience failure in meeting those requirements before they were ready for Jesus."

I thought I got it, so we moved on.

> When you are encamped against your enemies, keep away from everything impure. If one of your men is unclean because of a nocturnal emission, he is to go outside the camp and stay there. But as evening approaches he is to wash himself, and at sunset he may return to the camp.
>
> Designate a place outside the camp where you can go to relieve yourself. As part of your equipment have something to dig with, and when you relieve yourself, dig a hole and cover up your excrement. For the LORD your God moves about in your camp to protect you and to deliver your enemies to you. Your camp must be holy, so that he will not see among you anything indecent and turn away from you.
>
> —Deut. 23:9–14

I was again struck by the seeming incongruity of these verses. Did God view normal bodily functions as impure? Did Moses really mean God walked around in the camp, like a visiting dignitary on inspection, and saw indecent things?

Hal brought me back to where we had started the evening. "God was still talking about sacred space here, Chris," he said. "Only now it's movable space, more like Moses at the burning bush or the times you've felt God's presence in a place other than the temple or your European cathedrals.

"The Israelite army was about to cross the Jordan River and fight holy wars against God's enemies. We've already discussed that. And the secret of success in these wars is that God himself will go with them and fight for them. That's what makes them holy wars—not because some human being decided that the cause was just and God was on their side but because God himself declared the war and would fight it. The camp of God's army is sacred space.

"These are rules for the sacred space of the army camp, and they apply to the holy war that God has charged Israel to fight to conquer the land, exterminate the evil inhabitants, and fulfill the ancient promises to the patriarchs. Over and over again in Deuteronomy the teaching is that God will be with them, will fight for them, and will assure their victory."

"Armies in war are not neat and clean," I said. "I guess this army was different."

"Indeed," Hal said. "The Divine Warrior, God himself, led it and was present with it. The camp is a holy place, and the holy army had to maintain the purity that was suitable to such a place. That purity was to be physical, ritual, and moral. The requirement of ritual purification following a nocturnal emission is to focus the soldier on that purity and not let him be distracted by impure thoughts. The requirement of a latrine outside the camp is a good health rule, as modern people recognize, but it also keeps the camp clean in a manner that is consistent with the purity God requires. Observance of the purity laws kept soldiers aware of God's presence and of their dependence on God for success. The rules are summed up in the phrase 'Your camp must be holy.' Like the laws on purity of the assembly, the purity of the army camp is to give the soldiers an understanding of God's purity and perfection."

"What about the language about God 'moving about' and 'seeing' what is impure?" I asked. "It sounds like an anthropomorphic understanding of God, like he was really there, like a person, wandering around inspecting the camp like some visiting general. But this was God himself giving the laws through Moses."

"Remember chapter four, when we talked about God being both immanent and transcendent, here with us and at the same time so majestic he's beyond our ability to understand? This is the immanent sense of God: God with us. The language is, of course, metaphorical. It's like God 'walking in the garden in the cool of the day' in Genesis when he confronts Adam and Eve about their disobedience. God sees and knows the impurity of the camp and the impurity of the heart, whatever steps we may take to conceal them. He must not be driven away by his people's impurity."

"So how does this passage relate to us?"

"Holy war was for a limited time and place. That part doesn't have any application to us. But there's a lesson in the purity of the camp that's like the holiness of the assembly. The history of salvation that begins with man learning about God's holiness through laws like these ends very differently. True holiness is achieved only through Christ as God's gift. In the end man is unified with God by God's initiative on man's behalf, not by his ability to keep the laws—in that he is an abject failure.

"Now we're about to read something else about holiness."

> If a slave has taken refuge with you, do not hand him over to his master. Let him live among you wherever he likes and in whatever town he chooses. Do not oppress him.
> —Deut. 23:15–16

I was aware from my study that most commentators on this passage note a couple of distinctions about it. First, it is assumed that the fugitive slave is fleeing from a neighboring nation because servitude is mentioned elsewhere as existing in Israel. Second, it is contrary to what appears to be the universal practice elsewhere in the ancient near-east in which laws require the return of fugitive slaves, even to neighboring nations. Israel must not forget that it is a nation of fugitive slaves that has been given its freedom by God himself.

"But what," I asked Hal, "does this have to do with sacred space?"

"Do you remember our study in chapter twelve about the place where God would choose to place his name?"

I did, but I couldn't see the connection.

"The language God uses here," Hal explained, "to let the runaway slave 'live in whatever town he chooses' is the same language that's used in chapter twelve and elsewhere to refer to the place where God will choose to place his name. This is not accidental. Israel is to allow the weakest and poorest refugee the same freedom. The law of the fugitive slave is grounded in theology. As Jesus taught in Matthew, chapter twenty-six, if you have done it unto the least of these, so have you done it unto him. God is honored by honoring the less unfortunate—in this case, by giving them the freedom of location within the sacred space of the land."

We broke off the discussion while Hal made some decaf coffee and put together a plate of peanut butter cookies for us.

"They came in the mail," he said, offering them to me, "from Joan."

"I didn't know she could make cookies," I said.

"I don't know if she can," Hal replied. He showed me the note that came with them. It was a card from a gourmet food shop in our town. On it was Joan's neat handwriting:

> Your words and prayers have been in my mind and heart every hour since last Friday. I am reading the Bible and trying to learn to pray. I'm not very good at it, or at saying "thank you" or a lot of other things I should be better at than I am—things that got neglected while I was studying the more important matters of the law. I'm not very good at baking cookies either and don't know how else to thank you, but perhaps these cookies will at least let you know I think of you constantly. Love, Joan.

Joan's note brought me back to my earlier thought of how Hal had made an office conference room into sacred space and how this room we were in seemed like sacred space in his presence. Joan's gourmet cookies could almost be a communion wafer as Hal sampled them.

"I'll call her," he said. "She needs to be in church, in a worshipping body of believers. She'll find her own sacred space in time. I believe she'll stay in it."

"Like Julie?" I said, more as a remark than a question.

"They came to God from very different places," Hal said. "Julie was like Mary Magdalene or the woman taken in adultery, at the bottom of her life. Joan is on the opposite end of the social scale, but she needs the Lord just as much as Julie did. The problem is that most people in her position don't know it."

The cookies were gone, and we read on.

No Israelite man or woman is to become a shrine prostitute. You must not bring the earnings of a female prostitute or of a male prostitute into the house of the LORD your God to pay any vow, because the LORD your God detests them both.

—Deut. 23:17–18

"I see where this fits the 'sacred space' theme," I said. "Shrine prostitution and paying vows with the earnings of prostitution in the house of the Lord are desecrations of the sacredness of the place."

Hal agreed. "The connection here is pretty obvious. A lot of academic analysis had gone into trying to figure out exactly what constituted being a shrine prostitute and the difference between types of prostitution in these verses and elsewhere, but it doesn't really matter. Prostitution is a bad thing in God's eyes. It's a common metaphor all through the Old Testament for Israel's disloyalty and disobedience to God. It was as common in the ancient world as it is today—'the world's oldest profession'—and the Scriptures tell us about both religious and common prostitution. God's holy people were not to engage in it. End of story."

"It seems to me," I observed, "that not too many Christians would encounter this rule. I mean, people don't make vows to pay the Lord, and not many prostitutes are going to be seen in church anyway."

Hal disagreed with both of my points. "People do make pledges in many churches," he said, "and especially for things like building programs. They also make pledges for secular charities that may be doing God's work of caring for the sick and less fortunate.

"And as for there not being many prostitutes in church, there's a broader principle here. If the earnings of a prostitute are not to be brought into the Lord's house to pay a vow, one can infer that the Lord is not interested in the gift of any wrongful gain. People who make money by cheating others, by cheating on taxes, by wrongful conduct in business or the stock market, don't make any points with God by sharing it with the church or other good works. I sometimes wonder how much money comes into the offering plate that was earned in contempt of God's righteousness. There are a lot of people in church who are thought of as great philanthropists, but they'll find no favor with God under this law.

"The Scripture teaches that we are not to come before the Lord empty-handed, but it also teaches that we are not to bring blemished offerings to him, whether the defective animal or the fruits of improper economic activity.

"Now I want you to change your focus a little. We're done with teachings on sacred space and are moving on to some other principles."

> Do not charge your brother interest, whether on money or food or anything else that may earn interest. You may charge a foreigner interest, but not a brother Israelite, so that the LORD your God may bless you in everything you put your hand to in the land you are entering to possess.
>
> —Deut. 23:19–20

I recognized the prohibition on charging interest to a fellow Israelite as fitting with the law in chapter fifteen about lending freely and forgiveness of loans in the sabbatical year. Like the law forbidding the return of runaway slaves, this law was radically different from laws and practices among Israel's neighbors. I knew from my study that most commentators saw the limitation of the law to "a brother Israelite" as part of the fabric of laws by which members of the covenant community took care of their own and protected the poor. It did not apply to foreigners because they were likely involved in commercial activities in Israel, and the law's purpose did not apply to commerce, though other laws protected the poor and needy who were aliens in Israel.

"There are a number of laws in Deuteronomy," Hal said, "that challenge us in our most basic assumptions about economic life and our relation to our neighbors. This is one of them. The obligation of God's people to the poor and needy among them is to lend freely, at no interest, and to forgive the loan in the sabbatical year, whether or not it is paid. There is nothing comparable in modern social or economic theory or practice. All wealth is from the Lord, and it is to be shared as he would have it shared."

"As he has shared it, I suppose," I said. "After all, everything we have, from the food on the table to the ability to earn the means to buy it to life with the Lord in eternity, is a gift from God."

Hal smiled softly, a smile that told me he was pleased with his student. And I was pleased with myself, as you are when you realize that you get it, that you understand something that has been mysterious to you before, that the contents of some black box, the cogs and gears that make something happen, are suddenly laid out in a pattern that makes sense, as if it could only be this way, and now it all works in a pattern of perfect clarity.

The moment passed, and Hal was more somber as he read the next three verses.

> If you make a vow to the LORD your God, do not be slow to pay it, for the LORD your God will certainly demand it of you and you will be guilty of sin. But if you refrain from making a vow, you will not be guilty. Whatever your lips utter you must be sure to do, because you made your vow freely to the LORD your God with your own mouth.
>
> —Deut. 23:21–23

"This law," Hal said, "is about the commandment not to take the Lord's name in vain. Promises made to God must be kept."

"In court," I said, "we require witnesses to swear to tell 'the truth, the whole truth, and nothing but the truth, so help me God.' I suppose the oath of the witness comes out of this idea."

"Good point. Your oath in court assumes that there is such a thing as truth, and that God cares about that truth. It is based on the teaching that God expects truth and integrity from his people, and that there is guilt before God when you swear in his name to tell the truth and don't do so. Most modern people probably don't think a lot about guilt before God, though, when they take that oath."

"No," I said, "nowadays we have to rely on fear of perjury prosecutions, which hardly ever happen. There is a lot of perjury in court, but nothing generally comes of it."

"But the other part of this teaching is that vows are not always good things. People too often make oaths too quickly. If made rashly, they can have unfortunate results. We read the story of Jephthah in the eleventh chapter of Judges. He foolishly vowed to sacrifice to the Lord whatever came out of the door of his house when he returned home if the Lord would give him victory over the Ammonites. That vow led to the death of his only daughter. Perhaps for this reason, Numbers chapter thirty allows women to be relieved of vows by their father or husband, although no such relief applies to males. Proverbs and Ecclesiastes also warn against hasty vows."

"So people should avoid vows whenever they can?"

"There is a place for vows," Hal said, "such as at the marriage altar or in the courtroom. But it is limited. It remained for Jesus to teach against any vows. In Matthew five he said, 'Simply let your "Yes" be "Yes" and your "No," "No"; anything beyond this comes from the evil one.'"

"The extended principle here," I said, "is that a person's word, as the saying goes, should be his bond. We shouldn't be careless or casual about promises, to others as well as the Lord."

Hal's smile returned. He read the end of the chapter.

> If you enter your neighbor's vineyard, you may eat all the grapes you want, but do not put any in your basket. If you enter your neighbor's grain field, you may pick kernels with your hands, but you must not put a sickle to his standing grain.
>
> —Deut. 23:24–25

"Let me guess," I said. "This is like the rules about lending freely and not charging interest. It's part of God's plan for caring for those in need."

"You are correct," Hal said. "This rule protects the poor and needy by allowing them to eat food from someone else's field or vineyard but not to abuse the generosity of the law by gathering the grapes or cutting the grain. The rule also protects travelers. And Jewish tradition applies it to workers as well, like the law against muzzling the ox when it's treading out the grain."

"Are there any examples of applying this law in Scripture?"

"Sure. In Ruth chapter two, the impoverished woman goes into the field and picks grain that the harvesters have left. This is an application of this law, and another one in the next chapter.

"And, like almost everything else in Deuteronomy, this law shows up in the New Testament as well. Jesus and the disciples took advantage of it, as seen in Matthew chapter twelve, when they went into a grain field and picked heads of grain to eat. The Pharisees were upset with him, but not because he picked the grain. Rather, they were upset because he did it on the Sabbath. Jesus used the occasion as a teaching tool. There was a perceived conflict between this law and the law of keeping the Sabbath holy. Jesus resolved the conflict by his statement that 'the Son of Man is Lord of the Sabbath' and teaching that it is lawful to do good on the Sabbath. His statement of authority over the Sabbath, however, is an assertion of his divine authority. The passage in Matthew ends with the Pharisees plotting how they might kill Jesus. In their eyes, he had not only violated the Sabbath but was violating the laws against worshipping other gods or leading people into false religion by claiming his own divine authority. All of these are capital offenses under the law of Deuteronomy."

We had come to the end of another evening. Respect for the sacred nature of the space and things that belonged to God, care for the poor and needy, the importance of keeping our word, the connectedness of the teachings of Jesus and the events of his life to these laws in Deuteronomy—all filled my mind as I wrenched myself out of the tabernacle where Hal seemed so often to be face to face with God. I reentered the darkness outside.

Chapter Twenty-Four

"T"he Scriptures," Hal said, "are like a diamond, a precious stone. The more you look into them, the more you see. Every facet reflects the light a little differently, and there is a depth of beauty within that draws you into it when you see below the surface. But it's all in one stone, one object that ties it all together."

Darkness had long since fallen as we talked. But it had been one of those late winter days when bright sunlight glistened off new fallen snow, giving the world a glitter and sparkle that tied it together with a carpet of beauty. On days like that in New England, one could imagine existing inside a diamond world. The light reflected everywhere in an effervescent luminescence so bright that one had to shield the eye to bear it. Just as I was regretting turning to a passage of the law that seemed obscure if not offensive, Hal turned the thought around.

"This passage," he said, "is a good one to see how God ties it all together. Let's read."

> If a man marries a woman who becomes displeasing to him because he finds something indecent about her, and he writes her a certificate of divorce, gives it to her and sends her from his house, and if after she leaves his house she becomes the wife of another man, and her second husband dislikes her and writes her a certificate of divorce, gives it to her and sends her from his house, or if he dies, then her first husband, who divorced her, is not allowed to marry her again after she has been defiled. That would be detestable in the eyes of the LORD. Do not bring sin upon the land the LORD your God is giving you as an inheritance.
>
> —Deut. 24:1–4

With this curious law, we returned to the subject of divorce. Hal reminded me that divorce was an accepted custom in ancient Israel, but not a divinely ordained or approved event.

"I always tell couples I marry that divorce is not an option. The Old Testament assumes its existence but gives few laws concerning it. Jesus taught that only adultery justifies divorce, and those who divorce for any other reason and remarry are adulterers. This is true for both the husband and the wife. Moses permitted divorce only because of the hardness of people's heart, which is probably another way of saying that it was sometimes the lesser evil for marriages in which people were so disobedient to God that they were causing more sin by being together than they would apart. I've known many marriages like that and have even counseled divorce in some cases where I thought one of the parties was irredeemable within the marriage. Cases of spousal abuse and incest would be like that. But in every case of divorce, one or both of the spouses is at fault through selfish behavior."

"What is the prescription for a good marriage?" I asked.

"There is only one. A clear acceptance on the part of both the man and the woman that their marriage is a physical and spiritual union, making them 'one flesh,' figuratively in all respects, and literally in their sexual relationship and in the blessing of children. As Jesus said, 'What God has joined together, let man not separate.' The marriage must be consecrated to God and united in this purpose. There is a higher purpose in the union of man and woman than their own selfish interests, whether they are looking for economic advantage, legitimized sex, someone to have children with, or merely help and companionship. All these are legitimate objects of marriage, but the marriage is vulnerable if it's not grounded in a shared spiritual purpose."

"I grant the wisdom of that," I said, "and that it's all biblical and consistent with God's teaching. But what's really up with this law prohibiting remarriage? If another marriage is adultery, as Jesus teaches, I would think God would be pleased that the couple came back together in the original union. And how does this tie together with other Scriptures?"

"Some think this law is for the protection of the woman," Hal said. "Apparently there was a practice in Egypt—where the Israelites had most recently lived—of legitimizing what amounted to wife swapping by technical and basically phony divorces and remarriages. Women were passed around, so to speak, without really changing the basic family relationship. I've heard this is still done in some Muslim countries."

"This would be a logical explanation of prohibiting the practice," I said, "but it doesn't really fit the Scripture since the first divorce is grounded in the woman's indecent act, and the remarriage is prohibited even if the second husband dies."

"True," Hal said. "Another explanation of this law was that it was meant to protect the woman. By forcing the man to go through a formality, she may be protected from hasty action and have the legal evidence to justify her release from ties to him and legitimize another marriage. All this is true, but it still doesn't really explain why the remarriage is prohibited."

"Then what is the explanation?" I pressed.

"The key is in the woman's indecency, which was the ground of the first divorce. That's what it means when it says she has been defiled. It's usually presumed that this is something other than adultery, since the normal penalty for adultery is death. But a husband may not wish to press the matter, as Joseph didn't wish to press it with Mary when she was pregnant with Jesus before he understood the Holy Spirit impregnated her. The Gospels teach that he intended to put her away quietly, so we understand that the husband had some discretion in the matter. And Jesus' teaching that adultery justifies divorce presumes that capital punishment was not carried out automatically and that the husband could choose to divorce the woman instead. So it may be adultery, or it may be something less egregious—sexual behavior of some other sort, immodesty in dress, conduct, or speech, improper conduct with another man short of adultery, relations with another woman . . . the Scripture leaves it general. Whatever it is, the woman had despoiled her relationship with her husband to the point that he couldn't continue to live with her as his wife.

"God's message here is that when one has formed a moral judgment that something is unacceptable, he or she must not go back on that judgment. The unacceptable moral act had its consequences, and they can't be reversed. The lesson for us is that we are not to soften our moral resolution to gain some perceived advantage, including the company of someone we have loved and may still love. This is not about contrition or forgiveness. These may occur, but the divorce has happened and the woman has moved on into another marriage. The woman is not available until a second divorce or the death of the second husband. But even then, they are not to pretend that what happened didn't happen, or that the act of indecency and resulting divorce was not important, just to serve some mutual interest later on."

"So what you're saying," I said, "is that God's message here is moral consistency, not being double-minded."

"Yes," Hal said. "But it's more than that. The original law was probably meant to be applied literally, to teach that sin has consequences that can't be ignored or undone. But this law matures through the Scriptures to become one of the most profound teachings in the Bible."

"How so?"

"Often we can get some insight into the deeper meaning of passages like this by seeing what other parts of Scripture say about it, and God is not silent on this one. The prophets often used the metaphor of Israel as an unfaithful wife and analogize her disobedience to God, and especially her idolatry, as adultery."

He turned to Jeremiah 3 and read, "'If a man divorces his wife and she leaves him and marries another man, should he return to her again? Would not the land be completely defiled? But you have lived as a prostitute with many lovers. Would you now return to me?' declares the Lord."

"It sounds like the beginning of Deuteronomy twenty-four," I said.

"It is," Hal said. "God returned to this exact law in Deuteronomy hundreds of years later, through Jeremiah. The spiritual message of the law is clear. God's people can't lay him aside in favor of other objects of worship, and then pick him up again at their convenience."

"Is it hopeless, then," I asked, "for anyone who has betrayed God? Are we talking about the 'sin against the Holy Spirit' that Jesus said could not be forgiven?"

"No," Hal said. "The law that relates to taking back a woman divorced for indecency appears also in the book of Hosea. In Hosea, the reference to Deuteronomy is not as specific as in Jeremiah, but the idea is there. Let's look at it."

The prophet Hosea lived his life as a metaphor of Israel's life with God. At God's instruction, he married an adulterous wife, Gomer. Theirs was a marriage symbolic of God's relationship with Israel. Hosea, like the husband of the indecent wife in Deuteronomy 24, sent her away for her unfaithfulness, but then, again at God's direction, he bought her back to live with him in a proper relationship. The metaphor was one of marriage and adultery, but, in contrast to the law against remarriage, there was forgiveness and restoration of relationship.

"So God broke his own law?" I said. "How can that be?"

"Love overcomes the law," Hal said. "Hosea is taught to 'Love her as the Lord loves the Israelites.' God's action in breaking his own law is justified: 'For I am God and not man.' With man, it can't be done. But with God, all things are possible. The law of the indecent wife becomes a teaching on the depth of God's love for Israel."

"Is there more?"

"There is. In Matthew nineteen, a rich young man came to Jesus and asked what he must do to get eternal life. Jesus tested him with a superficial response by reminding him of some of the Ten Commandments: Do not murder, steal, commit adultery, or give false testimony. Honor your father and mother; and, he adds, love your neighbor as yourself. So far he was only talking about outward behaviors and relationships to others. The man said he had done all this but asked what he still lacked. Then Jesus told him that if he wanted to be perfect, he must sell his possessions and give them to the poor, and then follow him. At that the young man went away sadly.

"Jesus took him to his relationship with God and identified the thing that this man put before God. He showed him that his real God was his wealth and that he had violated the commandment to have no other gods before the Lord. After the young man went away, Jesus told his disciples that it's easier for a camel to go through the eye of a needle than for a rich man to enter the kingdom of heaven."

"I know that story," I said. "But I don't see what it has to do with Deuteronomy twenty-four."

"The disciples' response to Jesus' teaching was to ask, 'Who, then, can be saved?' Jesus' answer was the same answer God gave in Hosea with respect to the indecent wife: 'With man this is impossible, but with God all things are possible.' A teaching of unredeemable guilt on the part of a covenant partner in Deuteronomy was overcome by love triumphing over law in Hosea. Jesus then took the principle and made it applicable to all sin. Man can't overcome his sinfulness on his own, but with God, even this is possible. This is what Jesus taught when the disciples asked him how anyone could be saved. When you read the Scriptures about remarriage together, that is the message taught in the Old Testament, and Jesus teaches it again as a general principle of understanding God in the New Testament."

"One book, one story, one author," I said, echoing Hal's teaching. He nodded and read on.

> If a man has recently married, he must not be sent to war or have any other duty laid on him. For one year he is to be free to stay at home and bring happiness to the wife he has married.
>
> —Deut. 24:5

In chapter twenty, we had seen the exemption from military service for newly married men. Here it is repeated more specifically: The exemption is for one year and extends to unspecified duties other than military service.

Hal explained. "God had a purpose for the exemption of the newly married man from military or other public duties for a year: to bring happiness to his wife. The emphasis on the wife's happiness is in contrast to the notion that it is only the wife who has an obligation to bring happiness to the husband; that isn't mentioned. God's teaching in the Bible gives a different picture, and this passage is one of the parts of the picture. The happiness of the wife that God is referring to here is surely the complete happiness that is related to a good marriage. Conjugal relations are not the whole of it, but are surely part."

"Are we to think, then, that the popular idea is reversed, and it is the man who has an obligation to make his wife happy, not the other way around?" I asked.

"God isn't so unbalanced," Hal replied. "The obligation is mutual. Paul teaches in First Corinthians chapter seven that the husband should fulfill his marital duty to his wife, just as she should to him, and that the husband's body does not belong to him alone, but also to his wife, just as her body belongs to him. Anyone who thinks the Bible gives a man the unilateral right to impose himself on his wife has not read God's word on this subject or doesn't understand it. The God-ordained mindset of a husband on sexual matters is that his body is his wife's property, and is to be used for her satisfaction. His own satisfaction should be entirely secondary to him.

"Of course, the wife should understand that her husband owns her body, and she should see that it is used to satisfy him. They are not to withhold themselves from one another, except, as Paul teaches, by mutual consent for a time of devotion to prayer. Christian marriage should be a rich and fulfilling physical experience. When both parties are living their marriage in this respect, as God teaches, there should be little temptation to seek satisfaction anywhere else; they will be getting all the satisfaction they can handle right where they are."

"What a contrast," I said, "to the idea that the Bible just puts men in charge on everything."

"The Old Testament—and Christianity as well—are often seen as very male-oriented. The observation is correct to the extent that the culture and society was one in which men were expected to, and did, take leadership in the family, and in economic, religious, governmental, and military affairs. Women were not entirely absent from these positions, but they didn't dominate them or share them equally. The differences in gender roles were more distinct and knitted into the fabric of society than what we are accustomed to. Many laws were addressed primarily to males and assumed what was the reality of the time, that males would be the ones primarily affected by them and primarily enforcing them. But this passage in Deuteronomy—and others in the Bible—make it clear that biblical marriage is about reciprocal sharing and unselfishness. When the two become one flesh, the desire is to please the other—not just self—as part of that flesh."

Hal had a lot to say about marriage and sexuality. It was, he told me, the single greatest burden that people brought to him in a lifetime of pastoring. And it all could be avoided if people just followed God's teachings. What a wayward sort we are! And what a wonder that God loves us still.

"The second greatest burden," Hal said, "is money. And the Bible has a lot to say about that as well."

We read on.

> Do not take a pair of millstones—not even the upper one—as security for a debt, because that would be taking a man's livelihood as security.
>
> —Deut. 24:6

"Those millstones were household millstones that every home would have had for grinding the grain for bread. This teaching is straightforward: Those things that are necessary for a person to sustain himself and his family are not to be taken as security for debt."

I recognized the principle. In our bankruptcy law, certain things are exempt from creditors: $15,000 worth of a residence, household furniture, clothing, appliances, books, musical instruments, tools of the debtor's trade, etc. The principle was the same as the biblical one: debtors are never to be made totally bereft of property. Everyone needs certain basic things to keep going.

"Economic justice in the Bible," Hal said, "always favors the poor. We'll see even more of that principle before we're through."

> If a man is caught kidnapping one of his brother Israelites and treats him as a slave or sells him, the kidnapper must die. You must purge the evil from among you.
>
> —Deut. 24:7

Kidnapping, then as now, was a serious offense. It was part of the commandment against stealing, in this case stealing a person instead of his property. The law here did not refer to children, at least not exclusively.

"The death penalty," Hal explained, "was because kidnapping someone and selling him or her into slavery was the equivalent of social murder. Physical life might remain, but the opportunity to live a normal life as part of the covenant community was lost. This taking of life-opportunity was an offense worthy of the death penalty."

"There's not much controversy over kidnapping being a bad thing," I said. "No need for deeper analysis on this verse."

Hal didn't accept my quick gloss on a familiar evil. "We should reflect on other ways that one person can take the opportunity for meaningful life away from another. Kidnapping is not the only form of appropriating another's life for one's own advantage."

"Like what?" I asked.

"Like profiting from life-destroying addictions, especially drugs. Drugs have killed a lot of people and destroyed the lives of countless others who aren't physically dead. They have, in effect, kidnapped whole communities in some areas by destroying families, physical safety, economic life, and the things that make productive and meaningful life possible."

"Could you say the same for other addictions?" I asked. "Alcohol, tobacco, gambling, sex?"

"Each of these has the potential of great destructiveness. It's a matter of degree. Drug addiction is certainly the worst, the most powerful addicting agent. There are a lot of ways of kidnapping people."

While I pondered on the breadth of application of the law against kidnapping, Hal read the next two verses.

> In cases of leprous diseases be very careful to do exactly as the priests, who are Levites, instruct you. You must follow carefully what I have commanded them. Remember what the LORD your God did to Miriam along the way after you came out of Egypt.
>
> —Deut. 24:8–9

"Leprosy isn't much of a problem anymore," I said. "This law does seem like one that was relevant only to the people of the time."

Hal agreed that there wasn't much leprosy around but pointed out that the "leprous diseases" include many skin conditions other than leprosy. "The instructions," he said, "are given in detail in Leviticus thirteen and are assumed and not repeated here. Moses merely reminded the people to follow the instructions given elsewhere, and assumed their familiarity with them. But what do you think is the point of referring to Miriam here?"

"Didn't she get leprosy for some reason?" I asked, reaching through my memory for the story.

"The reference," Hal said, "is to the twelfth chapter of Numbers. Miriam and Aaron, Moses' siblings, were talking against him, supposedly because of his Cushite wife, but in reality seeking to replace him in his leadership role. God summoned the three of them to the Tent of Meeting, where he chastened Miriam and Aaron and struck Miriam with leprosy. She was cured only after Aaron pleaded with Moses—and Moses with the Lord—for her healing. Then she had to spend seven days of confinement outside the camp."

"So that's why she's referred to here," I said.

"The point of the admonition here is obedience, not teaching on leprosy," Hal said. "Miriam was a prophetess, the sister of Moses, and a leader in her own right. She was a VIP in Israel. But she wasn't exempt from God's punishment when she tried to take leadership matters into her own hands and promote herself. God is no respecter of persons. Being an important person doesn't exempt you from the consequences of sin and disobedience. David, Peter, and others of God's greatest people had to humble themselves and accept the consequences of their own failures. So did Miriam. So do we."

"Another theme that runs through the whole Bible," I said.

"One book, one story, one author," Hal replied. "God gave a lot of miscellaneous laws in this chapter, but they all connect to everything else."

We read the next section of chapter twenty-four.

> When you make a loan of any kind to your neighbor, do not go into his house to get what he is offering as a pledge. Stay outside and let the man to whom you are making the loan bring the pledge out to you. If the man is poor, do not go to sleep with his pledge in your possession. Return his cloak to him by sunset so that he may sleep in it. Then he will thank you, and it will be regarded as a righteous act in the sight of the LORD your God.
>
> —Deut. 24:10–13

"We're back on economic justice and debt," Hal said. "As with the law prohibiting taking the millstone as security for a debt, this law protects the dignity of the poor as well as their essential possessions. The cloak was both an outer garment during the day and a covering to sleep in at night. The creditor here is giving up what the debtor has offered him, on account of the poverty of the debtor. This is part of the theme that God repeats often in Deuteronomy and elsewhere of caring for the poor in the community and not insisting on rights. Righteousness consists of not taking advantage of the pledge."

"Another biblical concept that found its way into American law," I observed. "We have statutes that regulate collection agencies and protect debtors from harassing tactics to collect debts. I wonder if anyone thought of Deuteronomy when they passed them."

"Tell me if the concept of the next couple of verses got into American law as well," Hal said.

> Do not take advantage of a hired man who is poor and needy, whether he is a brother Israelite or an alien living in one of your towns. Pay him his wages each day before sunset, because he is poor and is counting on it. Otherwise he may cry to the Lord against you, and you will be guilty of sin.
>
> —Deut. 24:14–15

"It did," I said. "The concept of regular payment of wages has endured and been enshrined in modern law. There's a complex set of wage-and-hour laws on the federal and state level to protect the right of workers to be properly paid. Employers have less discretion in dealing with workers who are paid on an hourly than a salaried basis. Hourly workers must be paid regularly and are entitled to be paid minimum wages and extra pay for overtime.

"In this state, employers who don't pay workers when the wages are due can be subject to double damages. To pay wages less frequently than weekly requires a permit from the Labor Department. It's fascinating to find the origins of these basic employee justice laws given in God's teaching more than three thousand years ago."

Hal added, "The Old Testament frequently condemns employers who abuse workers by not paying them when they're due. Through a period of a thousand years, Leviticus, Isaiah, Jeremiah, and Malachi condemned such practices. In New Testament times, James repeated the condemnation."

He turned to James 5 and read, "'Look! The wages you failed to pay the workmen who mowed your fields are crying out against you. The cries of the harvesters have reached the ears of the Lord Almighty.'" Then he commented, "Unjust pay and working conditions are not just a matter of social or political controversy. They're sins before God. The Christian employer can no more mistreat his employees in this way than he can steal from people or cheat them."

"One book, one story, one author," I added.

Hal then read the next verse.

> Fathers shall not be put to death for their children, nor children put to death for their fathers; each is to die for his own sin.
>
> —Deut. 24:16

"I'm glad to know I'm not responsible for the sins of my ancestors," I said. "But aren't there some Scriptures that teach differently?"

"The principle of individual rather than generational responsibility for sin comes up elsewhere. It's repeated in Jeremiah, chapter thirty-one, and Ezekiel eighteen. In Second Kings, chapter fourteen, we see that King Amaziah spared the sons of his father's assassins based on this law. But you're right that there are scriptures that seem to contrast with this. Let's take a look at them."

Hal took us to four such instances. "In Numbers sixteen," he said, "we read of Korah's rebellion against Moses. There the earth opened up and swallowed the rebels, along with their households.

"In Joshua seven, Achan violated the divine command to destroy everything in the conquest of Jericho—he took some plunder for himself. When his violation of this holy obligation was discovered, he was stoned to death, along with his sons and daughters and livestock.

"In Second Samuel twenty-one, David turned seven descendants of Saul over to the Gibeonites to be executed in retribution for their father's attacks on the Gibeonites in violation of the agreement between Israel and Gibeon.

"And finally, in Deuteronomy thirteen, the inhabitants of Israelite towns that were led into worshipping other gods were destroyed."

"So how are these not violations of the principle of individual responsibility?" I asked.

"First," Hal said, "these accounts don't tell us the level of guilt that the executed individuals had in the matter. Certainly many of those who fell with the father or leader may have shared the guilt of the event that caused the death penalty. But, more importantly, these are all instances of events related to the holy wars in conquest of the land, those special wars where God himself led the battle. Korah's rebellion occurred against God's chosen leader on the way to the land; Achan's sin was a violation of the holy command to devote everything to destruction in the conquest; the sin of Saul against Gibeon was a violation of a covenant Israel made during the conquest; and the towns that were involved in false worship had rebelled against the God who has given them the land. Each of these was a holy offense that must be thought of like the conquest itself, where the sin of the Amorites had reached its full measure and justified the total destruction of the people. It was part of God's reclaiming his property for himself.

"As with the total destruction of the Canaanites in the conquest, these instances tell us nothing about how those among the destroyed people who were not personally involved in the offensive behavior are treated in eternity. We must trust God's justice to deal properly with them."

"So there was a time and place," I said, "when generational punishment was appropriate because of the special holiness of what was at stake."

"Yes," Hal said. "And on a broader scale, the principle here has great theological implications. We are all under a death sentence for Adam's sin. There is the ultimate corporate responsibility. But the death of the human race brought about by Adam's sin is reversed in Christ, whose death makes possible the salvation of sinners who deserve death. 'For as in Adam all die, so in Christ all will be made alive,' as Paul says in First Corinthians, chapter fifteen. Thus, corporate responsibility is acknowledged and atoned for. Individually, of course, we all deserve death for our own sin, apart from Adam's sin. But, again, Christ atoned for that sin, allowing us, if we accept that atonement, to live."

"One book, one story, one author," I said again.

Hal continued reading.

> Do not deprive the alien or the fatherless of justice, or take the cloak of the widow as a pledge. Remember that you were slaves in Egypt and the LORD your God redeemed you from there. That is why I command you to do this.
>
> —Deut. 24:17–18

"We just read about returning cloaks taken in pledge," I observed. "But if the debtor is a widow, you shouldn't even take it in the first place."

"It's another instance of God protecting the helpless," Hal said. "He comes back to it so many times and in so many different ways that it's hard not to get the point. Caring for the poor and helpless is one of the most consistent themes through all of Scripture. And God reminded the Israelites of their own history of slavery in Egypt when they needed help to escape. We've all been poor and helpless, if not in our own lives, then in those of our ancestors. We must remember this history when we think about our obligations to others."

"One book, one story, one author," I repeated.

> When you are harvesting in your field and you overlook a sheaf, do not go back to get it. Leave it for the alien, the fatherless, and the widow, so that the LORD your God may bless you in all the work of your hands. When you beat the olives from your trees, do not go over the branches a second time. Leave what remains for the alien, the fatherless, and the widow. When you harvest the grapes in your vineyard, do not go over the vines again. Leave what remains for the alien, the fatherless, and the widow. Remember that you were slaves in Egypt. That is why I command you to do this.
>
> —Deut. 24:19–22

"Didn't we talk about this in the last chapter?" I asked.

"Yes. It's the basis of the story of Ruth gleaning in the fields after the harvesters."

"I'm getting familiar with the principle," I said. "God really cares about how we treat the less fortunate, especially those without the means to establish or protect an economic stake in the society."

"And in Moses' time, the alien, the fatherless, and the widow were those who needed the most care. Once again, God reminds them of their own history and his blessings in rescuing them. If God did as much for them, how dare they not do the same for others? God's people are not to lapse back into slavery due to poverty or economic distress. He didn't lead them out of Egypt to become slaves again. At the heart of its moral and social values, the prosperous society must remember and acknowledge God and his blessings."

We closed our Bibles, and Hal prayed. While he was praying, my mind danced through the subjects we had covered: remarrying the indecent wife, happiness in marriage, proper treatment of debtors and the poor, depriving others of meaningful life, the need for the great as well as the humble to be obedient to God and admonished for their sins, proper employment practices, and individual versus corporate responsibility for sin. In each, these ancient laws given to a tribal people emerging from the desert into a settled land were repeated and expanded on throughout the Scriptures to become part of the foundation of a just and moral society today, and even part of the understanding of how God deals with us as we approach judgment and eternity.

One book, one story, one author!

CHAPTER TWENTY-FIVE

Hal's kitchen was dimly lit, but brighter than his study. He was sitting at the table when I came in; he invited me to sit with him. A jug of cider and two glasses sat on the table. Beside them were two books, one labeled "Tanakh" and the other "The New Testament."

"Do you know what these are?" he asked, pointing to the books.

"Well, I know what that one is," I said, indicating the New Testament. "But I never heard of Tanakh."

"You have," Hal replied, "but you don't know it by its Jewish name. Open it up."

I opened the volume and was surprised to find it was a Bible, or at least part of one, beginning with Genesis and ending with Chronicles.

"Tanakh," Hal said, "is a Hebrew acronym for the three major divisions of the Jewish Bible, the Torah, the Nevi'im, and the Kethuvim, meaning the Law, the Prophets, and the Writings. It's what Christians call the Old Testament and has all the same books as the Protestant Old Testament but arranges them in a different order. But it starts where the Old Testament starts, with the first five books in the same order."

"Interesting," I said. "But why are we looking at them as two separate books?"

"They're not, and that's the point. We've seen constant overlap and cross-references as we've gone along. I want to show you what I mean. You've heard me say before that the New Testament is sometimes called a commentary on the Old Testament. If this is true, it would profit us to study them together."

I picked up the Tanakh and found Deuteronomy in the usual location, between Numbers and Joshua, and read the first three verses of chapter twenty-five.

> When there is a dispute between men and they go to law, and a decision is rendered declaring the one in the right and the other in the wrong—if the guilty one is to be flogged, the magistrate shall have him lie down and be given lashes in his presence, by count, as his guilt warrants. He may be given up to forty lashes, but not more, lest being flogged further, to excess, your brother be degraded before your eyes.
>
> —Deut. 25:1–3

"So where is this taught in the New Testament?" I asked.

"It isn't taught," he replied, "but it is practiced. Read Second Corinthians eleven, twenty-four."

I did: "Five times I received from the Jews the forty lashes minus one."

"The practice of giving thirty-nine lashes as the maximum punishment was to ensure they didn't miscount and exceed the forty lashes permitted in Deuteronomy. The Jews followed Deuteronomy literally in this punishment. Paul, of course, was punished unjustly for preaching the gospel. His reference to the lashings is in a passage in which he wrote of his suffering for preaching Christ, and the strength he found in his weaknesses and suffering for the gospel. Thus, God's intended justice, when perverted to unjust purposes, still has a just result. God's power is made perfect in weakness."

"I don't think you'd get many takers for punishment by public flogging in this day and age," I said, "although I guess there are a few Muslim countries where it's still done."

"No," Hal said, "we wouldn't see it in a culture where it's out of fashion to even spank naughty children. But think about it. Are there any principles here that you recognize in our legal system?"

"Punishment for crime," I said. "That's about it."

"Look more closely. Verse one: Disputes are to be decided by courts and judges, not by arbitrary or homegrown or vigilante justice. Verse two: The guilty are to be punished proportionate to the crime. Verse three: Punishment is to have limits. The purpose of the limits is to protect the dignity of the guilty person. He still has the right to be treated humanely. Is this beginning to sound more familiar to you?"

What had sounded barbaric at first reading was beginning to sound less so as Hal pointed these things out. He went on to describe how the punishment was actually administered.

"Jewish tradition," he said, "recognized the restorative object of the punishment. During the flogging, certain verses of Scripture would be read, concluding with Psalm seventy-eight, verse thirty-eight." He took up the Tanakh and read: "'But He, being merciful, forgave iniquity and would not destroy; He restrained his wrath time and again and did not give full vent to His fury.'

"The guilty person," Hal went on, "would recite another verse, Jeremiah 10:24." He turned to the passage: "'Chastise me, O Lord, but in measure; Not in Your wrath, lest You reduce me to naught.'

"You see, Chris, guilt is before God as well as man. The human judge carries out divine instruction. He upholds society's holiness and righteousness. He restored an errant member. Guilt is acknowledged, guilt is punished, and guilt is over. The errant citizen can then resume a dignified place in society. How do you think that compares to our system of punishment?"

I had to admit that public flogging was looking better and better. "I guess the flogging wasn't that severe," I said. "The person being punished was still able to recite Scripture."

"He could," Hal said. "The idea of public flogging seems barbaric to modern Western people, although you're right that it's still practiced in some parts of the world. You could never restore it in this society that rejects any type of corporal punishment, and the religious nature of guilt and punishment could not be acknowledged in a society that strictly separates church and state. But it has a lot to recommend it, at least for crimes in which it's clear the offender is not dangerous to other people. The punishment is immediate, public, and over. There's no need for the cost of prisons that can turn people into worse criminals than when they entered. There's no interruption in the economic life of the guilty person, who can continue to support himself and his dependents. If any politician ever advocated it, I'd vote for him."

Hal poured us both a glass of cider while I read the next verse from the Tanakh.

You shall not muzzle an ox while it is threshing.
—Deut. 25:4

"Good practical advice," I observed. "I know that in Old Testament times grain was threshed or separated from the chaff by oxen treading on it or pulling a sledge over it. But how does the New Testament comment on this?"

"You are right that the plain meaning of this Scripture is a practical and humanitarian concern for the working animal. The animal must be able to eat while working and should not be unreasonably driven or deprived of sustenance. But this becomes a broader and important teaching in the New Testament. In First Corinthians nine, seven to twelve, Paul quotes it as authority for Christian workers to receive material support from those they serve. 'Is it about oxen that God is concerned? Surely he says this for us, doesn't he?' He revisits the Scripture for the same purpose in his letter to the young pastor, Timothy, in First Timothy five, seven to nine."

"Two references so far," I said, "and I recall our discussion of tithing and the Levites. If all Christians followed Old Testament teachings, there would be a lot of workers 'threshing.' So it's not just about animals. But is it only about supporting religious workers?"

I saw in this passage the broader principle of fair employment practices earlier in Deuteronomy, most recently in the teaching about prompt payment of wages. Hal agreed but had another insight.

"There's another lesson from this passage found in First Timothy," he said, "and it's totally different. It has to do with the authority of the Bible. Many skeptics question the authority of the Scriptures. This is the issue that is the principal division between what we may call the 'liberal' denominations and the conservative church—how seriously do you take the Bible? To answer that question we have to ask ourselves why the particular writings that make up the Bible have canonical status—that is, they're recognized as being authoritative. Why do we say these, rather than some other writings, are the words of God? Why are these writings, or the Bible as a whole book, entitled to more weight than what you or I might think about such matters, or what might be written by other religious leaders, such as Billy Graham or the Pope?"

CHAPTER TWENTY-FIVE

"Why, indeed?" I asked. "How does this passage answer that question?"

Hal read the full passage from 1 Timothy: "'For the Scripture says, "Do not muzzle the ox while it is treading out the grain," and "The worker deserves his wages."'"

"The first passage, which Paul describes as Scripture, is our passage from Deuteronomy. Remember, Jesus cited the Old Testament as authoritative. The second passage—'The worker deserves his wages'—states the same principle, only applied to people rather than animals. But this passage doesn't appear in the Old Testament. It's from Jesus' words in Luke's Gospel."

I didn't understand. "And . . .?"

Hal explained. "Paul was familiar with Luke's Gospel and considered it Scripture, just like the Old Testament Scriptures, which were well-known and called Scripture by Jesus. This means that, even in Paul's lifetime, Luke's Gospel was known and accepted as Scripture. The saying that 'the worker deserves his wages' appears nowhere else in Scripture."

"So you're saying that it enhances our confidence in the gospels by showing how old they are, how near to the life of Jesus, and how soon after his death they were recognized as Scripture, right?"

"Exactly," Hal answered. "The writings that make up the New Testament were determined by consensus of the church, but this passage shows how early in that history Scripture was being recognized."

"Are there any more passages like this?"

Hal referred me to 2 Peter 3:15–16, in which Peter wrote this about Paul's letters: "He writes the same way in all his letters, speaking in them of these matters. His letters contain some things that are hard to understand, which ignorant and unstable people distort, just as they do the other Scriptures, to their own destruction."

"Peter referred here to Paul's letters as Scripture, just as Paul referred to Luke's Gospel as Scripture. This shows us that, even in the time of the original apostles, those apostles recognized the gospels and epistles as Scripture."

At one time I had the impression that the New Testament was a somewhat arbitrary collection of writings selected from a sea of documents by a bunch of old men hundreds of years after Christ. As I had come to know the New Testament more fully, I had gained a new appreciation for its spiritual depth and the wisdom of those who had brought it to final form. I understood that at an early time the gospels and Paul's letters were in circulation as a corpus of Scripture, and that there had been widespread consensus about most of the New Testament contents in the earliest knowledge we have about the church. But Hal's insights showed me that from the cross-references within the New Testament Scriptures themselves, we could see how early that consensus was. Those who walked with Jesus understood when God the Holy Spirit had recorded his message through his servants for eternity.

As we finished the cider, we reflected on those faithful servants, Peter and Paul, reading Luke's Gospel—and undoubtedly the other Gospel accounts as well—and the letters they had written. We pictured them discerning God's Word being formed before their eyes. We had traveled a long way from the vision of the unmuzzled ox tramping around the threshing floor. Hal's lesson of the evening was beginning to sink in.

But what could he possibly find connected to the New Testament in the next passage from the Tanakh?

> When brothers dwell together and one of them dies and leaves no son, the wife of the deceased shall not be married to a stranger, outside the family. Her husband's brother shall unite with her: take her as his wife and perform the levir's duty. The first son that she bears shall be accounted to the dead brother, that his name may not be blotted out in Israel.

> But if the man does not want to marry his brother's widow, his brother's widow shall appear before the elders in the gate and declare, "My husband's brother refuses to establish a name in Israel for his brother; he will not perform the duty of a levir." The elders of the town shall then summon him and talk to him. If he insists, saying, "I do not want to marry her," his brother's widow shall go up to him in the presence of the elders, pull the sandal off his foot, spit in his face, and make this declaration: Thus shall be done to the man who

will not build up his brother's house! And he shall go in
Israel by the name of "the family of the unsandaled one."

—Deut. 25:5–10

"This," Hal said, "is the practice of 'Levirate marriage.' The term is
from the Latin for a husband's brother. It's found in various forms in
other ancient Middle Eastern cultures and even in some today. It's an
exception to the prohibition on marrying a brother's wife, found in
Leviticus twenty, twenty-one. If the surviving brother is unmarried, so
no polygamy is involved, it could be practiced today even in the United
States."

"I can't imagine it." I said. "Most Americans would be horrified at the
idea that God would expect this of them."

"There were conditions," Hal said. "It didn't apply to everyone whose
brother died. The brothers had to have been living together, so that
means an extended household, probably supported by inherited land,
not just a family relationship. That alone eliminates most families. And
there must be no surviving son, although Jewish interpretation reads
the meaning generically to include daughters, who could inherit in the
absence of sons. In Numbers, chapter twenty-seven, there is the story
of Zelophehad's daughters who inherited when there weren't any sons.
So it only applied if the brother who died had no children, and that
eliminated a lot of other families."

"OK," I said. "So it's only if they all live on the farm together and
the brother who dies is childless. But what's the point? Why doesn't the
widow just go marry someone else?"

"Looking at it economically," Hal said, "the law had a useful purpose
in providing for the widow within the family so she didn't have to rely
on remarrying, which might have been more difficult to do in that
society where brides were expected to be virgins. It also helped the
family by preventing the loss of inherited property by her marriage
outside the family. The result is that the widow is cared for and the
farm is kept intact."

"I have two questions," I said. "First, we started out tonight seeing
that the New Testament builds on the Tanakh, but so far I haven't seen
anything in this that relates to Jesus' teaching or the New Testament.

Second, God gave a law here that may require polygamy if the second brother is married. Surely there is something more to this spiritually, not just the economics of the farm or protecting the widow in her old age if she isn't remarriageable."

Hal smiled. "Let's talk about both of your questions. Have you heard what the difference is between those two groups of people, the Pharisees and the Sadducees, who constantly harass Jesus with questions to try to embarrass him or trick him?"

I hadn't.

"The Pharisees believed in life after death," Hal said, "and the Sadducees didn't. That's why they were sad, you see."

He grinned at his little joke and went on to discuss the levirate marriage in New Testament scriptures. "Jesus used this passage to teach us something about life after death," he said. "It appears in Matthew, chapter twenty-four. The Sadducees, who didn't believe in the resurrection of the dead, tried to stump Jesus with a question about the law of levirate marriage. They postulated a woman who was married successively to seven brothers, each of whom died in turn. Then they asked him whose wife she will be in the resurrection, since she had been married to all seven. Jesus used the occasion to teach on the resurrection, as well as to show the foolishness of the question. He told them, 'At the resurrection people will neither marry nor be given in marriage; they will be like the angels in heaven.'"

I knew the teaching, but I had never connected it to Deuteronomy. I asked Hal if the New Testament drew anything else out of the law of levirate marriage.

"Not directly," he replied. "But there is this. Augustine believed levirate marriage was the explanation for the apparent contradiction in the identification of the father of Joseph, husband of Mary the mother of Jesus, between Matthew, one, sixteen, and Luke, three, twenty-three. Matthew identified Joseph's father as Jacob, while Luke referred to his father as Heli. If Joseph was the son of a Levirate marriage, this contradiction would be reconciled. One would be his biological father, the other the deceased husband of his mother and the brother of his biological father."

"OK," I said, "but what about my second question? Does God have some purpose in mind here other than farm economics?"

"This law has something to teach us about the relationship between husband and wife. God teaches that in their union, they become one flesh. When the husband dies, having been one flesh with his wife, he lives on in her person. It is in this sense that her son, although fathered by the brother-in-law, will carry on the family line of the deceased husband. Marriage is much more than a contract—it is the union of two into one, and it endures past the death of the first."

He held up his hand to prevent my comment. "Now a clever or argumentative person will start in like the Sadducees here. So what about the second brother? Are both brothers one flesh with her? Are the brothers then one flesh with each other? And what about those polygamous relationships anyway? Who was the husband 'one flesh' with?"

"And . . .?" I said.

"They are futile arguments of the foolish," Hal said. "The point is that your relationship with your spouse endures in your union. 'Till death do us part' may refer to the death of the second person, not the first. That doesn't mean that no one should marry again when a spouse dies. There are a lot of good reasons why that should sometimes happen. But it does mean that there is something sacred, even past death, in the relationship between a husband and wife. That's all I mean to say about it."

"It must have been an important rule," I said, "considering all that spitting in the face and stuff with the sandal if the brother wouldn't do it."

Hal replied, "Some think the sandal symbolizes land, which was measured by tread. But biblical symbols are often earthier euphemisms, and this one probably is."

He led me to Genesis 38. There Judah's son, Er, dies, and Judah orders the next oldest son, Onan, to perform the duty of a brother-in-law to Er's wife, Tamar, to produce offspring for his older brother. Onan enters the levirate marriage, but avoids the consequence of progeny by spilling his seed on the ground when he has relations with Tamar.

"This passage," Hal said, "gave us the name 'Onanism,' for self-stimulation or masturbation, but that's really a misnomer. What Onan did was what we call 'coitus interruptus,' which is a natural birth-control method. The sin of Onan was not sexual; it was greed. He wouldn't impregnate his brother's wife because he knew the child would not be his. The point is that it would dilute his inheritance. He didn't want a child who would take his brother's share because the result would be less for him.

"When the rejected widow removes the sandal from the foot of the disobedient brother-in-law, she symbolically removes his right of sexual access to her. The foot and sandal symbolize the male and female organs. Her spit symbolizes Onan's spilling his seed on the ground, useless for procreation. The 'Family of the Unsandaled' is the family that has lost certain procreative rights or powers. The law does not prohibit the brother-in-law from rejecting the levirate marriage, but it exacts a high price in public and enduring humiliation if he chooses, for greed or other reasons, to do so."

I recalled to Hal, from the Iraq war, the television images in 2003 of Iraqis removing their sandals to strike the fallen statue of the evil dictator Saddam Hussein. "Yes," he said, "the custom of striking a person or thing with a sandal to convey insult or humiliation is widespread today in the Middle East. The ceremony—to be acted out at the town gate—of the widow removing the sandal of the brother who refuses to carry out the levirate duty, spitting in (or, some translators say, in front of) his face, and declaring his failure, has roots that persist."

"I understand the message about the husband and wife being one flesh," I said, "even if all the ramifications don't necessarily make sense. But is there any other lesson here?"

Hal took me to 1 Timothy 5:8: "'If anyone does not provide for his relatives, and especially for his immediate family, he has denied the faith and is worse than an unbeliever.'

"For us," Hal said, "the other teaching of the law of levirate marriage is that we are to provide for our family—not just spouse and children, but our larger family, including those to whom we are related by marriage. That doesn't limit our duty to care for other believers—or for the poor, the helpless, or the less fortunate, the widows, orphans, and aliens among us, as Deuteronomy so often instructs—but our own family has a special claim on our care."

"Home is the place where, when you go there, they have to let you in," I concluded, quoting Robert Frost's *Death of the Hired Man.*

Hal smiled. "Frost touched on a lot of religious themes," he said. "That's a discussion for another day. Let's read on."

> If two men get into a fight with each other, and the wife of one comes up to save her husband from his antagonist and she puts out her hand and seizes him by his genitals, you shall cut off her hand; show no pity.
>
> —Deut. 25:11–12

"I can't imagine this happening," I said. "I can't imagine a woman doing it, and I can't imagine the punishment being carried out if she did. What's going on here?"

"We can think of this in three ways," Hal said. "The literal, the symbolic, or the underlying teaching, as it is elaborated in the 'commentary' of the New Testament. Let's look at each one.

"Literally, the harshness of this law, which must have had only the rarest occasion for application, has puzzled even devout Jewish teachers from ancient times. The woman seems to be acting in an understandable way to assist her husband in his struggle. The attack would have been more practical in a time when men wore loose robes without underwear. The offensiveness of her particular act of seizing the genitals of her husband's opponent may stem from the immodesty of her conduct or from the threat to the procreative power of the man. The latter explanation would account for why Moses brought up the rule along with the law on levirate marriage. It's the only specific Old Testament instance of the 'eye for an eye' principle we talked about in chapter nineteen, although a literal 'eye for an eye' isn't possible in this case.

"Symbolically, some believe that the hand is a euphemism for the female genitals. That would implement the eye for an eye principle, although it isn't clear how exactly it would be done unless female circumcision is in mind. Others think that the hand substitutes for an equivalent 'eye for eye' punishment, which would be impossible to do literally. Some Jewish teachers have concluded that the real punishment was to be a fine the equivalent of the value of the woman's hand; others that the law referred to the right of the man whose genitals were seized to the self-defense of cutting off her hand to save his genitals if necessary. Still others think the law applies only to actions taken aggressively by the woman when her husband was not in danger."

"And what did Jesus think?"

"Jesus didn't cite this passage specifically," Hal said, "but he almost certainly had it mind in Matthew five." He turned to the chapter in his New Testament and read verse 30: "'And if your right hand causes you to sin, cut it off and throw it away. It is better for you to lose one part of your body than for your whole body to go into hell.'

"No one thinks Jesus intended that teaching literally," Hal said. "Just before it, he used the same principle in saying that if our eye causes us to sin, we should gouge it out. Yet we don't see Christians going around with missing eyes and hands, and most of us would be blind if we did apply it literally. Jesus is using hyperbole to show us the radical nature of sin and the need to take radical steps to deal with it. And that's the principle we should derive from this passage."

"I never would have connected that passage with this law," I said.

"Jesus often surprises us. The law of levirate marriage becomes a lesson on life in heaven, and a wife who doesn't fight fairly is an example of the severity of sin. And there's another principle here that both Jewish and Christian teachers have derived. It's the familiar principle that the ends don't justify the means. As Luther put it, 'Evil should not be done that good may come of it.' The goal of assisting her husband should not motivate her to the shameful and potentially injurious act of grabbing another man's genitals."

> You shall not have in your pouch alternate weights, larger and smaller. You shall not have in your house alternate measures, a larger and a smaller. You must have completely honest weights and completely honest measures, if you are to endure long on the soil that the LORD your God is giving you. For everyone who does those things, everyone who deals dishonestly, is abhorrent to the LORD your God.
>
> —Deut. 25:13–16

"Isn't this just a call to basic honesty?" I asked. "We have plenty of laws like that today."

"It is," Hal said. "The law of honest measures is a simple and direct command to commercial honesty. Some things haven't changed since biblical times. The inclination of men to dishonesty is evident throughout the Scriptures. Leviticus, Proverbs, Hosea, Amos, and Micah all condemn it. The weights and measures were how people did it in ancient times; now they're more sophisticated. The doctor who bills Medicare for reimbursement he isn't entitled to, the lawyer who pads his time, the merchant who inflates the bill or takes payment in cash and doesn't report it for taxes or who charges personal expenses to his business are all cheaters whose conduct God condemns."

"And what did Jesus say about this?"

Hal smiled. "With the measure you use, it will be measured to you," he responded. "In another words, you'll get what you deserve."

We then read the last law in this chapter, the law of the Amalekites.

> Remember what Amalek did to you on our journey, after you left Egypt—how, undeterred by fear of God, he surprised you on the march, when you were famished and weary, and cut down all the stragglers in your rear. Therefore, when the LORD your God grants you safety from your enemies around you, in the land that the LORD your God is giving you as a hereditary portion, you shall blot out the memory of Amalek from under heaven. Do not forget!
> —Deut. 25:17–19

I thought I knew a little about the Amalekites, and I was sure they weren't in the New Testament. Once again, Hal made the transition from Tanakh to the Scriptures that followed Jesus.

"The Amalekites," he said, "were an ancient enemy of God's people. We first see them in Exodus seventeen, when they attacked Israel on its way out of Egypt. Their particular technique was to attack stragglers, that is, the weak who are in need of assistance. They were a pirate nation, preying on those they should have been helping. They were also without fear of God; they committed their evil acts in defiance of divine righteousness and justice. In Exodus seventeen, fourteen, God declared that he would blot out the memory of Amalek from under heaven as a result of their nature. They were like the nations in the Promised Land that were to be destroyed."

"And were they?"

"Saul's failure to carry out the obliteration of the Amalekites earned him God's displeasure and rejection, as seen in First Samuel fifteen. The many battles with the Amalekites seem to have come to an end in the days of King Hezekiah, when five hundred Simeonites killed the remaining Amalekites, a story told in First Chronicles four. But some descendants persisted. The last mention of Amalekites in the Bible occurs in the book of Esther. The evil Haman, who plotted the death of all of the Jews in the kingdom of Persia, was described as an Agagite, a descendant of the Amalekite king Agag. At the end of the story, as a result of Esther's intervention with King Xerxes, Haman and his ten sons were hanged and their supporters destroyed, and the Jews 'did not lay their hands on the plunder.' This is the completion of the 'herem' destruction of this godless enemy of God and his people."

"So they were gone by New Testament times," I said, "and so is your lesson. On this one, the Tanakh has the last word."

"Not so fast," Hal said, smiling. "Amalek represents the original anti-Semite and the destroyer of God's people. He may be dead as a nation and a people, but he lives on in the satanic destroyers of God's people today. They prey on the weak and helpless and have no fear of justice. They live for their own pleasure and give no concern to what God has in store for them. And they will grow bolder, and the times will grow worse."

He turned to 2 Timothy 3 and read the following:

> But mark this: There will be terrible times in the last days. People will be lovers of themselves, lovers of money, boastful, proud, abusive, disobedient to their parents, ungrateful, unholy, without love, unforgiving, slanderous, without self-control, brutal, not lovers of the good, treacherous, rash, conceited, lovers of pleasure rather than lovers of God—having a form of godliness but denying its power.

"Having a form of godliness but denying its power," I repeated. My mind rushed through the churches I knew where the power of godliness, even the authority of the Scriptures, was denied. Hal read my thought.

"Amalek," he said, "lives on, even within the church."

The cider jug was empty, the chapter finished. Every subject touched on in the chapter, every thought of the Tanakh, reemerged in the New Testament

Scriptures. Sometimes they were simply background to understand Jesus' teachings or Paul's experiences. Sometimes they were reiterated for the same principle. Sometimes they emerged in surprising ways to be the basis of teaching a broader principle from God's mind. One book, I thought as we closed our two books. One story, one author.

Chapter Twenty-Six

M arch winds were blowing, but they were warm winds from the
south. The accumulated snow piles of the long bitter winter
were turning gray and black as they melted away, leaving the detritus
of dirt and bark and leaves concentrated on the remaining surface.
Days were getting longer, and daylight savings time was in sight again.
The sap was flowing in the New England maple groves, and the sugar
shacks performed the seasonal ritual, as cords of wood were consumed
under the long, shallow vats that boiled the watery liquid into the rich,
sweet, brown syrup we loved.

Hal came for dinner and insisted on clearing the table, much to
Anna's dismay. She had set out the china and crystal for him, but he was
indifferent to their value as his frail old hands clanked them together to
haul them to the kitchen.

"Hal," she said, "these are our wedding presents and our memories. I
love that you're helping, but why don't you let me take care of it?"

He set them down, chagrined that his desire to help had alarmed
her.

"You boys go to the living room and light a fire in the fireplace," she
said, assuming her maternal bustle. "I'll join you in a minute."

When the fire was lit and the light danced around the room, pushing
its warmth out from the red brick hearth, she joined us.

"Anna," Hal said, "did you ever make a covenant?"

"I suppose so; I married Chris."

"What do you remember about the ceremony?"

She smiled. "Would you like me to get out the pictures? Just kidding!
There was a lot of preparation: wedding dress, bridesmaids' dresses,
flowers, hair, rehearsal, and rehearsal dinner. We did it in church,
of course. The bridesmaids and maid of honor walked up the aisle

first. Then the organ flourish. I walked up the aisle with my father, and Chris was waiting for me with his best man. The minister went through the ritual: We were before God and the witnesses; I guess that was everyone. We recited the vows, to take each other, in sickness and health, for richer, for poorer, etc. I don't remember it all—till death do us part."

"Why did you marry Chris?" Hal asked. "Did you know him?"

"Silly question," she replied. "Of course I knew him. I wouldn't have married a stranger. In fact, I had known him since high school, and we had been dating for a year and a half before we got married."

"And do you ever celebrate the fact that you got married?"

"Every year," she said. "We always go out to dinner on our anniversary, and he always gives me something—sometimes a little thing, sometimes something really special." She held her right hand out, almost unconsciously, and the firelight glinted and sparkled off a band of tiny rubies and diamonds from our last anniversary.

"Would you like to discuss Deuteronomy with us?" he asked her. I could see Hal meant to include Anna in the discussion tonight, and his questions were not space-filling chatter.

"I'd love to, Hal," she said. "But I don't think I can contribute much. I haven't been in on all your discussions."

"You already have contributed," Hal said. "Did you know Deuteronomy is a covenant, like a marriage covenant?" She didn't, so Hal explained.

"The book of Deuteronomy," he said, "is more than a collection of history, teachings, exhortations, and laws set out or recapitulated to Israel by Moses in his last days. It has the form of an ancient covenant or contract, known as a sovereign-vassal treaty. Forms of such covenants have been found from the Hittite Empire in the second millennium B.C., contemporary with or before Moses' time. They've also been found from the Assyrian Empire, from around the seventh century B.C."

"I didn't know that. But how have I contributed to discussing this?"

"You understand the idea of a covenant," he said, "because you understand the covenant of marriage. Deuteronomy is a little like a big marriage ceremony between God and his people. In fact, the Bible uses marriage all the time as a metaphor for that relationship."

He had her attention. I threw some wood on the fire as he continued.

"The elements of the sovereign-vassal treaty are familiar and match the structure of Deuteronomy. They also are a lot like a marriage. First, there's a preamble. In Deuteronomy, that would be the first five verses of chapter one, just saying what's going on here, like the minister's opening 'dearly beloved' remarks. Second, there is a historical prologue, which recites the gracious acts of the sovereign to the vassal. That part is presumed in the marriage ceremony. It's the 'getting to know you' part. You get married because you know him and love him and trust him, based on your experience with him. It's the same way with Israel. They weren't marrying a stranger. Most of the first four chapters of Deuteronomy tell about the courtship, what God did for them and how he cared for them. Next are the general stipulations, which give the principles that are to guide the relationship, as in chapters five through eleven of Deuteronomy. Then there are the specific stipulations, which give the detailed conduct expected of the other. These are all the detailed laws in chapters twelve through twenty-six. The general and specific stipulations are pretty much like the wedding vows, where you recite how you will behave toward each other. In Deuteronomy, as in the other ancient covenants, there are then blessings and curses for obedience or disobedience of the covenant, as in chapters twenty-seven and twenty-eight. The wedding ceremony doesn't have anything quite the same as this, but there is usually a blessing of the marriage by the pastor or priest. Finally, there are witnesses to the covenant, as in chapters thirty to thirty-two, and your witnesses in the marriage ceremony are God and the wedding guests. The analogy isn't perfect, but you get the idea."

"I do," Anna said, "and I love the analogy. Were all the ancient covenants like that?"

"The covenant structure of Deuteronomy," Hal replied, "while following a form familiar in the ancient world, differs in one particular that makes it unique. In other known sovereign-vassal treaties, the sovereign was the king of the dominant partner: Egypt, Assyria, or the Hittite Empire. The treaty was made with this human sovereign, and obedience was owed to him. In Deuteronomy, the sovereign is no human king, but the Lord himself. In such a treaty, Israel was unique in the ancient world in declaring its allegiance to its God rather than a human ruler."

"Of course," he added, "your marriage may be a covenant, but it isn't a sovereign-vassal treaty."

"In Christ there is no male or female," Anna said, loosely quoting Paul's letter to the Galatians. "You have no idea how helpful that is to modern women coming to Christ."

"Another place where my analogy breaks down," Hal said. "Unlike a marriage, the sovereign-vassal treaty is not between equals."

"This is helpful," Anna said as she picked up her Bible. "So where are you guys, in the treaty or the covenant?"

"We're almost through the wedding vows," Hal said. "Chapter twenty-six is the end of the specific laws. After this we go on to the blessings and curses for obedience and disobedience and ceremonies to establish or commemorate the covenant."

Hal showed Anna that an important transition in the covenant structure occurs in chapter twenty-six. This chapter closes the specific stipulations, or detailed laws, that began with chapter twelve, concluding with two ceremonial celebrations of the covenant and a summary by Moses of the essence of the covenant itself. The chapter, he explained, mirrors chapter twelve, the opening chapter of the specific laws, with instructions for worship where the Lord will choose to place his Name after they have entered the land. The two chapters constitute a frame (bookends) around the law. Before the law was given, Israel was taught what its relationship to God was to be. After the law was given, Moses taught about the results of obedience or disobedience. In between are the laws, with their specific instruction on proper worship, holiness, government, justice, punishment of crimes, war, family relationships, and care for the poor.

"It's like a wedding," Anna observed. "First the bridesmaids, then the bride with her father walk up the aisle. Then after the ceremony she walks back down with her husband, followed by the attendants. I never thought of the balance to it, the mirror image in how it begins and ends."

I could smell the baking cookies; Anna excused herself for a few minutes. When she came back, she had a plate of fresh-from-the-oven chocolate-chip cookies, the chocolate still hot and melted in the warm, moist dough. She passed them around, and Hal took two. Then he read.

> When you have entered the land the Lord your God is giving you as an inheritance and have taken possession of it and settled in it, take some of the firstfruits of all that you produce from the soil of the land the Lord your God is giving you and put them in a basket. Then go to the place the Lord your God will choose as a dwelling for his Name and say to the priest in office at the time, "I declare today to the Lord your God that I have come to the land the Lord swore to our forefathers to give us." The priest shall take the basket from your hands and set it down in front of the altar of the Lord your God.

> Then you shall declare before the Lord your God: "My father was a wandering Aramean, and he went down into Egypt with a few people and lived there and became a great nation, powerful and numerous. But the Egyptians mistreated us and made us suffer, putting us to hard labor. Then we cried out to the Lord, the God of our fathers, and the Lord heard our voice and saw our misery, toil and oppression. So the Lord brought us out of Egypt with a mighty hand and an outstretched arm, with great terror and with miraculous signs and wonders. He brought us to this place and gave us this land, a land flowing with milk and honey; and now I bring the firstfruits of the soil that you, O Lord, have given me." Place the basket before the Lord your God and bow down before him. And you and the Levites and the aliens among you shall rejoice in all the good things the Lord your God has given to you and your household.
>
> —Deut. 26:1–11

"That doesn't sound much like our little anniversary dinners, Hal," Anna said.

"I told you my analogy was imperfect," Hal replied. "But it's still like an anniversary party. The ceremony of firstfruits was performed after the people had entered the land and taken possession of it, like you celebrate your anniversary after you have come into the marriage and experienced it. The people perform the ceremony in response to, and in fulfillment of, God's promise of the good land to them, just as marriage is the promise of the 'good land' of each other. They recite a liturgical prayer, acknowledging that they have come into the land of promise. The firstfruits are offered through the priest, and the worshipper utters another liturgical prayer. He remembers his homeless, wandering ancestry and his oppression in Egypt. He remembers God's mighty and miraculous acts in bringing him out of that place and into a land full of good things the worshipper did not create. He brings his offering before the Lord and rejoices in all the good things God has given him."

Hal's metaphor of the firstfruits ceremony as an anniversary was beginning to come through to me. "I know a lot of people are happy being single," I said, "but this resonates with me. Being single was like being a wandering Aramean, and getting married really was like coming into a land full of good things I didn't create."

"And so it should be," Hal said. "But let's take it a step further. The real analogy here isn't about the marriage covenant. I've been using it because you're both familiar with it. But this Scripture is rich with meaning for the Christian life.

"All Christian believers are the true Israel; they have been brought out of a life of sin and darkness, where they wandered and were oppressed, and into a land of light and life, where they have a home. They have been brought out, as Israel was from Egypt, by God's miraculous and powerful hand. When they worship properly, they have memory and gratitude. They acknowledge what God has done for them, their prior hopeless situation, and the good land he has brought them into, and they give their offering to him in rejoicing."

He rose and moved over to the table and took another cookie. "I'm too old to worry about the calories," he said. "I don't cut the fat off the meat either."

He looked at Anna. "Great cookies. I wish I still had someone to bake for me." He paused to enjoy them. I put another log on the fire.

"Anna," he resumed, "God is not just the God of nature who gives physical sustenance, the stuff you make your cookies out of, so to speak. He's also the God of history. He rescues us from oppression, whether that's the oppression of loneliness—like what I think Chris meant when he said he felt like a wandering Aramean before he met you—or the oppression of tyranny—like the Israelites experienced in Egypt—or the oppression of sin to which we are all subject. He is the giver of all good. This is a ceremony of remembering who we were and who we have become through God's gracious gifts to us."

Anna's face was somber. Hal's words were not bouncing off her but adhering and being absorbed. She was beginning to feel their power, as one who is immersed in the Scriptures comes to know the power of God's word, how it can be described as a sword, "dividing soul and spirit, joints and marrow, judging the thoughts and attitudes of the heart."

He handed her his Bible. "Now read the next four verses."

Anna read.

> When you have finished setting aside a tenth of all your produce in the third year, the year of the tithe, you shall give it to the Levite, the alien, the fatherless, and the widow, so that they may eat in your towns and be satisfied. Then say to the LORD your God: "I have removed from my house the sacred portion and have given it to the Levite, the alien, the fatherless and the widow, according to all you commanded. I have not turned aside from your commands nor have I forgotten any of them. I have not eaten any of the sacred portion while I was in mourning, nor have I removed any of it while I was unclean, nor have I offered any of it to the dead. I have obeyed the LORD my God; I have done everything you commanded me. Look down from heaven, your holy dwelling place, and bless your people Israel and the land you have given us as you promised on oath to our forefathers, a land flowing with milk and honey."
>
> —Deut. 26:12–15

"What's the difference between this section and the first?" Hal asked.

"This first part seemed to be directed more to God," Anna said hesitantly. "This section seems to be more about people."

"Good," Hal said. "The firstfruits ceremony is an act of 'vertical worship,' where the worshipper directs his attention and offering to God, the source of all good things he has granted.

"Now we're looking at the tithing ceremony of the third year," he continued. "It moves on to the 'horizontal' aspect of worship and obedience. This is the tithe that Chris and I studied back in chapter fourteen. It's commanded for the Levite, the alien or foreigner, the fatherless and the widow. There are many other provisions in Deuteronomy for the protection of these people who lack the means to sustain themselves. This is the fulfillment of the second greatest commandment—as Jesus says—of love of neighbor."

"Love God and love your neighbor. The two great commandments," Anna said.

"Just so," Hal replied. "And again there is a liturgy, a ceremony in which the worshipper declares his compliance with the law in respect to his tithe: He has provided it to the needy as instructed, he has withheld none of it, and he has not used any of it in an offensive manner. Providing for the needy is a sacred duty, a paradigm of love of God. Sacred rites don't make up for the disobedience of social wrongs.

"He concludes with a prayer for blessing, not for himself, but for the nation."

"Did they say all this in public?" I asked.

"Oh, yes," Hal replied. "There is a public accountability here for the tithe. The worshipper must bring it and declare before the Lord that he has done so in compliance with the law. The responsibility of the one who had been brought out of slavery to freedom was to provide the same for others."

Anna said, "I don't think many people in our church would welcome having to stand up in public and declare they had faithfully provided for the needy and not misused any of what God has given them."

"Nor in any other church," Hal said. "I sometimes wonder what would happen to our church treasuries if people had to engage in a public accountability before God like this."

"And the good things the church could do in the world," I added.

Anna and I looked at each other across the room. In the silent speech that people who have long been close to each other have, I knew she was telling me to recalculate the checkbook and be sure we were performing our responsibilities before God.

I acknowledged the thought, knowing, as her eyes searched my face, that she knew I was doing so. She looked back at Hal when the communication was complete. He was reading on. She closed her eyes and bowed her head as he spoke God's words.

> The LORD your God commands you this day to follow these decrees and laws; carefully observe them with all your heart and with all your soul. You have declared this day that the LORD is your God and that you will walk in his ways, that you will keep his decrees, commands and laws, and that you will obey him. And the LORD has declared this day that you are his people, his treasured possession as he promised, and that you are to keep all his commands. He has declared that he will set you in praise, fame and honor high above all the nations he has made and that you will be a people holy to the LORD your God, as he promised.
>
> —Deut. 26:16–19

It was as mutual as the covenant Anna and I had just made with our eyes. God's people declare that he is their God and that they will obey him. He declares that they are his people, that they are to keep his commands, and that he will set them in holy honor above the nations.

"These things," Hal said quietly, looking into the ebbing fire, "are to happen 'this day.' It's a term God uses a lot in Deuteronomy. Every day is 'today' in the believer's life. God's mercies are new every morning. Every day he commits himself to his people anew, and every day we undertake to obey him."

"And if we do," Anna said, paraphrasing the Scripture, "he'll set us 'high above all he nations he has made, and we'll be a people holy to the Lord.'"

"Yes," Hal said, "but understand that it's not for our glory but for his own. God's people are to be the light not hid under a bushel, the city on a hill, which will draw all men to God."

CHAPTER TWENTY-SIX

There was silence between us until Anna broke it abruptly.

"God," she said, "what a failure I am."

I knew her well enough to know she was speaking a prayer of confession to her Creator, not just using his name for thoughtless emphasis.

The look on her face told me she meant it. Every thoughtless ingratitude, every judgmental remark, every gossipy untruth, every selfish purchase that kept us from helping others, every moment of forgetting the abundance we had compared to our parents, or theirs before them, or even our own childhood, was written in pain on her face. If Hal hadn't been there I would have embraced her, reassured her, reminded her of all her kind and selfless moments, and kissed away her pain. But Hal was there, so I didn't move. Was her self judgment accurate? I wasn't sure. But Hal was.

"Of course you're a failure," he said. "We all are. We claim to love God, but we love our own life more. We think we obey him because we obey the law and do good things in people's eyes, but we don't really obey. We give to get our names in a book the charity publishes so everyone will know what generous people we are. If we're rich enough to give enough, we want buildings and scholarships and programs named after us. We forget his goodness to us, and that all we are and have comes from him. We don't thank him, or we do it perfunctorily. We let other people do the praying and the work for him, and even the giving, and think we're on the right side because we show up in church from time to time and stay out of jail. We give out of our surplus and not systematically. We couldn't honestly face human accountability, never mind God, who knows our hearts. It's not an excuse, and some do better than that. But yes, Anna, you are a failure."

He rose and went to her. Standing behind her chair, his gnarled fingers rested on her shoulders. The light from the fireplace shone on one side of them, illuminating Hal, but leaving Anna in the darkness of his shadow. They say some men are so close to their wives that they experience the physical distress of pregnancy when she does: nausea, food cravings, and the feeling of movement in the belly from the activity of the developing child. That night I experienced the spiritual distress Anna was feeling—that moment of looking down, as someone has said, and seeing the blood on your hands, of the companion who whispers, "Flee, all is discovered."[14] But I also felt Hal's hands on her shoulders as surely as if they rested on my own. I bowed my head and felt their strength flow into me, and I knew that the Holy Spirit that dwelled in Hal was even then flowing into Anna, as surely as if his blood was flowing out of his body and into hers.

"Anna," he said softly, "it is only in Christ that we have any hope of avoiding failure. Be immersed in him. Be in him now."

He bowed his head and prayed, the words low and indistinguishable, but flowing out like the Spirit itself. I bowed too and allowed myself to be bathed in a prayer I could not hear or understand but knew was present. As the low sound of Hal's words to his God and ours went forth, I could see the Hebrew farmer bringing his basket of produce up the temple steps to the priest and reciting the story of his people's salvation before his God—"My father was a wandering Aramean"—and making his tithe to the less fortunate with his declaration: "I have done everything you commanded me."

The fire was low, and a chill had set into the room, but a strange warmth rose up in me and surrounded me as I reflected on God's gifts. I considered life itself, the mind and body that enabled me to be all that I was, and to have all that I have—Anna; Hal and the knowledge of God he had brought into my life; the wonderful forgiveness and freedom I experienced when I first truly realized what it meant to say that Christ had died for my sins—and then my ingratitude, forgetfulness, disobedience, and failure to share the good things of God, both material and spiritual, with those in need.

When Hal had finished laying hands on Anna and praying, he wished us grace and peace from the Lord Jesus Christ, then picked up his coat and was out the door before we could say goodbye or offer him some cookies to take with him.

I put my arm around Anna's shoulder as we watched Hal disappear into the night. At last she turned her face up to mine. The pain was gone, and a certain beatitude had replaced it. "Now I know why you're doing what you're doing with him. What a man of God he truly is."

CHAPTER TWENTY-SEVEN

Anna was eager to get in on the remainder of our Deuteronomy study. "What should I do to catch up?" she asked over coffee the next morning.

"Well, you probably need to read the book up to here," I said, offering the obvious. "And then, well, how about asking Hal?"

We read Deuteronomy 27 and prayed together before going our ways for the day.

> Moses and the elders of Israel commanded the people: "Keep all these commands that I give you today. When you have crossed the Jordan into the land the LORD your God is giving you, set up some large stones and coat them with plaster. Write on them all the words of this law when you have crossed over to enter the land the LORD your God is giving you, a land flowing with milk and honey, just as the LORD, the God of your fathers, promised you. And when you have crossed the Jordan, set up these stones on Mount Ebal, as I command you today, and coat them with plaster. Build there an altar to the LORD your God, an altar of stones. Do not use any iron tool upon them. Build the altar of the LORD your God with fieldstones and offer burnt offerings on it to the LORD your God. Sacrifice fellowship offerings there, eating them and rejoicing in the presence of the LORD your God. And you shall write very clearly all the words of this law on these stones you have set up."

> Then Moses and the priests, who are Levites, said to all Israel, "Be silent, O Israel, and listen! You have now become the people of the LORD your God. Obey the LORD your

God and follow his commands and decrees that I give you today."

On the same day Moses commanded the people:

When you have crossed the Jordan, these tribes shall stand on Mount Gerizim to bless the people: Simeon, Levi, Judah, Issachar, Joseph, and Benjamin. And these tribes shall stand on Mount Ebal to pronounce curses: Reuben, Gad, Asher, Zebulun, Dan, and Naphtali.

The Levites shall recite to all the people of Israel in a loud voice:

"Cursed is the man who carves an image or casts an idol—a thing detestable to the LORD, the work of the craftsman's hands—and sets it up in secret."

Then all the people shall say, "Amen!"

"Cursed is the man who dishonors his father or his mother." Then all the people shall say, "Amen!"

"Cursed is the man who moves his neighbor's boundary stone."

Then all the people shall say, "Amen!"

"Cursed is the man who leads the blind astray on the road."

Then all the people shall say, "Amen!"

"Cursed is the man who withholds justice from the alien, the fatherless or the widow."

Then all the people shall say, "Amen!"

"Cursed is the man who sleeps with his father's wife, for he dishonors his father's bed."

Then all the people shall say, "Amen!"

"Cursed is the man who has sexual relations with any animal."

Then all the people shall say, "Amen!"

"Cursed is the man who sleeps with his sister, the daughter of his father or the daughter of his mother."

Then all the people shall say, "Amen!"

"Cursed is the man who sleeps with his mother-in-law."

Then all the people shall say, "Amen!"

"Cursed is the man who kills his neighbor secretly."

Then all the people shall say, "Amen!"

"Cursed is the man who accepts a bribe to kill an innocent person."

Then all the people shall say, "Amen!"

"Cursed is the man who does not uphold the words of this law by carrying them out."

Then all the people shall say, "Amen!"

—Deut. 27:1–26

Anna e-mailed Hal just as I had suggested. When I got home that night she showed me his response:

> Anna: When Chris first started studying Deuteronomy, he loved the history and geography of it. After he understood the road map, he was more open to the spiritual significance. Why don't you start the same way? Chapter twenty-seven is great for background. Read up on it, and let us know what

you find out. Remember always that God loves you and made you for himself. Blessings, Hal.

She looked at me expectantly. I pointed out the books on my shelf about Deuteronomy, and the ones I thought were the best. She scooped up an armful and retreated to the living room with them. Before Hal came over again, she had written a whole essay on the history and geography behind chapter twenty-seven and e-mailed it to Hal. This is what she wrote:

> Mount Ebal and Mount Gerizim, the mountains that are the scene of the ceremonies in the twenty-seventh chapter of Deuteronomy, are near the biblical town of Shechem. Shechem is an ancient crossroads town about forty miles north of Jerusalem. When the patriarch Abraham, then still known as Abram, came into the land of Canaan, his first recorded stop was at Shechem. It lies at the eastern end of an east-west valley, the only pass through the range of hills in the area, where north-south and east-west roads come together. Here God appeared to him—as told in Genesis 12—and first promised that he would give the land to Abram's off-spring. Here Abram built an altar to worship God, the first of several he built at spiritually significant sites.
>
> Abraham's grandson, Jacob, as told in Genesis 33 visited Shechem again.
>
> Jacob bought a plot of land there, pitched his tent, and built an altar he called El Elohe Israel, or "Mighty is the God of Israel."
>
> Shechem was the scene of the rape of Jacob's daughter, Dinah, by a man also called Shechem, the son of the ruler of the area, who, despite his ill-treatment of her, was taken with her and wanted to marry her. Dinah's brothers deceitfully agreed to the marriage if the men of Shechem would be circumcised. Three days after the circumcisions, while the men were still in pain, her brothers Levi and Simeon avenged her disgrace by killing every male in the unsuspecting city. The women

and children and everything else of the Shechemites were taken as plunder. Jacob, fearing retaliation by neighboring Canaanites and Perizzites, had his household turn over all their foreign gods to him, which he buried under the oak of Shechem; then they fled south to Bethel.

Jacob's son Joseph, before he died in Egypt, asked his brothers to carry his bones "up from this place." The Israelites carried his bones with them when they left Egypt. At Shechem the ancient promise to Joseph was fulfilled, when, as told in Joshua 24, his bones were buried in the tract that his father Jacob had bought.

Shechem is flanked by two mountains, Ebal to the north and Gerizim to the south, both around 3,000 feet in height, though Ebal is several hundred feet the higher. From the peak of Mount Ebal, one gets a view of most of the land, the Jordan valley to the east, the Mediterranean Sea to the west, Mount Hermon to the north, and the Jerusalem hills to the south. In Deuteronomy 27 the Israelites were directed to Mount Ebal—the site where God first promised the land to Abraham—for ceremonies to commemorate the fulfillment of the promise made hundreds of years earlier.

Shechem is about thirty miles from the Jordan Valley but sixty miles from the crossing point on the Plains of Moab where Israel entered the land. A literal rendering of the text of Deuteronomy 27 would have Israel accomplishing the commanded erection of the stones with the law written on them, and the altar, on Mount Ebal on the day of crossing, leading ancient Jewish commentators to speculate on the miraculous nature of their accomplishment in traversing the distance, erecting the stones and altar, and writing the law on them, all in one day. The NIV text probably captures the real meaning by simply saying that these things were to be done "when" they crossed the Jordan. In fact, as the book of Joshua relates, the Israelites camped at Gilgal near the crossing point and conquered Jericho and Ai before they enacted the ceremonies at Shechem prescribed by Deuteronomy, chapter twenty-seven.

Moses gave the command to build the stones and altar—and the commands that follow concerning the ceremony of blessings and curses on the two mountains—in conjunction with the elders of Israel and the Levite priests. This sharing of authority and instruction was appropriate to the circumstance: Moses was teaching about what would take place after his death. The elders and priests were the ones who would carry it out. The presence of the elders in this ceremony marking the fulfillment of the promise was also a tying-up of the acknowledgment of Moses' authority. In Deuteronomy 5, the elders ask Moses to represent them before a God who is so terrifying that they fear death in facing him. At this point, nearly forty years later, Moses had carried out the function they'd delegated to him, and, after he passes on, they appear to resume the reins of national leadership under Joshua.

The people were instructed to set up large stones, coated with plaster, on which "all the words of this law" were to be written. Such stones are called *steles*. The practice of writing on plaster-coated stones or steles was common in Egypt and was well known to these people. Paint for writing was made of ivory or bone black, from bones heated in closed containers. Much commentary, beginning with ancient Jewish sages, focuses on what exactly was to be written. Some, thinking the stones could scarcely accommodate the writing of all of the law that Moses had given, think only the Decalogue or some summary injunctions such as the Shema or the law against idolatry were inscribed. A line of fanciful Jewish thought—focusing on the statement in verse eight that the words of the law are to be written "very clearly"—postulates that the whole law was written in seventy languages, representing the communication of the Torah to the known peoples of the ancient world. Leaders of other nations are supposed to have come to read it. The rejection of Torah by the other nations justifies God's condemnation of them.

It is likely that what was written was the whole law given in Deuteronomy, written in legible Hebrew, a literal reading of the text and an instruction that certainly could have been carried out. Some ancient steles were large enough, especially if two were used together, to accommodate the writing of all the law of Deuteronomy. The use of such upright stone structures to publicly record law is known from various ancient sources and archeological digs. God was particular in a number of instances in Deuteronomy to use the written word to preserve his instruction: God himself inscribed the Ten Commandments on stone tablets in chapters five and ten, we see that the commandments were to be tied to the hands and foreheads and written on houses and city gates in 6:8–9 and 11:18–21, we see that the king was to write for himself a copy of the law taken from the priests and read it all the days of his life in 17:18–19 and in chapter 31 Moses himself wrote down a copy of the law and gave it to the priests for preservation and future reading. The recording of the law on a public stele for all to see and read was consistent with the whole thrust of Deuteronomy to teach through the word.

Along with the stele of the law, the people were instructed to build an altar of fieldstones (uncut or undressed stone) on Mount Ebal. The reason for using fieldstone is unclear, but is consistent with the instruction in Exodus 20:25. It is likely the purpose was either to distinguish it from Canaanite altars or to avoid having to call on Canaanite craftsmen to perform the work. In Joshua 17, we learn that the Canaanites had iron chariots, which the Israelites did not. Israel may have lacked the tools to dress the stone.

Whether the altar and the stone monument on which the law is to be written are the same or different structures has also occasioned controversy. Archaeological investigations on the top of Mount Ebal have discovered a fieldstone altar there some twenty by thirty feet in size, with walls four feet thick and nine feet high. This altar was filled with dirt and ashes, had a ramp to the top, and was surrounded by a courtyard and animal bones, consistent with the sacrifices Moses had instructed to be offered there. Pottery on the site dates to the thirteenth century B.C., near the time of Joshua.

The altar structure does not have the law inscribed on it. Either the inscription was on a different structure, or the writing was less permanent than other such ancient inscriptions. There is good reason to believe that this is indeed the altar of Deuteronomy 27.

The peaks of Mounts Ebal and Gerizim are only 2.2 miles apart. At the eastern end of the valley between them, the mountains are less than 1,700 feet apart, barely over a quarter of a mile. Farther west, they are about 4,300 feet apart, about eight-tenths of a mile. On the westerly approaches are two spots where natural amphitheaters face one another. At the easterly approach, or given the accommodating atmospheric conditions, at the westerly amphitheaters, the ceremonies of the Levites speaking to the tribes assembling on the two mountains, as described in chapter twenty-seven, or the tribes pronouncing blessings and curses to each other, can actually occur with all parties audible to one another. There is nothing fanciful in this ceremony. An 1839 lithograph by David Roberts kept in the Equinox Archives in Oxford and reproduced in Rogerson's Atlas of the Bible shows the entrance to Nablus, the modern West Bank town just west of the ruins, where ancient Shechem was. The two mountains come together at a pass just beyond the small town, minarets rise above the white stone houses, and a retinue of travelers on foot and camel are coming up the road toward the foreground. One can imagine the twelve tribes in the time of Joshua, assembled where the mountains approach each other, carrying out the antiphony of the ceremony.

After the conquest of Ai, as told in Joshua 8, Joshua led the building of the altar, copying the law onto stones, and the ceremony of recitation of blessings and curses at Mounts Ebal and Gerizim. There is no account of the conquest of Shechem under Joshua, leading to speculation that the destruction of the population in Jacob's time—in revenge for the rape of Dinah—was complete, or that a remnant of Israelites that never went to Egypt remained there and welcomed the Israelite conquerors. At the end of his life,

Joshua brought the people back to Shechem for a covenant-renewal ceremony; the story is told in Joshua 24. After reciting the glorious history of God's dealing with Israel, from Abraham to the conquest of the land, Joshua challenged them to choose between the Lord, who had done all this for them, and the old and foreign gods they served in Egypt and beyond the river Jordan. He concluded with this familiar declaration: "But as for me and my household, we will serve the Lord."

Shechem continued to be a pivotal site in many Old Testament historical events. In Judges 9:7, for example, Jotham climbed Mount Gerizim to speak to the people. A ledge on the mountain today is the traditional "Jotham's pulpit." Shechem was in the territory of the tribe of Ephraim and became part of Samaria or the Northern Kingdom when Israel divided into two kingdoms after Solomon. When the Assyrians conquered the Northern Kingdom and deported its population, they brought in peoples they were deporting from other parts of their conquests to live there. These people—either through contact with the Jews of the neighboring Southern Kingdom of Judah or with remnants of the Jewish population that survived the Assyrian conquest and deportation—developed what is known as the Samaritan Pentateuch, a virtual copy of the Jewish Torah except that it identifies Mount Gerizim as the place where God will place his name, as taught in Deuteronomy.

The Samaritan Pentateuch is an important document in biblical studies and is evident in John 4, when Jesus confronted the Samaritan woman at Jacob's well, near the plot Jacob had bought in Shechem nearly two millennia earlier. The woman at the well told Jesus, "Our fathers worshipped on this mountain, but you Jews claim that the place where we must worship is in Jerusalem." The mountain she is referring to is Gerizim, and her authority is the Samaritan Pentateuch. The conflicting interpretations between Samaritan and Jewish understanding of the meaning of the place where God would place his name were familiar to her. The issue she discussed with Jesus at the site of the ceremonies of Deuteronomy 27 was Deuteronomy.

Mount Gerizim has been the site of a Samaritan temple, a temple to Jupiter, and a Christian church. In modern times the several hundred surviving Samaritans sacrifice a lamb there yearly for Passover. The town of Shechem is the present-day West Bank city of Nablus, the site of ongoing controversy between Israelis and Palestinians, who are its principal inhabitants.

"This essay," Hal said, "would get an A in any Bible college. It should get an A in any college, but some professors wouldn't give you a good grade unless you found some ground to tear the text apart. Says more about them than their students, but that's the way it is."

He stopped for a muffin and a cup of coffee on a Saturday morning. He had to go to Boston that day, he said. But we could talk about Deuteronomy for a while.

He began the discussion by taking us back to the idea of structure. He reminded us of the marriage ceremony—framed by the bridesmaids, then the bride—coming up the aisle at the beginning, and coming down the aisle in reverse order at the end. "This chapter, along with chapter eleven, forms another frame around the law. Just as chapters twelve and twenty-six begin and end the law with instructions on worship, chapters eleven and twenty-seven both teach that there is to be a ceremony on Mount Ebal and Mount Gerizim, and that blessings and curses for obedience or disobedience are involved. Deuteronomy has structure throughout; nothing is accidental. There is the structure of the covenant treaty that we talked about last time: the prologue, the history of God's good things given to his people, the general then the specific rules, the ceremony of commitment, the blessings and curses, and the witnesses. But there is also the harmonic structure of the ebb and flow of the text, the chiasms, and the literary framework into which God's word is placed.

"Building the altar, writing the law, and ceremonies of blessings and curses at Shechem were fitting to the monumental and momentous nature of the occasion.

"Not only does this chapter mirror chapter eleven in framing the laws that are given in between, but it also mirrors promises made to Abraham hundreds of years earlier and repeated to Isaac and Jacob. These promises were first made here at Shechem. Here they were fulfilled through God's miraculous and gracious intervention. The people had been liberated from slavery, survived forty years in the desert wilderness, defeated their enemies, and entered the Promised Land. Now they return to Shechem, where Abraham first entered the land and received the promises, and pause to commemorate the event."

"I like the part about writing the law on the stones," I said. "That makes God's word a public monument that everyone can see."

"Yes," Hal said, "the public reminder of the foundation of the society was there for everyone to see. But you couldn't do that today, at least in this country. The Ten Commandments have been banned from classrooms and courtrooms. Any public reference to anything religious, any public symbolism of the spiritual, is driven from our sight. Religion, in the view of most Americans, is something to be kept to oneself, in the closet. Some people even think it's improper to rely on religious belief for judgments on any legal or moral issues, as if anyone could separate their core values as to what the universe is all about from those kinds of judgments."

I could see the fire in his eyes light up as Hal meditated on the foolishness of people who claim that their personal moral views can't be "imposed" on anyone else by law. "I suppose the Bible's prohibition of murder and robbery should prevent our society from doing likewise," he said. "Makes as much sense as saying we can't legislate against abortion because religions do so." He shook his head. "And intelligent people think that, or claim they do. What kind of education do they get in these supposedly great universities anyway?"

He looked away, gazing out the window as if seeing the corruption of education, logic, law, and human thought spread over the landscape before us. I once had a dream of Jesus doing the same thing. He was in the sky, and his head was hooded, his face slightly concealed. But he was looking out over his creation. He didn't speak or identify himself, but I knew who he was, as one does in dreams, and I could see his thoughts in his darkened face, as I could see Hal's at that moment. He was brooding over his creation, and I could almost hear his thoughts from the Scriptures: "O Jerusalem, Jerusalem, you who kill the prophets and stone those sent to you, how often I have longed to gather your children together, as a hen gathers her chicks under her wings, but you were not willing."

After a few moments, Hal turned back to us and resumed the discussion. "In the God-ordained society of Deuteronomy, we see how it ought to be. The law, spiritual as well as secular, is one, derived from God the Creator who teaches his people the nature of a society in harmony with his creation. Putting the law up for everyone to read is not a bad idea, even now.

"Besides," he continued, "even if we can't post the scriptural law in public, we can at least read it in our churches. One of the greatest failures of evangelical worship is the inattention to public reading of the Scriptures. In Judaism and in the liturgical churches, they are much more systematic in bringing the Scriptures forward in public reading. We evangelical types don't spend nearly as much time reading the Scriptures in worship. We just sort of assume people read their Bibles, so we spend sermon after sermon telling stories and illustrating this or that verse instead of making the whole thing part of the worship. Sometimes I'm surprised at how much people who may not believe it or follow the Bible know about it. They know it because they'd gone to a church where it is at least read."

"I know those people too," I said. "But it doesn't seem to have done much for them."

"That's because they were just read to and not taught," Hal said. "Anyone can hear it as an empty form and not make it part of their life. I once knew a pastor who had been in ministry for ten years before he was born again. It was an academic or traditional exercise for him up until then. After that it was part of his life. Then it became part of his church's life too. The church doubled in size in about three years."

Anna interrupted our digressions. "I have an observation," she said.

"Go ahead," Hal encouraged her.

"Last time, you showed us that the two ceremonies in chapter twenty-six, the firstfruits and the tithes, were vertical and horizontal. The firstfruits were a sacrifice to God, a thanksgiving for what he had done for them—the first commandment, to love God. It was the vertical relationship, man looking up to God. The tithes, then, were the horizontal relationship—serving others, loving neighbors, the gift for the needy in obedience to God's commands.

"Now, when I read this chapter, I see the same pattern. The two sacrifices to be made at the altar on Mount Ebal were vertical and horizontal. The burnt offering in verse six represents the vertical worship, our relationship with God. The fellowship offering, in verse seven, was to be consumed with others, like the horizontal nature of our duty to God, loving our neighbors. Together, these two sacrifices represent the first and second greatest commandments—love God, and love your neighbors."

"That's an A for class discussion," Hal said in his professorial mode. "You are a quick learner. The ceremonies in the last chapter are to be repeated. The ceremonies in this chapter are a one-time event, celebrating the fulfillment of the ancestral promises. But both sets of ceremonies follow the same pattern. They are first vertical and then horizontal, worshipping God and sharing with others. And both show us that we must remind ourselves regularly of our election and redemption. When we do that, we make the personal and historical facts behind them real, ongoing, and renewed."

I asked Hal what he thought about Anna's section on the woman Jesus met at the well in John 4.

"The meeting between Jesus and the woman at the well," Hal said, "occurred, as Anna pointed out, at the very place where this chapter sets the scene. There was to be a dramatic exchange of recited curses between the tribes, from mountain to mountain. When Jesus met the Samaritan woman, he stood on ground that had a long spiritual history. He used the historic location to teach some of the great truths about himself and God's relationship to humanity."

"And what are those truths?" Anna asked.

"The conversation was with a Samaritan woman," Hal said. "Jews hated the Samaritans, and it was thought inappropriate or beneath most Jewish males to have such a conversation with a Samaritan, or even with a woman. Jesus broke through both stereotypes in a setting that went back to the promise of the land to Abraham, made in this very location. In Christ there is no Jew nor Greek, male nor female. He also demonstrated his knowledge of her immoral lifestyle, although he didn't preach to her about it. Rather, he taught her about himself. The lifestyle would take care of itself if she came to him.

"Then he taught her a little theology. She was kind of a Pharisee, or a legalist. She thought it was important where God was worshipped and that Jews and Samaritans disagreed about that. It's kind of like the differences between charismatics and fundamentalists on how worship is to be conducted. Jesus cleared up her assumption that the physical location of worship is important to God. Rather, it is worship in spirit and in truth that is important. The object of that worship was right there before her. He is the living water she needed. At the end of the conversation, she became a missionary to her own people, bringing them the good news of Jesus Christ. God promised Abraham that through him all the nations of the earth would be blessed, and here, Jesus the Jew is extending the blessing to these hated Samaritans."

Our discussion then turned to the ceremony of blessings and curses, and the list of curses. The tribes' specific blessings and curses, to be exchanged on the opposing mountains, are not given. But the list of curses to be led by the Levites is given. In the "Cursed be . . ." formula, the people called divine sanction on wrongdoers, even if they were themselves.

The behaviors on which the Levites pronounced curses seemed to me a curious list. "It is selective," Hal said. "It's representative rather than complete, poetical, and designed for teaching and memory. It pretty much covers the spectrum of types of behavior that God condemns in Deuteronomy: idolatry, dishonoring parents, theft of property, taking advantage of the helpless or less fortunate, improper sexual relations, murder, and bribery. There are probably twelve behaviors selected for curses to reflect the twelve tribes, a symmetry of organization of the people with organization of the cursed behaviors.

"The 'Amen' that the people utter after each 'Cursed be . . .' is their affirmation of the cursed nature of the behavior, in effect condemning themselves if they are guilty of it. It's a pledge of obedience and an acceptance of judgment for guilt. In Jeremiah 28:6, 'Amen' is followed by the declaration 'May the Lord do so,' which probably captures the essence of the meaning."

"Like giving an oath in court?" I asked. "Promising to tell the truth, so help me God?"

"That's a good modern equivalent to it," Hal said. "In the 'so help me God' part of the court oath, it retains the nature of calling on a divine sanction for not telling the truth."

"Is there any common thread here?" Anna asked. "Anything that ties these curses together?"

Hal answered, "Jewish and Christian commentators have seen a common thread in these curses. They all curse behavior that is likely to be done in secret. Two of them are specific on this: casting and setting up an idol in secret, and killing a neighbor in secret. Moving a boundary stone would be a secret act. Leading the blind astray is an act, which, by its nature, makes it hard to identify the wrongdoer. Withholding justice from the alien, the fatherless, or the widow may be difficult to detect because the person treated unjustly may not understand the injustice, or may be powerless to do anything about it. The sexual behaviors condemned are ones that are easiest to commit without detection: bestiality in the field, where no humans are around, and sex with family members—stepmother, sister, mother-in-law—that a man would be around in the household normally. . . . And acceptance of bribes is, by its nature, secret."

"So what we have here is a condemnation of hidden sins," I said. "We've seen that before in Deuteronomy."

"Yes," Hal said. "God sees the heart, and he sees what we do when others aren't looking. The secret theft, the secret sexual sin, the secret betrayal of God, is not secret to him. Israel was, by these declarations, purging the community of guilt for undetected and unpunished crime, much as the ceremonies of chapter twenty-one absolved the community of responsibility for unsolved murders. Martin Luther said, 'If you look at the surface, he is holy; but if you look at the heart, there is no work so shameful that he would not do it if shame, fear and penalty were not in the way.' We honor God by behaving as he's told us to, even when no one else is looking."

"Why did he include leading the blind astray in verse eighteen?" Anna asked. "That seems a purposeless and rare form of wrong. Surely blind people don't spend a lot of time wandering around on the road. And what reason would someone have, other than pure meanness, to lead them astray?"

"From the earliest times," Hal replied, "this teaching has been generalized to instruct that we are not to lead astray anyone who can't see for himself. In religious terms, the church father Ireneaus applied it to the Gnostics, one of the heresies that abounded in the days of the early church. In First Thessalonians four, six, Paul applied the idea to sexual sins: 'in this matter no one should wrong his brother or take advantage of him.'

"And when Jesus taught that about the woes that come to those who cause 'little ones' to sin, I don't think he was limiting himself to children." Hal opened his Bible and read.

> Things that cause people to sin are bound to come, but woe to that person through whom they come. It would be better for him to be thrown into the sea with a millstone tied around his neck than for him to cause one of these little ones to sin.
>
> —Luke 17:1–2

"The blind are the little ones, the children, the ignorant, or the weak. They're to be the subject of our special concern, to protect them from going astray, from sin."

We talked for a bit about the sexual sins mentioned in the curses. Hal pointed out that the prohibitions on incest addressed practices that were actually followed in some of the ancient societies that surrounded Israel, including the royal house of Egypt, from which they had fled. There, brother-sister marriages were used to keep the royal family in power.

"And the ban on bestiality is not only because God and most people find it repugnant; it may go back to Genesis, chapter two. The Lord says in verse eighteen, 'It is not good for the man to be alone. I will make a helper suitable for him.' He then brings before him all the beasts of the field and the birds of the air, which Adam names, 'But for Adam no suitable helper was found.' The beasts were not 'suitable helpers' for the man."

"And then," Anna picked up, "God makes the woman of the same flesh as the man, and Adam declares that she will be 'bone of my bones and flesh of my flesh. It is for this reason that a man will leave his father and mother and be united to his wife, and they will become one flesh.'"

"Yes," Hal said. "In bestiality, animal life is equated with human life, as if they were 'one flesh,' but they are not. In bestiality, man, the bearer of God's image, is treated as one flesh with the beast, which bears no such image. This is the evil of bestiality. It's a violation of the God-given order of creation."

I asked, "Does some such concept also lie behind the biblical prohibition on homosexual conduct?"

"Deuteronomy does not talk about homosexuality specifically," Hal said. "But the same thinking that lies behind the prohibition on bestiality would apply to homosexuality. God did not make another man as a 'suitable helper' for Adam, and another man could not become 'one flesh' with him."

Finally, we looked at the last curse in chapter twenty-seven:

> Cursed is the man who does not uphold the words of this law by carrying them out.
>
> —Deut. 27:26

"Paul quoted this verse in Galatians three, ten," Hal said. "It's one of the most significant theological texts of the New Testament." He turned to it and read the following:

> All who rely on observing the law are under a curse, for it is written: "Cursed is everyone who does not continue to do everything written in the Book of the Law." Clearly no one is justified before God by the law, because, "The righteous will live by faith." The law is not based on faith; on the contrary, "The man who does these things will live by them"; Christ redeemed us from the curse of the law by becoming a curse

for us, for it is written: "Cursed is everyone who is hung on a tree." He redeemed us in order that the blessing given to Abraham might come to the Gentiles through Christ Jesus, so that by faith we might receive the promise of the Spirit.

Hal closed his Bible. "Here, in two texts from Deuteronomy, Paul explains the meaning of the Gospel. The last curse of chapter twenty-seven condemns everyone who violates any part of the law. Since everyone violates some part of the law, no one can be saved. That's where Deuteronomy leaves us. But Christ became the curse for us by being crucified and hanging on a tree. Our faith in him and the salvation he brings by taking on the curse for us is what allows us to be redeemed and share in God's blessings and promises.

"And now I must be on my way to Boston."

He made his goodbyes and headed out into the late winter morning, leaving Anna and me quiet in our thoughts.

"After Hal," I observed at last, "there's nothing more to say."

She moved next to me and slid her arm around my waist. "No," she said, "not after Hal. After Jesus. Hal's just the messenger. But a wonderful one. Jesus would be proud of him."

"Would be?" I asked, questioning her tense.

She let go and moved away, picking up the coffee cups. "Have you looked at the budget yet?"

CHAPTER TWENTY-EIGHT

It had been weeks since Hal and I had visited at the office. But now he was going to be in town again, so we decided to meet for lunch. I reserved a conference room and sent an e-mail around the day before to the group that had met when we discussed chapter twenty-two. Everyone except Tom—who was out of town—showed up, although a couple drifted in late, after finishing phone calls or other morning meetings. Paula, self-consciously, sat next to Hal and placed a very new and little-thumbed Bible on the table in front of her.

"I tried reading my old King James," she said quietly to him. "It was too hard to get into the old language, so I followed your suggestion and got a modern one." Hal picked it up and read the cover title: "Good News for Modern Man."

"This Bible," he told her, "is what we call a 'paraphrase' translation. Some people use the term 'dynamic equivalence.' It tries to express the thought of the Scripture in terms that are most easily understood by modern people. It's a good choice to start. Later, when you become more familiar with it, you may want to consider one of the translations that's more literal but uses current language, like the New International," he patted the Bible in front of him, "or the New American Standard. Did anyone else bring a Bible?"

No one had but me, though Jerry promised to bring one next time, and Joan said she had looked for one at home but hadn't found it.

"No matter," Hal said. "We've got three on the table, and that'll get us through lunch. But if you're serious about understanding your heavenly Father and having a relationship with him, you do need to get one and read it. And you don't have to spend a lot of money on it either. You can get them for a few dollars at the Bible Society office down the street."

He explained where we were in our study, and that the structure of Deuteronomy was in the form of the ancient sovereign-vassal covenant treaty, with God as the sovereign. He told them that the distinct form of the treaty was recognizable by its elements, always present and laid out in the same order: an introduction, a historical prologue, general then specific laws or stipulations, blessings and curses for obedience or disobedience, and witnesses.

"Like a will or a deed," Jerry said. "The form is pretty standard, although the content can vary a lot."

I added, "I remember the first day I worked as a lawyer. An older lawyer took me to the Registry of Deeds to do a title search. As we walked in the door, he asked me what the requirements were for a valid deed. I recited my law school learning: signature, witnesses, seal, and acknowledgment. Then he handed me a form that had a place to note all these things for each deed I would examine. I passed his test."

"Everything is in forms," Hal said, "if we know how to recognize them. Poetry, art, mathematics, scientific experiments, and papers about them. Some say the universe itself and everything in it is constructed in a pattern; we just haven't identified it yet. When we do, we'll know more about the mind of God than we can know from anything else except the Scriptures.

"When we met before, we were looking at one chapter among the fifteen chapters in Deuteronomy that give specific laws as part of this covenant between God and his people. We're through with that now. This chapter is the blessings and curses for obedience and disobedience. It's also a standard part of these covenants between a sovereign and subordinate state. Chris, why don't you read it to us?"

I read chapter twenty-eight in its entirety.

> If you fully obey the LORD your God and carefully follow all his commands I give you today, the LORD your God will set you high above all the nations on earth. All these blessings will come upon you and accompany you if you obey the LORD your God:
>
> You will be blessed in the city and blessed in the country.

The fruit of your womb will be blessed, and the crops of your land, and the young of your livestock—the calves of your herds and the lambs of your flocks.

Your basket and your kneading trough will be blessed.

You will be blessed when you come in and blessed when you go out.

The LORD will grant that the enemies who rise up against you will be defeated before you. They will come at you from one direction but flee from you in seven.

The LORD will send a blessing on your barns and on everything you put your hand to. The LORD your God will bless you in the land he is giving you.

The LORD will establish you as his holy people, as he promised you on oath, if you keep the commands of the LORD your God and walk in his ways. Then all the peoples on earth will see that you are called by the name of the LORD, and they will fear you. The LORD will grant you abundant prosperity—in the fruit of your womb, the young of your livestock, and the crops of your ground—in the land he swore to your forefathers to give you.

The LORD will open the heavens, the storehouse of his bounty, to send rain on your land in season and to bless all the work of your hands. You will lend to many nations but will borrow from none. The LORD will make you the head, not the tail. If you pay attention to the commands of the LORD your God that I give you this day and carefully follow them, you will always be at the top, never at the bottom. Do not turn aside from any of the commands I give you today, to the right or to the left, following other gods and serving them.

However, if you do not obey the LORD your God and do not carefully follow all his commands and decrees I am giving you today, all these curses will come upon you and overtake you:

You will be cursed in the city and cursed in the country.

Your basket and your kneading trough will be cursed.

The fruit of your womb will be cursed, and the crops of your land, and the calves of your herds and the lambs of your flocks.

You will be cursed when you come in and cursed when you go out.

The Lord will send on you curses, confusion, and rebuke in everything you put your hand to, until you are destroyed and come to sudden ruin because of the evil you have done in forsaking him. The Lord will plague you with diseases until he has destroyed you from the land you are entering to possess. The Lord will strike you with wasting disease, with fever and inflammation, with scorching heat and drought, with blight and mildew, which will plague you until you perish. The sky over your head will be bronze, the ground beneath you iron. The Lord will turn the rain of your country into dust and powder; it will come down from the skies until you are destroyed.

The Lord will cause you to be defeated before your enemies. You will come at them from one direction but flee from them in seven, and you will become a thing of horror to all the kingdoms on earth. Your carcasses will be food for all the birds of the air and the beasts of the earth, and there will be no one to frighten them away. The Lord will afflict you with the boils of Egypt and with tumors, festering sores and the itch, from which you cannot be cured. The Lord will afflict you with madness, blindness, and confusion of mind. At midday you will grope about like a blind man in the dark. You will be unsuccessful in everything you do; day after day you will be oppressed and robbed, with no one to rescue you.

You will be pledged to be married to a woman, but another will take her and ravish her. You will build a house, but you will not live in it. You will plant a vineyard, but you will not even begin to enjoy its fruit. Your ox will be slaughtered before your eyes, but you will eat none of it. Your donkey will be forcibly taken from you and will not be returned. Your sheep will be given to your enemies, and no one will rescue them. Your sons and daughters will be given to another nation, and you will wear out your eyes watching for them day after day, powerless to lift a hand. A people that you do not know will eat what your land and labor produce, and you will have nothing but cruel oppression all your days. The sights you see will drive you mad. The LORD will afflict your knees and legs with painful boils that cannot be cured, spreading from the soles of your feet to the top of your head.

The LORD will drive you and the king you set over you to a nation unknown to you or your fathers. There you will worship other gods, gods of wood and stone. You will become a thing of horror and an object of scorn and ridicule to all the nations where the LORD will drive you.

You will sow much seed in the field but you will harvest little, because locusts will devour it. You will plant vineyards and cultivate them but you will not drink the wine or gather the grapes, because worms will eat them. You will have olive trees throughout your country but you will not use the oil, because the olives will drop off. You will have sons and daughters but you will not keep them, because they will go into captivity. Swarms of locusts will take over all your trees and the crops of your land. The alien who lives among you will rise above you higher and higher, but you will sink lower and lower. He will lend to you, but you will not lend to him. He will be the head, but you will be the tail.

All these curses will come upon you. They will pursue you and overtake you until you are destroyed, because you did not obey the LORD your God and observe the commands and decrees he gave you. They will be a sign and a wonder to you and your descendants forever. Because you did not serve the LORD your God joyfully and gladly in the time of prosperity, therefore in hunger and thirst, in nakedness and dire poverty, you will serve the enemies the LORD sends against you. He will put an iron yoke on your neck until he has destroyed you.

The LORD will bring a nation against you from far away, from the ends of the earth, like an eagle swooping down, a nation whose language you will not understand, a fierce-looking nation without respect for the old or pity for the young. They will devour the young of your livestock and the crops of your land until you are destroyed. They will leave you no grain, new wine or oil, nor any calves of your herds or lambs of your flocks until you are ruined. They will lay siege to all the cities throughout your land until the high fortified walls in which you trust fall down. They will besiege all the cities throughout the land the LORD your God is giving you.

Because of the suffering that your enemy will inflict on you during the siege, you will eat the fruit of the womb, the flesh of the sons and daughters the LORD your God has given you. Even the most gentle and sensitive man among you will have no compassion on his own brother or the wife he loves or his surviving children, and he will not give to one of them any of the flesh of his children that he is eating. It will be all he has left because of the suffering your enemy will inflict on you during the siege of all your cities. The most gentle and sensitive woman among you—so sensitive and gentle that she would not venture to touch the ground with the sole of her foot—will begrudge the husband she loves and her own son or daughter the afterbirth from her womb and the children she bears. For she intends to eat them secretly during the siege and in the distress that your enemy will inflict on you in your cities.

If you do not carefully follow all the words of this law, which are written in this book, and do not revere this glorious and awesome name—the LORD your God—the LORD will send fearful plagues on you and your descendants, harsh and prolonged disasters, and severe and lingering illnesses. He will bring upon you all the diseases of Egypt that you dreaded, and they will cling to you. The LORD will also bring on you every kind of sickness and disaster not recorded in this Book of the Law, until you are destroyed. You who were as numerous as the stars in the sky will be left but few in number, because you did not obey the LORD your God. Just as it pleased the LORD to make you prosper and increase in number, so it will please him to ruin and destroy you. You will be uprooted from the land you are entering to possess.

Then the LORD will scatter you among all nations, from one end of the earth to the other. There you will worship other gods—gods of wood and stone, which neither you nor your fathers have known. Among those nations you will find no repose, no resting place for the sole of your foot. There the LORD will give you an anxious mind, eyes weary with longing, and a despairing heart. You will live in constant suspense, filled with dread both night and day, never sure of your life. In the morning you will say, "If only it were evening!" and in the evening, "If only it were morning!"— because of the terror that will fill your hearts and the sights that your eyes will see. The LORD will send you back in ships to Egypt on a journey I said you should never make again. There you will offer yourselves for sale to your enemies as male and female slaves, but no one will buy you.

—Deut. 28:1–68

When I finished the long chapter, everyone looked expectantly at Hal.

"We could spend a lot of time discussing the details of the blessings and curses," he said. "They're fascinating from a literary point of view, and I hope some of you will study them more if you get into some deeper Bible studies. Many of the blessings and curses mirror or reflect each other. They include chiasms, rhyme, alliteration, inversions, and poetry. Some of them tie in explicitly to other parts of the book."

"Like what?" Paula asked.

"For example," Hal responded, "verse thirty says, 'You will be pledged to be married to a woman, but another will take her and ravish her. You will build a house, but you will not live in it. You will plant a vineyard, but you will not even begin to enjoy its fruit.'

"In chapter twenty, which Chris will recall, these are the same three things that excuse a man from military service: being pledged to be married to a woman, building a new house that he hasn't dedicated, or planting a vineyard from which he hasn't begun to enjoy the fruit. These things—a home, marriage and family, crops to feed them—make life in the land worthwhile. It's not an accident that in the curses they're repeated as things that the disobedient will lose.

"In some respects, these blessings and curses are similar to blessings and curses in other ancient near-eastern sovereign-vassal treaties, which confirm the covenant or treaty nature of Deuteronomy. In this treaty form, one would expect blessings and curses at this point, and here they are. But they're also different, not mere copies of someone else's documents or ideas."

"So you're telling us," Kevin said, "that Deuteronomy is an international treaty between God and the nation called Israel? That's the nature of the document?"

"Exactly. Between Israel and the sovereign of the universe. The form was common at the time, but no one else made contracts with God, or their god or gods."

"I took a course in international law in law school," Jerry said. "I never expected to encounter it in the Bible."

"Be careful not to oversimplify, Jerry," Hal said. "Deuteronomy is— as we have discussed—an international treaty, and the presence of the blessings and curses appears to prove that; they're just at the place in the document where we'd expect to find them. But Deuteronomy is many other things, as well. Scripture may take certain literary forms, but it is never one-dimensional."

He turned to me. "Right, Chris?"

I unpacked my learning from our earlier sessions. "It's Moses' last words to his people, a summary of their history from the time they left Egypt. It's a prophecy of what lies ahead and a liturgy arranged in rhythmic patterns on both a macro and micro scale: large patterns in the whole book, small patterns in particular passages. It's a law book. It's a sermon. It's exhortation. It's teaching. It's a bridge between the earlier books of the Torah and the history and prophets that lie ahead. It's the most quoted book in the New Testament. It's—"

"OK," Jerry said, holding up his hand. "I get it. It's a big deal."

"What else can we learn from this chapter, Hal?" Paula asked.

Hal replied, "Chris and I have talked a lot in our studies about how the Bible is integrated internally and how once you understand what's going on in one part of the Bible, you see it popping up over and over again, sometimes in places that surprise you. This chapter is very much like that, but to understand it, you have to understand the history of Israel in the Old Testament. Anyone want to summarize that for us?"

No one volunteered, so Hal invited me to proceed. This is what I told them.

"Deuteronomy is set around 1400 B.C., at the end of Moses' 120-year lifespan, when Israel was on the Plains of Moab, on the east side of the Jordan River, poised to enter the Promised Land. After Moses' death, Joshua led the people across the Jordan in the conquest of the land, the history of which is told in the book of Joshua. Joshua is followed by the period of the judges, more than three hundred years in which Israel had no king, but successive leaders rose up to lead the Israelites in resisting various enemies and throwing off oppression. The history of the time of the judges is told in the book of Judges.

"The books of First Samuel through Second Kings—the 'former prophets,' as they're known in the Jewish Scriptures—tell of Israel under its kings, a story repeated by a different author in the books of Chronicles. Saul was the first king of Israel, around 1050 B.C., followed by David and Solomon in the era of the United Kingdom, when all Israel was one nation. On the death of Solomon, around 930 B.C., the Jewish people become divided into rival kingdoms. The northern kingdom, called Israel or Samaria, consisted of the territories of the ten northern tribes. The southern kingdom, called Judah, consisted of the territory of the tribes of Judah and Benjamin. The Assyrians conquered the northern kingdom in 722 B.C. and deported its people to other parts of the Assyrian empire. The prophets Isaiah and Hosea prophesied during this period.

"The Kingdom of Judah persisted for almost another 150 years. In 612 B.C., a new power emerged in the region. Babylon conquered Assyria and assumed dominance. Pharaoh Neco of Egypt marched north to assist the failing Assyrians and was met by King Josiah of Judah, who opposed him. Josiah died in a battle with the Egyptians at Megiddo, but at Carchemish the Babylonians defeated the Egyptians. Babylon's dominance was established in the region. The kings of Judah who succeeded Josiah then came under pressure to submit to Babylon. The prophecies of Jeremiah were given during the period leading up the fall of Judah.

"Babylon's dominance over Judah was asserted in successive confrontations. In 605 B.C., Nebuchadnezzar, King of Babylon, besieged Jerusalem and took captive King Jehoiakim and certain Israelites of royal birth, including the prophet Daniel. In 597 B.C., Jehoiakim's son, Jehoiachin, and some 10,000 Jews, including the prophet Ezekiel, were exiled to Babylon following another rebellion. The Babylonians placed Jehoiachin's uncle, Zedekiah, on the throne. In 586 B.C. his rebellion against his overlords led to the final destruction of Jerusalem and the temple and the exile of most of the remaining people to Babylon. The Book of Lamentations, which follows the book of Jeremiah and is usually attributed to him, speaks of the horrors of the 586 siege and the fall of Jerusalem.

"The period of the exile is the approximately seventy-year period in which the Jewish people were Babylonian exiles, with their homeland and religious center destroyed and distant. The exile ended when the Persian Empire succeeded Babylon. The Persian emperor Cyrus released the Jews to return home. The story of the return from exile and rebuilding of Jerusalem is told in the books of Ezra and Nehemiah."

"Impressive," Joan said. "I never heard anyone put it together like that."

"An A for your Old Testament history class," Hal agreed. "But the reason I had you recite all that history is to put this chapter into context with it. The teaching and prophecy of Deuteronomy is around 1400 B.C. Jeremiah lived and prophesied some eight hundred years later. The fall of Jerusalem, recorded in Second Kings and Lamentations, occurred in his lifetime. Most of the curses of Deuteronomy twenty-eight were literally fulfilled during this time. There's a straight line from Deuteronomy to Jeremiah to Lamentations: the distant prophecy of Deuteronomy about the result of disobedience, the near-term prophecy of Jeremiah to the same effect, and the fulfillment, as recorded in Lamentations."

"Show us," Joan said.

Hal took us through a number of illustrations.

"Deuteronomy twenty-eight, thirty-six, predicts the exile: 'The Lord will drive you and the king you set over you to a nation unknown to you or your fathers.' Jeremiah fifteen, fourteen prophesies: 'I will enslave you to your enemies in a land you do not know,' a prediction repeated over and over in Jeremiah. Lamentations one, three, says, 'Judah has gone into exile. She dwells among the nations.'

"In Deuteronomy twenty-eight, forty-eight, God says, 'He will put an iron yoke on your neck until he has destroyed you.' Jeremiah twenty-eight, thirteen, says, 'You have broken a wooden yoke, but in its place you will get a yoke of iron.' Lamentations one, fourteen, says, 'My sins have been bound into a yoke; by his hands they were woven together. They have come upon my neck and the Lord has sapped my strength.'

"In Deuteronomy twenty-eight, fifty-three, we read that the people will eat their own children in the siege. This has been described as the most gruesome scene in the Bible. It was literally fulfilled, and we can read the account in Lamentations two, twenty, and four, ten.

"In Deuteronomy twenty-eight, thirty-seven, Moses said Israel would become an object of scorn and ridicule among the nations. Jeremiah repeated this prophecy in a number of places, such as eighteen, sixteen. Lamentations two, fifteen, says, 'All who pass your way clap their hands at you; they scoff and shake their heads at the Daughter of Jerusalem.'

"Deuteronomy twenty-eight, forty-eight, tells of hunger and thirst. Jeremiah fourteen, three, prophesies lack of water. Lamentations four, ten, says, 'Because of thirst the infant's tongue sticks to the roof of its mouth.'"

Hal told us this was just a sampler. The horror, suffering, and despair of Jerusalem's siege and destruction—as well as the exile—are found throughout this chapter of Deuteronomy. From a distance of eight hundred years, God foretells through Moses exactly what will come as a result of disobedience.

"So you're telling us," Kevin said, "that this is prophecy, and it was fulfilled; it historically actually happened hundreds of years later."

"Eight hundred years later," Hal said. "Remember, the Bible is one book, with one ultimate author, God the Holy Spirit, despite the many human hands that wrote it down."

"One book, one story, one author," I added again. I could see interest instead of skepticism emerging on Kevin's face.

"Go on," he said to Hal, ignoring my summary.

"There were, of course," Hal said, "many disobediences and cycles of punishment, repentance, and restoration in the meantime. But the Bible leaves no doubt that what happened to the Jews in the Assyrian and Babylonian conquests—and exiles of Israel and Judah—was God-ordained, a direct result of their national disobedience to him. 'The Lord has brought her grief because of her many sins,' Lamentations says. The message here is that God is sovereign, and his actions in history are moral. We live in a universe in which right and wrong are rewarded and punished. It's a moral place, not a mindless abyss."

"We all want to believe that the universe is a moral place, Hal," Joan said. "And in our everyday lives, we all act as though we believe it. I mean, why else do you have laws and punish people who break them? And most of us think there's something after this life and that doing good things now will give us a better place then, even if we don't think we know much about the specifics."

"We have laws because of the 'social contract,'" Kevin interjected. "I won't kill you so you won't kill me, I won't steal from you so you don't steal from me. I don't know that it has anything to do with a moral universe. It's just the most convenient way for everyone to serve his own self-interest."

"I don't think so," Paula chimed in. "You're just parroting that Rousseau philosophy from the French Revolution, stuff you learned in college. But what happened in the French Revolution? As soon as one group got power, they started guillotining the other group until the whole idea collapsed. The idea that society is just an agreement for everyone to be nice to everyone else so everyone else will be nice to them is soft thinking. The reality is that whoever has the most guns does whatever he wants to do unless there is a belief in a moral universe, and then people find out what the moral rules require and try to live by them and institute them in society. That's the difference between us and dictatorships."

Kevin fell silent in the face of Paula's statement. I brought up my own question about the chapter.

"Is it as simple as a reward for doing right and punishment for doing wrong, Hal?" I asked. "If we simply obey God's commands, can we expect that our life will be filled with prosperity and good things?"

"The blessings and curses of Deuteronomy twenty-eight," Hal said, "were directed to one nation. The blessings are the natural consequences of a society and a culture that is God-fearing, God-honoring, and obedient to God's commands. The destruction of Jerusalem and the exile of the Jews happened to everyone as a consequence of a long history of national guilt and the failure of kings, priests, and prophets—both civil and religious leaders—to lead the nation in righteous paths. The Assyrians and Babylonians did not go around and figure out who was more or less godly, and treat them accordingly. They were not godly people themselves. God sometimes uses evil to chastise us."

He paused, and then gave them a message I had heard before from him. "I do fear that these blessings and curses have all too much relevance to our contemporary Western society. Christians need to pray for the nation and the culture, and do everything possible to be forces for goodness and righteousness in it. But too much evil for too long will cause our sin to reach its full measure, and when it does, we can certainly expect God to be against us."

He pointed us to verse sixty-three: "Just as it pleased the Lord to make you prosper and increase in number, so it will please him to ruin and destroy you."

And then to Lamentations 3:38: "Is it not from the mouth of the Most High that both calamities and good things come? Why should any living man complain when punished for his sins?"

Then Hal pointed out, "And if God could bring a cruel, godless people to destroy his chosen people, then he certainly can bring similar people against America."

"Like Islamic fundamentalists who want to destroy us and everything we stand for?" I asked.

"Just so," Hal replied. "They are evil people serving an evil cause. But God can use them, just as he used other such peoples to serve his purposes in history. I don't pretend to know the mind of God in the horrible attacks on the World Trade Center towers and the Pentagon on September eleventh, but the pattern is consistent with Israel's history. We are colossally mistaken in our understanding of God and the universe he created when we pretty him up and think it's in his job description to be nice to us."

"So is the message here just about nations?" I asked. "Does this have any relevance to individuals?"

"Nations are the sum of their individual citizens," Hal said, "although the governmental and religious leaders have more impact on their fate than individual citizens. But leaders, in our system at least, are chosen by their people. We get what we deserve in that respect.

"But, more important, perhaps, to us individually is this. Deuteronomy twenty-eight is, for individuals, a metaphor, or collection of metaphors, for heaven and hell. Read it with care and reflect on it. There are two possible responses. One is the response of good King Josiah. In Second Kings twenty-two, eleven, when the Book of the Law was found and read to him, he tore his robes to express his emotion, and then he set out to reform the kingdom. In Jeremiah thirty-six, on the other hand, when Jeremiah spoke similar prophecies to the wicked king Jehoiakim, he cut off the scroll and burned it in the fire. These same two responses occur today. Some people are moved by God's word and act on it to reform their lives. Some cut it out of their lives, or at least the parts of it that make them uncomfortable or that they don't like, and wind up with a much-reduced message or no message at all."

"I can see the metaphor," Jerry said. "Really more like hyperbole. Exaggeration. Moses was a preacher. Do good things and be rewarded. Do bad things and be punished. But no one believes in hell anymore, except a few religious nuts."

He looked at Hal, then at me and Paula, and then he blushed a little. "I don't mean to insult your beliefs; I don't even know what you believe about hell. But I can't see how anyone who believes in a loving God could think he could send anyone to burn in flames and all that stuff for eternity. It just doesn't make sense."

Hal replied, "It has become very unfashionable to preach about hell. Preachers don't preach the terrors of God's wrath anymore. We want to draw people to the good things of God, not scare them by preaching the hellfire-and-brimstone message of an earlier time."

"Do you believe there really is a hellfire and brimstone hell?" Jerry asked him. "I mean, a place where people who aren't Christians or haven't been good enough or whatever are tormented for eternity? Does your God really do that to people?"

Hal answered Jerry's question with a question. "Do you think anyone ought to be in such a place?"

Jerry paused. "Well, maybe Hitler, or the nine-eleven hijackers. Or serial killers. I don't know. But most people are basically good and try to do the right thing, even if some people don't think they have the right ideas about God. I can't see them getting thrown into hell because they didn't quite make the grade."

"You'd make a good Catholic, Jerry," Hal said. "The Catholic notion of purgatory really gets at your point. Some people haven't done or been or believed what God expects for entry into heaven, but they don't really merit eternal punishment either. So purgatory is a place of purification for them. There is some Scripture, but not much, to support this idea. But mostly it's a matter of what Catholics view as a logical necessity."

"Is that the only choice we have of beliefs?" Paula asked. "Either purgatory or eternal torment?"

"No," Hal said. "There are others, and they're based on understandings of various Bible passages and honest attempts to be faithful to Scripture while trying to solve the moral dilemma of thinking of God consigning people to eternal torment.

"One idea is to see the passages describing hell, mostly from the words of Jesus, as metaphors and not literal descriptions. For example, hell is described as both a place of fire and a place of darkness, sometimes at the same time, but these descriptions are contradictory. C.S. Lewis viewed hell as a metaphor, and a lot of people who believe the Bible would be surprised at how many other prominent evangelical thinkers agree. Hell is viewed as separation from God rather than a place of eternal torment. Separation from God, of course, may not seem like such a bad outcome to people who have never been joined to him. But the reality is not just a continuation of their disobedience in this world but an eternal accountability for it. Even in a metaphorical understanding, it would be pretty awful to spend eternity separated from the source of all goodness and happiness and truth and beauty."

"Are there other ways to think about hell?" I asked.

"The main other way," Hal said, "is to think that the wicked don't suffer eternally but are extinguished at some point. They just cease to be. You can interpret some passages of Scripture that way too. The alternative to eternal life is death, not eternal torment."

"And what do you think, Hal?" Paula asked.

All eyes were on him.

"God is perfect justice and perfect mercy. I believe in those perfections, and I trust him completely to accomplish them. I can read the Scriptures and the arguments about them and know only this: We will live beyond death, we will be accountable for who and what we are and do in this life, and the first thing God expects of us in this life is to believe him—to believe in him and in what he tells us, and that means, among other things, and first among those things, loving him and trusting Jesus as his son for our salvation. It also means obeying him. God's majesty, power, and holiness are far beyond our feeble powers to imagine. We are as helpless as an ant contemplating the glories of human achievement when we think about God. We can't imagine what it will really be like, either the good or the bad, after we die. The Bible gives us images to help us understand, but that's all they are. The real glory—and horror—is beyond our comprehension. Contemplate the images presented in this chapter we just read—the wondrous happiness of the blessed life and the horror of the cursed life. And then be sure you're on the side of the blessings. Don't get excited about the details; just be on the right side when the roll is called."

He closed his eyes, bowed his head, and reached his hands out, clasping Paula's hand on his right and Kevin's on his left. We all followed suit, linking hands around the table. As we did, I realized I had never joined with my law partners that way—ever. The currents of Hal's holy words seemed to flow around the circle from hand to hand and body to body, linking us as one person, as he spoke the words of Paul from Romans 8: "I consider that our present sufferings are not worth comparing with the glory that will be revealed in us. . . . He who did not spare his own Son, but gave him up for us all—how will he not also, along with him, graciously give us all things?"

Then he prayed for each of us, individually and personally, beseeching God to bring us before him cleansed and whole and holy; to bathe us in love and light and make us mirrors that would absorb and reflect that love back to him and out to each other; to immerse us in his word; to make Jesus a presence in our lives, whom we could look to in love and trust for every need and problem; to open our eyes to his beauty, our ears to his words, and our minds to his thoughts; to surround our understandings with those of the great cloud of witnesses who had gone before, and make us part of that cloud to our spouses and children and colleagues and clients and every soul whose life we touched. He prayed and he prayed, and I felt no impatience to start running the clock of remuneration or to return to the busyness that waited beyond the conference room door. At times during that prayer I felt uplifted, as though the six of us had somehow begun to rise, bodily—not out-of-body—to a light beyond, as though our feet had left the ground and we had risen, our legs passing through the table as if it were transparent, and a power drawing us that we were incapable of resisting. And when Hal finally closed with "in the name of Jesus Christ, our Lord and Savior, to whom be all power and honor and glory, forever and ever, Amen," I floated back to earth slowly but inexorably as the light faded. Paula gave my left hand a powerful squeeze before releasing it, silently signaling that she had felt it too. Jerry, on my right, whispered before getting up and rushing out, "We've got to talk."

And then it was over. Hal touched my sleeve gently as we moved to the door. "Tell Anna that God loves her."

And he was gone.

CHAPTER TWENTY-NINE

I suppose," Jerry said after entering my office and closing the door, "that I shouldn't say this to anyone. All my instincts tell me to keep my mouth shut and just quietly turn myself around. But I need to get some things off my chest, and our meeting with Hal the other day told me that the time to do it is now."

I had no idea what was coming next but had sensed from his comment when we closed our meeting that something deep was on his mind.

"I know you have something to say," I replied. "But why me? I don't run the place, and I'm not a pastor."

"Because," he said, "I don't know anyone else I can trust. I know you've been studying with Hal for months, and I know you understand spiritual things. I haven't gone to church in years. There's just no one in my life I can share these things with. I need someone to talk to."

Nothing in my previous thoughts or experience prepared me for what followed. Hal had warned me once—so casually I hardly took note of it—that once I started following God he would put me in strange places, places I never expected to be and didn't want to go. Anna had suggested the same thing when we had talked about what was happening to me and to us as we absorbed more and more of the spiritual life from Hal. This was one of those places.

The story Jerry spilled out was sordid. He confessed with tears that he had let himself become, as he put it, a sex addict. He had collected volumes of pornography and concealed it from his wife; he accessed it on the Internet at every opportunity, and he sought out liaisons and affairs with neighbors, female co-workers, and even prostitutes. It had become a way of life. Like an alcoholic or a drug addict, he concealed his actions, used money, and planned furtively to feed his addiction.

It dragged down his work productivity and interfered with his family life.

He had recognized for a long time that he had a problem but lacked the motivation to do anything about it. He had made abortive efforts to entice his wife into his lifestyle, suggesting that they seek out swingers groups and similar activity. Instead, she had started going to church and reading the Bible at home and enrolled their young children in Sunday school. Confronted with righteousness at home, his guilt deepened. One night he dreamed that he was in a dark street with women beckoning him from every doorway. The women were scantily clad and heavily made up, but he recognized in them the face of death and knew that he was being lured into his own destruction. Then he met Hal in our first session together and gained a sudden respect for the spiritual source that was pulling his wife in the opposite direction he had been going. The study of chapter twenty-eight was the last push that was needed. He saw the blessings and curses as real and personal. His life was a wasteland, and he wanted to make it a garden.

"Have you shared any of this with Barbara?" I asked, referring to his wife.

"No," he replied. "She knows I have this problem, but she has no idea of the depth of it. I'm afraid she'd leave me. But I've thrown out all my pornography and cleaned up my laptop. And I've ended all the affairs."

"She won't leave you," I said. "If she's turning to the Lord herself, she'll welcome having a partner in the journey. Spare her the lurid details, but let her know what's going on in your life. She's the best counselor you can ever have."

I didn't know Barbara well, and I had stepped out in faith a bit with this advice, but I knew as one knows at certain moments of crisis that it was the right thing to say. A woman who is living in faith will rejoice in seeing her life partner do the same. I had once gone on a men's retreat with a church group where we talked about the beginnings of faith in a married couple. Every man in the group affirmed that his wife had come to faith ahead of him and been instrumental, if only by example, in leading him to it. As one fellow put it, "I was sitting at home reading my Playboy while she was reading her Bible. Eventually it occurred

THE DEUTERONOMY PROJECT

to me that she might be onto something that I wasn't." Women have much more influence on the faith and righteousness of the men in their lives than most of them ever know.

I went on to advise him that addictions have a way of hiding for a while and then raising their ugly heads again in moments of weakness. That's why a recovered alcoholic won't ever take a drink. He needed some systematic ways of preventing a relapse. There are books, Christian counselors, and twelve-step groups that meet by phone—if there aren't enough local participants to meet in person—to help people deal with sexual addictions. He needed to plug into these resources and to be sure he had someone he could talk to regularly, and candidly, about these things, someone who could keep him accountable and help him keep himself accountable. And then I told him to immerse himself in Scripture and in prayer. I led him to 1 Corinthians 10: "No temptation has seized you except what is common to man. And God is faithful; he will not let you be tempted beyond what you can bear. But when you are tempted, he will also provide a way out so that you can stand up under it."

For all of this advice, I had no forethought or training or meaningful knowledge or experience, but it seemed right to me, and, I prayed, to the Holy Spirit. Jerry left looking much relieved, with a request that he join Hal and me for our next meeting on Saturday morning. I readily agreed.

By Saturday morning, the party had grown. Anna insisted on coming, and Paula had heard from Jerry that he was going and asked if she could join. Jerry and Paula came to our house and drove over with us. Jerry said Barbara was busy but delighted he was going somewhere to study the Bible. Anna and Paula sat in the back seat. While Jerry and I talked guy talk, I could hear out of one ear Paula telling Anna that her husband was a little annoyed at her becoming a "religious nut," but she didn't preach to him and just tried to show him by her caring for him and the way she lived that it was a good thing that was happening to her. "Pretty soon he'll come to church with me," she said. "Then I think we'll make some real progress."

Hal was happy about the growth in his little study group. The April sunshine was warm, even though some patches of snow remained in the shady corners of his yard and the surrounding woods. The sun's rays did penetrate, and the cold morning air seemed to warm perceptibly, even as we stood in it. The grass was starting to turn green again, and a few bulbs sent shoots poking through the recently thawed earth. Hal insisted we drag chairs out to the garden and enjoy a day in which spring appeared to be further along than it really was.

Then he had us read chapter twenty-nine.

> These are the terms of the covenant the LORD commanded Moses to make with the Israelites in Moab, in addition to the covenant he had made with them at Horeb.

> Moses summoned all the Israelites and said to them:

> Your eyes have seen all that the LORD did in Egypt to Pharaoh, to all his officials and to all his land. With your own eyes you saw those great trials, those miraculous signs and great wonders. But to this day the LORD has not given you a mind that understands or eyes that see or ears that hear. During the forty years that I led you through the desert, your clothes did not wear out, nor did the sandals on your feet. You ate no bread and drank no wine or other fermented drink. I did this so that you might know that I am the LORD your God.

> When you reached this place, Sihon king of Heshbon and Og king of Bashan came out to fight against us, but we defeated them. We took their land and gave it as an inheritance to the Reubenites, the Gadites, and the half-tribe of Manasseh.

> Carefully follow the terms of this covenant, so that you may prosper in everything you do. All of you are standing today in the presence of the LORD your God—your leaders and chief men, your elders and officials, and all the other men of Israel, together with your children and your wives, and the aliens living in your camps who chop your wood and carry your water. You are standing here in order to enter into a covenant with the LORD your God, a covenant the LORD is making with you this day and sealing with an oath,

to confirm you this day as his people, that he may be your God as he promised you and as he swore to your fathers, Abraham, Isaac, and Jacob. I am making this covenant, with its oath, not only with you who are standing here with us today in the presence of the LORD our God but also with those who are not here today.

You yourselves know how we lived in Egypt and how we passed through the countries on the way here. You saw among them their detestable images and idols of wood and stone, of silver and gold. Make sure there is no man or woman, clan or tribe among you today whose heart turns away from the LORD our God to go and worship the gods of those nations; make sure there is no root among you that produces such bitter poison.

When such a person hears the words of this oath, he invokes a blessing on himself and therefore thinks, "I will be safe, even though I persist in going my own way." This will bring disaster on the watered land as well as the dry. The LORD will never be willing to forgive him; his wrath and zeal will burn against that man. All the curses written in this book will fall upon him, and the LORD will blot out his name from under heaven. The LORD will single him out from all the tribes of Israel for disaster, according to all the curses of the covenant written in this Book of the Law.

Your children who follow you in later generations and foreigners who come from distant lands will see the calamities that have fallen on the land and the diseases with which the LORD has afflicted it. The whole land will be a burning waste of salt and sulfur—nothing planted, nothing sprouting, no vegetation growing on it. It will be like the destruction of Sodom and Gomorrah, Admah and Zeboiim, which the LORD overthrew in fierce anger. All the nations will ask: "Why has the LORD done this to this land? Why this fierce, burning anger?"

And the answer will be: "It is because this people abandoned the covenant of the LORD, the God of their fathers, the covenant he made with them when he brought them out of Egypt. They went off and worshiped other gods and bowed down to them, gods they did not know, gods he had not given them. Therefore the LORD's anger burned against this land, so that he brought on it all the curses written in this book. In furious anger and in great wrath the LORD uprooted them from their land and thrust them into another land, as it is now."

The secret things belong to the LORD our God, but the things revealed belong to us and to our children forever, that we may follow all the words of this law.

—Deut. 29:1–29

"All of you," Hal said, "have had a taste of Deuteronomy, but only Chris has been through it from the beginning. This is a good chapter for you to come in on because most of it is repetition. The symphony of Deuteronomy began with certain rhythms and melodies. Now we're past the heart of the book—the telling of the law—and the composition shifts back to the notes that were heard at the beginning. Moses reminds the people of the principles in which the law is grounded. It's like the old guideline for a good sermon: tell them what you're going to say, tell them what you have to say, then tell them what you said. In the literary structure called a chiasm, themes are repeated in reverse order on either side of the central message. It's like driving somewhere to see an attraction, then driving home again—you see the same scenery going home that you did on the drive out, but in reverse order."

"But not quite the same," Anna said. "When you travel in the opposite direction, the same scenery looks a little different."

"And that's so here, too," Hal said. "Themes aren't restated verbatim, but they're there and they're recognizable. Chris will see two or three new concepts in this chapter, but most of it is familiar from the early part of Deuteronomy, before we got into the law."

He paused and looked around, inviting questions, but the group was content to let Hal talk.

"Go on," Anna encouraged him.

And so he did. Through the warm spring sunshine we walked and rambled and strolled through the words, and through phrases and thoughts of the text; and we listened, listened as one does to those who know and love a thing and can talk of it, describe it, and express it so well that others learn through silence, by absorption. We were the Marys of the tenth chapter of Luke's gospel, sitting at the master's feet and listening to what he had to say.

Deuteronomy, Hal told us, is a document and a story of covenant—not just any covenant, but a solemn and binding contract between the sovereign Creator and a particular people of his creation whom he had selected for particular blessing as an example to all other peoples. In chapter twenty-nine, the covenant comes back into focus, in language and images that often mirror the early chapters of Deuteronomy. The history of God's powerful and redemptive actions had been set forth before. The Ten Commandments, and the general and specific laws that follow, had been given. Blessings for obedience and curses for disobedience had been invoked. Much of what had gone before is repeated here.

Moses begins by reminding the people that "these are the terms of the covenant." Originally, the covenant was made with this people at Horeb, that is, Mount Sinai, as described in chapter four. But this is an additional covenant, a renewal of that pledge and relationship that began forty years earlier, when God led the people out of bondage in Egypt. So a Christian who commits to the Lord would do well to remind himself often, as John Bunyan wrote, "of the beginnings of grace in his soul" and to renew his commitment on regular occasions.

Twice in this chapter, Moses reminded the people of what their "eyes have seen," or "you yourselves know," as he did in chapter four. They witnessed the miraculous liberation from Egypt, along with God's protection in the desert, and the "detestable images and idols" of Egypt and the lands they passed through on the way to this point. They had seen for themselves the power of the living God and the emptiness of manmade deities. They had defeated kings who had come out to fight them and refused to make peace with them. Powerful armies had fallen before them.

People learn by observation. The Israelites had learned by the things they had seen with their eyes and the mighty acts of God's power in the miracles of the Exodus and Conquest. Peter spoke of this in Acts, when he referred to the events of Jesus' life as things that "you yourselves know." The eyewitness testimony to Jesus' life, miracles, teachings, and resurrection permeate the New Testament.

God had done these things for a purpose: to show them that he was the Lord, their God. These are "apologetic" statements, reminders that their faith is based on personal, eyewitness observation, on their own history, not on human reasoning or philosophy. The Old Testament witness is the same as the New Testament. Just as Jesus' apostles and others spread the Christian gospel—based on their eyewitness to Jesus' teachings and miracles and his resurrection—so Israel's faith stood on its eyewitness to the miracles and wonders done in Egypt and in the desert, on God's profound and righteous teachings, and on their resurrection as a people.

All of the people were assembled for the covenant renewal—not just leaders, or males, but women, children, and aliens among them. The covenant included everyone in the community. All stood equally before God. And the covenant extended to their posterity—"those who are not here today." Just as the Sinai covenant forty years earlier was not just "with our fathers" but "with us, with all of us who are alive here today," as Moses taught in chapter five, so the present covenant renewal on the Plains of Moab reached into the future of God's people. God would be their God as he had promised them and their fathers before them. And they were to be his people, evidenced by following the terms of the covenant. God's relationship with his people is not interrupted by generations. Every day is "this day" for all of God's people of every age.

If anyone among them, whether an individual ("man or woman") or a group ("clan or tribe") turned away from the Lord to worship other gods, disaster would result. Some specifics of the curses from the previous chapter are repeated, though not verbatim. The message permeates the whole Bible: Be not deceived; God is not mocked (see Gal. 6:7). Such people might blind themselves to their danger, invoking "a blessing on himself," but it was no secret to God and would have its natural consequences. Just as obedience to the law in chapter four would invoke the admiration of the nations, so disobedience in chapter twenty-nine would reveal to the nations the consequence of Israel's abandoning the covenant and following other gods: calamities, disease, destruction of the land, and the uprooting of the disobedient people from the land.

The chapter concluded with a familiar but somewhat enigmatic statement: "The secret things belong to the Lord our God, but the things revealed belong to us and to our children forever, that we may follow all the words of this law."

As Hal wound down, a lone robin flew over our heads and landed in a nearby tree.

Silence prevailed. A light breeze cooled our faces; we were all deep in thought. The sun took temporary refuge behind a fair-weather cloud.

"What are your questions?" Hal said at last. "I'm sure you have some."

Anna spoke first. "What does it mean in verse four that 'the Lord has not given you a mind that understands or eyes that see or ears that hear'? If God gives understanding of the spiritual meaning of things, how could he curse and bring misfortune on those to whom he had not given such understanding?"

"Who," Jerry asked, "is the person who invokes a blessing on himself but brings on disaster? Why is the disaster on the whole community if only one is sinning?"

"How can God who forgives all and has forgiven this people, even for the idolatry of the golden calf and other rebellions, 'never be willing to forgive' this man who invokes a blessing on himself?" Paula asked.

"And what," I asked, "are the 'secret things' that belong to the Lord? What does the last verse of chapter twenty-nine really mean?"

"Let's begin at the end," Hal said. "Understanding the last verse will put the rest of the chapter in better perspective.

"There are two plausible meanings that can be attributed to verse twenty-nine. Both are theologically correct and important. The difference lies in who has the 'secret.'

"One meaning is that God will punish secret sins, but it's our responsibility—that is, the larger community—to deal with the wrongs that are known. The community or culture that disregards God's law does so at great peril, but God won't hold it responsible for those wrongs of which it is not aware, such as the person who thinks he can be all right with God, even if he's disobedient by 'invoking a blessing on himself.' This reading would be consistent with the teachings that went before it in this chapter.

"Another possible meaning is that we should not presume that we know all there is to know about God. His revelation to us is limited. What we know is just what we need to know, and what he in his infinite wisdom has chosen to reveal of himself to us. We are, however, responsible for the knowledge of God that is revealed, meaning the Scriptures, and for following and living by his instructions."

"Which do you think is correct?" I asked.

"I favor the latter interpretation," Hal said, "although the first is certainly consistent with the rest of the passage. God says that 'the things revealed belong to us and to our children forever.' That goes beyond accountability for the sin of others. It teaches the importance of living by what we know, the truths we've been given, and not trying to fill in the blanks by human reason or speculation. '"For my thoughts are not your thoughts, neither are your ways my ways," says the Lord. "As the heavens are higher than the earth, so are my ways higher than your ways and my thoughts than your thoughts."' Hal recited the verses from Isaiah 55.

"Much evil in the church—heresies and divisions—have come from people trying to make up their own systems out of the Scriptures, filling voids in revealed truth with their own fallible logic, and insisting on the absoluteness of disputable interpretations. There's no need to make of the Scriptures more than what they are. There are sacred mysteries that belong to our Creator and will remain with him unless he chooses to reveal them to us in the resurrection. Sometimes the best approach to difficult or puzzling passages is a prayerful silence."

He pointed out that this wasn't the only reference to sacred mysteries in the Bible. In Acts 1:7, Jesus said, "It is not for you to know the times or dates the Father has set by his own authority."

We moved back to Jerry's question about verses nineteen and twenty. Who is the person who invokes a blessing on himself but brings on curses?

"I have preached to churches full of such people," Hal said. "These are the secret idolaters, the people who worship something other than God. The strength of the original language does not entirely come through in translation. The word the New International Version translates as *idols* here—or *detestable images and idols*, to take the whole phrase—is similar to the Hebrew word for excrement, and some think that is the real sense here. In our society, worship of these images or idols that God equates to excrement does not usually mean people are bowing down to some man-made image they keep in their closet, as it may have in Moses' time, when such other gods abounded. But the false gods of modern man are very real, and they are in the pews of every church I have ever been in. They are all the things that people put before their Creator and Redeemer: gods of the flesh, whether gluttony, drunkenness, or lust; gods of materialism; the pursuit of wealth, consumerism, careers; gods of power; the egocentric person who insists on dominating his family or his church, who wants to be in control and have those around him follow or submit if not admire him. I'm not talking about the believer who loves the Lord but falls into sin from time to time—this happens to everyone, even pastors. I'm talking about the people who think they're all right because they go to church, because they sing the hymns or recite the prayers, or because they associate themselves with God's people, but whose hearts have never really been converted or committed. They paper themselves over with religion, but it is not who they are. The real person burns with jealousy, anger, greed, pride, and lust."

I recalled the words of C.S. Lewis in speaking of what he discovered in himself when he finally turned to God: a zoo of lusts, a bedlam of ambitions, a nursery of fears, a harem of fondled hatreds.

Hal then talked about a subject we had discussed before: distinguishing between individual and community responsibility. "A little yeast works through the whole batch of dough," he said, quoting 1 Corinthians 5:6. He cited Hebrews 12:15: "See to it that no bitter root grows up to cause trouble and defile many," a near quote from verse eighteen of this chapter. "God holds people accountable for their own disobedience," he said. "But at some point it affects the larger community. It may be, as these Scriptures suggest, that the disobedience of one person infects others. Gossip and slander is communicated to others. As James says, it corrupts the whole person. And the community is the sum of its parts. If enough of the parts are corrupted, the whole body becomes corrupt. At that point, the consequences of individual disobedience can become community consequences. And—in the story of Achan in the Book of Joshua, and of Jonah on the ship to Tarshish—individual disobedience brought consequences that did affect the community they were in."

We then turned to Anna's question and talked about the blindness, deafness, and lack of understanding that verse four presents. "The Scriptures are full of the blindness of man in the face of the knowledge of God," Hal said. He led us to Isaiah 6, where I read, "Be ever hearing, but never understanding; be ever seeing, but never perceiving."

"Isaiah," Hal said, "was following the thought of Deuteronomy twenty-nine here, and Jesus quoted this passage from Isaiah in Matthew thirteen. In discussing the difficulty of the Jews in accepting Christ, Paul quoted this Deuteronomy passage again in Romans eleven. From Moses to the prophets to Jesus to Paul, the same theme recurs. People hear of God but don't understand him, and see his works but don't perceive them."

Once again, I was reminded of C.S. Lewis, who described sin as being like a mist on the windshield that keeps you from seeing clearly when you're driving.

Hal agreed. "But we must understand these Scriptures in light of the Scriptures that say God will reward those who seek him. 'Seek and you shall find.' God opens the eyes and ears and understanding of those who want to see and hear and understand his way. He doesn't conceal himself from anyone who wants to find him."

Then he turned to Paula's question about God never forgiving the secret idolater who invokes blessings on himself.

"The language about the Lord never forgiving the secret idolater does not mean that such people are beyond becoming true believers, being redeemed in Christ, and being forgiven their sins. It means that the empty forms of belief, accompanied by the reality of unbelief, will never be effective. The consequences to them that are described here are, again, a metaphor for hell: curses, calamities, disasters, diseases, and a burning waste of salt and sulfur."

Finally, we talked again about the repetitive nature of Deuteronomy. "God is the great schoolmaster," Hal said. "One way people learn is by repetition. The same messages are repeated again and again throughout Deuteronomy, and elsewhere in the Bible, so people will learn. If God says it often enough, perhaps it will sink in."

"One book, one story, one author," I said.

The robin sang. The cloud had passed. In a few weeks, flowers would bloom in Hal's garden.

CHAPTER THIRTY

Another April Saturday morning. A light misty drizzle fogged the windshield just enough to make us turn the interval wipers on. I recalled again Lewis's analogy of sin's effect on our clarity of mind. What was our windshield wiper? For me, it was surely Hal. And Anna. And the Scriptures themselves, if I was faithful to read them. But why did I continue to need them? Why didn't I just learn God's ways once and be done with it? Anna and I drove into the driveway, a little ahead of Jerry and Barbara, who came with Paula. An unfamiliar vehicle was already parked there.

The old pickup truck had patches of rust and unrepaired dents. The front bumper drooped on the driver's side as if barely attached. Someone had scrawled *wash me* on the dirt-caked tailgate. We made our way around it, stepping over the puddles and getting our feet wet in the new growth of grass as we stepped onto the lawn here and there, choosing to have feet that were merely wet rather than feet that were also mud-covered.

Hal was bustling around the kitchen. The smell of breakfast was in the air. Bacon sizzled and scrambled eggs were almost ready. He was putting toast on the table for his guests: two men who sat at the table and stared silently at us as we entered. Their rough clothes matched their carriage: heavy plaid shirts, paint-stained jeans, one of them wearing a rumpled baseball cap from a biker's bar. Their clothing, unshaven faces, and reserved demeanor were too obvious a contrast to us. I was wondering who was at the wrong meeting when Hal greeted us.

"Meet Dewey and John," he said. "We're about to have breakfast. Can I fix you some?"

We had all eaten earlier, but we took a cup of coffee, found seats, and struggled through a conversation with Dewey and John as they wolfed the food Hal put in front of them. They were, we learned, "just passing through." They knew Hal from a church he used to pastor. They lived "up the road a piece," and did odd jobs for a living. Dewey spoke slowly and with a bit of a lisp and seemed to struggle for each thought and the means to express it. John let Dewey do most of the talking but provided his own commentary from time to time. Dewey, he told us, "ain't all there," but it was OK because he knew it, so we could say it in front of him. Dewey looked at him and nodded when he said it. The truck was John's, and the radiator was "no damn good," but he kept a water jug in the cab and stopped to fill it a lot, and they didn't have to go far anyway. They were vague on their destination that morning and, by the time breakfast was over, allowed that they ought to "get on home," a place they apparently shared. When they pushed back from the table, Dewey picked up a couple of pieces of toast and stuffed them in a jacket pocket. They shook hands deferentially with each of us and departed.

When we heard the engine of the pickup cough to life, Hal explained: Dewey was mildly retarded and had lived with his parents until they passed away. His only relative was a brother who lived out west somewhere and sent him some money from time to time. He lived with John in his family home, a bungalow that had gone downhill since his parents' death. John was a former drug addict. He had been through a successful rehabilitation, but his mind was permanently affected by years of pharmacological abuse. The two got some sort of government support, enough to keep them going at least. They did odd jobs for people who knew them. They had been in a church Hal had pastored, where he tried to bring in people living on society's margins. Even out here—maybe even more out here—in this rural community, there were a lot of folks like that. They didn't all live in some urban ghetto.

"That must have been a wonderful church, Hal," Paula said. "Bringing people like that into a real church. That's what living the gospel should be all about."

Hal smiled wryly. "Should be," he said. "Should be. But isn't. Problem was I was too successful, and pretty soon the other people started leaving. And they were the ones who had the money and kept the church going. Can't blame them, I suppose. No one really wants their children to come to church and be around people like Dewey and John. So, after awhile, the elders decided we couldn't be a family church and a mission church both, and sent me packing and got another fellow in there the moms and dads liked better. I think they're back being a family church now."

"What about Dewey and John?" Paula asked. "And the other people like them? Where do they go to church?"

"I try to keep in touch with them," Hal said. "If they live near enough to Concord, I send them to the Salvation Army; that's one place I know they'll be welcome. But it's hard. I visit; they come here; I do what I can."

"Like this morning?" I asked.

"Oh," Hal said, "this morning wasn't planned. They just showed up. When they get lonely or hungry they come by. I read the Bible a little and pray with them and give them a hot meal. We talk about repentance and loving God. It's probably all the church they have."

Anna began to clean up the table and the dishes and refused to listen to Hal's protests. His Bible was already on the table, and lay open.

"Go ahead," Anna told him. "I can hear you while I'm working."

So Hal read to us.

> When all these blessings and curses I have set before you come upon you and you take them to heart wherever the LORD your God disperses you among the nations, and when you and your children return to the LORD your God and obey him with all your heart and with all your soul according to everything I command you today, then the LORD your God will restore your fortunes and have compassion on you and gather you again from all the nations where he scattered you. Even if you have been banished to the most distant land under the heavens, from there the LORD your God will gather you and bring you back.
>
> He will bring you to the land that belonged to your fathers, and you will take possession of it. He will make you more prosperous and numerous than your fathers. The LORD your God will circumcise your hearts and the hearts of your descendants, so that you may love him with all your heart and

with all your soul, and live. The LORD your God will put all these curses on your enemies who hate and persecute you. You will again obey the LORD and follow all his commands I am giving you today. Then the LORD your God will make you most prosperous in all the work of your hands and in the fruit of your womb, the young of your livestock and the crops of your land. The LORD will again delight in you and make you prosperous, just as he delighted in your fathers, if you obey the LORD your God and keep his commands and decrees that are written in this Book of the Law and turn to the LORD your God with all your heart and with all your soul.

Now what I am commanding you today is not too difficult for you or beyond your reach. It is not up in heaven, so that you have to ask, "Who will ascend into heaven to get it and proclaim it to us so we may obey it?" Nor is it beyond the sea, so that you have to ask, "Who will cross the sea to get it and proclaim it to us so we may obey it?" No, the word is very near you; it is in your mouth and in your heart so you may obey it.

See, I set before you today life and prosperity, death and destruction. For I command you today to love the LORD your God, to walk in his ways, and to keep his commands, decrees, and laws; then you will live and increase, and the LORD your God will bless you in the land you are entering to possess.

But if your heart turns away and you are not obedient, and if you are drawn away to bow down to other gods and worship them, I declare to you this day that you will certainly be destroyed. You will not live long in the land you are crossing the Jordan to enter and possess.

This day I call heaven and earth as witnesses against you that I have set before you life and death, blessings and curses. Now choose life, so that you and your children may live and that you may love the LORD your God, listen to his voice, and hold fast to him. For the LORD is your life, and he will give you many years in the land he swore to give to your fathers, Abraham, Isaac, and Jacob.

—Deut. 30:1–20

When we had discussed the last chapter, we talked about the covenant of Deuteronomy. Jerry asked Hal if this chapter was part of the covenant.

Hal pointed out that the reference to "heaven and earth" as witnesses in verse nineteen completed the treaty text. Witnesses were a part of the ancient near-eastern treaties, but whom do you call upon to witness God's covenant? Here the answer is, in essence, the whole universe. God calls on his entire creation, the spiritual and material realm, as witness to his covenant with his people.

I recalled the law in chapter nineteen, where two witnesses were needed for conviction of a crime or offense.

"God," Hal said, "is true to his own law. The whole cosmos will testify against his people if they break his law. It follows the law as given in chapter nineteen."

He rose and moved to a CD player in the corner of the kitchen and pressed something. The strains of monastic chant flowed out, the Latin filling the air like the lingering textures of breakfast smells: coffee, bacon, and eggs. The melody rose, swelled, then faded and rose again. He closed his eyes for a minute, turning the volume up so it washed over us. Then he turned it down to a background level.

"There is a melody in Scripture," he said. "Can you see it here?"

I was trying to put the Latin together with Deuteronomy when Anna spoke: "It's the first ten verses," she said, "isn't it, Hal?"

He nodded. "Take it and read."

Anna read the verses aloud.

"I don't get it," Jerry said.

"Tell him, Anna," Hal said.

"It's the pattern we talked about last time, Jerry. It moves from one point in to a center, then back out in reverse order to the same point where it began.

"When you return to the Lord

He will restore you
Then you will love him
He will make you prosperous
When you obey."

I recognized the now familiar pattern, and more than that. The center was familiar: "so that you may love him with all your heart and with all your soul."

"It's the line from the Shema," I said, flipping back to chapter six. "Chapter six, verse five. It's the commandment Jesus called the first and greatest commandment. But what about circumcision of the heart? Didn't we talk about that before?"

"We did," Hal said, "in chapter ten. Remember that circumcision is the sign of the covenant. Circumcision of the heart means making the covenant internal, committing yourself to God with your whole person, not just outwardly."

The soft chant around us filled in the spaces in our conversation.

"O lux beatissima, reple cordis intima tu orum fidelium."

("O Blessed Light, fill the innermost parts of thy servants' hearts.")

"This chapter," Hal said, "is one of the most profound theological chapters of the Bible. It radiates beauty, hope, and redemption. In a mirror image of verses twenty-nine through thirty-one of chapter four, once again framing the law with the theological meaning and consequence, it teaches that the story does not end with the curses. It describes what actually happened to Israel in the exile and return from exile that lies some eight hundred to nine hundred years in the future. God always holds out the possibility of returning to him, as Israel did after the exile. When we turn to him with all our heart and obey him, he will restore, have compassion, regather, and renew prosperity. We have talked about how Deuteronomy follows the form of other sovereign-vassal treaties of the ancient near-east, but this is a respect in which it does not. Only the sovereign God offers his people a second chance."

"Sine tuo numine nihil est in homine, nihil est innoxium."

("Without thine aid there is nothing in man; there is nothing without sin.")

"There is a straight line from this passage to the New Testament, and it leads through the prophet Jeremiah. Chapters twenty-nine through thirty-one of Jeremiah are a prophetic message of restoration to the people who are about to be exiled. God's people, who are under the curse, will seek him with all their heart, and when they do, they will find him. God will make a 'new covenant' with them, which will not be like the old covenant he made with their fathers. He will put his law in their minds and write it on their hearts. And he will forgive their wickedness and remember their sins no more."

"Lava quod est sordidum, riga quot est aridum, sana est saucium."

("Cleanse that which is blemished; refresh that which is dry; heal that which is sick.")

"This is, of course, the new covenant Jesus spoke of, the new covenant in his blood, which was poured out for us. In the familiar parable of the prodigal son in Luke fifteen, Jesus taught God's willingness to restore his people. The son had squandered his inheritance in wild living, but when he repented and returned in humility, his father welcomed him back, killed the fatted calf, and celebrated his return from death to life."

"Flecte quod est rigidum, fove quod est frigidum, rege quod est devium."

("Bend that which is rigid; heat that which is cold; lead that which has gone astray.")

I asked Hal what the meaning of the circumcision of the heart was in this passage. Did it indicate that God alone was responsible for restoring his sinning people, or was it his response to their repentance and return to him?

"Da tuis fidelibus, in te confidentibus sacrum septenarium."

("To those who are faithful to thee, who trust in thee, give of thy sevenfold gifts.")

"In chapter ten," Hal said, "the people were told to circumcise their own hearts. In chapter thirty, God promises to do it for them and their descendants. But the passage begins the promise of restoration with the people's initiative in return and obedience in verses one and two, and ends with conditioning the restoration on obedience in verse ten. The difference is that their renewed love of God and obedience to him is enabled by God's action in circumcising their hearts. The meaning here is that God will remove obstacles or impediments to love and obedience."

"Da virtutis meritum, da salutis exitum, da perenne gaudium."

("Give virtue reward; give salvation in the final hour; give eternal joy.")

"There is only one way that those obstacles are removed, and that is by Jesus Christ taking on the burden of sin for us. Humans cannot save themselves through the law. Jesus is obedient for us, and the fulfillment of the law comes, for us, by believing in him. As Paul says in Romans ten, four, 'Christ is the end of the law so that there may be righteousness for everyone who believes.'

"You cannot separate or tip the balance between repentance and grace. God in his grace offers us circumcision of the heart, the path to righteousness, in Christ. We respond to the call. As Revelation three, twenty, says, 'I stand at the door and knock. If anyone hears my voice and opens the door, I will come in and eat with him and he with me.' Jesus certainly had this Deuteronomy passage in mind when he said in John five, forty-six, 'If you believed Moses, you would believe me, for he wrote of me.'"

"Amen. Alleluia."

The music faded, and Hal moved over to turn it off.

We turned to verses eleven through fourteen.

"I studied a lot of ancient epics in college," Jerry said. "In most of them, like the Gilgamesh epic in Babylon, the hero goes on a long search for elusive truth. That seems to be different here." Barbara put her hand over his as he spoke.

"Yes," Hal said. "Here God teaches that his commands, his word, require no search of distant places. They are very near, 'in your mouth and in your heart.' So Jesus taught in Luke seventeen, twenty-one, that the Kingdom of God is within you. And Paul referred to these verses in Romans ten, when he said, 'That if you confess with your mouth, "Jesus is Lord," and believe in your heart that God raised him from the dead, you will be saved. For it is with your heart that you believe and are justified, and it is with your mouth that you confess and are saved.'

"This is not a matter of great erudition. No special qualifications or training are required. God's revelation of himself to humanity is not mysterious, not part of the 'secret things' of Deuteronomy twenty-nine, twenty-nine. It's practical, realistic, understandable, and doable by the simplest person of faith."

"I'm reading the story of Watchman Nee," Barbara added. "He was a Chinese Christian who was killed by the Communists. A brilliant man. He wrote a lot of books. But at one point he went to a rural village and met an elderly woman who couldn't read or write. He listened to her prayers and talked to her and realized that in her simple faith she was way ahead of him spiritually. I guess that's a little of what the message is here: You don't have to go to seminary or be brilliant or make some extraordinary effort to understand God's word."

"Like a little child," Jerry said softly.

"Just so," Hal said. No more was needed.

The silence of comfortable friends enveloped us for a few minutes. Anna was through with the dishes and broke the silence as she sat down.

"We're at my favorite passage in Deuteronomy," she said: "Now choose life."

Paula read the fuller passage: "This day I call heaven and earth as witnesses against you that I have set before you life and death, blessings and curses. Now choose life, so that you and your children may live."

I knew exactly where Anna was coming from on this one. Our ten-year-old daughter had just come to understand what abortion was. The horror of the discovery was the shipwreck of innocence. Mothers, doctors, and the justice system her father worked in conspired to tear children apart and destroy them in what should have been the safest place they would ever be. We had been struggling to find ways to explain, but there was no explanation. How, I wondered, did people who approved of abortion explain it to their children? "Pro-choice and pro-child," read the bumper sticker. I didn't understand it any more than little Elizabeth did.

Paula and Anna looked expectantly at Hal.

"Now choose life!" he repeated softly. "It is a ready-made catchword for the pro-life movement. It jumps at you out of the pages of chapter thirty. In context, of course, it was not about abortion but an exhortation that captures the message of the entire Bible. Our Creator God has from the beginning put before man and woman—the beings he created in his own image—the choice of life and death. In the second chapter of Genesis, he told Adam that his disobedience in eating from the Tree of the Knowledge of Good and Evil would bring about his death. Our primordial parents' disobedience led to the fulfillment of the sentence, for them and their descendants: 'dust you are and to dust you will return.' And yet it does seem particularly appropriate to think of the choice of life and death in terms of this paradigm, almost primordial, evil of our time."

"Does Jesus ever talk about it?" I asked.

"Not about abortion as such," Hal said. "It would have been so unthinkable that he wouldn't have needed to. It was one of things that doctors were forbidden to do under the Hippocratic Oath, which dates to hundreds of years before Jesus' life on earth. But the presentation of the choice of life or death, prosperity or destruction, blessings or curses, probably was in Jesus' mind in Mark three, four, when he asked, 'Which is lawful on the Sabbath: to do good or to do evil, to save life or to kill?' And he confirmed the choice that Moses presented when he taught in Mark sixteen, sixteen, that whoever believes will be saved, but whoever does not believe will be condemned. The teaching harks back to Abraham, who believed God, and it was credited to him as righteousness."

We came to abortion, and Hal had this to say: "Somewhere in eternity are the souls of tens of millions of aborted children. God deals with them in his mercy and justice. And there are tens of millions of people who bear the guilt of those abortions, whether they are the mothers who chose them, the fathers or family members who urged or financed them, the medical personnel who performed them, or the judges, legislators, or the political leaders who made them lawful and threw the robe of government protection around them.

"We have already seen from Deuteronomy that God views child sacrifice as one of the most horrible evils man can commit. In this chapter, we can see that the knowledge of right and wrong, of the content of God's law in this regard, is not elusive or mysterious but in plain sight. Even children can understand it. God puts a plain choice before people of life and good, or death and evil. The choice of abortion is a plain choice for death and evil.

"Polls show that even most women who have had abortions believe it's morally wrong. They have made a choice that is tragically, horribly wrong, murdering their own children for a perceived greater, but selfish good. It is the embarrassment, the inconvenience, the expense, the loss of freedom, in bearing and raising a child that drives abortion, along with the conviction that women—and, incidentally, the men who would bear legal and financial responsibility for the child—should be able to engage in sexual activity freely without having to bear the natural consequences.

"And yet, even for as great a sin as this, God holds out the possibility of restoration. One can turn to him and be restored. Forgiveness is available. Jesus can bring even the thief on the cross to himself, and into paradise, if he believes and confesses."

The CD chant had long since stopped. But the voices echoed in my mind as they echoed through the vaults and chambers of the cathedrals and monasteries where they first sang:

Kyrie eleison.
Lord have mercy.
Lord have mercy.
Lord have mercy.

CHAPTER THIRTY-ONE

I t was several weeks before we came back together at Hal's. Easter intervened, and people were busy. Hal put me off until all of the growing group could gather. It was no longer just him and me, he told me. What had been important to me was just as important to the rest of them. One could be selfish even about the things of God, which, above all things, were meant to be shared.

When we finally did meet, it was May. The snow had disappeared even from the plow piles and south sides of the fields, where borders of trees made winter linger for a few weeks and gradually recede away from the sunlit north sides. Buds were visible on the maples and cherry trees. A warmth we hadn't felt since October blanketed the land.

And so we came, Anna and I, Jerry and Barbara, Paula and—to my surprise—her husband, Mike, a local newspaper editor. And, to my further surprise, Julie. Apparently Hal had invited her, and when I saw her drive in, I was embarrassed that I had not thought of it. At the office, a certain hierarchy was observed between the staff and the professionals, although she seemed to move easily around it, respectful but friendly and not deferential to the lawyers. Here among three of her "bosses," Jerry, Paula, and I, and our spouses, she was one with us, and we, unselfconsciously, with her. "No Jew nor Greek," I thought, "no slave nor free." Our oneness in Christ needed neither thought nor effort.

"Thanks for waiting, Hal," I overheard Paula say to him as he directed us again to haul chairs out to the rose garden. "Mike couldn't have come any sooner."

As we arranged our circle and opened our Bibles, I noticed Hal had been pruning the bushes and raking up winter mulch. "The dark and snow cover makes fungus grow," he explained, observing me observing his handiwork. "You have to get rid of the old mulch and air the soil around the plant so it will get a healthy start on the new season. Then you can put a little new mulch on—clean, healthy mulch, so it gets some protection. Same with pruning: Cut off the dead wood, and adjust the growth of the rest of it so it grows healthy, not all crooked and scraggly. You'll never get good blooms if you just leave it alone. It grows every which way."

Then he read.

> Then Moses went out and spoke these words to all Israel: "I am now a hundred and twenty years old and I am no longer able to lead you. The LORD has said to me, 'You shall not cross the Jordan.' The LORD your God himself will cross over ahead of you. He will destroy these nations before you, and you will take possession of their land. Joshua also will cross over ahead of you, as the LORD said. And the LORD will do to them what he did to Sihon and Og, the kings of the Amorites, whom he destroyed along with their land. The LORD will deliver them to you, and you must do to them all that I have commanded you. Be strong and courageous. Do not be afraid or terrified because of them, for the LORD your God goes with you; he will never leave you nor forsake you."
>
> Then Moses summoned Joshua and said to him in the presence of all Israel, "Be strong and courageous, for you must go with this people into the land that the LORD swore to their forefathers to give them, and you must divide it among them as their inheritance. The LORD himself goes before you and will be with you; he will never leave you nor forsake you. Do not be afraid; do not be discouraged." So Moses wrote down this law and gave it to the priests, the sons of Levi, who carried the ark of the covenant of the LORD, and to all the elders of Israel. Then Moses commanded them: "At the end of every seven years, in the year for canceling debts, during the Feast of Tabernacles, when all Israel comes to appear before the LORD your God at the place he will choose, you shall read this law before them in their hearing. Assemble the people—men, women, and children, and the

aliens living in your towns—so they can listen and learn to fear the LORD your God and follow carefully all the words of this law. Their children, who do not know this law, must hear it and learn to fear the LORD your God as long as you live in the land you are crossing the Jordan to possess."

The LORD said to Moses, "Now the day of your death is near. Call Joshua and present yourselves at the Tent of Meeting, where I will commission him." So Moses and Joshua came and presented themselves at the Tent of Meeting.

Then the LORD appeared at the Tent in a pillar of cloud, and the cloud stood over the entrance to the Tent. And the LORD said to Moses: "You are going to rest with your fathers, and these people will soon prostitute themselves to the foreign gods of the land they are entering. They will forsake me and break the covenant I made with them. On that day I will become angry with them and forsake them; I will hide my face from them, and they will be destroyed. Many disasters and difficulties will come upon them, and on that day they will ask, 'Have not these disasters come upon us because our God is not with us?' And I will certainly hide my face on that day because of all their wickedness in turning to other gods.

"Now write down for yourselves this song and teach it to the Israelites and have them sing it, so that it may be a witness for me against them. When I have brought them into the land flowing with milk and honey, the land I promised on oath to their forefathers, and when they eat their fill and thrive, they will turn to other gods and worship them, rejecting me and breaking my covenant. And when many disasters and difficulties come upon them, this song will testify against them, because it will not be forgotten by their descendants. I know what they are disposed to do, even before I bring them into the land I promised them on oath." So Moses wrote down this song that day and taught it to the Israelites.

The LORD gave this command to Joshua son of Nun: "Be strong and courageous, for you will bring the Israelites into the land I promised them on oath, and I myself will be with you."

After Moses finished writing in a book the words of this law from beginning to end, he gave this command to the Levites who carried the ark of the covenant of the LORD: "Take this Book of the Law and place it beside the ark of the covenant of the LORD your God. There it will remain as a witness against you. For I know how rebellious and stiff-necked you are. If you have been rebellious against the LORD while I am still alive and with you, how much more will you rebel after I die! Assemble before me all the elders of your tribes and all your officials, so that I can speak these words in their hearing and call heaven and earth to testify against them. For I know that after my death you are sure to become utterly corrupt and to turn from the way I have commanded you. In days to come, disaster will fall upon you because you will do evil in the sight of the LORD and provoke him to anger by what your hands have made." And Moses recited the words of this song from beginning to end in the hearing of the whole assembly of Israel.

—Deut. 31:1–30

"You're at a disadvantage, Mike," Hal said, after finishing the reading. "You're starting the book at the end. Only Chris has been studying it from the beginning. Still, the end of Deuteronomy in many ways reflects the beginning. I've been teaching the group about pattern and structure in Deuteronomy. One of the things—the many things—that gives us confidence in the integrity of the text is its conformity to pattern. Like a symphony or a sonnet. You don't know what the notes or the verses will be, but you know they'll fall into a particular form. Beauty is found in form, and so are truth and goodness."

"Help me out," Mike said.

I knew Mike well enough to know that he understood and appreciated classical music and had a first-rate education. There was a certain arrogance in his bearing not uncommon to those who believe they have achieved a measure of worldly knowledge not shared by most around them, a supreme confidence in the rightness of their opinions confirmed by the indoctrinations of the illiberality of what passed for liberal education in some institutions. But Hal had used the right concepts to capture his attention. There was something more here than met the eye, and Mike, too, could be privy to it and could gain a special knowledge consistent with his belief in the excellence of the things he respected.

Hal reviewed the chapter for Mike's benefit and, to a degree, for everyone's, in light of what had gone before.

Chapter thirty-one, he explained, begins the closing sequence of Deuteronomy, what some students of the book call the "outer frame." The first part of the outer frame was made up of chapters one through three, where the historical prologue introduced the law. "Think of it like crossing a river," he said. "You go through the outer frame of the first three chapters, then the inner frame of the general stipulations through chapter eleven. The deep central part is made up of the law chapters, twelve through twenty-six. Then the inner frame on the other side of the chapters, twenty-seven through thirty. Now we approach the far bank, the outer frame of chapters thirty-one through thirty-three. The difference is that on the other side of the river, in the first three chapters, Moses was looking back at where they had been, teaching by history, by the experiences they had actually had. Now, as he approaches the far bank, he reminds them of that history, but these three chapters, thirty-one to thirty-three, look ahead. He is now going to teach by prophecy. While the historical prologue focused on the people's past experience—leading up to the time of entry into the land—the concluding chapters focus on the future: the need for obedience, the inevitability of rebellion, and the response of God, who has given them the good things they're about to possess, and of their rejection of him."

"Go on," Mike said.

"There are many similarities between the beginning and the end of the book," Hal said. "Both parts are introduced as the words of Moses. Both contain the assurance of God's leading in the victories that lie ahead, the prohibition of Moses' entering the land, the transition of leadership to Joshua, and his involvement in dividing the land. The concluding ceremonies of the covenant were reenacted by Josiah in Second Kings and by Nehemiah after the Exile.

"This chapter fulfilled and finished the covenant, committing it to writing and entrusting the copy to the Levites and the elders, who were to place it beside the Ark of the Covenant containing the tablets of the Ten Commandments. The Levites and elders to whom it was entrusted were the religious and civil authorities responsible for its ongoing fulfillment.

"This chapter also establishes the ceremony of public reading at the Feast of Tabernacles in the year of forgiveness of debts. We studied that in chapter fifteen. That's the time when thankfulness and personal commitment should be at a height. The entire community was included in the ceremony. The law of the two witnesses reappeared when Moses again called 'heaven and earth,'—as well as the two writings, the scroll of the law, and the Ten Commandments—to witness against the people in their future disobedience.

"The song that was given became yet another witness against them in their future failures. And this chapter repeats the prophetic inevitability of failure, based on God's knowledge of the people's hearts. It referred to prostitution or sexual infidelity as metaphors to describe the people's turning to other gods in violation of the covenant. It foresaw prosperity leading to their lapse of commitment, as they had been warned against in chapters six and eight. It sees the irony of the very blessings given by God leading to them forgetting God's graciousness in granting those blessings, and that adversity is often a better teacher than prosperity."

"So far, so good," Mike said. "But what do you make of the one-hundred-twenty-year lifespan of Moses? Surely you don't believe he did all this stuff when he was a hundred and twenty years old? One good reason not to believe the Bible is these crazy lifespans it gives people in the Old Testament . . . Methuselah and all that."

Hal replied, "One hundred twenty years is the limit of a man's life according to Genesis six, three. I saw an article recently in which someone had done a study and determined that one-hundred-twenty years is about the maximum length of time the human body can last. And I've read many newspaper articles about the death of this or that person who was the oldest person known in the world, usually well past a hundred and usually not in a nursing home but still functioning up to the end in some Asian country. So I guess it can happen, even if it's unusual, without anything miraculous being involved. And Moses was an unusual man."

"I'll agree to that," Mike said.

"As to 'Methuselah and all that,'" Hal continued, "there are old genealogies from other cultures as well as the Bible that give similar extraordinary lifespans for the ancients. So either something was going on then that allowed people to live to extraordinary ages and we just don't understand it, or there were some literary conventions at work in which the numbers given for their ages have some other meaning that's lost to us now. Neither alternative gives me reason to question the Bible. Psalm ninety says, 'The length of our days is seventy years—or eighty, if we have the strength.' That certainly is more typical for most people."

I added, "I once heard the philosophy that the first twenty-five years are for learning, the second twenty-five for earning, and the last twenty-five for relaxing and enjoying the fruit of the earning."

"That's not the biblical model," Hal said. "God gives no retirement age in the Bible. Moses spent the first third of his life learning in Egypt, as in your model. The next third was his time of separation from his people. But it was in the last third of his life that he did all his great work. His leadership of Israel through the confrontations with Pharaoh, the exodus out of Egypt, the wilderness wanderings in the desert with all the hardships, and the battles with Sihon and Og, began when he was eighty. By this model, applied to the typical lifespan of Psalm ninety, our most useful work for the Lord would begin around age fifty. It's not for nothing that the term *elders* is used for leaders of God's people in both the Old and New Testaments. Joshua himself lived to be a hundred and ten and continued in leadership throughout that time. While his exact age on assuming leadership isn't certain, it was at the end of the Exodus, and he had been an adult at the beginning, so he must have been at least sixty when he was commissioned to take over from Moses. The time of rest for believers is after this life, not during it."

"I know a lawyer who is well into his seventies," I said. "He's devoted his useful years after retiring from his active law practice to developing Christian legal aid clinics throughout the country. He's developed the models, written the guidebooks on how to do it, and traveled the country recruiting and training lawyers to carry it out."

"There," Hal said, "is a Moses. He knows the meaning of these Scriptures where God says he will 'cross over ahead of them' and 'go with them.' For us, that presence of God with us is Jesus, the Immanuel, or 'God with us,' prophesied in Isaiah seven, fourteen, and fulfilled in him, as Matthew teaches. And your lawyer friend must also know the meaning of the teaching to be 'strong and courageous' that God gave repeatedly to Israel, and to Joshua in this chapter. Motivating lawyers to do biblically-based legal aid sounds like no small task."

"Motivating lawyers," I said, "to even acknowledge their Christian faith by belonging to an organization like the Christian Legal Society or committing a couple of hundred dollars a year to dues that sustain some voice of believers in the legal profession is difficult enough. It takes a lot of strength and courage to get people to do more than that and actually give some of their time to the work of the Lord in their professional field."

"Well," Hal said, "you lawyers are busy and under a lot of pressure. Don't judge your colleagues too harshly. Anyway, your point was that lawyers can serve the Lord in their senior years, like your friend who's out starting Christian legal aid services. That's not just a point about lawyers. God's great people in the Bible all died 'with their boots on,' as the saying goes."

We went on to talk about the writing of the law and its transmission to the Levites and elders, the assembly of all the people—men, women, and children—to hear it read every seven years in the year of canceling debts at the Feast of Tabernacles, and the deposit of the written law beside the Ark of the Covenant.

"I'm amazed that they included women," Mike said. "Women didn't get any respect in the Bible."

A quick look passed between Anna and Julie, a look I could easily read. They knew far too much about the Bible to fall into the thinking that it slighted women. Paula and Barbara, newer to the faith, looked at Hal, curious for his response.

"It is significant," he said, "that the law was to be read to women, children, and aliens, as well as the men of Israel. The notion that women were not to be taught God's word in the same manner and to the same extent as men is not from the Bible. Some of the Greek and Roman views about women's inferiority seeped into Jewish and Christian thinking. To the extent that it did, it is simply error.

"And it is significant not only that the law was to be read to the whole people but that the whole law was to be read. The book of Deuteronomy can be read aloud in a few hours. Most evangelical churches read very little Scripture, often only the verse or verses the pastor is preaching on that Sunday. But the public reading of Scripture is a biblical practice and command. There are whole parts of the Bible that some evangelical churches never read or teach. Biblical literacy in the larger society is nearly non-existent, but even in Bible-centered churches it's shockingly deficient. Our spiritual life tends to be as rich as the time we spend in the word of God. No matter how long and at what depth you've studied the Bible, you can't spend time in the word without learning something new. It's as true of churches as it is of individuals. One of the advantages of the more liturgical churches is the more systematic and repetitive exposure of people to the Scriptures."

"I've never seen the point of having separate men's and women's Bible studies," I said. "I'd rather learn and study with my wife."

"There may be some practical reasons for separate studies sometimes," Hal said. "I don't have a problem with it as long as people don't think they're doing it out of some biblical command. There are some subjects about which people may feel freer to express themselves or share their experiences or problems when they are not in mixed company. And there are some gender differences in what men and women tend to be interested in that lend themselves to separate groups for certain kinds of fellowship. But God's teaching is that learning his word is in no way a matter of male exclusiveness or priority."

"And children, too," Julie said.

"Especially children," Hal said. "Things learned at an early age tend to be remembered. Deuteronomy consistently teaches the need to communicate God's word to children. They are to be present in the great assemblies of reading the law and remembrance of God's gracious acts. If these were done every seven years, each child would hear the whole law read and participate in the ceremonies at least twice before reaching the age of adult understanding."

"I remember some things well from the Sunday school of my youth," I said. "Especially 'Jesus loves me.' That song is engraved in my consciousness forever. I love to hear it sung, even now. It may seem childish, but it's so basic, so reassuring, so connected to Jesus himself and everything he means; it's a key part of my life in faith from the earliest memory."

Hal leaned back and closed his eyes to the morning sun. Then he sang it out in a soft voice. One by one we joined him, off key and on, soprano and bass, alto and tenor, calling back the message of God from our childhood and the childhoods of millions of other children:

> Jesus loves me,
> This I know,
> For the Bible tells me so.
> Little ones to him belong.
> They are weak
> But he is strong.
> Yes, Jesus loves me.
> Yes, Jesus loves me.
> Yes, Jesus loves me.
> The Bible tells me so.[15]

Paula joined in, but Mike listened silently, expressionless. What was he thinking? Was he afraid to take on Hal's statement about Greek and Roman thought versus biblical teaching? Was he confused to find people as well-educated and sophisticated as he was singing "Jesus Loves Me"? Did he wonder what he had gotten himself into by coming? He gave no hint. As the familiar melody faded, Hal resumed.

"Music," he said, "is an especially good device for memorizing. We remember songs when we don't remember prose. This chapter anticipates the next, in which God told Moses to write down the words of a song God would teach him, and to teach it to the people because, as verse twenty-one says, 'it will not be forgotten by their descendants.'

"Jewish tradition," he added, "interpreted the instruction to write down the song rather broadly. Verse nineteen says, 'write down for yourselves,' a plural command that clearly required someone more than Moses alone to write it. You might think it meant Moses and Joshua, since Joshua was present and was being commissioned to succeed Moses. But the Jewish sages concluded, based on various kinds of reasoning, that what was required to fulfill this was that every Jew was to write down a copy of the Torah for himself, much as we saw in chapter seventeen that the king was required to do. The text doesn't really bear this meaning, but it's a wonderful learning device. It wouldn't be a bad exercise for school children to write a copy of a book of the Bible." He paused.

"Programs that teach children Bible memory have the same objective: to find ways of engraving God's word, as the Scripture says, 'in their mouth'—that is, to memory, and 'in their heart'—that is in the understanding and commitment of the mind. Hosea four, six says, 'My people are destroyed for lack of knowledge.' It's still true."

Then he brought us back to the writing. Twice in this chapter Moses is said to have written down the law. In addition, God instructed them to write down the song that becomes chapter thirty-two. Several times before in Deuteronomy, God had told them to write down the law. God himself wrote the Ten Commandments. The people were to write the law on their wrists and foreheads, on the doorposts of their houses and on the city gates; the king was to write the whole law so he would have his own copy that he could read and follow in his governance. In this chapter we see that Moses wrote down the law and deposited it for posterity, as well as writing down the particular song that became chapter thirty-two for a witness against the people in their anticipated disobedience and for their remembrance.

Mike came back to life as he contemplated the writing of the law.

"So what did he really write?" he asked. "And how do we know he wrote it down anyway? Anyone could have written that he wrote it."

"Anyone could," Hal said. "I could write a book and say Moses wrote it. But I don't think anyone would believe me. Here the text says Moses wrote down the law. From the earliest knowledge we have, the Jews have believed that Moses was the author of the first five books of the Bible. It seems reasonable to think that the people closest in time to the writing would have known."

"But what about . . ." Mike began.

Hal held up his hand to stop him. "Besides," he said, "Jesus implied that Moses wrote the first books of the Bible. He's a pretty good authority. He talked about most of the parts of the Old Testament that modern people have the greatest trouble believing with no hint that they didn't happen: Adam and Eve, Noah, Jonah, Sodom and Gomorrah. Now maybe he was just using them to make a point and wasn't trying to distinguish between history, metaphor, and allegory. But he took them seriously, and so should we.

"Unless," he looked at Mike, "we don't take Jesus seriously. And that is quite another matter."

Mike avoided the pointed comment. "It all comes down to the Bible, doesn't it? I mean, even believing in Jesus basically requires you to believe the Bible. Why should we? Why is it any more believable than any other book?"

"People often wonder," Hal replied, "how the Bible came to be and how we can have confidence in it. Well, here in Deuteronomy thirty-one is an account of the beginning of the canon of Scripture—the creation, preservation, and recognition of the writings that embody God's word and instruction."

"But it doesn't even say what he wrote," Mike said. "If it's the beginning of creating Scripture, we ought to know what was created."

"It's true," Hal said, "that there is no table of contents for what Moses wrote. It refers to writing 'this law' and 'the words of this law from beginning to end.' Some think that what was written down by Moses was the whole Torah—that is, the first five books of the Bible. In Jewish understanding, that is what 'the law' is. Others think it was only Deuteronomy. Either way, it is clear that sacred writing was being created here, writing that was meant to be preserved and used for teaching, rebuking, correcting, and training in righteousness, as God says in Second Timothy."

"Do you think," Mike asked, "that Moses even wrote parts that talk about himself, like where it says 'After Moses finished writing'?"

"No, of course not," Hal replied. "It's unlikely that Moses wrote about himself in the third person or wrote the account of his own death, which appears in chapter thirty-four. And there are other places in Deuteronomy that show the mark of a later editor, like where something is said to be there 'until this day.' The Scriptures show us that other biblical writers, including Jeremiah and Paul, had secretaries, if you will, who recorded much of their writing for them. None of that should affect your confidence in it. Knowing that others contributed to the final form of the text shouldn't affect our belief that the first five books were basically Moses' work."

"So how did it all get to be the Bible?" Mike asked.

Hal replied, "The Jews' original sacred writings were later added too, so they included not only the first five books, known as the Torah or, in Greek, the Pentateuch, but also the collections known as the former prophets, the latter prophets, and the writings. The former prophets are what we usually call the historical books, from Joshua through Second Kings. The latter prophets are what we call the prophets: Isaiah, Jeremiah, and Ezekiel, the 'Major Prophets,' and the 'Book of the Twelve,' or the 'Minor Prophets.' Finally are the writings, the collection of 'festal scrolls' of praise and instruction that included Psalms, Proverbs, Job, Ruth, The Song of Songs, Ecclesiastes, Lamentations, Esther, Daniel, Chronicles, Ezra, and Nehemiah. Together, these scrolls, or books, that constitute our Old Testament, were, by the time of Jesus, well recognized as the sacred or canonical Scriptures. They were Jesus' Bible, and he often referred to them as 'the Law and the Prophets,' or 'the Law of Moses and the Prophets.' In Luke twenty-four, forty-four, he says, 'Everything must be fulfilled about me that is written in the Law of Moses, the Prophets and the Psalms.' These writings comprising the Old Testament or Hebrew Bible are sometimes referred to as the Tanakh, an acronym of the first letters of the Hebrew terms for the law, the prophets, and the writings.

"The Old Testament Scriptures were originally written on scrolls, which lent themselves to reading in the temple or the synagogues. Christians initially saw the New Testament as an additional section of the Tanakh and began writing the Scriptures in the form of a codex or book in which pages were written on both sides and bound together. One reason for this was to facilitate reference to other portions of the Scriptures for teaching and persuasion. It was the missionary task of the early church to show the Jews and the Gentiles that Jesus' credentials—who he was, what he did, and the meaning of his life, death, and resurrection—were grounded in the Old Testament teachings and prophecies.

"A study of the details of how the Bible came to be is way beyond what we can do here today, Mike, although I would love to help you with such a study. I'll give you a book on it before you leave. But the short answer to your question is that the Bible was the product of consensus. The thirty-nine books of the Old Testament, written over a span of a thousand years, were the consensus of the Jewish community as to what was canonical—that is, authoritative—as God's word. The twenty-seven books of the New Testament represented the consensus of the church about the canonical teachings of Christianity, in addition to the Old Testament. There were plenty of other writings around, but these were the ones that were judged authoritative, suitable for teaching and reading in church, and that could be relied on to prevent errors and heresies. For the most part, the consensus was broad-based and arrived at early. Some of the New Testament consensus was even within the lives of the original apostles. And, while it may not be something you can understand right now, the consensus was arrived at with the guidance of God, the Holy Spirit, whom Jesus promised to send and who would lead us into all truth."

The sun was high in the sky. We had shed sweaters and jackets to enjoy the warmth on our arms and faces, white with winter pallor. The morning had worn on, and it was time to part.

Mike said, "I want to hear you again on this subject."

The others left, but Hal delayed Mike's departure until he had pulled several books out of his library for him. As Mike and Paula drove off, Hal stood beside me, watching.

"Mike thinks he's had the greatest education money can buy," Hal said. "And he's proud of it. And he's right, too, if you only see with the eyes of men. But he has no idea the education he's about to get. He'll count the rest of it rubbish before he gets through."

"What makes you think he'll get that other education, Hal?" I asked.

"Skepticism is thin ice to skate on for a lifetime," Hal replied. "He sees the cracks in it, and he knows its cold and dark underneath. Besides, he's got that girl—Paula. She's got a good hold on him, and she's headed in the right direction. She won't let him fall through the ice."

CHAPTER THIRTY-TWO

W e were nearing the end of our study of Deuteronomy, Hal and I. But the others were just beginning. Fired up by the times they had sat with Hal, each had been studying independently and had acquired a commentary or two and a study Bible to help them. E-mails passed between us day to day on this point or that. Jerry and Paula and Julie all stopped by my office a time or two to share insights. Jerry looked happier and more relaxed than I remember seeing him since we had begun working together, and I guessed he was doing well in dealing with the matters he had confessed to me weeks before.

It was a couple of weeks before we could get together with Hal again. For the first time since I had begun studying with him, he put me off a couple of times before scheduling a study. When he did, he insisted it be at his house. On a Friday evening, we gathered: Jerry and Barbara, Paula and Mike, Julie, Anna, and me. We found Hal in his old red chair in the study and squeezed ourselves into the room with him. Julie and Jerry wound up on the floor for lack of chairs or space to put them. No fire burned in the fireplace. I asked Hal if he would like me to light one, and he agreed. I had to gather wood from his porch and find some old newspapers in the kitchen to start it. When its flames were dancing, we read chapter thirty-two in turns.

> Listen, O heavens, and I will speak; hear, O earth, the words of my mouth.
>
> Let my teaching fall like rain and my words descend like dew, like showers on new grass, like abundant rain on tender plants.
>
> I will proclaim the name of the LORD.

Oh, praise the greatness of our God!

He is the Rock, his works are perfect, and all his ways are just. A faithful God who does no wrong, upright and just is he.

They have acted corruptly toward him; to their shame they are no longer his children, but a warped and crooked generation.

Is this the way you repay the LORD, O foolish and unwise people? Is he not your Father, your Creator, who made you and formed you?

Remember the days of old; consider the generations long past. Ask your father and he will tell you, your elders, and they will explain to you.

When the Most High gave the nations their inheritance, when he divided all mankind, he set up boundaries for the peoples according to the number of the sons of Israel.

For the LORD's portion is his people, Jacob his allotted inheritance.

In a desert land he found him, in a barren and howling waste. He shielded him and cared for him; he guarded him as the apple of his eye, like an eagle that stirs up its nest and hovers over its young, that spreads its wings to catch them and carries them on its pinions.

The LORD alone led him; no foreign god was with him.

He made him ride on the heights of the land and fed him with the fruit of the fields.

He nourished him with honey from the rock, and with oil from the flinty crag, with curds and milk from herd and flock and with fattened lambs and goats, with choice rams of Bashan and the finest kernels of wheat. You drank the foaming blood of the grape.

Jeshurun grew fat and kicked; filled with food, he became heavy and sleek. He abandoned the God who made him and rejected the Rock his Savior.

They made him jealous with their foreign gods and angered him with their detestable idols.

They sacrificed to demons, which are not God—gods they had not known, gods that recently appeared, gods your fathers did not fear.

You deserted the Rock, who fathered you; you forgot the God who gave you birth.

The LORD saw this and rejected them because he was angered by his sons and daughters.

"I will hide my face from them," he said, "and see what their end will be; for they are a perverse generation, children who are unfaithful.

They made me jealous by what is no god and angered me with their worthless idols.

I will make them envious by those who are not a people; I will make them angry by a nation that has no understanding.

For a fire has been kindled by my wrath, one that burns to the realm of death below. It will devour the earth and its harvests and set afire the foundations of the mountains.

"I will heap calamities upon them and spend my arrows against them.

I will send wasting famine against them, consuming pestilence and deadly plague; I will send against them the fangs of wild beasts, the venom of vipers that glide in the dust.

In the street the sword will make them childless; in their homes terror will reign.

Young men and young women will perish, infants and gray-haired men.

I said I would scatter them and blot out their memory from mankind, but I dreaded the taunt of the enemy, lest the adversary misunderstand and say, 'Our hand has triumphed; the Lord has not done all this.' "

They are a nation without sense, there is no discernment in them.

If only they were wise and would understand this and discern what their end will be!

How could one man chase a thousand, or two put ten thousand to flight, unless their Rock had sold them, unless the Lord had given them up?

For their rock is not like our Rock, as even our enemies concede.

Their vine comes from the vine of Sodom and from the fields of Gomorrah. Their grapes are filled with poison, and their clusters with bitterness.

Their wine is the venom of serpents, the deadly poison of cobras.

"Have I not kept this in reserve and sealed it in my vaults?

It is mine to avenge; I will repay. In due time their foot will slip; their day of disaster is near and their doom rushes upon them."

The Lord will judge his people and have compassion on his servants when he sees their strength is gone and no one is left, slave or free.

He will say: "Now where are their gods, the rock they took refuge in, the gods who ate the fat of their sacrifices and drank the wine of their drink offerings? Let them rise up to help you! Let them give you shelter!

"See now that I myself am He! There is no god besides me. I put to death and I bring to life, I have wounded and I will heal, and no one can deliver out of my hand.

"I lift my hand to heaven and declare: As surely as I live forever, when I sharpen my flashing sword and my hand grasps it in judgment, I will take vengeance on my adversaries and repay those who hate me.

"I will make my arrows drunk with blood, while my sword devours flesh: the blood of the slain and the captives, the heads of the enemy leaders."

Rejoice, O nations, with his people, for he will avenge the blood of his servants; he will take vengeance on his enemies and make atonement for his land and people.

Moses came with Joshua son of Nun and spoke all the words of this song in the hearing of the people. When Moses finished reciting all these words to all Israel, he said to them, "Take to heart all the words I have solemnly declared to you this day, so that you may command your children to obey carefully all the words of this law. They are not just idle words for you—they are your life. By them you will live long in the land you are crossing the Jordan to possess."

On that same day the LORD told Moses, "Go up into the Abarim Range to Mount Nebo in Moab, across from Jericho, and view Canaan, the land I am giving the Israelites as their own possession. There on the mountain that you have climbed you will die and be gathered to your people, just as your brother Aaron died on Mount Hor and was gathered to his people. This is because both of you broke faith with me in the presence of the Israelites at the waters of Meribah Kadesh in the Desert of Zin and because you did not uphold my holiness among the Israelites. Therefore, you will see the land only from a distance; you will not enter the land I am giving to the people of Israel."

—Deut. 32:1–52

Looking back on that evening now, I can't help but feel how full of ourselves we all were. We were so young but thought we were so old, so green but thought we were so mature, so eager to share and yet so slow to receive. We had read the book, not just the Bible itself but our books about the Bible. Our cups were overflowing with someone else's knowledge. But in the end what mattered was that we were there. We had crossed the Zered Valley and we were ready for what lay ahead. And Hal was still our leader.

But Hal did little leading for most of the evening. He let us go, as a choir director might let young men and women have a twilight sing, while he stared silently into the fire. From time to time, he would intercede to correct our melody, or add a note, usually bringing us into the New Testament or some other Scripture that related to our thoughts.

My own eye had become more practiced and my study more intense as I neared the end of Deuteronomy. In the "Song of Moses" I could see themes and images we had encountered before, but also a rich tapestry that wove together the message of the whole book: the favor God had bestowed on his people; their foolish rejection of him; the seductiveness of wealth and ease; God's punishment of the rebellious nation but granting of favor to it again. I tried to give the "big picture."

Mike had discovered in his commentaries the various theories of when and by whom Deuteronomy was written. He clung to the academic analyses, eschewing the spiritual. And yet, he conceded, of all the riches of Deuteronomy, the Song of Moses in chapter thirty-two has captured more attention from scholars and Bible students than any other. Other parts of Deuteronomy, and the book as a whole, have been the subject of academic claims that the book dates much later than the time of Moses, perhaps to the time of King Josiah in the seventh century B.C. Some even claim it was composed as late as the exile or after it. No one made such claims about the song. Almost everyone attributes it to an early date, certainly before the monarchies of Saul, David, and

Solomon, if not from the time of Moses himself. Like the blessings and curses of the earlier chapters, it contains a strikingly accurate portrayal of later events of Israel's apostasy and exile, even from the early date that Mike conceded it had been written.

Jerry wanted to talk about the song in a lawyerly fashion. He followed the commentators who saw it as a "covenant lawsuit" of the sovereign against his people, a fitting follow-up to the covenant now concluded. God brought forth witnesses and accusations against Israel, and recited his acts of benevolence or compliance with the covenant. Then he listed Israel's acts of infidelity and noncompliance, and called down punishment on the violator. However, the lawsuit has an uncharacteristic end. The sovereign's love and mercy for his people win out over punishment. The rod of discipline is the rod of healing. The ungodly people who have been the instruments of punishment of God's people are themselves punished for their ungodliness. The vision of the future is expanded to include "the nations," indicating God's purpose to bless all the nations of the world through Israel.

Anna saw the song as art. Some, she told us, had analyzed it as a careful composition of three series of twenty-three verses each, matching the number of letters in the Hebrew alphabet. The total, with the summary added in, matched the seventy members of Jacob's family that went down into Egypt, as well as the seventy "nations of the ancient world." Whether or not it was intended to fit this pattern, it is poetry of a high order. It is said to be spoken or recited but, undoubtedly, as the term *song* implies, was put to music and sung as part of Israel's liturgy and worship. Hebrew manuscripts set the song off in a different presentation than the rest of the biblical text, and it is read or recited in Jewish practice with the other Song of Moses in Exodus 15.

The language of the song, Barbara noted, is rich in metaphor and message. It calls on the now familiar two witnesses of heaven and earth in verse one. The teaching of the song is to be like rain, dew, showers on new grass, or abundant rain on tender plants in verse two—nourishing and giving growth to those to whom it comes. It moves on to praise God, who is described as "the Rock," for his perfection, uprightness, and justice. His perfections are contrasted with the corruption and crookedness of the foolish and unwise people, who are, as a result, no longer his children.

At the mention of children, Hal came to life. He reminded us of the description of Israel as God's "firstborn son" in Exodus 4:22. Then he led us to the first chapter of John's gospel in which Jesus comes to those that are his own but they do not receive him: "Yet to all who received him, to those who believed in his name, he gave the right to become children of God—children born not of natural descent, nor of human decision or a husband's will, but born of God."

After connecting the children of God in the song to those who received Jesus and believed on his name in the New Testament, Hal lapsed back into silence.

Julie picked up the thread. The foolish people were rebuked for their behavior toward their Creator. They were urged to remember "the days of old" and to ask their fathers and elders for explanations. "Jews would understand," she said, "that this refers to the glorious, powerful, and even miraculous acts by which God brought their ancestors out of Egypt, through the desert, and into the Promised Land."

"Good," Hal said. "The song is for the young, for the future generations. God showed himself to the Jews in history by these things, just like he showed himself to us in Christ."

Mike brought up the meaning of verse eight, the curious language about dividing up and setting boundaries for mankind "according to the number of the sons of Israel." He had learned that the Masoretic text—the transmitted Hebrew text from which our versions of the Old Testament are translated—uses the term *sons of Israel*. Some early translations, particularly the Septuagint (the pre-Christian Greek translation of the Old Testament) and the Dead Sea Scrolls, which date to around the time of Jesus, render the term *sons of Israel* as "sons of God." I pointed out that either translation indicates—as I had learned in chapter two about other peoples inhabiting the lands around Canaan in the time of Moses and before—that God is responsible for dividing humanity into nations and giving them places to live in their time.

"Read Acts seventeen, twenty-six," Hal interjected. "When Paul talked to the men of Athens on the Areopagus, he referred to this verse from the Song: 'From one man he made every nation of men, that they should inhabit the whole earth; and he determined the times set for them and the exact places where they should live.'"

"Which version is correct?" Mike asked. "Is it 'sons of Israel' or 'sons of God'?"

"If the 'sons of Israel' translation from the Masoretic text is correct," Hal replied, "then the reference is to the seventy nations established in Genesis ten, from the descendants of Noah after the Flood. Traditional Jewish understanding is that these correspond to the seventy families of Jews, from the seventy members of Jacob's family who went down to Egypt with him, as seen in Genesis forty-six, twenty-seven. Hence, the division of the nations matches the numbers of the sons of Israel.

"If the 'sons of God' translation is correct, then the passage refers to a different notion. Each nation has an angel or divine being, a 'son of God,' who oversees it. Hence the division of the nations matches the number of the 'sons of God.' This understanding is supported by Daniel, chapter ten, when the 'man' in Daniel's vision speaks of being detained by 'the prince of the Persian kingdom' and receiving help from 'Michael, one of the chief princes,' who later helps him fight against the 'prince of Greece.' These princes are apparently supernatural beings who exercise some authority with respect to the nations."

"I guess I better study Daniel," Mike said. I knew Hal had left him behind in his explanation. He was just beginning serious Bible study and wasn't even sure yet that he believed what he was reading. Understanding the descendants of Noah, the family of Jacob, or the dramatic heavenly and earthly events of Daniel was well in the future for him.

Julie and Anna took us through verses ten through twelve. Jacob, that is Israel, was the special "portion" or "inheritance" of God himself. Israel was distinguished from the other nations by God's special favor. God finds him "in a barren and howling waste," and shields and cares for him as "the apple of his eye." This familiar phrase is an English transliteration of the Hebrew idiom "little man of his eye," indicating the pupil, which must be shielded and protected above all. The blessings God brought to his special people are described in terms both literal and figurative. Israel is cared for by God like an eagle cares for its young, spreading its wings to catch them and carrying them on its pinions, reminding us of the metaphor in Exodus 19:4 of how God carried his people "on eagle's wings and brought you to myself."

"An allegory," Hal said. "The spreading wings of the eagle are an allegory of Christ with his arms stretched out on the cross, caring for and catching and carrying his people."

Paula pointed out that verse thirteen's reference to God making his people "ride on the heights of the land" is a likely reference to them triumphing over the cities and fortified places that were often located on high places for defense. "Get honey from rock and oil from the flinty crag," may refer to literal honey from bees nesting in rocky caverns or to olive trees growing in craggy hills. The drink wine, described as "the foaming blood of the grape," is an image that calls to mind the similes of Revelation 14, where the angel harvests the ripe grapes of the earth and throws them "into the great winepress of God's wrath," where the blood flows out to the height of the horses' bridles.

I told them that the reference to Israel as "Jeshurun" in verse fifteen is a pet name that sounds similar to Israel but means, ironically, "the upright one." This upright one, however, becomes a beast that "grew fat and kicked"; that is, it rebelled in response to its blessings. Prosperity led it astray, and it abandoned its Creator God who had given it blessings in favor of "gods they had not known, gods that recently appeared, gods your fathers did not fear." All of this was a warning that had appeared in Deuteronomy before.

God's "sons and daughters" faithless behavior angered him. Paula was quick to pick up that just as women are to learn the covenant and law, so are they held responsible for its violation.

As Israel made him jealous by serving "what is no God," he will make them envious by "those who are not a people." When we touched on this verse, Hal told us that Paul quoted it in Romans 10:19, in conjunction with Israel's rejection of Jesus.

We noted that in verses twenty-two to twenty five, God's wrath is described in terms as horrific as the curses of the previous chapters, but terms that accurately describe what happened to Israel and Judah in the sieges and exile that followed its idolatry and disobedience. God's wrath is as profound as his love. "It is," as Hebrews 10:31 teaches, "a dreadful thing to fall into the hands of the living God."

"But the tide of God's thought starts to turn in verse twenty-seven," Anna said. "God protected his own honor by turning his wrath against

Israel's enemies. It's obvious that the misfortunes that befell Israel in the face of its enemies could not have happened unless the Lord 'had given them up.'"

"And that brings us back to Romans," Hal said. "The language here is like Romans one, where God 'gave over' to shameful lusts those who chose to worship created things rather than the Creator. But 'it is mine to avenge; I will repay,' God says in language Paul quoted in Romans twelve, nineteen, to urge Christians to seek peace and not revenge. Hebrews ten, twenty-nine, quotes the same verse to describe the punishment of one who has 'trampled the Son of God under foot' and 'treated as an unholy thing the blood of the covenant that sanctified him, and who has insulted the Spirit of grace.'"

Hal was gaining energy and began to resume his customary leadership of the group.

"In Israel's despair, when 'their strength was gone,' God invited them to get help from their false gods. He mocked the idea of sacrifices to gods who need food and drink. Then God declared, 'See now that I myself am he! There is no god besides me.' It's like what he told Moses when, in Exodus, chapter three, he asked what he was to tell the people the name of God is. The answer: 'I AM WHO I AM.'"

I added my own analysis, "'I put to death,' God said (recalling Adam), 'and I bring to life,' (foretelling Christ and the resurrection of believers to eternal life). 'I have wounded and I will heal,' he asserted, speaking his sovereignty over evil as well as good. 'No one can deliver out of my hand,' he said.

"Finally, God called on the 'nations' to rejoice with his people over the just vengeance he would take on his enemies. The fulfillment of the promise to Abraham that all the nations of the world will be blessed through him was in view. As Jesus the Jew said to the Samaritan woman at the well in John four, twenty-two, 'Salvation is from the Jews.' The Scriptures come back to this message in Romans fifteen, ten, where Paul quoted verse forty-three of the song to show that the Gospel of Jesus Christ is for the Gentiles as well as the Jews.

"Moses and his designated successor, Joshua, then recited the song to the people. 'They are,' Moses tells them, 'not just idle words for you—

they are your life.' The words represent the mind of God, who, Moses told the people in the same language in chapter thirty, 'is your life.'"

I recited all this, full of my knowledge of the song. Hal was duly impressed, but he was not interested in discussing the points I had made.

"The song," he said, "is, as one commentator said, 'Hauntingly beautiful, even in translation.'[16] But it's not meant to be studied; it's meant to be read aloud, or sung, over and over, until the words and message are part of the memory of each member of God's covenant community."

He lit two candles that were mounted on sconces attached to the dark wood that framed his fireplace. Then he turned off the lights so the flickering candlelight was all that illuminated the room and little else could distract our attention. And then Hal began to recite the song. At first I thought he was reading it. I closed my eyes to let the verses and phrases, the poetry and metaphor of the mind of God, wash over me. When I opened them occasionally and looked at Hal, his eyes were closed. He was not reading the song; he was reciting it. It was part of his mind and consciousness, like the Lord's Prayer or the twenty-third Psalm. His soft voice was a monotone, but the words lost no force on that account. Phrases that had become familiar to me from my study rolled into the dim room like old friends:

"Let my teaching fall like rain . . ."

"I will proclaim the name of the Lord."

"Is he not your Father, your Creator,

Who made and formed you?"

"In a desert land he found him . . ."

"He made him ride on the heights of the land . . ."

"Jeshurun grew fat and kicked . . ."

"They sacrificed to demons . . .

Gods that had recently appeared . . ."

CHAPTER THIRTY-TWO

"You forgot the God who gave you birth . . ."

"They made me jealous by what is no god . . ."

"They are a nation without sense,

there is no discernment in them."

"It is mine to avenge; I will repay."

"See now that I myself am He:

There is no god besides me.

I put to death and I bring to life,

I have wounded and I will heal,

And no one can deliver out of my hand."

"Rejoice, O nations, with his people . . ."

When he finished, there was silence. He did not open his eyes.

"Now you say it, Chris," he said to me, his eyes still closed. I tilted my Bible so the dim light fell on it enough to read, and read as he had recited. As I did, his old head nodded in rhythm with the phrases, and some of them came to me naturally enough so my eye slid past them, my mind having already captured the words in memory. When I had finished, his eyes opened. He looked into a dark corner of the room where the flickering candlelight barely reached. His old piano rested there. He rose and went to it.

"It is a song," he said, "and it should be sung. I don't know—no one knows—what the tune was. But someone sang it once without a piano or a degree in music. Maybe we can do as much."

I don't know music, but Hal's old fingers had never seemed soft on the keys when I had heard him play in church. He had music in front of him for the old hymns, though I don't know if he ever actually looked at it. But tonight, he had no music, and could hardly have seen it if he had. He sat and played notes and chords that at first seemed random but settled into a pattern, a soft pattern of melody that began to assume a shape. And then he began to sing, to sing the Song of Moses, to sing the mind of God as it was, and is, and ever will be. The song began softly, then rose to the words of praise, clashed over the language of disobedience, retreated to a gentle, lilting melody of God's care for his people, hammered through their forgetting of God, and rose to a demanding crescendo in the language of wrath. Then it stopped, and resumed tentatively as God reasoned with himself and his wayward people. It built again through the verses of vengeance on God's enemies to a soaring height of his deep bass voice as God declared himself as the one who put to death and brought to life. Then it tapered down to the end, with the soft, fulfilling call to the nations to rejoice with God's people.

When he was finished, he sat slumped over the old piano. He said nothing, nor did any of us. I thought of all the trite and foolish things I could have said. I could have praised him for the beauty and power of his composition, but I knew there was no composition. I could have told him to write it down, perform it in church, that it was a shame for such a piece not to be shared. But I knew he could not write it down and would never perform it again, that we had shared a moment that no one else would ever share. Worse, I could have applauded, my lone handclaps feebly trying to express an approval for that for which there was no expression. Approval, most of all mine, was as irrelevant as gods that needed food and drink.

He rose at last, as did the rest of us. He took a few steps toward me. Tears were streaming down his face. I did not have to ask why. He gave me a brief hug—the first time he had done so in our several dozen meetings. "Go now," he said. "Go home and leave an old man in peace."

And we did.

CHAPTER THIRTY-THREE

I t was for them, you know," Anna said.

Several days had passed since our evening with Hal and the Song of Moses. The litter of breakfast cluttered the kitchen table. The kids had rushed out to catch the school bus. I was finishing my coffee before making my own way off to meet the needs of clients and demands of courts. Anna turned away from replacing boxes of cereal and jelly jars, rested against the counter, and looked at me with a gaze that told me she had a trunkful of thoughts, one of which was untidily poking out from under the cover.

"We don't talk about it," she added, "and we should."

I was still mentally retreating from the headlines in front of me—the crimes, wars, politics, and sundry outrages that were, or passed for, the news.

"What was for them?" I asked. "And who is them? And what don't we talk about?"

"Hal," she replied, "and the other night. The song. You know what I mean. Don't tell me you weren't affected too."

Now I knew what she meant—or thought I did. Yes, I had been affected. No, we didn't talk about it. Why not? Did we know each other too well, so we didn't need to? We did, after all, almost always know exactly what the other was thinking. And we rarely disagreed on important things. Almost never on spiritual matters. Or was it too deep, too personal, to want to share even with the one to whom you were closest? If that was what I thought, however subliminally, she was challenging me. We needed to talk. I tried to respond.

"It was for them," I said. "For Paula, for Mike, for Jerry . . . for all of us."

She shook her head. "No," she said. "It wasn't for us. That's my point. I thought it was at first. But it wasn't. It was for them." She motioned her head toward the door where Willy and Lily had just disappeared. "Willy and Lily," our own pet names, our "Jeshuruns," for our little ones, our William and Elizabeth, those most precious little people that our Lord had created from our bodies and entrusted to our care.

"It was for them, and Jerry and Barbara's kids, and Paula and Mike's, and the ones Julie teaches in her catechism class. It was like . . . what do you lawyers call it when you do estate plans where there's no tax until the next generation?"

"A generation-skipping trust," I said. Even though I didn't do estate plans, I knew the term.

"That's it," she said. "Hal was passing something on to us to give our children. And their children. We have to understand it ourselves to pass it on. But it isn't our own salvation, getting ourselves into heaven; that's the main point. It's making sure our children grow up in the right place with God. And that they'll do the same for their children. If we take care of ourselves only, we're the most selfish of all; it's against everything Jesus taught."

I had an appointment and couldn't linger for the time the conversation demanded. "We'll talk more about this," I said. "But we do have to look out for ourselves. If we're not right with God, if we don't understand and believe, how can we help Willy and Lily? Or anyone else?"

We parted for the day, a parting that was more reluctant than usual. Anna's thoughts consumed me until I hit the rush of legal business that awaited.

The conversation and e-mails among our group were more subdued that week. It was as if all of us were reflecting on what happened at Hal's. We did agree to come together with Hal again soon for chapter thirty-three, the blessing of Moses on the tribes, and that each of us would try to study one or two of the tribes and understand the blessing of that tribe to share with the others.

Toward the end of the week, Julie stopped by my office to talk about Hal.

"Did you see it?" she asked.

"See what?" I responded. I was trying to match her enigmatic query with Anna's thoughts.

"I guess you didn't," she responded. "No one else seems to have. But I'm not going crazy. I know it was there."

"What was there, Julie?"

"The glow. When he was singing the song and playing the piano, his whole face began to glow—just a little luminescence, like there was some light inside coming out, or surrounding him, I don't know. I've never seen it before. I don't just have visions like that."

"Maybe a reflection from the fire," I offered. "Or the candles."

She shook her head. "No, that was my first thought. But it wasn't. I know it wasn't. I wish we could have that evening back, but I'm afraid we won't."

"We're meeting at Hal's again Friday night," I said. "Maybe you'll get your wish."

"Yeah," she said, "to study the tribes. It's not the same. It won't be the same. I just want it back—what happened that night."

"It wasn't for us," I said, remembering Anna. "It was for your child and all those children you teach every Saturday. Don't covet spiritual highs; just worship him in spirit and truth, and he'll give you what you need to experience." I was sounding too much like Hal, I thought. But maybe that was the whole idea.

I'd have to talk to Anna about that.

Friday night at Hal's.

We settled into our places in the study, squeezed together as before. Hal seemed even less animated than he had at the beginning of our study the week before, and he let us go ahead with little guidance. We were more sober, less ebullient, as well. There was little of the frivolous chitchat that usually accompanied gatherings. We plunged into the Blessings of Moses, each in turn speaking to the tribe or tribes whose blessings they had studied.

I read the introduction.

> This is the blessing that Moses the man of God pronounced on the Israelites before his death. He said:
>
> "The LORD came from Sinai and dawned over them from Seir; he shone forth from Mount Paran. He came with myriads of holy ones from the south, from his mountain slopes.
>
> Surely it is you who love the people; all the holy ones are in your hand. At your feet they all bow down, and from you receive instruction, the law that Moses gave us, the possession of the assembly of Jacob. He was king over Jeshurun when the leaders of the people assembled, along with the tribes of Israel.
>
> —Deut. 33:1–5

Then I shared my learning about the first few verses I had read. At the end of chapter thirty-two, Moses was instructed as he had been at the end of chapter three, to ascend Mount Nebo. From there he would view the Promised Land that he had been forbidden to enter, and on this mountain he would die. Before he carried out this last command from his God, he gave his blessing to the tribes he had led for forty years. These blessings, presented in chapter thirty-three, are the last words of Moses recorded in the Bible. Like the song of chapter thirty-two, the blessings are in the form of poetry.

Moses' blessing on the tribes is often compared to Jacob's blessing of his sons. Jacob's blessings appear in Genesis 49. He blessed his sons as their physical father. Moses blessed Jacob's sons' descendants as their spiritual father. Jacob's blessings looked back, and in some instances were disapproving. Moses' blessings looked forward and were prophetic; they promised good and not bad. Moses was done with the curses and warnings of the evils that would befall them for disobedience. This was the time—his final time with them—to call for them to have every success. His blessings were redeeming rather than judgmental, a prayer—as he has prayed repeatedly in the past—for a prosperous, successful, and obedient people.

Hal interrupted me to point out that in Luke 24:50–53, Jesus, too, blessed his disciples when he left them.

Then I continued. In the opening verse, Moses is described as "the man of God." The phrase is used in the Old Testament to identify prophets, as Moses is identified in chapters eighteen and thirty-four. His blessing begins with a vision of God dawning and shining forth from the southern mountains from which Israel had trekked to the Promised Land: Sinai (the only use of this term instead of Horeb in Deuteronomy), Seir, and Paran. God was not alone but came with "myriads of holy ones."

Hal spoke up again. "It was from this," he said, "that the inspired writers of the New Testament Scriptures—Luke reporting the speech of Stephen to the Sanhedrin in Acts seven, fifty-three, Paul in Galatians three, nineteen, and the writer of Hebrews in Hebrews two, two—understood that the giving of the law through Moses was mediated by angels."

Jewish sages who puzzled over the mystery of God's selection of Israel for special blessing as his chosen people saw additional significance in this verse. Paran was the traditional home of Ishmael, Abraham's son by Sarah's maidservant Hagar, who became the father of the Arabs. Seir was the home of the descendants of Jacob's brother Esau. They deduced from this that the Torah had been offered to the descendants of Ishmael and Esau, but they refused it. Because Israel, under Moses, accepted it, Israel was the subject of God's special favor. The story has no biblical support and is contrary to the teaching of Deuteronomy 7, which says it is not on account of Israel's righteousness that God chose her. But it shows the moral agony that the Jews themselves had over their favored place in God's eyes.

In verse three, the term *holy ones* refers to the people God loves. Some think the verse, in context, must refer only to Israel. Others see in it the missionary function for which the "Israel of God"—the church, which fulfilled the promise to Abraham of the blessing of the nations through him—was destined with the coming of Christ. The "people whom God surely loves" is stated generically, with no special reference to Israel.

At this Hal broke in again. "When Moses said, 'All the holy ones are in your hands,' he expressed the same thought Jesus did in John ten, eight, when he said, 'No one can snatch them out of my hand.' Then Jesus went on to say, 'No one can snatch them out of my Father's hand.' He was telling them that he and the Father are one, and then he said it explicitly: 'I and the Father are one.' Jesus has the holy ones in his hands, just as Moses said."

I resumed my teaching. Verse four ("the law that Moses gave us, the possession of the assembly of Jacob") together with Deuteronomy 6:4, make up the first words a Jewish child is supposed to be taught when old enough to begin speaking. It expresses Moses giving the law, the heritage of the law, and the possession of it by the whole of Israel.

"Why," Mike asked, "does verse four refer to Moses in the third person when he is supposedly speaking the blessing?"

I was stuck, but Hal came to my rescue. "It's an antiphony," he said. "A responsive reading. This is music and poetry from God. Hear it that way, and you will understand." I wasn't sure Mike did, but I went on to point out that verse five uses Jeshurun again as the "pet name" for Israel, as does verse twenty-six.

When I had finished talking about the introduction to the chapter, Anna picked up with the tribe of Reuben in verse six: "Let Reuben live and not die, nor his men be few."

Reuben's blessing, she told us, seems to be a reversal, or restoration, of Reuben from the blessing of Jacob. Reuben was guilty of the sin of sleeping with his father's concubine, as reported in Genesis 35:22, which earned his father's condemnation—"you will no longer excel"— in Genesis 49. According to the censuses of Numbers, chapters one and twenty-six, the number of Reubenites had declined by three thousand in Moses' time. Hence the blessing of Moses that he "live and not die, nor his men be few."

Mike then discussed the tribe of Judah in verse seven:

And this he said about Judah:

"Hear, O LORD, the cry of Judah;

bring him to his people.

With his own hands he defends his cause.

Oh, be his help against his foes!"

The blessing of Judah, he taught, may reflect the fact that Judah was designated in Numbers 2:9 to go first among the tribes, and presumably to be the first to encounter an enemy. The blessing would then be Moses' plea that God would be with them in battle and bring them back safely to the rest of the people.

He also talked about the tribe of Simeon, which was omitted from the list. Jacob had cursed the tribe because of its bloody avenging of the rape of Dinah in Shechem, and, according to Joshua 19, took away its territory from the share of Judah. It may have become absorbed into that tribe. Its numbers were reduced from 59,300 to 22,200, according to the two censuses in the Book of Numbers. Jewish tradition sees a reference to Simeon in the verses pertaining to Judah. The "hear" of verse seven—the "shema" familiar from chapter six—is from the same Hebrew word root as Simeon, which probably means "one who hears." Martin Luther reports that the Latin father Jerome speculated that Simeon was omitted because Judas Iscariot came from this tribe. The speculation is interesting, Mike said, but it has no biblical support.

Julie had the priestly tribe of Levi, from verses eight through eleven.

> About Levi he said:
>
> "Your Thummim and Urim belong
>
> to the man you favored.
>
> You tested him at Massah;
>
> you contended with him at the waters of Meribah.
>
> He said of his father and mother,
>
> 'I have no regard for them.'
>
> He did not recognize his brothers
>
> or acknowledge his own children,
>
> but he watched over your word

and guarded your covenant.

He teaches your precepts to Jacob

and your law to Israel.

He offers incense before you

and whole burnt offerings on your altar.

Bless all his skills, O LORD,

and be pleased with the work of his hands.

Smite the loins of those who rise up against him;

strike his foes till they rise no more."

Julie had much to teach about Levi. He had participated with Simeon in the slaughter of the Shechemites after the rape of Dinah, and Jacob condemned him, along with his brother, for his role in the affair. Nevertheless, the tribe of Levi became the priestly tribe and received an extensive blessing from Moses. The Thummim and Urim were stones that were kept in the priests' breastplate to make decisions by casting lots. An instance of application appears in 1 Samuel 14, when the lot was cast to determine who was guilty of sin at a time of confrontation with the Philistines. Proverbs 16:33 teaches, "The lot is cast into the lap, But its every decision is from the Lord."

In the first chapter of Acts, the choice of an apostle, Matthias, to replace the treacherous Judas, was done by casting lots. It may be counterintuitive to most Christians, but Scripture seems to approve casting lots, at least by holy men, to enable God's people to make difficult decisions.

The message of verse nine—that Levi had no regard for his father and mother, and did not recognize his brothers or acknowledge his own children—is set in the context of his duty to watch over God's word and guard his covenant. It is not a statement of disregard for family but a clarifying of priorities. God, the sovereign Creator and master of all, is more important than family, and especially so to those who are charged with the responsibility for his ministry.

"Jesus," Hal interceded, "teaches the same principle in several passages of the Gospels. In Matthew, chapter ten, for example, he teaches that anyone who loves his father or mother, son or daughter, more than him is not worthy of him. These passages follow the principle of Deuteronomy thirteen that even the closest members of one's family in the covenant community of Israel must be put to death if they entice a person to worship other gods."

Julie went on. The functions of the tribe of Levi include decision-making before the Lord, teaching, and leading in worship. Such ministers must die to the world to be effective in these divine charges. Small wonder, she said, that Moses takes special care to pray for blessing on the skills and the work of the hands of the Levites, and the destruction of those who oppose such work. Verse eleven is a model of the prayer we should all have for our clergy and religious leaders.

Barbara was next, on Benjamin in verse twelve.

> About Benjamin he said:
>
> "Let the beloved of the LORD rest secure in him,
>
> for he shields him all day long,
>
> and the one the LORD loves rests between his shoulders."

Benjamin is said to be "beloved of the Lord." This, she said, may reflect Genesis 44:20, where Benjamin was beloved of Jacob. He was the only one of Jacob's sons born in the holy land, and the only one who did not participate in the sale of Joseph into slavery. The reference to him resting between the Lord's shoulders is likely a simile of a father carrying his son on his back, or on his chest. Jewish tradition suggests it is a metaphor for the temple, which was in the territory of Benjamin.

Paula read verses thirteen through seventeen, which talked about Joseph:

> About Joseph he said:
>
> "May the LORD bless his land
>
> with the precious dew from heaven above

and with the deep waters that lie below;

with the best the sun brings forth

and the finest the moon can yield;

with the choicest gifts of the ancient mountains

and the fruitfulness of the everlasting hills;

with the best gifts of the earth and its fullness

and the favor of him who dwelt in the burning bush.

Let all these rest on the head of Joseph,

on the brow of the prince among his brothers.

In majesty he is like a firstborn bull;

his horns are the horns of a wild ox.

With them he will gore the nations,

even those at the ends of the earth.

Such are the ten thousands of Ephraim;

such are the thousands of Manasseh."

The blessing of Joseph, she told us, is the most prolific of the blessings in material prosperity and military success. The reference to "the favor of him who dwelt in the burning bush" is the only biblical reference, outside of Exodus 3, to God's appearance to Moses in that form. The sons of Joseph—Ephraim and Manassah—were included in the blessing. Apparently the tribe of Joseph was gradually splitting into the two half-tribes. In his blessing, four hundred years earlier, Jacob mentioned Joseph but not his sons. By the time of the judges, the tribes of the sons were mentioned without Joseph.

Jerry picked up on Zebulon and Issachar in verses eighteen and nineteen:

About Zebulun he said:

"Rejoice, Zebulun, in your going out,

and you, Issachar, in your tents.

They will summon peoples to the mountain

and there offer sacrifices of righteousness;

they will feast on the abundance of the seas,

on the treasures hidden in the sand."

The blessings on Zebulon and Issachar, he taught, are combined, Zebulon being blessed in "going out" and Issachar "in your tents." Modern Bible students see this as a "merism," that is, a literary device that intends to be all-inclusive. Jewish tradition took the blessing to mean that the tribe of Issachar stayed in its tents, studying Torah, and Zebulon supported it. Zebulon is associated with the sea in the blessing of Jacob in Genesis 49:13–15, and the major seaport of modern Israel, the city of Haifa, is in the territory of Zebulon. The reference to summoning peoples to the mountain where they will offer sacrifices is a likely a reference to the sanctuary city of Tabor, also in Zebulon's territory. Like the reference to "the people" at the beginning of this chapter, it carries the intriguing sense of the broader outreach of Israel to others in drawing them to worship of the one true God.

Anna had Gad, verses twenty and twenty-one:

About Gad he said:

"Blessed is he who enlarges Gad's domain!

Gad lives there like a lion,

tearing at arm or head.

He chose the best land for himself;

the leader's portion was kept for him.

When the heads of the people assembled,

he carried out the LORD's righteous will,

and his judgments concerning Israel."

She told us that the blessing of Gad may refer to the fact that Gad already had its territory east of the Jordan but crossed over with the other tribes to fight to secure the rest of the Promised Land. Jewish tradition says "the leader's portion" meant that Moses' tomb was located in the territory of Gad, a speculation for which there is no other biblical support.

Mike then did Dan in verse twenty-two:

> About Dan he said:
>
> "Dan is a lion's cub,
>
> springing out of Bashan."

He had studied the history of the tribe. The cryptic reference to Dan as "a lion's cub, springing out of Bashan," may refer to the later movement of the tribe of Dan to the area near Bashan as documented in chapter nineteen of Joshua and chapter eighteen of Judges.

He passed the ball to Barbara to talk about Naphtali in verse twenty-three:

> About Naphtali he said:
>
> "Naphtali is abounding with the favor of the LORD
>
> and is full of his blessing;
>
> he will inherit southward to the lake."

The blessing of Naphtali, she shared, refers to the richness of the land this tribe would inherit, though the correct translation of the blessing has vexed scholars and is uncertain.

Jerry had Asher, verses twenty-four and twenty-five.

> About Asher he said:
>
> "Most blessed of sons is Asher;
>
> let him be favored by his brothers,
>
> and let him bathe his feet in oil.

The bolts of your gates will be iron and bronze,

and your strength will equal your days."

It was like Naphtali, he told us. The blessing of Asher, whose name means "blessed," refers to his prosperity in the land. Washing the feet was a necessity in the hot, dusty land. To bathe the feet in oil is a metaphor for wealth or prosperity.

"Washing the feet occurs in the New Testament as well," Hal added. "Jesus demonstrated service to others and humility by bathing the feet of the disciples—as seen in John, chapter thirteen—and taught on priorities and values when his own feet were washed by a woman with a jar of expensive perfume."

It was my turn again, for the conclusion.

"There is no one like the God of Jeshurun,

who rides on the heavens to help you

and on the clouds in his majesty.

The eternal God is your refuge,

and underneath are the everlasting arms.

He will drive out your enemy before you,

saying, 'Destroy him!'

So Israel will live in safety alone;

Jacob's spring is secure

in a land of grain and new wine,

where the heavens drop dew.

Blessed are you, O Israel!

Who is like you,

a people saved by the LORD?

He is your shield and helper

and your glorious sword.

> Your enemies will cower before you,
>
> and you will trample down their high places."
>
> —Deut. 33:26–29

The end of the chapter, I told them, is a great hymn to the power of God and the security he brings to his people. As he dawned and shone forth in the images from the beginning of the chapter, now he rides on the heavens and the clouds in his majesty, for the purpose of helping his people. The wonderful image of the "everlasting arms" gave birth to the Christian hymn "Leaning on the Everlasting Arms."

"Jacob's spring" is a metaphor for Israel, the offspring of Jacob. Christians have always understood the church to be the "Israel of God," as Paul taught in his letters, such as in Galatians 6:16. The chapter concludes with the declaration of the uniqueness of the people who have been saved by the Lord, a declaration that every Christian believer could share, and the images of conquest of their enemies and trampling down their high places, that is, the places of false worship. The enemy—sin, in all its powerful and corrupting forms—is subject to the greater power of the Lord our God.

After we recited our learning to each other, Hal nodded approvingly.

"Your study and understanding has come a long way," he said. "You, Chris, have gained a real grasp of Deuteronomy, and I think the rest of you are getting there too. You understand something of its literary form, its relation to the earlier history of Israel and the patriarchs, and the extent to which the later history plays out against it as a background and fulfills the prophetic aspects of it. You can see how deeply and consciously rooted Jesus' teachings—and the whole New Testament—are in it. And I think you have some feeling for the beauty and power of the language, especially the metaphors: God 'dawning' and 'shining forth' and 'riding on the heavens' and keeping his people secure with the 'everlasting arms' under them to catch them when they fall.

"But this is not a time of study; it's a time of prayer. Moses' blessings are a prayer, a prayer of praise for God who has been Moses' life, and, whether they understand it or not, is life itself for his people. And, along with the prayer of praise, it is a prayer conveying Moses' intercession for God's blessings on them, blessings that are appropriate to the situation of each. Moses has no power to confer blessings, only to ask them of God. Pray with me now."

We bowed together. And then Hal slid out of his chair to his knees. For a moment I was alarmed, as he had seemed feebler each time we had met in recent weeks. I started to rise to assist him, but his eyes were closed, and he was beginning to speak to his God. I realized his posture was not a physical collapse but moving to his knees to humble himself before him who was before all things.

I dropped to my own knees in my place. The others followed.

Hal's prayer that night was a recapitulation of his entire life in ministry. As with his music of the song, I had thoughts of what a spiritual treasure would have existed if I could have recorded it—and what a sacrilege it would have been to do so. This was a man of God before his God. No one could break the bond of communication that flowed at that moment, and no attempt to transmit, capture, or commit it to any medium could do anything but taint with the vain material of human striving the purity of spirit that was present. I have thought in later years of trying to write it down from what I remember of it but realized it would be equally vain.

For more than an hour he prayed, and if there was any individual or body his spiritual life had touched for whom he did not pray, I could not tell it. He had served seven churches in his career in ministry, and they had not all been kind to him. Some had fired him, and others encouraged him to leave. I knew a little of some of them from comments he had made, or things Julie had told me. He had left one church that he had built up into a dynamic ministry in a middling town on the outer fringes of metropolitan Boston. The church leaders insisted on hiring an assistant minister who was the son of one of them, and who was not, in Hal's view, ready for ministry leadership. Another had voted to fire him when he invited a nonprofit day-care center to use the church's facilities as temporary housing while the building was vacant during the week. They preferred their property remain empty rather than risk the possibility of damage from little children of poor mothers who needed to work to stay off welfare. Still another encouraged him to move on after only a couple of years of ministry because some longtime church members could not adapt to his preaching style or informal attire. This was, after all, New England, and even a lifetime New Englander like Hal could offend people who thought they owned the pews.

But it had not all been thus. He began one of the churches as a mission in an area of New Hampshire that was, at the time, devoid of gospel-preaching churches. He started it in his home and worked a full-time job to support himself and his family while it was starting. He started an informal food pantry, and served open meals on Wednesday and Saturday nights. Most of the early parishioners were the down-and-out people of the community who needed the food. They didn't own any "Sunday best" and wouldn't have been comfortable in the established churches to which Hal referred as "the denominations." Gradually, the ministry grew as some students from a nearby college who were Bible-believing Christians discovered it, the community began to understand the work that was going on there, and some of Hal's early "rice Christians" got traction in their lives and became missionaries to the community.

Another of his favorite churches was one to which he had been called after its members had, to a person, voted to leave one of the "denominations." The previous pastor had been engaged in behaviors that the congregation thought unbecoming a pastor: giving undue attention to young men who were invited to the parsonage to spend the night, and renting X-rated videos at the local video store. When the denominational leadership treated their complaints with derision, they decided they did not need the denomination. As is often the case with denominational churches, the legal documents of the denominational affiliation provided that the title to the church rested in the denomination, even though it had been built and paid for entirely by the local congregation. Hal came to the church as it met in a local garage. Although advised by an attorney that they might have grounds to challenge the denominational title to the building they had built, the congregation had decided to follow Paul's advice of avoiding litigation and living in peace. "We built one church building; we can build another," was the summary of their attitude. The old church stood empty, and eventually the denomination sold it to the city for a community center. The people, under Hal's leadership, built a newer, larger building, which became the center of the religious life of the little community for years to come.

Hal prayed for each of these and the other churches he had served. He prayed for them by name, and he prayed for their pastors and their leaders by name—he still knew who most of them were, even those he had left decades earlier. He prayed for the people he had known and to whom he had ministered in each of them, the faithful workers who had taught the children in Sunday school, led the music and sang in the choirs and praise groups, organized and taught Bible studies, led youth groups, staffed the offices, swept the floors, and painted the clapboards. And he prayed for those who brought the church out of the building and into the community; those who organized the food pantries and soup kitchens, the vacation Bible schools, the athletic and other programs for youth, the marriage and parenting clinics, the seven-step groups, the day-care centers, and the pregnancy-care and counseling centers, and those who gave voice to righteousness in the halls of government, the legislature, and the courts, and by speaking on behalf of God's people for those things that were just and right in his eyes, and against what was not.

He prayed for children who had learned the most basic Bible lesson by singing "Jesus loves me," even before they could read and go to school, and who had memorized Scripture verses as soon as they could read, while their hearts were still soft and well able to retain such things. He prayed for the young people who were going through the greatest times of temptation and trial in their teens and twenties, that they would remember the Lord in the days of their youth. He asked God—on behalf of church members, believers, and non-believers alike—to remove scales from eyes, unplug ears, and open hearts to the Gospel of Jesus Christ, to take God's teachings to heart, to love God with all of their hearts and minds and souls and strength, and to pursue righteousness, belief, and the purity of true religion by the way they cared for their own and those around them. He prayed for blessings on each and all of these persons and ministries and many others, too many for me to remember. He prayed for those who had treated him badly, as well as those who had followed and honored his leadership. He prayed that their ministries and spiritual lives would be prosperous, that their teachings would nourish others, that they would have the skills to minister and communicate effectively, that they would not be deterred or tarnished by the temptations of sin, and that they would stand strong against the assaults that the Evil One surely brings against those who oppose him. He prayed and he prayed.

And then he prayed for each of us. He prayed for us individually, by name, as if placing us on the altar where we could not escape God's attention. And his prayer for each touched the particular needs and backgrounds and place in the spiritual walk where we were.

When at last he came to an end, I had no words of my own, and none were offered by others. So complete and moving had Hal's prayer been that I could only say, "Thank you, Lord, for this man of God, this servant of yours. Thank you for bringing him into my life, and the life of so many others. Amen."

"Amen," the others repeated.

Hal rose slowly, slower, I thought, than just the slowness that attends an aging body. He sank back into his chair and looked weak, almost confused at beholding the material world of his study, and us, again after soaring in the spirit with his God for so long. I asked if he was all right, and he assured me that he was, though I was not entirely convinced.

We had one more chapter to study, chapter thirty-four, on the death of Moses.

Hal asked us to meet him early on the following Saturday morning and plan to spend the day with him for our final study. Paula and Mike had to cancel some weekend plans but said they would do so gladly.

Hal asked Anna and me to stay behind for a few minutes after the others left. Dewey and John, he told us, had been coming by every day to help a little but couldn't make it that day. Could we just pick up the kitchen for him, he asked—so the food wouldn't stay out overnight— and help him to his bedroom?

Anna plunged into the kitchen and cleaned it up, while I helped Hal to his bedroom.

"I'll be all right now," he said, sitting on the edge of the bed. He refused our offer to come back in the morning. "I just get a little tired at the end of the day," he said. "And Dewey and John will stop in tomorrow. It's OK. Go on home, and don't worry about me."

CHAPTER THIRTY-FOUR

The e-mail came on Monday morning. *Dress warm. Winter coats. Leave your Bibles. My house. Saturday morning at 8:00. Hal.*

"What is he thinking about?" I asked Anna. "It's June. It's going to be in the eighties. Winter coats?"

"You know Hal," she replied. "It's one of his mysteries, but there will be something to learn from it."

"And leave your Bibles?" I added. "How can we finish the study without our Bibles?"

"You finish it," she said. "And write about it. But do as he says. Leave your Bible at home on Saturday."

I spent Tuesday and Wednesday evenings, and half of Thursday evening following Anna's suggestion. I studied chapter thirty-four, I wrote about it, and I tried to put it in the setting of the history of Israel and the whole Bible. Then I printed it out and folded a copy to tuck into my pocket for Saturday.

We rolled into Hal's yard early Saturday morning, warm clothing in hand. The late spring morning was warm, and summer was in the air. Robins hopped along the lawn among the dandelions and grass that was overdue for mowing. An eleven-passenger blue van was parked in the yard with the words, "God Loves You! Barrington Community Christian Church" printed on the side. I knew it was Hal's last church. No driver was in sight.

Hal walked out of the house briskly, showing little sign of the frailty of our evening meetings of recent weeks. He greeted us warmly, pulled open the van door, and motioned us in. Seeing the keys in his hands, I realized he meant to drive and offered to take the wheel.

Hal would have none of it, waving off all our offers. "Come on," he said. "I want to take you on a trip." When all seven of us were loaded in, he climbed behind the wheel, started it up, and was on the road. He gave no hint of our destination but asked if any of us had anything we wanted to talk about on the journey.

"Why don't you share your writing?" Anna asked.

I pulled the folded sheets of computer paper out of my pocket and, with the others' consent, read chapter thirty-four and my summary of it.

> Then Moses climbed Mount Nebo from the plains of Moab to the top of Pisgah, across from Jericho. There the LORD showed him the whole land—from Gilead to Dan, all of Naphtali, the territory of Ephraim and Manasseh, all the land of Judah as far as the western sea, the Negev and the whole region from the Valley of Jericho, the City of Palms, as far as Zoar. Then the LORD said to him, "This is the land I promised on oath to Abraham, Isaac, and Jacob when I said, 'I will give it to your descendants.' I have let you see it with your eyes, but you will not cross over into it."
>
> And Moses the servant of the LORD died there in Moab, as the LORD had said. He buried him in Moab, in the valley opposite Beth Peor, but to this day no one knows where his grave is. Moses was 120 years old when he died, yet his eyes were not weak nor his strength gone. The Israelites grieved for Moses in the plains of Moab thirty days, until the time of weeping and mourning was over.
>
> Now Joshua son of Nun was filled with the spirit of wisdom because Moses had laid his hands on him. So the Israelites listened to him and did what the LORD had commanded Moses.
>
> Since then, no prophet has risen in Israel like Moses, whom the LORD knew face to face, who did all those miraculous signs and wonders the LORD sent him to do in Egypt—to Pharaoh and to all his officials and to his whole land. For no one has ever shown the mighty power or performed the awesome deeds that Moses did in the sight of all Israel.
>
> —Deut. 34:1–12

Moses had been instructed, before the blessing of the tribes, to "go up into the Abarim Range to Mount Nebo in Moab," where he would be allowed to view Canaan and then would die. The instruction had been given before, as reported in chapter three, where he was told to "go up to the top of Pisgah" for the same purpose. Now he carries out the command, going up from the Plains of Moab, climbing Mount Nebo "to the top of Pisgah."

The word *Pisgah* means a ridge or serrated ridge. Pisgah is part of the Abarim Range of mountains lying north and east of the Dead Sea. There are a number of peaks in the Abarim/ Pisgah heights. Nebo, at a little over 2,600 feet, is described as the high point, or one of two high points, of the ridge. The tribe of Reuben settled the nearby town of the same name, and in later times it was part of Moab. It is in modern Jordan, as are all of the plains of Moab. A Franciscan basilica and monastery stand today on the traditional height of Nebo. Christian buildings have occupied the site since the late 300s A.D.

Modern observers agree that one cannot see from the top of Nebo all of the territory that the Lord showed Moses in the first three verses of chapter thirty-four. You can see much of it: Mount Hermon one hundred miles to the north, Tabor and Gilboa to the northwest, Mount Ebal and Mount Gerizim and the central hills to the west, the Mount of Olives, Jericho, and much of the Dead Sea to En Gedi, about two-thirds of the way down the western shore. But the Mediterranean is not visible, cut off by the central hills, nor is Zoar at the south end of the Dead Sea. These conflicts between the text and reality contributed to the non-scriptural hagiographies of Moses that claim that he ascended into heaven like Elijah and Jesus himself, and hence was able in the heights of his ascension to see what could not be seen from the mountain. These accounts conflict with the direct teaching of the chapter that "he," that is, the Lord, buried him in Moab, in the valley opposite Beth Peor. And they are unnecessary to understand the text. God may well have given Moses a vision of the land that transcended his physical ability to see. Or the language may be metaphorical or hyperbole, figures of speech to denote the completeness of the view. Or it may be merely descriptive of the areas of which he could see part—that is, Judah that extends to the sea, and the region of Jericho, which extends to Zoar.

Whatever reason reconciles the view and the text, the importance of the passage lies in its connection to the past and the future: God reminds Moses that this is the land he had promised to give to the patriarchs Abraham, Isaac, and Jacob. The fulfillment of those promises made so many hundreds of years before—going back to the twelfth chapter of Genesis and repeated so many times thereafter—is in view as Moses views the land. And, as Moses looks ahead to the future fulfillment of promises that he will not experience, the view of the whole Old Testament is before us. Hebrews, chapter eleven, recites the litany of experiences of the Old Testament saints who lived by faith: "They did not receive the things promised; they only saw them and welcomed them from a distance. And they admitted that they were aliens and strangers on earth."

God said they were "longing for a better country—a heavenly one." So Moses' vision is the vision of the people of faith of all of the ages past who longed for that better thing that was received in Christ Jesus. And it is the vision of every believer of every age who longs to enter into God's rest, into the heavenly country the Father has prepared for us.

Moses then died "as the Lord had said." The language is taken in Jewish tradition as meaning Moses died by God's will—not of old age or sickness. He is said to have died "with a kiss from the mouth of God." The Hebrew idiom "death by a kiss" refers to a sudden and painless death in old age.

The anonymity of his grave is commonly ascribed to God's wanting to keep the people from the idolatry of worshipping his burial place or remains. Alternatively, it may be to prevent the people from bringing his remains into the land that he was forbidden to enter, or to prevent Israel's enemies from desecrating the grave, or to prevent the pride that might attend the tribe with jurisdiction over the burial place. The little book of Jude in the New Testament refers in verse nine to the archangel Michael disputing with the devil about the body of Moses. Some think this cryptic reference is to Satan's desire to corrupt Israel by making a shrine of Moses' burial site.

Moses, although 120 years old, retained his eyesight and vigor. Few indeed are the elderly who do not suffer from infirmity of vision, addressed in the modern world by eyeglasses, corneal implants, and a variety of surgical techniques. The vigor that Moses retained is thought by some to refer to his sexual potency, by others to a lack of the wrinkling of the flesh that normally attends old age. In its most straightforward meaning, he was simply a man who still had physical strength. He had recently led Israel in successful military campaigns against the armies of Sihon and Og, and was able to ascend a 2,600-foot mountain, apparently unassisted. Although he says in Deuteronomy thirty-one, two, "I am no longer able to lead you," the reference seems more to the prohibition on his crossing the Jordan than to physical frailty.

Moses' authority had been transferred to Joshua by the laying on of hands, a ceremony performed in many contexts throughout the Bible. Israel mourns its lost leader for thirty days, apparently a customary or prescribed period of mourning at the time.

The last few verses are a eulogy to Moses. No such prophet arose in Israel after Moses until Jesus himself, the new Joshua. The name *Jesus* is the Greek version of the Hebrew name *Joshua*. The Lord knew Moses "face to face," which undoubtedly means directly, without a mediator or intermediary. The miracles and mighty acts the Lord sent him to do are ascribed to him. The eulogy ends on an apologetic note:

These acts were done "in the sight of all Israel"; hence, there is no excuse for the people not to follow the instructions of Moses and the God who communicated to them through him.

The nation founded by Moses under God's instruction and power survived for eight hundred years, until the early sixth century B.C., when the forces of Nebuchadnezzar conquered the last remnants of it and carried it into exile. The former and latter prophets—as well as the historical and prophetic books of the Old Testament—are clear, specific, and repetitive in teaching that this ending was a direct consequence of the disobedience to God's covenant commands, stated or summarized in Deuteronomy. Although the Jews returned from exile under the authority of later Persian rulers and rebuilt Solomon's temple, they did not regain national independence. The lesson of the exile was "over-learned," and Judaism slid into legalistic religion, making up rules to implement those that were given and emphasizing form over substance. Much of the Gospel teachings and dialogues between Jesus and the Pharisees and other Jewish groups came from this overemphasis. Jesus called them back to the true religion of Moses: seeking the heart commitment of loving God and neighbor—which is what God desires—rather than religious formalities. A few decades after Jesus' crucifixion, the second temple was destroyed, as Jesus had prophesied, and the Jews were again scattered to the nations.

Israel was not an independent nation again until 1948, when the British partitioned Palestine after the Second World War. The modern nation shows little evidence of commitment to the faith of its fathers. Although the Orthodox have much influence, Israel is largely a secular democracy in which Jewishness is a national more than religious heritage, much like being, say, Norwegian.

However, Moses did enter the land. In the story of the transfiguration of Jesus—told in the gospels of Matthew, Mark, and Luke—Jesus went up onto a mountain with Peter, James, and John. His appearance changed, his face shone like the sun, and his clothes become as bright as lightning. Moses and Elijah then appeared with him "in glorious splendor," talking about his departure, which was near. That which was denied to Moses in life was granted to him in eternity.

As Moses passed from the scene, he left a people with their mission at hand but unfulfilled. So it is with every believer at every moment in time. The blessings are still before them. The promise is still good. But they still have to keep the covenant, to act in obedience, to follow where God leads them, to receive it. And, in the end, although they have many successes, their sinful hearts make failure inevitable. Only through the intervention of God himself—becoming flesh in Jesus Christ to take on the burden of all flesh—is the circle of the history of every person and every people broken.

Here Deuteronomy ends. There is a certain despair, a hope-lessness, in the situation. The reader knows where the story is going and what actually happened in later history. But redemption has been hinted at, promised even in the depths of failure. Chapter four and chapter thirty have told them that the story is never over. Deuteronomy ends with God's people needing a savior. It will be 1,400 years before he is delivered, in a stable in Bethlehem.

My van mates applauded as I refolded my essay and put it back in my pocket. The group talked about it while I turned my attention back to Hal. By now it was clear that we were headed in a northerly direction, but he offered no clue as to the destination. I rattled on to the others about my studies in chapter thirty-four. Hal grunted his acknowledg-ment but offered little more. Finally, I pressed him on where we were going.

"Mount Washington," he replied.

Mount Washington, at 6,288 feet, is the highest mountain in the northeastern United States, and the second highest east of the Rockies. It is the presiding peak of the Presidential Range of mountains in northern New Hampshire, with Monroe and Eisenhower to the south, and Madison, Adams, John Quincy Adams, Jefferson, and the recently named Mount Reagan to the north. Mount Washington is about two and a half times the height of Mount Nebo.

To New Hampshire's Native American peoples, before the time of European settlement, Mount Washington was known as "Agiochook." It embodied the sense that so many peoples have had that there is something sacred, closer to God or their gods, about high places. Agiochook was the dwelling place of the Indian gods, the hill to which they lifted up their eyes and from whence they sought help.

A touching legend involving Agiochook attends the death of Passaconaway, the great chief and leader of the New Hampshire Native Americans at the time of the first European settlements. A sled pulled by a team of white wolves is said to have pulled up before his lodge on a cold winter night. The old chief recognized its purpose, got into it, and was pulled to the top of Agiochook, from where he and his mystical team ascended into heaven. Europeans, as well as his own people, attributed miraculous powers, not unlike those of Moses, to Passaconaway. Whether the reports of miraculous acts are true or not, it is clear he had a prophetic vision for his people and his land. He understood the inevitability of the progress of European settlements, and preached peace with and accommodation to the new settlers. He became a Christian believer in his late years. The most realistic account of his death is that he passed away while doing mission work among the Indians of Maine, and they buried him on Mount Agamenticus, a small mountain in southern Maine.

From post-colonial times to the present, Mount Washington has retained its appeal. Although it remains a peak achievement for climbers, there are two ways to access its summit without walking: an auto road and the Cog Railway. The cog track allows coal-fired engines to climb to the top, at angles up to forty-five degrees. At one time it had a summit hotel, and now it has a weather station that is manned year-round. It still has the record for the highest wind speed ever recorded in North America, in excess of 230 miles per hour.

Its appeal to climbers has been costly. Over the years, many an ill-prepared climber has lost his life in its treacherous weather. Even in mid-summer, when gentle warmth pervades the valleys below, at the upper reaches high winds and sudden storms can overcome climbers with wintry conditions. Hence Hal's e-mail about winter coats.

"I have climbed Mount Washington seven times," Hal said, "mostly with youth groups that could do it in half the time I could, even when I was younger. I haven't been there for years. I just wanted to see it again."

As we approached the Presidential Range, Hal took the turn that led us up Pinkham Notch on the east side of the range. To my dismay, he turned onto the auto road that allows one to drive to the summit, paid the fee at the gate, and started up.

At every turn the Mount Washington auto road is a six-mile experience in defying death. It twists its way back and forth along unprotected precipices that drop hundreds of feet. It has that quality of leading drivers around outside curves with nothing but sky in front of them that make you feel as though you were about to drive off into space. Below every turn, one believes, there is surely a whole junkyard of twisted metal from previous vehicles that didn't get around the bend successfully. It made me uncomfortable to sit in the passenger seat; I had driven the road once years before and vowed I would never do it again. Like Hal, I had climbed the mountain several times, and I much preferred to do it on foot.

Hal pressed resolutely ahead, the old blue church van laboring and his own breathing coming heavier as we mounted the height. At last it was over, and we pulled into the small parking area below the summit buildings. Hal got out slowly. We made our way up the short walk to the summit. After a rest, he insisted we ascend the observation tower.

That was where he settled in, pulling his sweater and jacket on for protection against the stiff, cold wind. From that summit, there is a 360-degree view, a forest of surrounding peaks, the nearby valleys, and the distant lower hills beyond. On a clear day, you can see the Atlantic Ocean, some ninety miles to the southeast. Maine, Vermont, Massachusetts, and Quebec, as well as New Hampshire, are in view. Hal took it in slowly and studiously. Then he took my arm and led us to the southeast corner of the platform. One by one, he pointed out the hills and valleys where lay each of the seven churches and communities he had served.

Pastors, good pastors at least, never tell stories that would betray the confidences of the people who come to them for counseling, and Hal betrayed no confidences that day. But he told us stories—stories of his successes and failures in each of the churches he had served. He told us of the people who had come to him and come to the Lord under his ministry, of the good things they had done and tried to do. He also told us a bit about those who had opposed him, who had fought the fight of the Pharisees to keep legalism ahead of the love of the heart for God and to contain God in the pristine walls of their building instead of bringing him to the weak and poor and sin-ridden people that surrounded them.

His stories went on, and so did the day. Lunchtime came and went, but we didn't go to the small restaurant that served the summit visitors. Time stood still for those hours, like the sun in the days of Joshua.

Hal was getting chilled and tired. Paula and Anna urged him to go down. He had one more thing to say. He pointed south of the southeastern view, from which we barely could discern the gleam of the distant ocean.

"There's Boston," he said. "We minister the Lord's way in these hills and little towns, and that's good, but the people are in the cities. God's heart is everywhere the people are, and the more so as they need him. The Lord went from the little towns of Galilee to Jerusalem, and there he died. It was from Jerusalem that the gospel went out to the world. It's well to live God's way in Galilee, but don't forget Jerusalem."

With that, he took my arm and signaled he was ready to depart. I helped him down the steps, and he went much slower than he had ascended. I sensed that something had gone out of him, that he had risen to the task of driving up the mountain and climbing to the summit, and to his hours of reminiscing over the life he had lived out in the land we were viewing. But it was over.

Barbara insisted we stop at the restaurant. He sat with us and sipped a little cocoa and nibbled at a sandwich but ate little. Then he gave me the keys to the van and let me drive us down the mountain and home.

EPILOGUE

I never saw Hal again.

After our day on Mount Washington, I got caught up with my work. It was several weeks before I took the time to call him. When I did, I found the phone had been disconnected. I drove over to his house and found it deserted, with a "for sale" sign on it. When I called the real estate office whose number was listed on the sign, they told me that the owner had passed away recently, and his daughter had listed the property for sale. I asked for her name and address, but they refused. If I was interested in the property, they said, I had to go through them. And if I was that good a friend of Hal's, I should know how to find his daughter on my own.

I found her address in the Probate Registry of his county, where the estates of deceased persons are processed. It gave the name of an Aimee Bonenfant and an address in Dorchester, Massachusetts. The name and address added to my curiosity as to what had happened to Hal. I got directions from Mapquest on my computer and, on another Saturday morning, Anna and I set out for Dorchester to find out.

Dorchester is part of the city of Boston and, with neighboring Roxbury, comprises much of the section of that city populated largely by African-Americans. I knew that before I started and surmised that Aimee Bonenfant was Hal's daughter by Edith and had somehow found her way to the African-American community of our nearest major metropolitan center. As we left the interstate just south of the central city and made our way along the inner city streets to our destination, it was apparent that my surmise was correct. There were many people on the streets, and almost none were white. Our out-of-state license and obviously Caucasian appearance made us the object of some attention as we passed slowly along the walk-up tenements and street-front stores of the minority neighborhoods. Anna self-consciously locked our car doors.

Finally, we turned a corner and saw the street numbers give out. Where the number for which we were looking should have appeared, there was a red brick structure of recent construction. Out front was a sign that read "L'Eglise Evangelique du Jesus Christ et Centre de Ville." My high school French was good enough to translate it as "The Evangelical Church of Jesus Christ and Community Center." We had seen some other storefront and business signs in French in the surrounding blocks as I approached. I realized that the neighborhood we were in was Haitian.

The church and community center took up most of a city block, with rambling brick structures of one and two stories tacked onto each other in a seemingly haphazard fashion. Pulling into the small parking lot, I searched for an entrance. Around a corner on a side street, people seemed to be coming and going through a swinging glass door that appeared to be the main entrance. We went in to a small foyer with halls leading in several directions. When I asked a woman passing through if we could find Aimee Bonenfant there, she directed me down one hallway into a large cafeteria area with an open kitchen behind a serving counter.

I knew Aimee as soon as I saw her. She was in the kitchen with a shower cap covering her hair and medicinal gloves for food handling, helping and giving directions to several men and women who were serving soup-and-sandwich lunches. People wandered in alone, in pairs, and occasionally in small families—usually just a mother and two or three children. They passed down the serving line and helped themselves. At the end of the line was a donation box. Some people put something in; others did not. It was a community soup kitchen, serving food to those who needed it, and Aimee was in the middle of it.

She was a woman of perhaps forty, with a soft, kind face that showed only the slightest sign of age around her eyes. Her skin was light, the lightest of any around her, and her Caucasian features betrayed her mixed parentage. A few wisps of gray had crept into her hair, but her step was lively, and she was obviously in command of the scene. I could see Hal in her eyes and mouth, and the mannerisms of her movement.

We stepped into the kitchen and asked if she was Aimee, and introduced ourselves.

"So you are Chris and Anna," she said. "I've been meaning to get in touch with you. Dad talked about you a lot over the last year."

"He didn't talk about you," I blurted and immediately regretted the implication of what I had said.

She smiled and was not embarrassed. "No," she said, "he wouldn't have. It's not that he didn't love me, and he certainly wasn't embarrassed about me. We talked every week by phone, and he came here often to visit. He loved this place and what we do here. But he's a pastor, and he always thought it distracted from his ministry to talk about his family. He didn't do it from the pulpit. I'm not surprised he didn't do it with you. Anyway, I'm glad to get to meet you. You meant a lot to him, you know. He said the time he spent with you was the best time of his week."

She took us through the lunch line, and we sat over sandwiches and coffee. She told us about growing up in small New England towns where she and her mother were often the only black people in town. She told us that Hal and Edith had met at a conference on worship in Boston after his first wife died. She talked about her mother and father's devotion to each other and how they learned to be immune to those in the church and outside who looked askance at their racially mixed marriage.

"How did you get to be here?" I asked.

"I met Maurice at a conference also," she said. "I'm so glad I took French in high school. He had just immigrated, and his English wasn't very good at the time. But he swept me off my feet, and here we are. Maurice is the pastor here. We just decided we would serve the Haitian community as best we can. My first name is really A-M-Y, but I use the French spelling to be more a part of the community here. We started with a storefront church, and it grew from there. Now we have the food kitchen, a day care center, a counseling center, a homeless shelter, and temporary housing to help people get on their feet. We host job-training and twelve-step programs. We even have some lawyers who come down here every Friday afternoon and do legal counseling—something called the Christian Legal Society. And we've been rehabilitating the housing in the neighborhood and getting people into decent housing that they own themselves. That's a slow and expensive process, but the next two blocks down the street have gone through it."

I expressed surprise at the success of their evangelical mission. "I thought Haitians were Catholic," I said.

"Most are," she replied. "But they're like everyone else—lost sheep that need a shepherd. We shepherd them and anyone else who comes in. If they want to worship in a Catholic church, that's OK with us; we take them to St. Marie's down the street and introduce them to Father Jean. They don't have a native priest, but he's from Quebec and speaks the language."

"Some people think sending people to a Catholic church is the road to perdition," Anna said half-jokingly. "They may get taught salvation comes by good works and find they're not saved at all."

Aimee's look hardened slightly. "People who think that can have their little heresy," she said. "I never confuse belief in Christ with doctrines about the theology of salvation. Besides," she said, her tone turning lighter, "Father Jean plays a pretty good game of cribbage; we get together every Monday night."

Just then a tall, heavy-set, broad-shouldered man with skin as black as Africa came in and approached us. He was neatly dressed and, like Aimee, walked with an air of being in charge. She introduced us to Maurice, her husband and partner in the church and mission. Together they gave us a tour of the church and facilities. We walked around the blocks of rehabbed housing and the facilities for all the programs they were sponsoring.

"How do you afford it?" I asked. "It seems like a lot more money being invested here than this community can afford."

"Our people tithe," Maurice said. "You'd be surprised what you can afford, even in a poor community, when people tithe. We get some mission support from others. We get some help from government and other programs for some things we do, like the soup kitchen and homeless shelter. Down here, no one worries too much about separating church and state; there's just too much need to bog down in that. And we use groups like Habitat for Humanity in the rehab projects. There are a lot of resources out there, if you know how to tap them—and she does." He nodded at Aimee.

"Hal and Edith didn't send me to college for nothing," she said. "But Maurice is the real dynamo here. I'm just the helper."

"I love the Sunday morning worship," Maurice said. "But I only spend about ten percent of my time on that. God has too many things for us to do. I let the music take care of itself; I have great people for music leadership. I just give the message. It's never hard to find something the Lord wants me to say to these people."

Anna was tugging on my arm. She pointed at the flower bushes blooming around the houses.

"What?" I asked.

"They're roses," she said. "Every house has roses. And they're the same roses that are in Hal's garden. Around every house."

It was mid-afternoon, and we had taken enough of their time. We invited them to visit us in New Hampshire, but somehow I knew they never would. And they invited us to come back again, any time, but I knew it was not our place. I resolved to send them money as part of our own tithe. Maurice gave us a warm handshake, and Aimee embraced both of us as we parted.

On the long drive home, I found myself in another world. I couldn't get Aimee and Maurice and the blessings and prosperity they were bringing to that Boston neighborhood out of my mind. I recalled Hal's words on the summit of Mount Washington: "Remember Boston; that's where the people are." I hadn't realized at the time how personal his comment was. And then I remembered that I had never asked Aimee where Hal was buried. But it didn't matter anymore; we had gone looking for a shrine, a place to visit to remember the holiness we had touched through Hal. And we had found what God wanted us to find there—not a grave or a statue but a living, dynamic memory, spreading the message and the blessing of the God of Israel and the Israel of God to the nations.

These, I thought, were the words that Moses spoke.

STUDY QUESTIONS

CHAPTER ONE

1. In your own words, explain how the prayer "Lord Jesus Christ, have mercy on me" summarizes the gospel message.

2. Why did the author refer to Deuteronomy as a "transitional book"?

3. In an e-mail to Chris, Hal wrote, "The Bible is a whole book, not a series of disconnected texts. Like all good stories, it has a beginning, a middle, and an end; protagonists and antagonists." List similarities and differences you see between Deuteronomy and most other literature (apart from the Bible).

4. What is a "chiasm"?
   Try to write something in chiastic form:

5. Hal told Chris, "Someone has observed that all stories ever told could be titled either 'I Took a Trip' or 'A Stranger Came to Town.' The story contained in the Hebrew Scriptures—the Old Testament, the Bible that Jesus read—is of the 'I Took a Trip' nature." Explain how the Old Testament is of the "I Took a Trip" nature. List at least three Old Testament stories that support your answer.

6. Hal also told Chris, "For you, Chris, that means it [the message of Deuteronomy] is addressed to you personally and to every other individual human being. But the heir to the Israel of Moses is not the modern state of Israel, nor the United States, nor any other contemporary nation. It is the church." Do you agree or disagree with Hal's statement? Explain.

7. In your own words, restate Hal's definition of "anagogical."

8. Are you in the "Promised Land" or on your way? Reflect a bit on your journey.

CHAPTER TWO

1. From this section of Deuteronomy, list several examples of people groups (other than Israelites) driving other groups from their lands.

2. At what point (geographically) did the Israelites leave the territory of their "brothers" and enter truly "hostile territory"? Find this area on a map of the ancient near-east.

3. In a sense, Hal took Chris to task for focusing too much on the geography and history of the Deuteronomy text. On what did Hal want Chris to focus? Are geographical and historical facts irrelevant? Explain the relationship between biblical facts and their interpretation and application in your life.

4. What "irony" did Hal point out in certain people groups dispossessing others from their lands, while the Israelites failed to do so? Recall a time when you've seen unbelievers act more honorably than believers.

5. In your own words, explain the principle of "herem." Why did God call for this "herem"?

6. Why did Chris struggle with Hal's anagogical explanation of the herem seen in Deuteronomy, and why did Hal refer to the importance of context in answering Chris's question?

CHAPTER THREE

1. In Deuteronomy three, Moses recalled, "I commanded you at that time: 'The LORD your God has given you this land to take possession of it. But all your able-bodied men, armed for battle, must cross over ahead of your brother Israelites.'" If God had already given them the land, why did he tell them to prepare for battle to take the land?

2. Why was there nearly a conflict between the tribes of Reuben and Gad and the rest of the Israelites? How was the conflict averted?

3. Referring to the lessons from this chapter of Deuteronomy, what did Hal say was "one of the most basic and consistent teachings of the Scriptures"?

4. Deuteronomy seems to say that the Israelites, *together with Moses*, were responsible for Moses' exclusion from entering the Promised Land. How did Hal explain this?

5. If you can recall a time in your life when you worked faithfully toward a good goal that won't be completed in your lifetime, write a paragraph or two about it.

Chapter Four

1. In your own words, define transcendence and imminence. List a time when you've felt God's imminence.

2. How did Hal answer Chris's question about Jesus' adding to the (Old Testament) Scriptures?

3. What does the term *apologetics* mean, and how does it relate to Deuteronomy 4?

4. Why is it important that the Bible is rooted in real historical events with real eyewitnesses?

5. Explain why you agree or disagree with Hal about what makes a nation great.

6. How did Hal relate the ban on idol worship to present-day life?

CHAPTER FIVE

1. Why did God use fire as a backdrop when he gave the Israelites the Ten Commandments?

2. How did Hal answer Chris's question about why God actually *wrote* the Ten Commandments?

3. What are some ways people use God's name in vain? Why is proper use of God's name so important?

4. In what ways is the commandment about the Sabbath different from the rest of the Ten Commandments?

5. Summarize Hal's reflection on the logical order of the Ten Commandments.

CHAPTER SIX

1. What passages make up the "Shema"? What is the Tetragrammaton?

2. What does Elohim mean, and why is it important in understanding the concept of the Trinity?

3. Why does Deuteronomy focus so much on the need for parents to teach their children about God?

4. What is the anagogical meaning—the timeless principle—behind the Deuteronomy 6 passage about inheriting lands someone else cultivated and houses others built?

5. According to Deuteronomy 6:24, why does God want his people to keep his laws? How did Jesus summarize what's needed to obey the many Levitical laws?

Chapter Seven

1. Why did God choose the Jews? How did Abraham fit into this choice?

2. As exemplified in a "Peanuts" comic strip, what is the irony of humility?

3. According to Hal, why didn't God choose to work through one of the great nations of the time?

4. How did Hal explain—and perhaps reconcile—Calvin's doctrine of predestination and Arminius' doctrine of foreknowledge? Think particularly about Hal's reference to God's relationship to time ("God doesn't need a crystal ball to predict the future").

5. What do you think when you gaze at the night sky? Do you relate it to the Lord? Do you have fear or joy? Why?

CHAPTER EIGHT

1. Why was God so concerned that the Jews remember their history?

2. According to Hal, why did God want the Jews to remember their difficult times in the desert?

3. Why is pride the most dangerous sin?

4. How does Chris's dream encapsulate the basic doctrines of sin and salvation?

5. Hal told Chris, "Grace isn't a once-in-a-lifetime event." Write down some of God's acts of grace in your life.

CHAPTER NINE

1. Hal said Deuteronomy 8 revealed that God did not choose the Jews because of their power or position, and chapter nine explains that he did not choose them because of their righteousness and integrity. How did Hal relate this principle to the church?

2. Write about a time when you were on the "giving" or "receiving" end of a "pear-tree" event.

3. How did Hal reply to Chris's question about "original sin"?

4. How did Hal explain God's promise to Abraham that his descendants would have to wait to take the Promised Land because "the sin of the Amorites has not yet reached its full measure"?

5. In this chapter, Moses recalled the golden calf incident (when he had brought the Ten Commandments down from the mountain). Apart from idolatry itself, what was significant about the calf image?

6. According to Hal, why did Moses recall the golden calf incident?

7. In this chapter of Deuteronomy, Moses also recalled the stories of Massah or Meribah. Where are those stories first found, and what are they about?

8. How was Moses' prayer for the people like Chris's dream?

CHAPTER TEN

1. How did Hal answer Chris's question about the apparent contradiction in the timeline of the Ten Commandments and the Ark of the Covenant (and about the builder of the ark)?

2. What is the "documentary hypothesis," and how did Hal refute it?

3. Summarize how Hal contrasted "academic orthodoxy" with truly "advancing in knowledge of the Lord."

4. What comparison did Chris draw in the legal profession's "burden of proof" doctrine and critical analysis of the Bible?

5. How did Hal answer Chris's question about God's appearing to change his mind in response to Moses' prayer?

6. What did Hal say is a "fundamental New Testament teaching" about sin and salvation?

7. What did Hal say was the purpose of physical circumcision for the Jews?

CHAPTER ELEVEN

1. What did Hal say is the pattern found in Deuteronomy 11?

2. Diagram the chiasm (pattern) found in this chapter.

3. How did Hal answer Chris's question about the modern-day application of visible, physical displays of God's laws?

4. Why did Hal refer to chapters five through eleven as a "transition point" in Deuteronomy?

INTERLUDE

1. Summarize Hal's reasoning for his statement "This was God giving his chosen people rules through his chosen leader, Moses."

2. Hal told Chris and Anna, "Sometimes it ['the law'] refers to the specific laws given by Moses. It can also be used to refer to all of God's will or revelation, as in 'the law of God,' or 'the law of Christ.'" What did he say was the key to discerning between the two?

CHAPTER TWELVE

1. In his studies of Deuteronomy 12, Chris discovered that scholars with "a low view of Scripture" believe Josiah created the "lost" book of the law for what purpose?

2. According to Hal, when God said he would place his name in a location, what did he mean? In the long term, the "name" refers to whom?

3. How does this chapter of Deuteronomy correlate with John 17?

4. Explain why you agree or disagree with Hal's assessment of Deuteronomy 12 and John 17.

5. Explain Hal's criticism of the teaching that "it's only right doctrine that leads to salvation." Do you agree or disagree? Why?

CHAPTER THIRTEEN

1. What is a "sovereign-vassal covenant," and what was unique about Israel's "sovereign-vassal covenant"?

2. According to Hal, who was Israel's "real enemy"?

3. Why did Hal relate Israel's idol worship to treason?

4. According to Hal, how does Acts 15 relate to Deuteronomy 13?

5. Hal said Deuteronomy 13 "provided the scriptural authority for the Jews to seek Jesus' execution." Explain his reasoning.

6. How did Hal answer Chris's question about Christianity being a "different religion [from Judaism]"?

7. Hal said, "Theocratic government will return" when?
   "In the meantime, we live under the law of _____, rather than the law of _____."

CHAPTER FOURTEEN

1. Explain why you agree or disagree with Julie's answer to Chris's question about kosher food laws.

2. How did Hal respond to Anna's thoughts about the reasons for the kosher food laws?

3. According to Hal, why did Jesus override the kosher food laws?

4. Chris and Anna thought the second part of chapter fourteen seemed unrelated to the first part. How did Hal explain the relationship between the two parts?

5. How did Hal explain the developing relationship of chapters 12 through 14?

6. Have you complied with the food laws, as Hal has explained them?

CHAPTER FIFTEEN

1. What is the *shemitah*?

2. List some of the ways the Jews tried to avoid keeping the shemitah.

3. According to Hal, what is the central thought of "supply him" or "put upon his neck"?

4. What were some of the stipulations attached to the "sacrifice of the firstborn"?

CHAPTER SIXTEEN

1. List some of the things you learned about Passover from Hal's explanation of it to Chris and Anna.

2. How did Hal answer Anna's question about the significance of Pentecost to Christians?

3. What are some other names for the Feast of Tabernacles? To what American holiday did Hal compare it and why?

4. According to Hal, in the figurative sense, who appears empty-handed before the Lord?

CHAPTER SEVENTEEN

1. Summarize what you learned from Hal about hierarchical church governance.

2. Explain why you agree or disagree with Hal's statement that the elder-based leadership model "may have been appropriate in its original context, and may still be appropriate for mission churches today. But it is less clear that it is appropriate for established churches with a membership of believers."

3. What is syncretism, and why would it be an issue for the Jews as they entered the Promised Land?

4. How did Hal relate syncretism to Christians today?

5. Why were two or more witnesses required for capital cases? List some examples of how this law came into play in the New Testament.

6. What did Hal say was a "standoff in ideas" from Deuteronomy?

7. How did Hal answer Chris's question about the religious significance of abortion?

Chapter Eighteen

1. What did Hal say was remarkable about the structure of government called for in Deuteronomy 16 through 18?

3. What are some of the occult practices this passage lists as "detestable"?

4. According to this passage, what verifies that a prophet has "spoken by the LORD"?

5. According to Hal, how was the foretold prophet going to be like Moses?

6. List some New Testament passages that refer or allude to Deuteronomy 18.

CHAPTER NINETEEN

1. What is "*natural* law," and how does it relate to Deuteronomy 19?

2. What did Hal say about natural law based on Romans 1?

3. What was Hal's modern-day application to the section about a man who accidentally kills a neighbor when the axe head flies off the handle?

4. How did Hal answer Chris's question about "eye-for-an-eye justice"?

5. How did Hal respond to the notion that not everyone agrees on what natural law is? If it's *natural* law, then why is there disagreement over it?

Chapter Twenty

1. According to "Apologetics 101," what are the first two reasons to believe the Bible is God's Word?

2. According to Deuteronomy, why should the Israelites not be afraid when they see superior opposing forces in a battle? How might this principle apply to Christians today?

3. Why did God reduce the size of Gideon's army? How does Gideon's story in Judges 7 relate to Deuteronomy 20?

4. "The story of Gideon is the story of the _____ _____ put to _____." What was Hal teaching by this?

5. How did Hal answer Chris's question about why the priest was involved in "Gideon's battle"?

6. How did Hal answer this question from Chris: "Am I one of the ones who will get to fight, Hal," I asked, "or will I be sent home?" How might Hal's answer comfort you?

7. How does the story of the Gibeonites relate to the second part of chapter twenty?

8. How did Hal answer Chris's question about what the distant cities in the Promised Land represent?

9. What is the literal purpose behind not cutting down fruit trees in a conquered land? What might be the spiritual reason behind this command?

CHAPTER TWENTY-ONE

1. According to Deuteronomy 21, what were the leaders of the nearest town to do if a man was found dead (apparently from foul play) in a field? What was the purpose in such an action?

2. How did Hal explain this "strange" practice to Chris?

3. Why was this ceremonial law abandoned after the exile?

4. How did Hal reply to this question from Chris: "If God holds us accountable together for all the wrongs of the land, how do we respond?"

5. How did Hal reply to Chris's comment that the law about treatment of and marriage to women taken captive in battle is irrelevant today?

6. How did Hal explain God's apparent sanction of polygamy?

7. How did Hal relate the passage about punishing rebellious children to the fifth commandment?

8. How did Hal connect the curse of being hung on a tree to the New Testament and Jesus?

CHAPTER TWENTY-TWO

1. Explain how Jesus customized the first passage in Deuteronomy 22 to tell his Good Samaritan story.

2. Summarize the discussions the attorneys had about how this prin-
    ciple from Deuteronomy 22 might or might not apply today.

3. "The ancient rabbis always recognized that this law is not just
    about _____.
    It's about '_____,' and that certainly includes
    reputation. But reputation is still not our most precious posses-
    sion." According to Hal, what is our most precious possession?

4. Explain why you agree or disagree with Hal's application of this
    verse: "A woman must not wear men's clothing, nor a man wear
    women's clothing, for the LORD your God detests anyone who does
    this."

5. How did Hal reply to Chris's question about whether this pas-
    sage means that "men and women are separate and have different
    functions, and people should not confuse them"? Explain why you
    agree or disagree with Hal.

6. In addition to the environmental application, what principle did
    Hal see in the passage about the bird's nest?

7. What general principle of Jewish law did the parapet on the roof represent?

8. What kind of modern-day application did Hal see in the prohibitions of "mixing"?

9. How is the story of Jacob and Rebekah related to the section about a husband's discovery that his wife was not a virgin at the time of marriage?

10. When Hal told the attorneys, "Much of the teaching in Deuteronomy is about this," to what did he refer?

11. What was the penalty for a man who had sexual relations with another man's wife? Why was this referred to as a "paradigm law"?

CHAPTER TWENTY-THREE

1. What was the assembly of the LORD, and why were Ammonites and Moabites excluded from it?

2. How did Hal answer these questions from Chris: "Why should we assume that these categories of people don't or can't share the thoughts—or are excluded from salvation?"

3. What did Hal say was the purpose of the purity laws and rituals?

4. According to Hal, why didn't the Father just skip over all these laws and rituals and send Jesus sooner?

5. How was the Israelite army in the time of Deuteronomy different from other armies?

6. Summarize Hal's explanation of the modern application of these purity laws for the Israelite army.

7. How does the fugitive slave law relate to the teaching on sacred places?

8. What spiritual behavior among the Israelites did prostitution commonly depict?

9. How did Hal reply to Chris's comment that there aren't many shrine prostitutes in today's churches?

10. How did Hal relate the passage about keeping one's vows to the commandment not to take the Lord's name in vain?

Chapter Twenty-four

1. How did Hal rephrase Moses' allowance for divorce?

2. How did Hal answer this question from Chris: "What is the prescription for a good marriage?"

3. What were some of the explanations Hal gave for prohibiting "remarriage"?

4. What did Hal say was the spiritual message to be drawn from Deuteronomy 24 and Jeremiah 3?

5. How is it that (as seen in Hosea) God broke his own law about remarriage?

6. How did Jesus draw from Deuteronomy 24 to answer his disciples' question about who can be saved?

7. What was the reason for exempting a man from military service for one year after his wedding?

8. What was the purpose behind not taking a man's millstones as a debt security?

9. Explain the relationship Hal showed between the Deuteronomy passage on wage payment and James 5.

10. Chris said, "So there was a time and place when generational punishment was appropriate because of the special holiness of what was at stake." Hal agreed but said a broader principle applied. What is that principle?

CHAPTER TWENTY-FIVE

1. What is the Tanakh, and how is it divided?

2. How does Deuteronomy 25 relate to 2 Corinthians 11:24?

3. What practical and modern-day justice principles did Hal draw from the first verses of this chapter?

4. What are some of the advantages Hal listed for corporal judgment? Explain why you agree or disagree with his thoughts.

5. Besides the plain, practical meaning of "You shall not muzzle an ox while it is threshing," what did Hal see as a timeless application of the message?

6. How did Hal tie together this passage about the ox with Luke's gospel and 1 Timothy to show the authority of the Bible?

7. What is a Levirate marriage, and what principles might be drawn from it and applied today?

8. What was Hal's take on this statement from Jesus: "And if your right hand causes you to sin, cut it off and throw it away. It is better for you to lose one part of your body than for your whole body to go into hell."

9. Review some of Hal's discussion with Chris about the Amalekites.

10. How did Hal relate the Amalekites to today's church?

CHAPTER TWENTY-SIX

1. Hal said, "Deuteronomy is like _____ _____."
   List some of the similarities between these covenants.

2. Chapter 26 mirrors what earlier chapter in Deuteronomy? Explain how it does so.

3. Hal said, "This Scripture is rich with meaning for the Christian life." Explain.

4. What did Hal mean when he said the first section of the chapter deals with the "vertical" relationship, while the second half deals with "horizontal" relationships?

5. What did Hal mean when he said to Anna, "Of course you're a failure"?

6. Do you have a Hal in your life? Are you a Hal to anyone else?

Chapter Twenty-seven

1. As seen in Genesis 12, who was Shechem, and what was his relationship to Jacob (Israel)?

2. Why might it be significant that the Israelites at this time found themselves in the place called Shechem (also see Joshua 24)?

3. What was Anna's conclusion about the reason the Israelites "were instructed to build an altar of fieldstones (uncut or undressed stone) on Mount Ebal"?

4. Hal said, "Not only does this chapter mirror chapter eleven in framing the laws that are given in between, but it also mirrors promises made to Abraham hundreds of years earlier and repeated to Isaac and Jacob." Explain.

5. Anna said this was the same type of vertical-then-horizontal pattern in this chapter that they'd seen in the previous chapter. Explain why you agree or disagree with her.

6. Why is it significant that Jesus taught the Samaritan woman at the well in the very site to which this chapter refers?

7. According to Hal, what is the common thread Jewish and Christian commentators see in the curses called out in this chapter?

8. How did Hal tie together the last curse in this chapter with Galatians 3:10?

Chapter Twenty-eight

1. As seen in Chris's Old Testament summary, what "led to the final destruction of Jerusalem and the temple and the exile of most of the remaining people to Babylon"?

2. List some of the passages that show the fulfillment of the curses for disobedience, as seen in Deuteronomy 28.

3. How did Hal answer this question from Chris: "If we simply obey God's commands, can we expect that our life will be filled with prosperity and good things?"

4. How did Hal respond to Jerry's skepticism about a literal hell?

5. What did Hal think about the reality of hell in eternity?

Chapter Twenty-nine

1. About what did Moses remind the people twice in this chapter?

2. What did Hal mean when he spoke of "apologetic statements" God had made to the Israelite people?

3. How did Hal reply to Chris's question about the meaning of the last verse in this chapter?

4. How did Hal answer Jerry's question about the person who invokes a blessing on himself but brings on curses?

5. How did Hal answer Anna's question from verse four about blindness, deafness, and lack of understanding?

6. How did Hal answer Paula's question about never forgiving the secret idolater who invokes blessings on himself?

CHAPTER THIRTY

1. Who witnessed God's covenant with Israel (as outlined in Deuteronomy)?

2. According to Jeremiah 29–31, what will happen when God's people seek him with all their heart?

3. How did Hal reconcile the fact that, in Deuteronomy 30, God first told the people to circumcise their own heart, and then he told them he would circumcise their heart?

4. How did Hal tie together this chapter, Mark 3:4, and the abortion debate?

5. Do you recognize who really understands the word of God? How?

CHAPTER THIRTY-ONE

1. How did Hal explain Deuteronomy's "outer-frame" structure?

2. What are some of the similarities Hal listed between the beginning and end of Deuteronomy?

3. How did Hal respond to this statement from Mike: "Women didn't get any respect in the Bible"?

4. What did the Jewish sages conclude verse 19 ("Now write down for yourselves this song and teach it to the Israelites and have them sing it, so that it may be a witness for me against them") meant?

5. Referring to Deuteronomy, Mike said, "If it's the beginning of creating Scripture, we ought to know what was created." How did Hal respond to this statement?

6. Hal told Mike Scripture was approved by "consensus." But he said another element was involved in developing the Bible. What was that other "element"?

CHAPTER THIRTY-TWO

1. How did Hal answer the question about whether the reference to "the song" in this chapter refers to "the sons of Israel" or "the sons of God"?

2. How did Hal interpret the metaphor of Exodus 19:4 (that God carried Israel "on eagle's wings and brought you to myself")?

3. What did this chapter teach you about Jeshurun?

4. Why did Anna say, "It's obvious that the misfortunes that befell Israel in the face of its enemies could not have happened unless the Lord 'had given them up'"?

5. What is the connection between Romans 15:10 and verse 43 of this chapter?

6. Reflect on Hal's singing of the song of Moses. Has your life ever experienced this?

CHAPTER THIRTY-THREE

1. Summarize what Anna meant when she said, "It's for them."

2. From what part of this chapter did the New Testament writers learn that the giving of the law through Moses was mediated by angels? List some New Testament passages that allude to this passage.

3. What are two explanations about the term *holy ones* in verse three of this chapter?

4. How did Moses "restore" the blessing Jacob had taken away from Reuben? Might there be an eternal principle here you can apply in your life?

5. What was the context of the message in verse nine: "Levi had no regard for his father and mother, and did not recognize his brothers or acknowledge his own children"?

6. How does Deuteronomy 33 conclude?

CHAPTER THIRTY-FOUR

1. List two explanations for the differences between what Moses was said to have seen from the top of Mount Nebo (just before his death) and what observers can see from there now.

2. As Moses looked out over the lands, what did God remind him about?

3. What is a likely reason why no one knows for sure where Moses was buried?

4. According to the prophets, why were the last remnants of the Jewish people carried off into exile eight hundred years after Moses' death?

5. What similarities did you see between Moses and Hal as Hal took "his people" up Mount Washington?

EPILOGUE

1. How did Aimee and Maurice fulfill Hal's dream (and in the process, fulfill one of the primary themes in Deuteronomy)?

2. Why was it appropriate that Chris forgot to ask Aimee where Hal was buried?

BIBLIOGRAPHY

Braun, Mark E., *Deuteronomy*. St. Louis: Concordia Publishing House, 1995.

Brown, Raymond, *The Message of Deuteronomy*. Downers Grove, IL: InterVarsity Press, 1993.

Brueggemann, Walter, *Deuteronomy*. Nashville: Abingdon Press, 2001.

Cairns, Ian, *Deuteronomy: Word and Presence*. Grand Rapids: Wm B. Eerdmans Publishing Co., 1992.

Calvin, John, *Sermons on Deuteronomy* (1583 facsimile edition). Edinburgh: The Banner of Truth Trust, 1987.

Christensen, Duane L., Ed., *A Song of Power and the Power of Song: Essays on the Book of Deuteronomy*. Winona Lake, IN: Eisenbrauns, 1993.

Christensen, Duane L., *Deuteronomy 1:1–21:9*. Nashville: Thomas Nelson Publishers, 2001.

———, *Deuteronomy* 21:10–34:12. Nashville: Thomas Nelson Publishers, 2002.

Clements, R.E., *Deuteronomy*. Sheffield, England: JSOT Press, 1989.

Craigie, P.C., *The Book of Deuteronomy*. Grand Rapids: William B. Eerdmans Publishing Company, 1976.

Driver, S.R., *A Critical and Exegetical Commentary on Deuteronomy*. Edinburgh: T&T Clark, 1901.

Gaebelein, Frank E., Ed., Vol. 3, *The Expositor's Bible Commentary*. Grand Rapids: Zondervan Publishing House, 1992.

Hamilton, Jeffries M., *Social Justice and Deuteronomy*. Atlanta: Scholars Press, 1992.

Henry, Matthew, Vol. 1, *Commentary on the Whole Bible*. Hendrickson Publishers, Inc., Fourth Printing, 1996.

Interpreter's Bible, The New, Vol. II (The Book of Deuteronomy: Introduction, Commentary, and Reflections by Ronald E. Clements). Nashville: Abingdon Press, 1998.

Keil, C.F. and Delitzsch, F., Vol. I, *Commentary on the Old Testament in Ten Volumes*. Grand Rapids: William B. Eerdmans Publishing Company, reprinted 1980.

Knight, George A.F., *The Song of Moses: A Theological Quarry*. Grand Rapids: William B. Eerdmans Publishing Company, 1995.

Levinson, Bernard M., *Deuteronomy and the Hermeneutics of Legal Innovation*. New York: Oxford University Press, 1997.

Lienhard, Joseph T., Ed., *Ancient Christian Commentary on Scripture, Old Testament III: Exodus, Leviticus, Numbers, Deuteronomy*. Downers Grove: InterVarsity Press, 2001.

Luther, Martin, Vol. 9, *Luther's Works, Lectures on Deuteronomy*. St. Louis: Concordia Publishing House, 1960.

Mann, Thomas W., *Deuteronomy*. Louisville: Westminster John Knox Press, 1995.

Maxwell, John C., *The Communicator's Commentary: Deuteronomy*. Waco: Word Books, 1987.

Mayes, A.D.H., *Deuteronomy*. Grand Rapids: William B. Eerdmans Publishing Company, 1979.

McConville, J. Gordon, *Grace in the End: A Study in Deuteronomic Theology*. Grand Rapids: Zondervan Publishing House, 1993.

———, *Deuteronomy*. Downers Grove, IL: InterVarsity Press, 2002.

McGee, J. Vernon, Vol. I, *Thru the Bible*. Pasadena: Thru the Bible Radio, 1981.

Merrill, Eugene H., *Deuteronomy*. Broadman & Holman Publishers, 1994.

Millar, J. Gary, *Now Choose Life: Theology and Ethics in Deuteronomy*. Grand Rapids: William B. Eerdmans Publishing Company, 1998.

Miller, Patrick D., *Deuteronomy*. Louisville: John Knox Press, 1990.

Munk, Elie, *The Call of the Torah: Devarim*. Brooklyn: Mesorah Publications, Ltd, 1995.

Nachshoni, Y., *Studies in the Weekly Parashah*. Brooklyn: Mesorah Publications, Ltd, 1989.

Nelson, Richard D., *Deuteronomy*. Louisville: Westminster John Knox Press, 2002.

Patrick, Dale, *Old Testament Law*. Atlanta: John Knox Press, 1985.

Payne, David F., *Deuteronomy*. Philadelphia: The Westminster Press, 1985.

Pressler, Carolyn, *The View of Women Found in the Deuteronomic Family Laws*. New York: Walter de Gruyter, 1993.

Rashi, *The Torah: with Rashi's Commentary, Deuteronomy*. Brooklyn: Mesorah Publications, Ltd, 1998.

Ridderbos, J., *Deuteronomy*. Grand Rapids: Zondervan Publishing House, 1978.

Rofe, Alexander, *Deuteronomy*. London: T&T Clark, 2002.

Schneider, Bernard N., *Deuteronomy: A Favored Book of Jesus*. Winona Lake, IN: BMH Books, 1970.

Thompson, J.A., *Deuteronomy: An Introduction and Commentary*. Downers Grove, IL: InterVarsity Press, 1974.

Tigay, Jeffrey H., *Deuteronomy*. Philadelphia: The Jewish Publication Society, 1996.

Von Rad, Gerhard, *Deuteronomy*. Philadelphia: The Westminster Press, 1966.

Walton, John H. and Matthews, Victor H., *The IVP Bible Background Commentary: Genesis-Deuteronomy*. Downers Grove, IL: InterVarsity Press, 1997.

Weinfeld, Moshe, *Deuteronomy 1–11*. New York: Doubleday, 1991.

Willis, Timothy M., *The Elders of the City: A Study of the Elders-Laws in Deuteronomy*. Atlanta: Society of Biblical Literature, 2001.

Wilson, Ian, *Out of the Fire: Divine Presence in Deuteronomy*. Atlanta: Scholars Press, 1995.

Wisdom, Jeffrey R., *Blessing for the Nations and the Curse of the Law*. Tubingen: Mohr Siebeck, 2001.

Wright, Christopher, *Deuteronomy*. Peabody, MA: Hendrickson Publishers, Inc., 1996.

ENDNOTES

1 J.G. McConville, *Deuteronomy* (Downers Grove, IL: InterVarsity Press), p. 10.

2 Martin Luther, *Luther's Works: Lectures on Deuteronomy* (St. Louis, MO: Concordia Publishing House), p. 48.

3 Prov. 30:6

4 Rev. 22:18–19.

5 Charles C. Finney, *The Autobiography of Charles G. Finney* (*Helen Wessel, Ed*) (Minneapolis: Bethany Fellowship), pp. 21–22.

6 Ibid at 26.

7 Arthur Green, *These Are the Words* (Woodstock, VT: Jewish Lights Publishing), p. 3.

8 C.S. Lewis, *Mere Christianity* (New York: The Macmillan Company), p. 109.

9 Martin Luther, *Luther's Works: Lectures on Deuteronomy* (St. Louis, MO: Concordia Publishing House), p. 96.

10 "Amazing Grace," public domain.

11 Saint Augustine (John K. Ryan, translator), *The Confessions of St. Augustine* (New York: Doubleday), p. 202.

12 Christopher Wright, *Deuteronomy (New International Biblical Commentary; 4)* (Peabody, MA: Hendrickson Publishers), pp. 177–78.

13 "And Can It Be?", public domain.

14 Robert Penn Warren, *All the King's Men* (New York: Bantam Books), p. 270.

15 "Jesus Loves Me," public domain.

16 Duane Christensen, *Deuteronomy 21:10–34:12* (Nashville: Thomas Nelson Publishers), p. 785.

About The Author

R ichard B. Couser is an author, speaker, and attorney. His earlier book, *Ministry and the American Legal System,* received the "Book of the Year" award and has been recognized as "the best church and law text in print." Couser has also written publications, news columns, magazine articles, chapters in other books, and teaching texts. He has spoken frequently to churches, Christian service groups, and attorneys. He is past president and board member of the Christian Legal Society, a national organization of Christian attorneys, judges, law professors, and law students, and has been a speaker at national conferences.

Couser graduated from Phillips Exeter Academy, Yale University, and Stanford Law School. His professional experience has included serving more than seventy churches and other Christian organizations. He has been listed as one of "America's Leading Lawyers for Business" and "The Best Lawyers in America" by national publishers.

Couser's wife, Linda, is accomplished in music, painting, and other forms of art work. Their daughter, Alison, is married with three children, and their son, Jonathan, is married with four children. Couser's entire family are believing and faithful Christians.

The Deuteronomy Project follows seminary level courses and some fifteen years of study of Deuteronomy through the books listed in the bibliography, virtually all of the texts available in English. He is particularly pleased to see it in print at this time due to his health issues with cancer and his reliance on the Lord, and the prayers and support from so many.

To order additional copies of this title call:
1-877-421-READ (7323)
or please visit our Web site at
www.winepressbooks.com

If you enjoyed this quality custom-published book,

drop by our Web site for more books and information.

www.winepressgroup.com

"Your partner in custom publishing."